Aristotle, W. Ogle

Aristotle on the parts of animals

Aristotle, W. Ogle

Aristotle on the parts of animals

ISBN/EAN: 9783337019341

Printed in Europe, USA, Canada, Australia, Japan

Cover: Foto ©Thomas Meinert / pixelio.de

More available books at **www.hansebooks.com**

ARISTOTLE

ON

THE PARTS OF ANIMALS.

TRANSLATED, WITH INTRODUCTION AND NOTES,

BY

W. OGLE, M.A., M.D., F.R.C.P.

SOMETIME FELLOW OF CORPUS CHRISTI COLLEGE, OXFORD.

*Præclare cum illo agitur, qui non mentiens dicit, quod ab Aristotele responsum est sciscitanti Alexandro, quo docente profiteretur se scientem: 'rebus,' inquit, 'ipsis, quæ non norunt mentiri.'—*VARRO.

LONDON:
KEGAN PAUL, TRENCH & CO., PATERNOSTER SQUARE.
1882.

PREFACE.

The biological treatises of Aristotle are more often quoted than read; and, it may be added, more often misquoted than quoted correctly. None perhaps have fared worse than the "De Partibus Animalium," which forms the central portion of that great trilogy, in which are set forth successively, the phenomena presented by animals in life, the causes that have determined their structure, and the process of their generation and development. The crabbed and obscure style in which this treatise is written, its corrupt text, and, generally, the difficulties of language have kept off the biologist, while the simple Aristotelian has been deterred by a subject-matter, as a rule alien to his tastes. Yet to both the treatise offers much of interest. In it the Aristotelian will find some of the best examples of his master's method; while the biologist can scarcely be void of curiosity as to the first serious attempt to assign its function to each separate part of the animal body. It has been hoped therefore that this volume may be welcome to both; offering to the one a faithful and intelligible rendering of the text, and to the other a body of notes, which have been made much fuller than would have been necessary, had they been meant for those only, who had already some acquaintance with physiology.

In neither part of this undertaking can I hope to have escaped many a blunder. It is indeed the consciousness of this that has caused me to keep the following sheets in my desk unpublished, though written many years ago. And even now, when I have been induced by friends to venture on publication, I do so with extreme diffidence and misgiving. Of this, however, I feel assured; that those persons, who are most competent to detect my shortcomings, will also be those most disposed to make full allowance for them. For they will best know, how difficult a task the preparation of a volume of this kind is in reality, easy and simple as it may seem to one who has never tried it.

THE TRANSLATOR.

N.B.—The references in the introductory essays and in the notes are to Bekker's octavo edition of Aristotle, published by the Clarendon Press. At the bottom of each page of the translation there has also been added a reference to the corresponding place in the Berlin quarto edition.

CONTENTS.

	PAGE
PREFACE	v
INTRODUCTION	i
THE MAIN GROUPS OF ANIMALS	xxi
SYNOPSIS	xxxv
TRANSLATION.—Book I.	1
,, ,, II.	19
,, ,, III.	57
,, ,, IV.	92
NOTES.—Book I.	141
,, ,, II.	150
,, ,, III.	186
,, ,, IV.	217
ERRATA	254
INDEX TO NOTES	255

INTRODUCTION.

How came these adaptations about, is a question coeval, we may be sure, with the first recognition of the adaptations themselves. The answers to it fell of old, as ever since, into two main divisions. One group of philosophers there was, who fancied that they found an adequate cause for the phenomena in the necessary operations of the inherent properties of matter; while another sought a solution in the intelligent action of a benevolent and foreseeing agent, whom they called God, or Nature, as the case might be. Look, for instance, said these latter, at the back-bone. See how marvellously it has been constructed to suit the animal's requirements; not made of one solid mass, as is the femur or the humerus, but subdivided into small pieces, so as to allow of the animal making such motions and bendings as it may require; while at the same time, in spite of its subdivision, so firmly bound together are its parts, as to supply a rigid support to the frame.[1] Or look again at the alimentary canal and at the blood-vessels. Each part requires a supply of matter for its due nourishment. What but foresight and intelligent purpose can have made these channels throughout the body to meet that necessity? Or see again your hand. Notice how admirably it is made; what an exquisite instrument for the purposes of an intelligent animal, and how useless for one without such mental capacity; and then consider that it is man, and man alone, that has been endowed with it. Is it possible not to discern a foreseeing intention in this limitation of the organ to the creature that alone can use it with advantage? In all this, said the materialist, you are mistaken. The fœtus in its mother's womb is straitened for space, and forced to lie in a bent attitude. Its backbone gives way to the bendings, and is necessarily broken up into a series of short pieces.[2] The animal then makes the best use of it it may. As for the stomach, the intestines, and the blood-vessels,[3] they are simply formed by the fluid in the animal substance, driven hither and thither by the motions of that substance,

[1] D. P. ii. 9, 4. [2] D. P. i. 1, 16. [3] D. P. i. 1, 21.

making channels for itself where it can most easily escape. The hand, again, was not given to man because he was already intelligent; but an animal among the millions of possibilities chanced to develop a hand, and, having it, made use of it, and by its means became intelligent.[1] But, said the teleologist, if this be so, if all be due to chance combinations which the multiform play of the laws of matter brings about, how comes it that we everywhere see adaptations? Combinations there should be without adaptations; combinations, even, where the organs and the life are ill suited for each other. And are there not such, said the materialist, partly anticipating Darwin, as before he had partly anticipated Herbert Spencer; are there not such about you on every side? You have but to open your eyes and you will see them everywhere. When the rain falls in seed-time you say the gods send it that the crops may grow; but you shut your eyes to the storms that come in harvest and wreck the farmers' hopes. The rain, whether it do good or harm, is alike the result of necessity. So also is it with things that live. All kinds of combinations are produced, but those alone survive that have the necessary conditions of survival; the rest perish.[2] Even of such as are able to survive, is it true that all are suited for their life, in the sense that your hypothesis of an intelligent creative power would require? Do we not see on all sides living monstrosities and deformities, whose existence is incompatible with design, and only explicable if referred to blind necessity? These, if such there be, are no more, said the teleologist, much as Paley[3] said after him, than the blunders of an artist. You will find errors in the composition of the best writer; faults

[1] D. P. iv. 10, 19.
[2] Cf. Phys. ii. 8, 4, where is a remarkable passage in which A. thus states the materialistic view. "Why, however, it must be asked, should we look on the operations of Nature as dictated by a final cause, and intended to realise some desirable end? Why may they not be merely the results of necessity, just as the rain falls of necessity, and not that the corn may grow? For the uprising of the watery vapour, its cooling when thus raised, and its fall as rain when cooled, are all matters of necessity; and though the rain makes the corn grow, it no more occurs in order to cause that growth, than a shower which spoils the farmer's crop at harvest-time occurs in order to do that mischief. Now, why may not this, which is true of the rain, be true also of the parts of the body? Why, for instance, may not the teeth grow to be such as they are merely of necessity, and the fitness of the front ones with their sharp edge for the comminution of the food, and of the hind ones with their flat surface for its mastication, be no more than an accidental coincidence, and not the cause that has determined their development? And so with all the other parts, wherever there is an appearance of final causes? In short, whenever accident caused all the parts of the body to be developed spontaneously in this suitable manner, to be developed, that is, just as they would have been had design presided over the formation, the resulting wholes survived; but when this was not the case they perished, and still do perish, as Empedocles insists when speaking of certain monstrosities."
The explanation suggested in this passage will be found recurring in after-ages. A similar hypothesis, for instance, is started in Diderot's "Letter on the Blind for the use of those who can See," where it is put in the mouth of the blind Sanderson. The relation in which the hypothesis stands to that of Darwin may thus be expressed; the old philosopher insists on the survival of the fit, Darwin on the survival of the fittest. What a vast difference underlies the apparent similarity in the introduction of a single short syllable scarcely needs to be pointed out.
[3] Nat. Theol. i. 2.

in the work of the best sculptor.[1] But the presence of these will not prevent you from believing that writer and sculptor worked with a preconceived intention and for a definite end.

So began, and so was carried on, that venerable strife, which ever since has divided thinking men into two factions, and which still, though twenty centuries have passed away, is fought with unchanged weapons, and with increasing bitterness, and in which neither side has ever succeeded in reducing an opponent to submission, while each has never failed to claim complete victory.

Between these two opposite views Aristotle had now to decide. He had already in his Historia Animalium set forth the phenomena of animal life. He had now to consider to what cause or causes these phenomena were attributable. Were they due to mere necessity, or to the action of intelligent foresight, or at any rate of some principle that acted as intelligent foresight would do? To neither, he says, exclusively, but to both, though in very unequal degrees. The motions of the heavenly bodies are governed by necessity, and by necessity alone. But in the works of Nature, that is in the phenomena of terrestrial life, this necessity is a comparatively unimportant factor. Most is the outcome of design. Still some part, though but a small one, is the result of necessity. There is indeed one sense in which everything in the animal body may be said to be the result of necessity. When a man builds a house, he must, in order to realise his plan, of necessity have walls, roof, and the like. To have these he must first have bricks, stones, mortar, and what not; and, again, to furnish these, clay, lime, and the other necessary materials must be previously forthcoming. So is it with the animal body. The design of Nature cannot be carried out without the necessary antecedents.[2] In this sense then all the parts of the body, and all the successive stages by which they are developed one after the other, may be said to be the result of necessity; for all must necessarily be there, if the plan of Nature is to be realised.

This "hypothetical or conditional necessity" is, however, clearly not what is meant by Democritus and the Materialists when they say that all organisms are the result of necessity. They speak of absolute, not of hypothetical necessity. They mean, that is to say, that organisms are evolved as necessary consequences of the inherent properties of matter; not merely that the existence of the organism implies the pre-existence of the necessary conditions for its production; in short, that the antecedents determine the end, and not the end the antecedents. Is this, asks Aristotle, in any degree true? In some measure, he answers, it is; but that measure, as already said, is but a small one.

---

[1] Phys. ii. 8, 11.   [2] D. P. i. 1, 12.

Nature in making plants and animals can but use such material substances as exist. Now these substances have many properties. Suppose then that Nature has selected one or more of them for a given purpose, in virtue of their having this or that suitable property; she must take them not only with this desirable property, but with all their other characters, whatsoever these may be; and these other properties, which were not the cause of the selection, will afterwards assert themselves, and give rise to necessary consequences not included in her design. Thus "we must not expect to find everything in the body made for a purpose. Its parts are mostly the result of final causes; but their material constitution entails as necessary consequences much that is incidental and undesigned."[1] These incidental and unforeseen results may be perfectly useless,[2] nay, may even sometimes be baneful;[3] but, on the other hand, they may be laid hold of by Nature, and incorporated in her scheme, though not originally included within it.[4] The excreta, for instance, are the result of necessity; for the body wears away, and the products of its decay, together with the surplus and the indigestible parts of the food, must necessarily be eliminated. But these excreta are in many cases utilised, and converted into means of defence.[5] Or, to give another example; the formation of the skin is the necessary consequence of the exposure of the external surface to friction and evaporation,[6] and the growth of hair upon the scalp is the necessary and incidental consequence of certain arrangements in the skull, which were intended by Nature to answer another purpose.[7] But this skin when once formed, and this growth though undesigned, are utilised by Nature, and turned to account in furnishing a protection to the parts beneath against excess of heat or cold. In other words, then, Nature does the best she can with the materials that are at hand; but the properties of those materials are beyond her control, and such consequences as follow upon those properties are the results of necessity.[8]

[1] D. P. iv. 2, 8. So also De Animâ, iii. 12, 2: "Everything given by Nature is either itself given for an end, or is the incidental accompaniment of something else which is given for an end."
[2] Those characters of an organism, says A. (De Gen. v. i.) that are essential, that is, that form part of its natural design, are fixed and immutable; those that are unessential, casual, and outside the plan, are variable. Thus, an eye is essential to an animal that is intended by Nature to see, and is invariably present in such; but the precise colour of the eye is, speaking generally, unessential, and therefore variable, being left to the uncontrolled action of material causes.
[3] D. P. iii. 2, 19.
[4] D. P. iii. 2, 15. "The necessary results of existing material conditions are made available by rational nature for a final cause."
[5] Cf. iii. 2, note 8.   [6] D. G. ii. 6, 26.   [7] D. P. ii. 14, 6, and ii. 7, 19.
[8] "Magnopere hallucinantur, quicumque eas (*final causes*) physicis causis adversari aut repugnare putent. Nam causâ redditâ, quod *palpebrarum pili oculos muniant*, nequicquam repugnat altera illa, quod pilositas soleat contingere humiditatum orificiis. Neque causa reddita, quod *coriorum in animalibus firmitudo pertinet ad cæli injurias prepulsandas*, adversatur illi alteri, quod illa firmitudo fit ob contractionem pororum in extimis corporum per frigus et deprædationem aeris, etc."—*Bacon, De Augm. Scient.* iii. 4.

A similar notion of the limitation of creative power runs through the whole of the Timæus. The gods in making man and animals do the best they can, but they deal with a more or less intractable material, which often baffles their efforts. "Let us always, and in all that we say," says Plato, "hold that God made them as far as possible the fairest and best, out of things which were not fair and good."[1]

Galen, also, some centuries later, took much the same position, when criticising the Mosaic cosmogony.[2] Moses, he says, teaches us that the Creator is lord over the necessary properties of matter, and that he can suspend or modify them at his will. He tells us that the Creator can make an animal of any matter he may please, a man from a stone, an ox from dust. This we deny. The laws of matter are antecedent to the Creator, and obligatory upon him. He can only work in harmony with them. He can choose the best which they allow, but not the best absolutely.

Aristotle, then, admits that necessity is a factor in the world of life; and this not merely in the sense that living bodies consist throughout of ordinary matter, retaining its original properties unaltered; but also in the sense that some parts of living structures are the simple outcome of such properties, uncontrolled and undirected by design or final cause. What he denies is that the whole organism, or more than an inconsiderable part of it, can thus be explained. It is ridiculous, he says, to suppose that such phenomena as those of organic life are merely the result of chance; meaning by chance, as I understand him, no separate mysterious agency, but such uncoordinated combinations of necessary causes as are too tangled for man to unravel, and whose results are therefore not to be predicted. The very essence of chance is its uncertainty. Chance is the principle of the inconstant. But the phenomena in question present a high degree of constancy, and can be foretold with more or less precision. It is quite plain that besides the necessary forces of matter, there is something else at work which guides and coordinates these, so as to make them converge to a predetermined end. If a man cannot see this, it is absurd to argue with him; as well try and convince a man born blind, who denies the existence of colour.[3] You see a house or a ship, and without hesitation you infer that such house or ship was made for the purposes to which ships and houses are subservient. Why? Because they are manifestly adapted to those purposes. Why, then, when you see a plant or an animal with equally manifest adaptations, do you hesitate to draw a similar inference? True, in one case you can see the agent at work, while in the other the agency is invisible. But, why should this make

---

[1] Jowett's Transl. ii. 546. [2] De Usu part. xi. 14. [3] Phys. ii. 1, 5.

any difference? The agency in the latter case is invisible, because it is an internal force, a something acting inside the material. It is as though the visible shipwright were away, and his art were inherent in the timber itself. It is the case of a physician getting well, not that of a physician curing another person. Moreover, if the agency itself be out of sight, the model from which it works is visible enough; is as visible and palpable as the model of the ship or the plan of the house, and, like them, examinable before either is constructed. For the germ or seed will not develop after any chance pattern,[1] but will grow in the likeness of its parent. Nature's model is that parent form. The seed of an olive will not produce any chance plant, but an olive like that from which it came. Man gives rise to man, and horse to horse. The doctrine of Empedocles ignores this fact.[2] You say, or Empedocles said, that the multiform interaction of the countless combinations of matter gives rise to every conceivable form of being; but that those forms alone survive that have the necessary conditions of survival.[3] Be it so. But the olive and the man are not the only beings that have these conditions. Why, then, do they always produce offspring like themselves?[4] Why not any one of the other countless possible forms of life? Clearly because there is something else than the chance combinations of necessary properties of matter, guiding and directing these to a preconcerted end. This something else is what I call Nature. I grant that, as Nature is invisible, her existence is an hypothesis, but her works are visible and the hypothesis is founded upon the contemplation of these.[5] If you ask me whether this hidden force acts, as the builder or the shipwright, with conscious deliberation, and conscious adaptation of means to ends, I do not know. Even art is not always deliberative.[6] The highest art goes straight to its end without deliberation. So, too, the swallow builds its nest and the spider its web without deliberation, and yet each in nicest adaptation to its wants.[7] Why may not Nature be a similar force implanted in matter, undeliberating though guiding to a rational end? All I assert is, that there is something at work in living bodies more than the common necessary properties of inanimate matter, something which, whether deliberative or not, acts as would an intelligent agent, selecting the best end, and reaching it by the most appropriate means. "Invariably, however, when there is plainly some final end to which a motion tends, should nothing stand in the way, we say that such final end is the aim or purpose of the motion."[8] In other words, in the works of Nature, as in those of Art, it is the desirability of the end, which in some way or other determines the antecedent processes that lead to it. But you say, that what I call

[1] Phys. ii. 8, 13.   [2] D. P. i. 1, 16.   [3] Phys. ii. 8, 4.   [4] Phys. ii. 8, 13.
[5] D. G. v. 8, 4.   [6] Phys. ii. 8, 15.   [7] Phys. ii. 8, 9.   [8] D. P. i. 1, 37.

Nature occasionally produces deformities and monstrosities. Does the artist, your builder, let us say, or your shipwright, never make a blunder?[1] Do such blunders make you infer that the artist had no definite end in view? Monstrosities are Nature's mistakes; or, rather, they are her failures; for they are due not to any imperfection or uncertainty in her action, which is invariable and faultless, but to the uncertainty of her materials. The substances in which she works are of indefinite composition, and her work cannot therefore possibly be uniform. The monstrosity is not Nature's work; it is the victory of matter over Nature.[2] Thus it is that though there is nothing of haphazard or of chance in Nature herself, Nature being invariably the source of order,[3] yet her operations appear to be liable to exceptions, and her rules to be of general rather than of universal application. "In all our speculations, therefore, concerning Nature, what we have to consider is the general rule. For that is natural which holds good either universally or generally."[4]

There is an apparent difficulty here which requires a moment's consideration. Aristotle held the properties of the elementary forms of matter to be fixed and immutable. How, then, could he explain Nature's occasional miscarriages by the indefinite character of the materials? Clearly, if the properties of the elementary bodies are fixed, when once an organism has been formed from them with a certain degree of perfection, any failure thereafter to attain at any rate to an equal degree must be attributable not to the necessary properties of matter, but to the faulty selection of material. For the properties of matter manifestly cannot be inconsistent with such perfection as has actually once been realised. Nature, therefore, must have been held by Aristotle either to have been an influence acting with limited intelligence, or to have been in some way or other hindered in her choice of materials; to have had, that is, her freedom narrowed by something more than the ultimate properties of elementary matter. The latter was, undoubtedly, Aristotle's view; and the limitation consisted in the materials with which Nature had to deal not being the ultimate elements themselves with their immutable properties, but those compound substances which were in reality the simplest actually producible bodies in existence, the pure elements themselves never being actually presentable as such, in a condition, that is, of isolation.[5] Had Nature been able, as a modern chemist, to take so much of each or any of the elementary substances as she pleased, and to form from them compounds of fixed composition, and therefore of fixed properties, her

---

[1] Phys. ii. 8, 11.   [2] D. G. iv. 4, 11, and iv. 10, 10.
[3] De Cælo, ii. 8, 2; Phys. viii. 1, 16; De Gen. iii. 10, 18, etc.
[4] D. P. iii. 2, 16.   [5] Cf. ii. 1, note 3.

operations would have had a fixed basis, and her invariable purposes have been carried out with invariable precision. But, in making earthly organisms, she had to deal with materials as they actually exist on earth; and such were of indeterminate composition,[1] and therefore of indeterminate properties. For it must be borne in mind that though Aristotle distinguished chemical union from mere mechanical intermixture,[2] he had of course no notion either of combination in definite proportions, or even of preferential affinities. There was no such thing as definite composition, or definite compound substances. One piece of compound matter might more or less nearly resemble another, but that it should be identical with it in composition, and therefore in properties, was in the infinity of possibilities not to be dreamed of. Every sample of material would differ more or less from every other; and organisms made from such materials could never be precisely alike. The heavenly bodies being formed of a single pure uncombined elementary substance were free from such variability, and their phenomena were therefore absolutely fixed and eternal. But earthly substances were all compound, and therefore all indeterminate. Their compound character introduced an element of chance, which often thwarted Nature's efforts, the faulty matter refusing to take the form she would impress upon it.

There is a question to which one would gladly find an answer, but to which no sure answer is forthcoming. Did Aristotle suppose that there stood anything in the background behind this mysterious organising force which he personified as Nature? And, if so, what was it? That the force which constrained the material of each individual organism to develop into the form most suited to the requirements was the same force which, acting on a larger scale, brought the fishes of the sea, the fowls of the air, the plants of the earth, and in short all forms of life, more or less completely into harmonious relations with each other,[3] and established an ascending scale of interdependence, in which plants should minister to animals, and animals to man,[4] may be fairly assumed. But this is only to remove the question one stage back. Whence did this universal Nature (ἡ τοῦ ὅλου φύσις) derive its principle of harmony and excellence? Was it a something self-existing, or something, like the orderly discipline of an army, which, though apparently inherent,

---

[1] D. G. iv. 10, 10. [2] Cf. ii. 1, note 4.
[3] Met. xi. (xii.) 10, 2. The passage is worth quoting, if only for the "noblesse oblige" simile. "The universe is not so constituted that there is no interdependence between one thing and another. Such relation does in truth exist. For all things have been ordered together as part of one whole; and all things, the fowls of the air, the fishes of the sea, and the plants of the earth, have been in some wise brought into harmony with each other, though not all in equal degree. It is as in a household; where the masters are by no means at liberty to act by chance, but in all or most of their doings are guided by fixed rules; while the slaves and animals do some little for the common weal, but for the most part act by chance, and follow the dictates of their individual natures."
[4] Polit. i. 8, 11.

INTRODUCTION.   ix

is in reality dependent on a general in the background? Aristotle himself asks[1] the question, but gives no answer. This much, however, seems clear. The general, if general there were, could not be the extra-cosmic God whose existence is postulated in the Metaphysics, the "Unmoved that causes motion as an object of desire;" for his life was an undisturbed ecstacy of self-contemplation. But whether there were other divine essences of less serene attributes, answering to the inferior gods who in the Timæus are interposed between the Demiurgus and mortal beings, of whose intelligent activity Nature was but the expression, is a question which, whatever surmise we may form from a few stray and hazy passages, admits of no definite solution. In the biological treatises there is no reference whatsoever to the relation in which, if in any, Nature stands to God. In these Aristotle limits himself to the teachings, or supposed teachings, of the senses. These revealed to him the phenomena of animal life, and he wrote of them. They showed him also, or seemed to show him, as plainly as his eyes showed him the existence of colour, that these phenomena were not explicable by reference to the ordinary properties of inanimate matter, but implied the action of some other and co-ordinating force. They told him also something of the conditions and limitations under which this force acted, and with these, also, he deals. But they told him nothing of the origin of this force, and, whatever may have been his ideas as a metaphysician, as a biologist he was silent.

Having in the first book of this treatise laid down his general position, Aristotle proceeds in the rest of the work to deal with the application of his views to particulars. With this purpose he takes the various parts of the body, both tissues and organs, one after the other, into consideration, and professes to examine in each case how far the structure is the outcome of necessity, how far of apparent design. Such, I say, is his profession. His actual practice is merely to see if it be possible to find any use, real or imaginary, for a given structure, and if such can be devised, at once to claim that structure, without further argument, for design. Seeing how fertile was his fancy in generating final causes, it will be readily understood how scanty a margin remained after this process as the share of necessity. One set of structures indeed there was which seems to have caused him much difficulty. These were the organs which we now-a-days know as rudimentary parts. The inutility of these was too striking to escape notice, and seemed to exclude them from the predesigned plan of Nature, that "makes nothing without a purpose." Were they then the offspring of mere necessity? To this question Aristotle never gives a definite answer. He speaks in many

[1] Met. xi. (xii.) 10, 1.

places as though Nature worked under some kind of restraint, the obligation of which is never clearly defined, whether, that is, it is self-imposed or dictated from without. This restraint consists in the existence of certain definite types or patterns, in more or less close accordance with which each organism must be made. Nature, for instance, can fashion this or that bird to fit the exact mode of life which is pre-ordained for its species; but in so fashioning it she must not transgress certain limits. Each and all birds, through all their varieties, must present in form and composition[1] the essential characters of the ideal bird which constitutes the avian type. If any part in this type be useless to the special animal created, nay, even if its presence be actually prejudicial,[2] yet it must still be there in some shape or other, "by way of token" (σημείου χάριν). The most that Nature in such a case can do is to reduce its size; and, inasmuch as the ultimate composition of all the animals in a given class is precisely, or almost precisely, alike, she can only do this by diverting the material which should have gone to the full formation of the useless or prejudicial part into some other organ where it may be of use, or at any rate not equally injurious. So that, in fact, the organisation of an individual species of animals is not always the best conceivable, but the best of which the essential type of the class to which that species belongs admits.[3] Aristotle, as I have said, never expresses himself clearly on this matter. Did Nature herself make these types, and adhere to them in her after-work with the obstinacy of a prejudiced inventor; or, was there some external necessity coercing her, and driving her against her own better judgment to make her products in part futile? I take it that Aristotle was not himself clear as to his own views on the matter; that his opponents, or his own mind, had pointed out the impossibility of reconciling the existence of rudimentary organs with the strictly teleological position, and that he met the difficulty with a phrase, "by way of token," leaving it really unexplained.

The giant share which Aristotle allots to final causes, and the almost complete exclusion of necessity from consideration, make the main portion of his treatise to consist of little more than an attempt to assign to each part of the animal body a definite use; so that the work becomes rather one on the functions of parts than on the causes of their existence, and might almost have been styled, as was Galen's later work, a treatise "De Usu partium." Very possibly it was on this account that the designation by which Aristotle himself[4] refers to the work, "On the Causes of the Parts of Animals," was in time superseded by the vaguer title "De Partibus," which it has ever since borne.

[1] D. P. iv. 12, 28.   [2] D. P. iii. 2, 5.   [3] De Incessu. 2, 1, and 8, 1.   [4] D. G. v. 3, 6.

We have now to enquire how it fared with Aristotle in his search after final causes, in his attempt, that is, to assign to each organ its proper function.

It must be confessed that his success, as measured by what has been attained in modern times, was but small. In dealing, indeed, with the external parts he was more happy. His account, for instance, of the adaptation of the visible parts of birds to the varied modes of life in this class of animals is admirable, and reads like a chapter from Cuvier, whose unstinted praise was lavished on it. But with the internal organs it was otherwise. The most that can be said is that he devised an ingenious system, which included in its range pretty fairly all such facts as were known to him, but which in its conclusions was far wide of the truth as now ascertained. This was indeed inevitable. He was trying to solve the complex problems of biology, while the ancillary sciences were yet unknown. Anatomy was still in its first infancy, physics embryonic, and chemistry hardly as yet conceived. What possibility was there that digestion or respiration should, under these conditions, find an adequate interpretation? This explanation of Aristotle's failure to assign to the several internal parts their several functions seems to me a sufficient and a true one. It is more usual, however, to account for it on other grounds, and to attribute it to his carelessness in the observation of individual facts, his hastiness in generalisation, and the imperfection of his method. A few words on each of these alleged causes of defeat; and, first, as to his supposed inaccuracy of observation. I cannot but think that this has been, to say the least, enormously exaggerated. Were we indeed to suppose that Aristotle had committed all the extravagant blunders which critics have laid to his charge, the accusation would have to be admitted as just. But a very large proportion, at any rate, of his supposed mistakes have no other ground than the careless mode in which his writings have been studied. They are not mistakes of Aristotle, but mistakes of his critics. To give a few examples. It is laid to his charge that he represented the arteries as void of blood and containing nothing but air; the aorta as springing from the right ventricle; the heart as beating in man and in no other animal, and as not liable to disease; the gall-bladder as situated in some animals on or close to the tail; reptiles as having no blood; and so on, till the list might be swollen with almost every conceivable absurdity. In reality not one of the errors here enumerated was made by him. Still I am far from denying that there are strange misstatements of simple facts to be found in his works. That there is but a single bone in the neck of the lion and of the wolf; that there are more teeth in male than in female animals; that the mouth of the dolphin is placed, as in rays and sharks, on the under surface of the body; these and the like are strange blunders, however they originated. This much, however, seems to me beyond question: these were not the personal observations of the same man who had noted the heart beating in the embryonic chick as a "punctum saliens" on the third day of incubation; who had distinguished the allantoidean development of birds and reptiles from the non-allantoidean development of fishes; who had unravelled with fair accuracy the arrangement of the bronchial tubes and their relation to the pulmonary blood-vessels; and who had not only given zoological and anatomical details concerning the cephalopods, which both Cuvier and Owen regard as "truly astonishing," but had described nine species of them "with so much precision and happy a selection of their distinctive characters as to enable modern naturalists to identify pretty nearly all."[1]

Is it possible to believe that the same eye that had distinguished the cetacea from the fishes, that had detected their hidden mammæ, discovered their lungs, and recognised the distinct character of their bones, should have been so blind as to fancy that the mouth of these animals was on the under surface of the body? Although a statement to this effect occurs twice over in the Greek text, yet it is to me as incredible that it should have been actually made by Aristotle, as it would be that Professor Huxley should make a similarly palpable misstatement about an animal with which he was perfectly familiar. If it be asked how we can account for the presence of the erroneous statement in the text, we have not to go far for, at any rate, a very possible explanation. We have only to remember the strange vicissitudes to which the original manuscripts of Aristotle's treatises are said to have been subjected. Hidden underground in the little town of Scepsis, to save them from the hands of the kings of Pergamus, who were then collecting books to form their famous library, and who, in so doing, apparently paid but little regard to the rights of individual owners, they were left for the better part of two centuries to moulder in the damp, "blattarum et tinearum epulæ;" and when they were at last again brought to light, fell into the hands of Apellicon of Teos, a man who, as Strabo says, was a lover of books rather than a philosopher, and who felt no scruples in correcting what had become worm-eaten, and supplying what was defective or illegible.[2] To what extent this corruption of the very fountain head took place, we have now absolutely no means whatsoever of ascertaining. We are, however, I think, justified in assuming with much confidence that such palpable absurdities, as the one which has just been mentioned were due to this sacrilegious interference with the text, and should be put not to the account of Aristotle, but to that of the incompetent Apellicon, or his fellow transcribers and emendators.

[1] Todd's Cyclop. i. 561. [2] Grote's Arist. i. 51.

Similarly would I explain another blunder already mentioned, namely, the statement which occurs in the Historia Animalium, that in certain species of animals, namely men goats sheep and swine, the teeth are more numerous in the males than in the females, a blunder which has been quoted, with others, by Mr. Lewes, as an instance of Aristotle's carelessness in observation. That this statement is due to interpolation or correction of the original manuscript I feel the more assured, because in other passages, in the De Partibus, when the distinctions between males and females as regards their horns, teeth, and their offensive and defensive weapons generally, are discussed,[1] no such erroneous statement is to be found. It is said, and said correctly, that horns and tusks are often larger in the male than in the female, and horns frequently wanting in the latter when present in the former; but as to any difference in the number of the teeth, there is not a single word. We can readily conceive how an incompetent editor, finding in the manuscript a half legible passage relating to the teeth of male and female animals, may have so filled up the gap as to convert a difference of size into a difference of number.[2] Some of the more striking blunders in Aristotle's treatises, especially such as occur only in single instances, may, I think, be fairly thus explained. As to others, we must remember that Aristotle, like every writer on a vast subject, had to rely in great measure on the statements as to matters of facts made by others, and this the more implicitly as the opportunities of verifying these statements were but rare, neither menageries nor museums of anatomy having as yet come into existence.

There is indeed a tale that Alexander supplied Aristotle with animals from all the countries into which his expeditions led him; but this story is so plainly fabulous that it might be passed over entirely without notice, had it not received the sanction of the great Cuvier. "On voit en effet," says he,[3] "par l'exactitude avec laquelle Aristote décrit plusieurs animaux de l'Inde et de la Perse, qu'il a eu sous les yeux les objets eux-mêmes." Five animals are mentioned[4] as examples of this statement, the elephant, the camel, the hippelaphus, the hippardium, the buffalo. As regards the first two of these, the description given by Aristotle is fairly complete; and inasmuch as these animals, being tamed, would present no difficulty in transportation, it is not impossible that Aristotle may actually have seen them. I can, however, find no evidence that he had done so, there being nothing in the description

---

[1] D. P. iii. 1.
[2] There are, it may be noted, some species in which the males have more teeth than the females; in the sense that teeth which are more or less highly developed in the males are, if not absent, yet rudimentary in the females. The narwhal is a well-known instance, the horse is another.
[3] Hist. d. Sc. Nat. i. 137.   [4] Ibid. p. 154.

xiv   INTRODUCTION.

which might not easily have been communicated by others, while some remarks are made which seem to me much more compatible with the latter view than with the former. As regards the other three animals, it is astonishing how Cuvier can speak of their being so accurately described as to imply actual examination. They are only mentioned once, all together, in a few clauses (H. A. ii. 1, 20, 21, 22); just as they might be if Aristotle were citing a passage of a letter from his pupil Callisthenes, who accompanied Alexander, and with whom Cuvier himself supposes Aristotle to have kept up a continuous correspondence.[1] The hippelaphus may be identified with much probability, though no actual certainty, with the nylghau, and the wild oxen are undoubtedly buffaloes. But the details given in this passage are quite insufficient to determine what animal is meant by the pardium or hippardium; and to prove this it is enough to say that Cuvier, who must have been speaking at second-hand, and relying upon some utterly untrustworthy authority, actually identifies it with the "tigre chasseur," or cheetah, whereas it is said by Aristotle to have a cloven hoof and horns, in this resembling the hippelaphus, and has been supposed by some to correspond to the giraffe! Cuvier the historian of science is, as I have often found, an authority of very different value from Cuvier the biologist.

Whether Ptolemy Philadelphus, not very many years after Aristotle's death, instituted a museum with a zoological garden attached to it, more richly supplied with animals than any that has since existed, as is stated,[2] may be doubtful; but that no such collection was open to Aristotle is, I think, indisputably shown by the utter absence of any allusion to it in his treatises. Thus Aristotle, in all probability, had never had the opportunity of personally examining any of the larger carnivora, either alive or dead. The stories of hunters, always prone to exaggeration, were the only source of information as to the habits of these animals in life; and if a chance skin, hung up in a temple to commemorate an escape from a perilous encounter, may perhaps have sometimes given a more direct notion of their external aspect, yet the internal parts—spirits of wine or other preservatives of organic structures not having as yet been discovered—must have been entirely beyond the reach of investigation. A hunter, noticing the thick and solid neck of the lion and the wolf, jumped to the conclusion that it contained but a single bone, and did not hesitate to report as an actual anatomical

---

[1] I do not know on what authority Cuvier makes this probable statement. I presume, however, that he relied on a passage in Simplicius, where it is stated that Callisthenes forwarded certain ancient astronomical observations to Aristotle from Babylon. Cf. Simpl. Comment. ex recens. Karstenii, p. 226.
[2] Hist. d. Sc. Nat. i. 174.

observation what was in reality a mere supposition.[1] Nor does it imply any great credulity on the part of Aristotle, that he should unhesitatingly have accepted such a report. For it is not the actual falseness of a statement, but its inconsistency with our previous experience, which makes the ready acceptance of it to be an act of credulity. A modern naturalist knows from an examination of a vast number of species that, as a rule to which there is scarcely an exception, the mammalian neck contains seven vertebræ, and that in no known instance are there less than six. Possessing this knowledge, he would show great credulity were he to accept without further question any account of a mammal with but one cervical bone. But to Aristotle, who had not this previous knowledge, there would seem nothing strange in such an account; and as there was nothing in it to rouse his suspicions, he would accept it without question. In no instance do we find similar outrageous errors, when Aristotle, as he often does, states a fact to have been derived from his own observation. So far, indeed, as I can judge, he seems to have been anything rather than a careless and inaccurate observer. It cannot, of course, be maintained that he was able to observe with the precision of a modern man of science. His substratum was insufficient for this. To observe, unless the phenomena be of the very simplest, it is not enough to keep the eyes open and to watch with honest intention for what may turn up. To be effectual, observation requires a stock of previous knowledge. He that has most of this will see best and most. Tell me, said even the long-experienced Faraday, when asked to be witness of an intended experiment, tell me what you expect me to see, that I may be able to see it.

A second source of Aristotle's failure is found in his habit of hasty generalisation. That he was constantly generalising on a very scanty basis of facts cannot be denied. The stage to which biology had then attained made this a matter of necessity. The first stage in every new science is the simple accumulation of facts. The next, if it may be called next, seeing that it must go hand in hand with the first, is the rough sorting of these facts and the reduction of their chaos to some kind of order. This is effected by temporary generalisations, which, though they may be very far from the ultimate truth, yet serve for the time the necessary purpose of enabling the observer to manage his otherwise unwieldy material. All that can fairly be demanded at this period is that there shall be diligence in the collection of facts, and that the temporary generalisations shall not be obviously untrue. As regards Aristotle's

[1] Possibly, however, not a mere supposition, but a hasty generalisation from some single example, in which the cervical vertebræ had been affected as they are occasionally in the hyæna, and become anchylosed. And this is the more possible, inasmuch as the anchylosis has actually given rise to a similar belief concerning the hyæna, namely, that it has but one bone in the neck. Cf. Règne Animal, i. 160.

diligence there can be no doubt. Every chapter in his treatises bears testimony to it. What proportion, indeed, of the huge array of facts there stored was due to his own personal observations, to his dissections, vivisections, and occasional experimentations, what was borrowed from others, it is impossible to say with any exactness. For the works of his predecessors and contemporaries have perished almost completely; and the laudable custom of citing the authority on which a statement is made had not yet been established. As yet there was no mistrust of other observers, because as yet it was not known how easy it is for an observer to be misled. Aristotle does indeed occasionally mention a name, but it is the name of some one whose statement he rejects, and very rarely, if ever, the name of one whose statement he borrows.[1] Nor must it be supposed that Aristotle's generalisations, though often false, were utterly puerile. Among them are not a few that, with little or no modification, have stood the test of time; and some even that, restated by moderns in ignorance of his writings, have been claimed by themselves or their admirers as deserving high credit. The law of organic equivalents, for instance, the general statement, that is, that Nature must save in one part if she spends in another, be it true or false, has been claimed for Goethe and for Geoffroy St.-Hilaire. Yet it had been stated in unmistakable terms over and over again in this treatise of Aristotle's.[2] The advantage of physiological division of labour "was first set forth," says Milne-Edwards,[3] "by myself in 1827;" yet Aristotle had said repeatedly that it is preferable when possible to have a separate organ for a separate office; and that Nature never, if she can help it, makes one organ answer two purposes, as a cheap artist makes "spit and candlestick" in one.[4] That the position of an organism in the kingdom to which it belongs is not to be settled by a single differentia, but by a consideration of its aggregate characters;[5] that the complexity of life varies with the complexity of the organisation;[6] that the structural differences of the alimentary organs are correlated with differences of the animal's alimentation;[7] that no animal is endowed with more than one adequate means of defence against its enemies;[8] that there is an inverse relation between the development of horns and of teeth;[9]

---

[1] Thus, when A. borrows the account of the hippopotamus (H. A. ii. 7) almost verbatim from Herodotus, he makes no mention of his authority; neither does he when he takes from the same source the account of a skull without sutures (H. A. iii. 7, 3); but on three occasions, when he contradicts him, he mentions in so doing his name (H. A. iii. 22, 1, D. G. ii. 2, 11, and iii. 5, 15). From Ctesias he takes without acknowledgment the account of the parrot, and very probably of the elephant; but whenever he mentions Ctesias by name, it is to contradict him flatly. His treatment of Plato is exceptional. For though he frequently, in the De Partibus, alludes to statements in the Timæus to reject them, he always forbears in so doing to mention his former teacher's name.
[2] Cf. ii. 9, note 9.   [3] Leçons sur la Phys. i. 16.   [4] Cf. iv. 6, note 15.
[5] D. P. i. 3, 14.   [6] D. P. iv. 7, 1.   [7] D. P. iii. 14.
[8] Cf. iii. 2, note 9.   [9] Cf. iii. 2, note 19.

that no dipterous insect has a sting;[1] that there is an inverse relation between growth and generation;[2] that the embryo is evolved by a succession of gradual changes from a homogeneous mass into a complex organism,[3] and that the development of an organism is a progress from a general to a special form;[4] these and numerous others are instances of generalisations made by Aristotle, and which have lasted, with but slight modifications of his terms, to the present day.

There remains yet the faulty method. Mr. Lewes, in an interesting chapter, traces Aristotle's failure to the absence of verification from his method of enquiry. Again, however, I would say that verification does not find its proper sphere in the early condition of a nascent science, when the generalisations are merely provisional, and though false yet necessary precursors of more accurate ones. How far, indeed, Aristotle himself recognised the true character of his biological work, may be a matter of doubt. Few men care to look on the results of their hard toil as provisional and ephemeral. I can, however, find no passage in which he betrays any confidence in the finality or permanence of his conclusions. In the absence of such it seems but simple justice to credit him with at least the same degree of modesty as he evinced when speaking of his much more successful labours in another branch of science. "I found," he says, "no basis prepared; no models to copy . . . . Mine is the first step, and therefore a small one, though worked out with much thought and hard labour. It must be looked at as a first step, and judged with indulgence. You, my readers or hearers of my lectures, if you think I have done as much as can fairly be required for an initiatory start, compared with other more advanced departments of theory, will acknowledge what I have achieved, and pardon what I have left for others to accomplish."[5]

So far the comparison has been between Aristotle and his successors in modern times; for it is only in contrast with their achievements that we can speak of his results as failures. Such a comparison might serve in estimating their claims, but not in estimating his. For it is the gap that separates a man from his predecessors, not that which lies between him and his successors, that gives the true measure of his position. Let any one then compare Aristotle's physiology with that of the Timæus, which Plato, as Galen tells us,[6] borrowed from Hippocrates, and which we may therefore fairly take to represent the general views of the most prominent authorities immediately antecedent to Aristotle.

In passing, then, from the Timæus to Aristotle's treatises, one is

---

[1] Cf. iv. 6, note 13.   [2] D. G. iv. 4, 20 ; i. 8, 4.   [3] D. G. ii. ch. 4, 5, and 6.
[4] "The embryo of man or horse or other animal is not at first man or horse or other animal, but only assumes the specific form at a final stage," being first living thing, then animal, then special kind of animal. D. G. ii. 3, 4 ; ii. 6, 29 ; iii. 9, 2.
[5] Soph. El. xxxiv., as rendered by Grote, ii. 133.   [6] De Usu Part. i. 8.

conscious of passing into an entirely new order of things. In the former we have airy and fanciful constructions, in which imagination alone supplies the foundation, and in which facts, if introduced at all, are introduced merely as ornamental additions, in no wise essential to the fabric. In the latter the positions have been inverted. What was the ornament has become the foundation; what was foundation has been converted into ornament. It may, indeed, be that sometimes these new foundations are but slight and weak in comparison with the structure they are made to support, but they are at any rate substantial, and of the right material. "Jamais," says Cuvier,[1] speaking of his great predecessor, "jamais il ne pose une règle à priori;" and even if we allow, as perhaps we must, that exceptional cases may be found in which this too general statement hardly holds good, and in which Aristotle seems to lapse into the faulty methods of earlier writers, yet it must at the same time be conceded that these occasions are at most but rare; and that when they do occur, it is because, as with other men so with Aristotle, practice falls somewhat short of principle. Neither should we forget that in most minds there exists an æsthetic craving after completeness, or, when this is not to be had, after its semblance, a craving which leads men almost irresistibly to fill up the gaps in their systems with such makeshifts as come to hand; and this weakness may be forgiven them, if only they are ready to pull down their stop-gaps and cart them to the rubbish-heap, so soon as better materials can be obtained. That Aristotle, who manifestly felt this desire most acutely, and who in those early days of science had but scanty means of giving it legitimate satisfaction, should occasionally have had recourse to this palliative, can scarcely be a matter of surprise. But how ready he was to abandon it for better things the following passage, amongst others, shows. "Such," he says, after speaking of the reproduction of bees, "such is the conclusion to which we are led à priori, and facts apparently support it. I say apparently, for the actual facts are not yet sufficiently made out. Should future research ever discover them, we must surrender ourselves to their guidance, rather than to that of theory; and theories must be abandoned unless their teachings tally with the indisputable results of observation" (De Gener. iii. 10, 25). It was by thus altering the basis of enquiry, and substituting facts for theories, more than by actual observations, that Aristotle made a huge step in advance of his biological predecessors. And if, some two thousand years later, Bacon gained for himself an immortal name by insisting still more peremptorily upon the value of induction, it must be remem-

[1] "Toutes les propositions générales, qu'il exprime, sont des inductions, résultant de l'observation et de la comparaison des faits particuliers; jamais il ne pose une règle à priori."—Hist. d. Sc. Nat. i. 143.

bered that the instrument in his own hands was at any rate not more successful than in those of Aristotle. By the skilful use of scientific method to discover new truths is a noble achievement; but far nobler is it to discover the method itself, by which alone such achievements are made possible; and to have done this is Aristotle's glory. That the method as left by him was not perfect, that there were flaws which the fuller experience of after-ages detected, and gradually remedied, may be allowed. Seldom, if ever, does a great invention come fully armed from the brain of its first author. Weak points there invariably are, which trial alone will reveal. To detect and strengthen these is to confer a benefit on mankind; but is a service which can never be put on a par with that rendered by the original conception. "Inventions," to quote from a treatise[1] already once cited, "are either the final shapings of what has been partly elaborated by others, or they are original discoveries, and but roughly shaped. The latter are the most important. The first step, according to the proverb, is the grand thing and the most difficult; for first beginnings are as small and inconspicuous as they are potent. When they are once accomplished, the remainder is easily added or developed."

[1] Arist. on Fallacies. Poste's transl., p. 95.

THE MAIN GROUPS OF ANIMALS.

ARISTOTLE has left us no systematic classification of animals. It will nevertheless be convenient to arrange the chief groups recognised by him in a tabular form; and the form which seems most consistent with his views is that in which these groups are placed in linear series, according to their supposed degrees of excellence.

Before, however, doing this, it will be well to consider very briefly what Aristotle means when he speaks, as he so often does, of one animal being superior to or more noble than another; and also to enquire what were the external characters by which he thought such superiority could be recognised. When we have done this, we can proceed to apply Aristotle's tests of comparative excellence to his various groups with the fair expectation of being able to arrange them in much the same order as he would himself have done.

(1). The basis of all excellence is the presence of a soul, that is, the possession of life. "Anything nobler or better than the soul cannot possibly exist;"[1] and again, "to be is better than not to be; to live than not to live; things with a soul than things without; the soul itself than the body."[2] As things that live are superior to things that are lifeless, so also things with much life are superior to things with little. "Souls differ from each other in their degrees of honour;"[3] and the difference is thus set forth. "The faculties of the soul are many; and though everything that lives has a soul, yet have not all souls all these faculties. In some souls there is but one faculty, in others several, in some all. The faculties are the Nutritive, the Sensitive, the Appetitive, the Motor, the Intellectual. In plants there is no other faculty than the Nutritive, but in all animals there is not only this, but the Sensitive, and, as a necessary consequence, the Appetitive as well. Some animals there are, again, that possess also the Motor faculty; and a few, such as man and any other creature, if such there be, that equals or surpasses him in

---

[1] De Animâ, i. 5, 15.   [2] De Gen. ii. 1, 2.   [3] De Gen. ii. 3, 11.

honour, in whose soul there is still further the Intellectual faculty and Reason."[1] In proportion as the soul includes more or fewer of these successive faculties will its possessor's place be higher or lower in the scale of excellence. At the bottom will come organisms whose life is confined to nutrition; next, those that are also endowed with sensation; then, such as besides feeling are also capable of locomotion; and, lastly, those who add to these endowments the possession of reason. The few groups thus obtained will again be divisible into smaller groups, according to the degree in which each successive faculty is developed. There are degrees of Nutritive power, of Sensibility, of Motility, of Intelligence; and the question next to be considered is, what were the external characters by which Aristotle thought that he could determine these degrees.

(2). The Nutritive soul manifests itself, of course, in growth and reproduction; and the tests of its power are the bulk of the body,[2] and the duration of life, which is usually proportionate to the bulk. "For, as a rule, big animals are long lived, though not invariably."[3] The number of the progeny is not so good a measure as might be expected, because the requirements of a large body on the nutritive material may prevent an animal of great size from being prolific.[4] The sensitive soul is of course certainly present, if the organism have external organs of sense. But a doubt may arise when, as in the sponge,[5] there are none such. The test in such a case is to see whether the organism shrinks when irritated. The degrees of sensibility must be judged of by the number and perfection of the organs of sense, and especially of those senses from which are derived the perceptions, which conduce most to knowledge.

As to the Motor soul, and the Intellectual, the tests are self-evident; and may therefore be passed over.

But besides these special tests, applicable to the several parts of the soul, Aristotle had other more general ones, by which he gauged the excellence of the soul as a whole. Foremost among these was the temperature of the body. For though Aristotle would not allow,[6] with Democritus, that heat was identical with the soul, that is, with life, yet he admitted that heat was its necessary agent, so that the two were inseparably conjoined, and the degree of the one became a measure of the degree of the other. "The nobler an animal is, the greater is the amount of heat it possesses. For with greater heat there must of necessity be combined a nobler soul."[7] But how was the temperature to be measured? As Aristotle had no thermometer, he could only form a

[1] De An. ii. 3, 1. [2] De Gen. ii. 1, 7. [3] De Long. vitæ 4, 3; De Gen. iv. 10, 1.
[4] De Gen. iv. 4, 20, and i. 8, 4. [5] H. A. i. 1, 18. [6] D. P. ii. 7, 5.
[7] De Resp. 13, 2.

notion of the relative temperatures of different animals either directly by touch, or indirectly by inference from structure. On touch, though sometimes used by him, he apparently placed but little reliance. For, as he says,[1] it could not tell whether the heat was intrinsic, or whether it was merely accidental and derived from without. Moreover, even supposing that touch were a sufficient measure of ordinary heat, it by no means would necessarily follow that it would be an equally good test of "vital heat," which was something in Aristotle's opinion quite distinct in its efficacy from common heat,[2] and would require to be measured by its own appropriate standards. He relied therefore mainly on inference from structure. The presence or absence of blood, and its relative abundance, gave him indications[3] in which he had absolute confidence. No less certain was the evidence given by the presence or absence of a lung, and by its degree of development. For, by his theory of respiration, the whole purpose of a lung was to temper the excess of heat. "Those animals," he says, "are the more perfect that have the greater amount of heat; and in animals that have blood the measure of natural heat is the lung. For those that have a lung are invariably hotter than those that are without one; and among such as possess one, those in whom it is richly supplied with blood and soft in texture are hotter than those in whom it is bladdery or hard, or contains but little blood."[4]

Besides the blood and the lung, Aristotle had a third structural measure of temperature in the brain, which shared, as he thought, with the lung the office of reducing excess of heat. The close connection, however, of the brain with the higher sense organs, and its delicate sympathy[5] with the heart, made its presence and size a measure of the intellectual faculty rather than of the excellence of the soul as a whole.

A fourth measure of animal heat, on which Aristotle placed great reliance, was the condition of the embryo when liberated from the mother's body.[6] Impressed by the manifest action of heat in effecting the development of the eggs of birds and reptiles, he erroneously though not unnaturally inferred that the more mature condition of the mammalian embryo at the time of birth was mainly due to its having been subjected to a higher temperature in its mother's womb; and similarly that all other ovipara must be colder than birds and reptiles, inasmuch as their eggs were, as he thought, deposited in a still less advanced state. This, however, we shall have to consider at greater length hereafter.

There remains yet a fifth among Aristotle's thermometers, which, almost childish as it now appears, yet requires a moment's notice. One of the primary axioms upon which all his notions of the material world

---

[1] D. P. ii. 2, 20. [2] Cf. ii. 6, note 7, and D. G. ii. 3, 13. [3] D. P. iii. 6, 9.
[4] D. G. ii. 1, 16. [5] Cf. ii. 7, note 27. [6] D. G. ii. 1, 17, etc.

were built was that it was the inherent property of heat, and therefore of everything possessing heat, to mount upwards. He fancied that varying indications of such a tendency were to be traced in the ordinary attitudes of animals. At the bottom of the scale came those humble creatures in whom there was so little elevating heat that their bodies lay prostrate on the ground,[1] or were even, like plants, actually attached to it; while at the other end came man of all animals alone erect and of all the one with most heat; while between these two extremes came animals in intervening gradations of heat and corresponding differences of bodily attitude.

Such were Aristotle's tests of vital heat. The relative warmth of animals was not, however, his only, though his main, guide in judging of the soul's excellence. Another, to which he not unfrequently refers, was the degree of complexity of the organism. The nobler the soul the more varied its activities, and the more numerous the instruments it requires. "For when the functions are but few, few also are the organs required to effect them. For this reason animals present a greater complexity of structure than plants; and this complexity is again more marked in some animals than in others, being most varied in those to whose share has fallen not mere life but life of high degree."[2] Nature might, of course, use one organ for many purposes, and so endow a simple organism with complex activities. Sometimes, indeed, she does so.[3] But as in handicrafts so in the body; it is better to have special instruments for special operations, than single instruments for multiple uses. Nature never, therefore, when she can help it, acts like the artisan, who for cheapness makes "a spit and lamp-holder" in one.[4] In the more perfect animals, then, there are numerous organs, each with its separate office; whereas in less perfect ones such division of labour is much less complete, and in some is so slight that, when the body is cut into bits, each separate fragment can continue to live independently for a short time; there being scarcely more unity between them than if the animal had been a plant or an aggregation of distinct animals into a single mass.[5] "But in animals of the most perfect conformation no such phenomena as these are observable, because their nature has attained to the highest possible degree of unity."[6] Thus centralisation of vitality becomes a test of excellence as well as complexity of structure, the one like the other implying division of labour.

(3). These tests we may now proceed to apply. But it is important to bear in mind that no one of them was supposed by Aristotle to be sufficient by itself. The true nature of any group is not to be defined

---

[1] D. P. iv. 10, 16, and iii. 6, 9.   [2] D. P. ii. 10, 3.   [3] D. P. iii. 1, 11, and ii. 16, 6.
[4] D. P. iv. 6, 13.   [5] De Resp. 17, 4; D. P. iii. 5, 3.   [6] De Juvent. 2.

by a single differentia, but requires many.[1] That is to say, its position in regard to other groups must be determined by a consideration not of one but of all its characters, and by striking a balance between those points in which it excels and those in which it shows inferiority. How inadequate a single test may be, and into what confusion it may lead, Aristotle points out in the De Generatione (ii. 1, 15), selecting the apparent degree in which the instruments of the motor soul are developed as an example. So also he admits that the test on which he chiefly relies in that treatise in judging of the heat of animals,[2] namely, the condition in which the young are produced, is not a perfectly sure one; other conditions, such as moisture,[3] having some influence, and even cold itself sometimes producing indirectly the same result as heat.[4]

But though Aristotle thus refused to accept any one test of excellence as sufficient, yet it is clear that he held some of his tests to be much more trustworthy than others. What was wanted was a test that should gauge the soul. But the soul is incorporate in matter, and such is the uncertain character of matter that the bodily organs do not always correspond with perfect strictness to the soul within. This makes it "impossible to classify by functions common to body and soul."[5] As we can only judge of the soul through the body, every one of the tests has this failing. This is partly obviated by taking many tests in place of one, and by selecting those which give most direct information about the soul, that is to say, with the least implication of matter.

Aristotle divides all terrestrial things into three great primary groups: (a) things without a soul, i.e. the Inorganic kingdom; (β) things with a purely nutritive soul, i.e. the Vegetable kingdom; (γ) things with a soul that is not only nutritive but sensitive, i.e. the Animal kingdom. These three groups, he says, are not separated from each other by deep-cut lines of demarcation; but Nature passes from one to the other so gradually and imperceptibly that it is sometimes difficult to say under which heading a given object should be classed.[6] What group it was with such dim vestiges of life as to bridge over the interval which divided plants from the inorganic world, Aristotle does not say. We may, however, fairly suppose that he had in his mind the Lichens and the Mosses, of which latter Lord Bacon spoke as interposed between corruption and life.[7] But as to the transition from Plants to Animals he is more explicit; placing between them the indiscriminate collection of organisms, which in after-times were confused together as zoophytes,

[1] D. P. l. 3, 14. [2] D. G. ii. 1, 23. [3] D. G. ii. 1, 18. [4] D. G. i. 10, and i. 11, 1.
[5] D. P. i. 3, 12. [6] H. An. viii. 1, 5; D. P. iv. 5, 42.
[7] Nov. Organ. xxx. "Moss, which holds a place between putrescence and a plant." And in another passage, "Moss, which is but a rudiment between putrefaction and a herb."

but for which Aristotle had no common name. This group, then, in which he included Sponges, Sea-anemones, Jelly-fishes, Holothurias, and Star-fishes, stood at the bottom of his scale of animal life. Their inferiority was shown by even their common sensibility being so scantily developed as to become sometimes of doubtful presence, while in none of them were there any organs whatsoever of higher sense.[1] None of them, moreover, possessed organs for active locomotion. Such of them as changed place at all did so at the mercy of the waves and currents, floating passively about "like plants detached from the soil"; to which the rest were more or less permanently fixed. As to the reproduction of these animals Aristotle says but little. He supposed them to be developed spontaneously,[2] and to be altogether without organs of generation, a character which, with the absence of a vent and their simple structure generally, approximated them closely to plants.

From this intermediate group we pass insensibly to true animals, that is, to organisms whose sensibility is indisputable. These form two great groups, those that have blood, and those whose nutritive fluid is not true blood but something[3] analogous to it; a division which coincides with the modern one, introduced by Lamarck, into Vertebrata and Invertebrata. To this division of animals, into those with blood and those without, it is objected that the one group has but a negative character. The objection is drawn from Aristotle's own quiver, and is equally fatal to Lamarck's Invertebrata. Aristotle's division may, however, be so expressed as to avoid this criticism. Animals whose nutritive fluid is red, and animals whose nutritive fluid is white or colourless. But to this again it is objected that some worms have coloured blood, and it may be added that there is a fish whose blood is colourless. Similarly we might object to Lamarck's division that there are fishes whose chorda dorsalis is never replaced by vertebræ. Nomenclature is after all to a great extent a matter of simple convenience; and, when a convenient name has been found for an undoubtedly natural group, exceptional cases to which it scarcely applies, though they require to be noted, yet hardly suffice for its displacement. "Vertebrata" will probably be retained in spite of the exception to its accuracy given above; nor are we likely to discard the familiar "Reptilia," though the Pterodactyle flew and though the Turtles swim. I am by no means sure then that Aristotle would have abandoned his group-names even had he known of the exceptions to their accuracy. But did he know of them? Of the fish with colourless blood, it need scarcely be said, he was ignorant. But earth-worms can hardly have escaped his notice. It is strange, however, that he never makes definite mention of them. It may be, nay probably is, the case,

[1] D. P. iv. 5, 43, etc. [2] H. A. v. 15, 21. [3] D. G. iv. 1. 30; D. P. ii. 3, 12.

that the animals he once[1] alludes to as popularly called "entrails of the earth" are earth-worms. If so, we have another explanation of his division. For, sad to say, he thought that these were embryonic forms of eels, that is, of animals with red blood.

The Bloodless animals are in every respect less perfect than the Sanguineous, and inferior to them. They are, as a rule, of smaller[2] size, and live for a shorter time.[3] They are colder, as is shown not only by their want of blood,[4] but also by the almost universal absence of any special provision for refrigeration, such as gills and lungs and brain; the simple bathing of the surface with air or water sufficing, as a rule, to temper their small heat.[5] Another proof of this cold nature is furnished by the immature condition in which they produce their young. None of them deposits a perfect ovum, an ovum, that is, which has attained its full growth; but if they produce an ovum at all, it is at best an imperfect one, an ovum, that is, that increases in size after it is deposited; and though this is true of some of the least perfect among the Sanguineous animals, namely, the scaly fishes, it is true of all the Bloodless kinds.[6]

It should be said in explanation of this latter ground of distinction, that the ova of fishes and mollusca, and other animals that lay their eggs in water or damp situations, sometimes increase considerably in size after being deposited. This increase was supposed by Aristotle to be due to actual growth,[7] whereas it is in reality attributable to mere imbibition of water. This explanation applies to most of his classes of Bloodless animals, but not to Insects. These he thought produced something even less mature than the imperfect ovum of the water animal, and to it he gave the name of Scolex. The scolex was distinguished from the ovum not only by being less mature, but by being metamorphosed as a whole into the perfect animal; and not, as the true ovum, serving partly for the nourishment of the embryo, partly for its development. It has been supposed from this that Aristotle had in some extraordinary way overlooked the eggs of insects, and fancied that these animals produce primarily grubs or maggots. This, however, was not so. He says that there are two kinds of scolex, one capable of motion, in other words a grub or maggot, the other incapable of motion, and so excessively like an ovum in shape, size, and consistency, as to be indistinguishable from it, excepting by considering its ulterior changes.[8] The insects which produce the moving scolex or grub are

[1] D. G. iii. 11, 24. Aratus also uses the term "entrails of the earth," apparently in reference to earth-worms.
[2] H. A. i. 5, 13; De Gen. ii. 1, 7.   [3] De Long. V. 4, 2.   [4] D. P. ii. 7, 8.
[5] Cf. iii. 6, note 3.   [6] D. G. ii. 1, 17, etc.
[7] So also Pliny, ix. 74: "piscium ova in mari crescunt, quædam summâ celeritate."
[8] D. G. iii. 9, 5.

those viviparous species, in which, as in the flesh-fly, the ovum is hatched into a grub before being extruded from the parent's body; while the ordinary oviparous insects and spiders are those which produce the motionless egg-like scolex. Why, however, it will be asked, should Aristotle have considered the scolex, whether in shape of egg or of grub, to be more immature than an ovum ? Simply because the condition of scolex was antecedent to and preparatory of the condition of chrysalis or pupa; and the chrysalis or pupa which neither ate nor grew, and was the motionless form which immediately gave rise to the perfect animal,[1] was supposed by him to correspond to the true ovum of other animals.[2] Though, however, it corresponded to an ovum, it differed from one because the whole of it was converted by metamorphosis into the perfect animal. Still less mature than the scolex was the generative product of certain Testacea. This consisted at most of a slimy fluid produced asexually, and scarcely differing from the inorganic mud, which could itself generate these animals spontaneously, though its power of so doing was somewhat increased by the addition of this excretion.[3] The slimy substances to which Aristotle alludes are the agglutinated egg-masses of Gasteropodous molluscs. Although he failed to see that these masses consist of a multitude of distinct ova, and are not a simple homogeneous slime, yet in recognising them as the generative products of Testacea, he was in advance of the naturalists of the eighteenth century, who described these egg-masses as distinct species of animals, and gave them separate names.[4]

The ova of other Testacea completely escaped Aristotle's observation; and he supposed these animals to be generated either spontaneously, or by budding[5] from the parent; which is actually true of some of the animals included by him in the group, but which he also supposed to be true of the bivalved molluscs, such as Oysters and Mussels, which live in large communities and are often found adhering to each other's valves in masses, as though they had budded from each other.[6]

There was thus a regular[7] series of gradations in the degree of maturity reached by the generative product of different animals at the time of birth, corresponding generally with similar gradations in the natural

---

[1] D. G. iii. 9, 8, 9.
[2] D. G. ii. 1, 25. "The scolex after a time assumes the form of an egg; for the so-called chrysalis is equivalent to an egg." And again, iii. 9, 6. "The scolex as it becomes matured and of larger size invariably at last assumes the condition of an ovum; for its outside hardens into a shell, and at this period it becomes motionless. This is readily seen in the case of bees and wasps, and of caterpillars. The explanation lies herein; that the nature of these animals is imperfect, and that their eggs are consequently produced before the due time, the scolex being as it were an ovum, still soft and in process of growth."
[3] H. A. v. 15, 3; D. G. iii. 11, 12. etc. [4] Cf. M. Edwards, Leçons s. l. Phys. ix. 367.
[5] D. G. iii. 11, 12.
[6] The spat of oysters was apparently first observed in the time of Pliny. "Nuper compertum in ostreariis humorem iis fetificum lactis modo effluere."—N. H. ix. 74.
[7] D. G. ii. 1, 23.

heat of the parents. In only one instance did the two series fail to coincide, namely, in the case of the ovoviviparous fishes, which exception is elsewhere explained. Omitting these, the series runs: (1) the fully developed fœtus of Vivipara, *i.e.* of Mammalia; (2) the perfect ovum of Birds and Reptiles; (3) the imperfect ovum of bony Fishes, of Cephalopods, and of Crustacea; (4) the scolex of Insects; (5) the generative slime of certain Testacea; (6) the bud, as in Bivalves, Ascidians, etc.; (7) the absence of all generative product and consequently spontaneous generation, as in all lower groups; and even occasionally in the higher, up to Fishes.

The Bloodless animals are divided by Aristotle into four great groups, the Testacea, the Insecta, the Crustacea, and the Mollusca [1] ($\mu a \lambda \acute{a} \kappa \iota a$). This last group corresponds to the modern Cephalopoda, and in the following pages will be called by that name, to avoid the confusion into which we should be led by retaining Aristotle's name Mollusca, this title having acquired a different significance in modern times. At the bottom stand the Testacea, in which are included all the modern Mollusca excepting the Cephalopods, and also the Ascidians and the Echini. Their inferiority to the rest is shown by their being completely or almost completely incapable of locomotion; by their having, that is, no motor soul, or only dim traces of it; so that they are repeatedly spoken of as Sedentary ($\mu \acute{o} \nu \iota \mu a$), in opposition to all other true animals, which are Locomotive ($\kappa \iota \nu \eta \tau \iota \kappa \acute{a}$). In this respect they resemble plants rather than animals, as also they do in many other points, such as the absence of sexual distinction,[2] there being only one species, namely, the Snails, in which there are any grounds for believing such distinction to exist;[3] and in their mode of origin. For, like plants, they are generated either spontaneously, or by budding, or from an excretion produced, like the vegetable seed, asexually.[4] So nearly in fact do they resemble plants, that they seem intended by Nature to occupy in the sea the place which these occupy on the earth; so that they may almost be spoken of as sea-plants, while plants may be similarly looked on as land testacea.[5] They graduate insensibly into plants through the Zoophytes; the Echini and Ascidians, which are usually reckoned by Aristotle as Testacea in virtue of their external covering, being sometimes apparently included by him in the group of Zoophytes. Still further signs of the inferiority

---

[1] Aristotle having called these animals Mollusca, because their body consists of an uniformly soft substance, tries also to define and name the three other groups according to their consistence. The Ostracoderma (*shell-skinned*), or Testacea, were soft within, and hard without. The Malacostraca (*soft-shelled*), or Crustacea, were also soft within and hard without; but the hardness was that of a *crusta*, not of a *testa*. There remained the Insecta. These, says Aristotle boldly, are uniformly hard throughout. But the statement is so manifestly untenable, that he does not again insist upon it, nor attempt to give the group a name expressing so false a notion.

[2] D. G. i. 23, 10.   [3] D. G. iii. 11, 18.   [4] D. G. iii. 11, 11.   [5] D. G. iii. 11, 5.

of the Testacea, as compared with animals capable of greater locomotion, are furnished by the simplicity of their structure,[1] which accords with the simplicity of their life, and by the absence, or at any rate the doubtful presence, of the higher senses, hearing and sight.[2]

Next above the Testacea come the segmented animals or Insecta, in which group Aristotle included not only Insecta, Myriapoda, and Arachnida, but also intestinal parasites, and in fact all such Annulosa as were known to him, with the exception of Crustacea.

These were superior to the Testacea; in the first place, because they were capable of locomotion; secondly, because they had all[3] the five senses; and thirdly, because they presented generally, though not[4] invariably, distinctions of sex, and reproduced their species by congress. They were inferior to the other two groups of bloodless animals in being occasionally sexless and spontaneously developed; and in producing, when sexual, a less perfect generative product, viz. the Scolex. They are therefore distinctly stated by Aristotle to be the coldest of all animals[5] that give off generative products, that is, of all animals excepting the Testacea. Their low position in the scale was also shown by their want of vital centralisation; for after they have been cut into pieces, each segment continues to live independently for a space, as though the animal were a plant, or an aggregation of distinct animals united into a mass. The only reason, says Aristotle, that such a piece does not live still longer, is that it has not got the necessary organs of nutrition, such as mouth and the like.[6]

Of the two remaining groups of Bloodless animals, the Crustacea and the Cephalopods, it is not so easy to decide which was held by Aristotle to be the more perfect. In most respects they were on a par; for in both the sexes were always distinct, and in both the generative product was an equally immature ovum. Probably, however, the first place must be assigned to the Cephalopods, in virtue of the great size to which they occasionally[7] attain, and still more in virtue of their having a brain,[8] a mark of superiority distinguishing them from all other bloodless animals.

We come now to Aristotle's second group, the Sanguineous animals, the Vertebrata of Lamarck and his successors. These doubtless from time immemorial have been popularly divided into Beasts, Birds, Reptiles, and Fishes. Aristotle adopted the popular[9] division, in the formation of which men had been guided by a happy instinct; and in so doing he has been followed by all zoologists, until almost in our own day the Amphibia have been separated from the Reptiles, and made to form a

[1] D. P. iv. 7, 1.   [2] H. A. iv. 8, 32.   [3] H. A. iv. 8, 25.
[4] H. A. iv. 11, 4.   [5] D. G. ii. 1, 25.   [6] D. Juvent. 2, 6, etc.
[7] H. A. i. 5, 13.   [8] D. P. ii. 7, note 9.   [9] D. P. i. 3, 14.

fifth class. First, however, he divided his Sanguineous group into two subdivisions, the Vivipara and the [2]Ovipara. Of these the Vivipara, including the biped Man, the quadrupedous Beasts, and the apodous Cetacea, were manifestly superior to the Ovipara; for their more perfect organs of respiration, and the more mature condition of their young at birth testified indisputably to their greater heat.

The Ovipara include the Birds, the Reptiles, and the Fishes. Of these the Fishes were clearly at the bottom. The stunted character of their external form,[1] the absence of lungs and the substitution for them of an inferior organ of refrigeration, were unmistakable signs of inferiority. But more than all was this shown by their ovum being deposited in an imperfect condition. It was true that in one great subdivision of Fishes the ovum was not so deposited. These fishes were ovoviviparous, that is, the ovum was hatched inside the body, and in some cases the embryo even formed a kind of[2] placental attachment to the mother. But, says Aristotle, such ovoviviparity is not to be taken like viviparity for a sign of heat. On the contrary, it is a sign of cold. These fishes are of so cold[3] a nature, that they have not enough heat to harden the outside of their ovum into a shell. Their egg remains soft; and if extruded in this condition would soon be destroyed. It is therefore retained in the parent's body for security.

There remain the Reptiles and the Birds. It is not easy to decide offhand which of these was held by Aristotle to be the higher in the scale. One would have thought that the manifest warmth of the one to the touch, and equally manifest coldness of the other, would at once have decided the matter. But, strange as it seems, there is no passage, so far as I can ascertain, in which Aristotle recognizes this difference. Yet he had most certainly laid his hand on a living chameleon, and on a living tortoise, for he describes[4] their vivisection; and it is impossible to imagine that he had never touched a living bird. The explanation, I think, is to be found in the fact, already stated, that Aristotle drew a wide distinction between ordinary heat and vital heat; and would not allow that touch was any measure of the latter. Tried by his main vital standards the two groups were on a par. Each had red blood; each breathed by a lung, and in each this lung was of a bladdery and therefore an inferior character.[5] In each the sexes were invariably separate. Each was oviparous, and in each the ovum was a perfect one, that is, had attained its full size at the time of deposition. The similarity between the ova went moreover still farther. For in each it consisted of a white part and a yellow part;

[1] D. P. iv. 13, 1.
[2] D. G. iii. 3, 9. This statement of Aristotle regarding the smooth galeus (Mustelus lævis) has been shown by Müller to be true.
[3] D. G. i. 10 and 11.   [4] H. A. ii. 11, 11; D. Resp. 17, 4.
[5] Aristotle mistook the bladder-like air-sacs of Birds for their lungs, cf. iii. 6, note 10.

and in each the embryo was provided not only with an umbilical vesicle, but also with an allantois.[1] In all these characters Birds and Reptiles resembled each other, and differed from Fishes.[2] The two groups then were on a par in all their main characters. Still we may, I think, fairly assume that the greater vivacity of Birds, their rapid locomotion, their more varied life, and their comparatively erect position, as contrasted with the grovelling attitude of Reptiles, cannot but have led Aristotle to assign to the former the place of honour. And this accords with a passage[3] where he classes animals by the degrees in which the parental instinct is developed. The purpose of Nature, he says, is to give such an instinct to all animals. But in the lowest kinds the instinct ceases to act with the deposition of the eggs. This applies to the Bloodless animals, and as a rule to Fishes. In the next group the instinct lasts till the eggs are hatched, and then ceases. This applies to the Reptiles, whom he describes as laying their eggs on the ground to be hatched by the heat of the soil, and coming backwards and forwards at intervals to see that no mischief happens to them. A step farther and we have animals of higher intelligence, that continue their care until their young have not only been hatched, but have attained full growth. Such are the Birds; and most Mammals. While lastly come man and some few animals of high intelligence, who retain their affection for their young throughout life.

Such were the main groups recognised by Aristotle, and such the order in which he apparently placed them. It would, I think, not be impossible, nor even very difficult, to apply the same tests to his minor groups, and arrange these also pretty much in the order in which he would himself have placed them. The zoophytes, for instance, would have been classified by him, it may almost be said were[4] classified by him, according to their apparent degrees of sensibility, their freedom from attachment, and generally their less or greater resemblance to plants; the fixed sponges with their doubtful signs of feeling being at the bottom, and the free and more manifestly sensitive star-fishes at the top, while between them came groups less freely motor than the latter, and yet more clearly sensitive than the former, which were "in fact virtually plants, and nothing more"; namely the Holothuriæ and Sealungs, which, though not actually fixed, yet floated at the mercy of the waves like "detached plants," and were as insensible as sponges, and the Acalephæ, which, though usually attached to the rocks, could, some or all, detach themselves at will. Of the Testacea, again, we can hardly be wrong in supposing that Aristotle would have placed the motor, and occasionally

---

[1] Cf. iv. 12, note 15.
[3] D. G. iii. 2, 14.
[2] D. G. iii. 1, iii. 2; iii. 3.
[4] D. P. iv. 5.

sexual, Turbinata at the top, and the[1] sedentary and asexual Bivalves at the bottom, while the Univalves or limpets, usually fixed but capable of locomotion, would have held the middle place. The greater or less power of locomotion, the presence or absence of the higher senses, the degrees of vital centralization, of which the number of legs formed a criterion, and the position of the body in regard to its elevation above the ground, would have given to the subdivisions of his Insecta the following order: Intestinal worms; Myriapoda; Spiders; Hexapodous Insects. So we might go on with the other groups. But it is hardly worth while to do so, seeing what space the necessary collection of passages would occupy, and how much conjecture after all would have to be allowed. It will be as well therefore to limit ourselves to the main groups; and these may now be presented in the following tabular form :—

i. SANGUINEOUS ANIMALS [*Vertebrata*].
   A. Vivipara [*Mammalia*].   1. Man.
                                           2. Quadrupeds.
                                           3. Cetacea.
   B. Ovipara.
      a. With perfect ovum.   4. Birds.
                                           5. Quadrupeds and Apoda [*Reptiles and Amphibia.*]
      β. With imperfect ovum. 6. Fishes.
ii. BLOODLESS ANIMALS [*Invertebrata*].
      a. With imperfect ovum.   7. Malacia [*Cephalopods*].
                                           8. Malacostraca [*Crustacea*].
      β. With scolex.   9. Insecta [*Remaining Arthropoda and some Vermes.*]
      γ. With generative slime; buds; or spontaneous generation.   10. Ostracoderma or Testacea [*Mollusca excepting Cephalopods*].
      δ. With spontaneous generation only.   11. [*Zoophytes.*]

---

[1] Or rather "the usually sedentary Bivalves"; for Aristotle was acquainted with the peculiar motion of the Scallop, cf. H. A. iv. 4, 8.

SYNOPSIS.

INTRODUCTORY MATTER. i. 1—i. 5.

i. Scientific methods a part of general education ... ... i. 1.
ii. The method of biology and questions relating thereto.
   α. Whether generic or specific characters should be first considered.
   β. Whether phenomena or their causes should be first considered.
   γ. The materialistic view of previous writers, and the several meanings of "necessity."
   δ. The relative importance of the material and final causes, and the propriety of taking both into account.
   ε. The insufficiency of Dichotomy or division by a single differentia, and the advantages of the natural method or classification by many differentiæ ... ... i. 2—i. 4.
iii. A defence of the study of animal structure, as not ignoble ... ... i. 5.
iv. The plan of this treatise to take the parts in succession, and enquire what share Necessity and the Final Cause respectively have in their formation.

THE THREE DEGREES OF COMPOSITION ii. 1—end of treatise.

i. The mutual relations of the three ... ... ii. 1.
ii. The first degree. Physical substances ... ... ii. 2—ii. 3.
   2. *Hot and cold.* 3. *Solid and fluid.*
iii. The second degree. Homogeneous parts or tissues ... ... ii. 4—ii. 9.
   4. *Blood.* 5. *Fat.* 6. *Marrow.* 7. *Brain.* 8. *Flesh.* 9. *Bone.*
iv. The third degree. Heterogeneous parts or organs ... ... ii. 10—end of treatise.

  A. **In Sanguineous Animals** ... ... ii. 10—iv. 4, and iv. 10—end of treatise.
    α. Organs of the Head ... ... ii. 10—iii. 2.
      10. *Brain and organs of sense.* 11, 12. *Ears.* 13, 14, 15. *Eyelids and Eyelashes.* 16. *Nostrils, Lips.* 17. *Tongue.*
      iii. 1. *Teeth.* 2. *Horns.*
    β. Organs of the Neck ... ... iii. 3.
      3. *Œsophagus; Trachea; Epiglottis.*
    γ. Visceral Organs ... ... iii. 4—iii. 13, iv. 1—iv. 4.
      4. *Heart.* 5. *Blood vessels.* 6. *Lung.* 7. *Liver, Spleen.* 8. *Bladder.* 9. *Kidneys.* 10. *Diaphragm.* 11. *Fibrous membranes.* 12. *Viscera of different groups compared.* 13. *Viscera compared with flesh.* iv. 1. *Peculiarities of viscera in ovipara.* 2. *Gall bladder.* 3. *Omentum.* 4. *Mesentery.*
    δ. External parts ... ... iv. 10—iv. 14.
      10. *In vivipara.* 11. *In reptiles.* 12. *In birds.* 13. *In fishes and intermediate groups, cetacea, seals, bats.* 14. *In the ostrich.*

  B. **In Bloodless Animals** ... ... iv. 5—iv. 9.
    α. Internal parts ... ... iv. 5.
    β. External parts ... ... iv. 6—iv. 9.
      6. *In insects.* 7. *In testacea.* 8. *In crustacea.* 9. *In cephalopods.*

BOOK I.

(Ch. 1.*)* Every systematic science, the humblest and the noblest alike, seems to admit of two distinct kinds of proficiency; one of which may be properly called scientific knowledge of the subject, while the other is a kind of 'educational acquaintance with it. For an educated man should be able to form a fair offhand judgment as to the goodness or badness of the method used by a professor in his exposition. To be educated is in fact to be able to do this; and even the man of universal education we deem to be such in virtue of his having this ability. It will, however, of course, be understood that we only ascribe universal education to one who in his own individual person is thus critical in all or nearly all branches of knowledge, and not to one who has a like ability merely in some special subject. For it is possible for a man to have this competence in some one branch of knowledge without having it in all.[1]

It is plain then that, as in other sciences, so in that which enquires into nature, there must be certain canons, by reference to which a hearer shall be able to criticise the method of a professed exposition, quite independently of the question whether the statements made be true or false. Ought we, for instance, to give an illustration of what I mean, to begin by discussing the specific characters of each kind of animal—man, lion, ox, and the like—and by describing separately the distinctive features of each, or ought we rather to deal first with the characters which all these animals have in common, and thus form a basis for the consideration of them separately? For genera[2] that are quite distinct yet oftentimes resemble each other in many of their phenomena; in sleep, for instance, in respiration, in growth, in decay, in death, and in other similar affections and conditions, which may be passed over for the present, as we are not yet prepared to treat of them with clearness and precision. Now it is plain that if we discuss each kind of animal separately, we shall frequently be obliged to repeat the same statements over and over again; for horse and dog and man present, each and all, every one of the phenomena just enumerated. A discussion therefore of these several animals separately would necessarily involve frequent repetitions as to characters, themselves identical, but recurring in animals specifically distinct. (Very possibly also there may be other characters which, though they present specific differences, yet come under one and the same category. For instance, flying, walking, swimming, creeping, are plainly specifically distinct, but yet are all forms of animal progression.) We must, then, have some clear understanding as to the manner in which our investigation is to be conducted; whether, I mean, we are first to deal with the common or generical characters, and afterwards to take into consideration special peculiarities; or whether we are to start straight off with the ultimate species. For as yet no definite rule has been laid down in this matter. So also there is a like uncertainty as to another point now to be mentioned. Ought the writer who deals with the works of nature to follow the plan adopted by the mathematicians in their astronomical demonstrations, and after considering the phenomena presented by animals, and their several parts, proceed subsequently to treat of the causes and the reason why; or ought he to follow some other method? And when these questions are answered, there yet remains another. The causes concerned in the generation of the works of nature are, as we see, more than one. There is the final cause and there is the motor cause. Now we must decide which of these two causes[3] comes first, which second. Plainly, however, that cause is the first which we call the final one. For this is the Reason, and the Reason forms the starting-point, alike in works of art and in works of nature. For consider how the physician or how the builder sets about his work. He starts by forming for himself a definite picture, in the one case mental, in the other actual, of his end—the physician of health, the builder of a house—and this he holds forward as the reason and explanation of each subsequent step that he takes, and of his acting in this or that way as the case may be. Now in the works of nature the good end and the final cause is still more dominant than in works of art, such as these, and necessity is a much less constant factor in their production; though it is to this that almost all writers would seek to refer their origin, though they do not distinguish the various senses in which the term necessity is used. For there is absolute necessity, manifested in eternal phenomena; and there is hypothetical necessity, manifested in everything that is generated by nature as in everything that is produced by art, be it a house or what it may. For if a house or other such final object is to be realised, it is necessary that such and such material shall exist; and it is necessary that first this and then that shall be produced, and first this and then that set in motion, and so on in continuous succession, until the end and final result is reached, for the sake of which each prior thing is produced and exists. As with these productions of art, so also is it with the productions of nature. The mode of necessity, however, and the mode of ratiocination are different in natural science [and in art] from what they are in the theoretical sciences;[4] of which we have spoken elsewhere. For in the latter the starting-point is that which is; in the former that which is to be. For it is that which is yet to be—health, let us say, or a man—which, owing to its being of such and such characters, necessitates the pre-existence or previous production of this and that antecedent; and not this or that antecedent which, because it exists or is generated, makes it necessary that health or a man shall come into existence. Nor is it possible to trace back the series of necessary antecedents to a starting-point, of which you can say that, existing itself from eternity, it has determined their existence as its consequent. These, however, again are matters that have been dealt with in another treatise. There too it was stated in what cases absolute and hypothetical necessity exist; in what cases also the proposition expressing hypothetical necessity is simply convertible, and what cause it is that determines this convertibility.[5]

Another matter which must not be passed over without consideration is, whether the proper subject of our exposition is that with which the ancient writers concerned themselves, namely, what is the process of formation of each animal; or whether it is not rather, what are the characters of a given creature when formed. For there is no small difference between these two views.[6] The best course appears to be that we should follow the method

640 a.

already mentioned, and begin with the phenomena presented by each group of animals, and, when this is done, proceed afterwards to state the causes of those phenomena, and to deal with their evolution. For elsewhere, as for instance in house building, this is the true sequence. The plan of the house, or the house, has this and that features; and because it has this and that features, therefore is its construction carried out in this or that manner. For the process of evolution is for the sake of the thing finally evolved, and not this for the sake of the process. Empedocles, then, was in error when he said that many of the characters presented by animals were merely the results of incidental occurrences during their development; for instance, that the backbone was divided as it is into vertebræ, because it happened to be broken owing to the contorted position of the fœtus in the womb.[7] In so saying he overlooked the fact that propagation implies a creative seed endowed with certain formative properties. Secondly, he neglected another fact, namely, that the parent animal pre-exists, not only in idea, but actually in time. For man is generated from man; and thus it is the possession of certain characters by the parent that determines the development of like characters in the child. The same statement[8] [namely, that the process of production occurs for the sake of the thing produced] holds good also for the operations of art, and even for those which are apparently spontaneous. For the same result as is commonly produced only by art may sometimes occur spontaneously. Spontaneity, for instance, may do the work of the physician and bring about the restoration of health. As a general rule, however, the products of art are such as cannot possibly be produced spontaneously; for they require the pre-existence of an efficient cause homogeneous with themselves, such as the statuary's art which must necessarily precede the statue; art indeed consisting in the conception of the result to be produced before its realisation in the material. As with spontaneity,[9] so with chance; for this also occasionally produces the same result as art, and by the same process of evolution.

The fittest mode, then, of treatment is to say, a man has such and such parts, because the conception of a man includes their presence, and because they are necessary conditions of his existence, or at any rate of his perfection; and these conditions in their turn imply other prior conditions. Thus we should say,
640 b.

because man is an animal with such and such characters, therefore is the process of his development necessarily such as it is; and therefore is it accomplished in such and such an order, this part being formed first, that next, and so on in succession; and after a like fashion should we explain the evolution of all other works of nature.

Now that with which the ancient writers, who first philosophised about Nature, busied themselves, was the material principle and the material cause. They enquired what this is, and what its character; how the universe is generated out of it, and by what motor influence, whether, for instance, by antagonism or friendship, whether by intelligence or spontaneous action,[10] the substratum of matter being assumed to have certain inseparable properties; fire, for instance, to have a hot nature, earth a cold one; the former to be light, the latter heavy. For even the genesis of the universe is thus explained by them. After a like fashion do they deal also with the development of plants and of animals. They say, for instance, that the water contained in the body causes by its currents [11] the formation of the stomach and the other receptacles of food or of excretion; and that the breath by its passage breaks open the outlets of the nostrils; air and water being the materials of which bodies are made; for all represent nature as composed of such or similar substances.

But if men and animals and their several parts are natural phenomena, then the natural philosopher must take into consideration [not merely the ultimate substances of which they are made, but also] flesh, blood, bone, and all the other homogeneous parts;[12] nor only these, but also the heterogeneous parts, such as face, hand, foot, and the like; and must examine how each of these comes to be what it is, and in virtue of what force. For to say what are the ultimate substances out of which an animal is formed, to state, for instance, that it is made of fire and water, is no more sufficient, than would be a similar account in the case of an inanimate object, such as a couch or the like. For we should not be content with saying that the couch was made of bronze or wood or whatever it might be, but should try to describe its design or mode of composition in preference to the material; or, if we did deal with the material, it would at any rate be with the concretion of material and form. For a couch is such and such a form of this or that matter, or such and such a matter

640 b.

with this or that form; so that its shape and structure must be included in our description. For the formal nature is of much greater importance than the material nature.

Does, then, configuration and colour constitute the essence of the various animals and of their several parts? For if so, what Democritus says will be strictly correct. For such appears to have been his notion. At any rate he says that it is evident to every one what form it is that makes the man; as if man were constituted by a certain recognisable shape and colour. And yet a dead body has exactly the same configuration as a living one; but for all that is not a man. So also no hand of bronze or wood or of any but the appropriate materials can possibly be a hand in more than name. For like a physician in a painting, or like a flute in a sculpture, in spite of its name, it will be unable to do the office which that name implies. Precisely in the same way no part of a dead body, such I mean as its eye or its foot, is really an eye or a foot. To say, then, that shape and colour constitute the animal is an inadequate statement, and is much the same as if a woodcarver were to insist that the hand he had cut out was really a hand. Yet the physiologists, when they give an account of the development and causes of the animal form, speak very much like such a craftsman. What, however, I would ask, are the forces by which the hand or the body was fashioned into its shape? The woodcarver will perhaps say, by the axe or the auger; the physiologist, by air and by earth. Of these two answers the artificer's is the better, but it is nevertheless insufficient.[13] For it is not enough for him to say that by the stroke of his tool this part was formed into a concavity, that into a flat surface; but he must state the reasons why he struck his blow in such a way as to effect this, and what his final object was; namely, that the piece of wood should develop eventually into this or that shape. It is plain, then, that the teaching of the old physiologists is inadequate, and that the true method is to state what the definitive characters are that distinguish the animal as a whole; to explain what it is both in substance and in form, and to deal after the same fashion with its several organs; in fact, to proceed in exactly the same way as we should do, were we giving a complete description of a couch.

If now this something that constitutes the form of the living being be the soul,[14] or part of the soul, or something that without the soul cannot exist; as would seem to be the case, seeing at any rate that when the soul departs, what is left is no longer a living animal, and that none of the parts remain what they were before, excepting in mere configuration, like the animals that in the fable are turned into stone; if, I say, this be so, then it will come within the province of the natural philosopher to inform himself concerning the soul, and to treat of it, either in its entirety, or, at any rate, of that part of it which constitutes the essential character of an animal; and it will be his duty to say what this soul or this part of a soul is; and to discuss the attributes that attach to this essential character. Again, nature is spoken of in two senses, and the nature of a thing is either its matter or its essence; nature as essence including both the motor cause and the final cause.[15] Now it is in the latter of these two senses that either the whole soul or some part of it constitutes the nature of an animal; and inasmuch as it is the presence of the soul that enables matter to constitute the animal nature, much more than it is the presence of matter which so enables the soul, the enquirer into nature is bound on every ground to treat of the soul rather than of the matter. For though the wood of which they are made constitutes the couch and the tripod, it only does so because it is capable of receiving such and such a form.

So far as has yet been said it remains a debatable question, whether it is the whole soul or only some part of it, the consideration of which comes within the province of natural science. Now if it be of the whole soul that this should treat, then there is no place for any other philosophy beside it. For as it belongs in all cases to one and the same science to deal with correlated subjects —one and the same science, for instance, deals with sensation and with the objects of sense—and as therefore the intelligent soul and the objects of intellect, being correlated, must belong to one and the same science, it follows that natural science will have to include the whole universe in its province. But perhaps it is not the whole soul, nor all its parts collectively, that constitutes the source of motion; but there may be one part, identical with that in plants, which is the source of [change of quantity or] growth, another which is the source of feeling or change of quality, while still another, and this not the intellectual part, is the source of [change of place or] locomotion.[16] I say not the intellectual part; for other animals than man have the power of locomotion, but

641 b.

in none but him is there intellect. Thus then it is plain that it is not of the whole soul that we have to treat. For it is not the whole soul that constitutes the animal nature, but only some part or parts of it.[17] Moreover, it is impossible that any abstraction[18] can form a subject of natural science, seeing that everything that Nature makes is means to an end. For just as human creations are the products of art, so living objects are manifestly the products of an analogous cause or principle, not external but internal,[19] derived like the hot and the cold [and the other material elements of our bodies] from the environing universe.[20] And that the heaven, if it had an origin,[21] was evolved by such a cause, there is even more reason to believe, than that mortal animals so originated. For order and arrangement and constancy are much more plainly manifest in the celestial bodies than in our own frame; while change and chance are characteristic of the perishable things of earth. Yet there are some who, while they allow that animals were all generated by nature, nevertheless hold that the heaven was constructed to be what it is by chance and spontaneity; the heaven, in which not the faintest sign of hap-hazard or of disorder is discernible![22] Again, whenever there is plainly some final end, to which a motion tends, should nothing stand in the way, we always say that such final end is the aim or purpose of the motion; and from this it is evident that there must be a something or other really existing, corresponding to what we call by the name of Nature. For a given germ does not give rise to any chance living being, nor spring from any chance one; but each germ springs from a definite parent and gives rise to a definite progeny. And thus it is the germ that is the ruling influence and fabricator of the offspring; for the offspring is that which in the course of nature will spring from it. At the same time [in the order of thought] the offspring is anterior to the germ; for germ and perfected progeny are related as the developmental process and the result, [and result is in thought anterior to evolution]. Anterior, however, to both germ and product is the organism from which the germ was derived. For every germ connotes two organisms, the parent and the progeny. For germ or seed is both the seed of the organism from which it came, of the horse, for instance, from which it was derived, and the seed of the organism that will eventually arise from it, of the mule, for example, which is developed from the seed of the horse. The

641 b.

same seed then is the seed both of the horse and of the mule, though in different ways. Moreover, the seed is potentially that which will spring from it, and the relation of potentiality to actuality we know [to be that of consequent to antecedent].[23]

There are then two causes, namely, necessity and the final end. For many things are produced, simply as the results of necessity. It may, however, be asked, of what mode of necessity [24] are we speaking when we say this. For it can be of neither of those two modes which are set forth in the philosophical treatises.[25] There is, however, the third mode, in such things at any rate as are generated. For instance, we say that food is necessary; because an animal cannot possibly do without it. This third mode is what may be called hypothetical necessity. Here is another example of it. If a piece of wood is to be split with an axe, the axe must of necessity be hard; and, if hard, must of necessity be made of iron, or bronze, or the like. Now exactly in the same way the body, which like the axe is an instrument—for both the body as a whole and its several parts individually have definite operations for which they are made—just in the same way, I say, the body, if it is to do its work, must of necessity be of such and such a character, and made of such and such materials.

There are then, as before said, two modes of causation, and both of these must, so far as possible, be taken into account in explaining the works of nature.[26] At any rate it is plain that an attempt must be made to include them both; and that those who fail in this tell us in reality nothing about nature. For the main factor in the nature of an animal is much more the final cause than the necessary material. There are indeed passages in which even Empedocles hits upon this, and following the guidance of fact, finds himself constrained to speak of the final cause as constituting the essence and real nature of things. Such, for instance, is the case when he explains what is a bone. For he does not merely describe its material, and say it is this one element, or those two or three elements, or a compound of all the elements, but states the law or plan of their combination, and takes this to constitute the bone. As with a bone, so manifestly is it with the flesh and all other similar parts.

The reason why our predecessors failed in hitting upon this method of treatment was, that they were not in possession of the notion of formal cause, nor of any definition of essence.[27] The

642a.

first who came near it was Democritus, and he was far from adopting it as a necessary method in natural science, but was merely brought to it, spite of himself, by constraint of facts. In the time of Socrates a nearer approach was made to the method. But at this period men gave up enquiring into the works of nature, and philosophers diverted their attention to political science and to the virtues which benefit mankind.

Of the method itself the following is an example. In dealing with respiration we must show 'that it takes place for such or such a final object; and we must also show that this and that part of the process is necessitated by this and that other stage of it. By necessity we shall sometimes mean hypothetical necessity, the necessity, that is, that the requisite antecedents shall be there, if the final end is to be reached; and sometimes absolute necessity, such necessity as that between substances and their inherent properties and characters. Thus it is necessary [if we are to live] that there shall be alternating discharges and returns of heat from and to the body, and a necessary condition for this is the inflow of air. Here at once we have a necessity [in the former of the two senses]. But the reduction of the internal heat by refrigeration produces [as a necessary result] the outflow of the air, while *vice versâ* the reduction of the cold by the internal heat produces an inflow. [This is a necessity in the second of the two senses.] [28]

In the foregoing we have an example of the method which we must adopt, and also an example of the kind of phenomena, the causes of which we have to investigate.

(Ch. 2.) Some[1] writers propose to reach the definitions of the ultimate forms of animal life by bipartite division. But this method is often difficult, and often impracticable.

Sometimes the final differentia of the subdivision is sufficient by itself and the antecedent differentiæ are mere surplusage. Thus in the series Footed, Two-footed, Cloven-footed,[2] the last term is all-expressive by itself, and to append the higher terms is only an idle iteration.

Again it is not permissible to break up a natural group, Birds for instance, by putting its members under different bifurcations, as is done in the published dichotomies, where some birds are ranked with Animals of the water, and others with Animals of the air. The group Birds and the group Fishes happen to be named, while other natural groups have no popular names; for instance the groups that we may call Sanguineous and Exsanguineous are not known popularly by any designations. If such natural groups are not to be broken up, the method of Dichotomy cannot be employed, for it necessarily involves such breaking up and dislocation. The group of the Many-footed, for instance, would, under this method, have to be dismembered, and some of its kinds distributed among land animals, others among water animals.[3]

(Ch. 3.) Again privative terms inevitably form one branch of dichotomous division, as we see in the proposed dichotomies. But privative terms in their character of privatives admit of no subdivision. For there can be no specific forms of what is nonexistent, of Featherless for instance or of Footless, as there are of Feathered and of Footed. Yet a generic differentia must be subdivisible; for otherwise what is there that makes it generic rather than specific? There are to be found generic, that is specifically subdivisible, differentiæ; Feathered for instance and Footed. For feathers are divisible into Barbed and Unbarbed, and feet into Manycleft, like those of a bird, or Twocleft, like those of an ox, or Uncloven and Undivided, like those of a horse. Now even with differentiæ capable of this specific subdivision it is difficult enough so to make the classification, as that each animal shall be comprehended in some one subdivision and in not more than one; but far more difficult, nay impossible, is it to do this, if we start with a dichotomy into two contradictories. (Suppose for instance we start with the two contradictories, Feathered and Unfeathered;[1] we shall find that the ant, the glow-worm and some other animals fall under both divisions.) For each differentia must be presented by some species. There must be some species, therefore, under the privative heading. Now specifically distinct animals cannot present in their essence a common undifferentiated element, but any apparently common element must really be differentiated. (Bird and Man for instance are both Two-footed, but their two-footedness is diverse and differentiated. So any two sanguineous groups must have some difference in their blood, if their blood is part of their essence.) From this it follows that a privative term, being insusceptible of differentiation, cannot be a generic differentia; for, if it were, there would be a common undifferentiated element in two different groups.[2]

643 a.

Again, if the species are ultimate indivisible groups, that is, are groups with indivisible differentiæ, and if no differentia be common to several groups, the number of differentiæ must be equal to the number of species. If a differentia though not divisible could yet be common to several groups, then it is plain that in virtue of that common differentia specifically distinct animals would fall into the same division. It is necessary then that none of the differentiæ that belong to the ultimate or indivisible groups shall be common; for otherwise, as already said, specifically distinct animals will come into one and the same division. But this would violate one of the requisite conditions, which are as follows. No ultimate group must be included in more than a single division; different groups must not be included in the same division; and every group must be found in some division. It is plain then that we cannot get at the ultimate specific forms of the animal, or any other, kingdom by bifurcate division. If we could, the number of ultimate differentiæ would equal the number of ultimate animal forms, [which is inconceivable]. For assume an order of beings whose prime differentiæ are White and Black. Each of these branches will bifurcate, and their branches again, and so on till we reach the ultimate differentiæ, whose number will be four or some other multiple of two, and will also be the number of the ultimate species comprehended in the order.

(A species is constituted by the combination of differentia and matter. For no animal, nor portion of an animal, is purely material or purely immaterial, in other words purely corporeal or purely incorporeal, as repeatedly observed.)

Further the differentiæ must be elements of the essence, and not merely properties or attributes. Thus if Figure is the term to be divided, it must not be divided into figures whose angles are equal to two right angles, and figures whose angles are together greater than two right angles. For it is only an attribute of a triangle and not part of its essence that its angles are equal to two right angles.

Again the bifurcations must be contradictories, like White and Black, Straight and Bent; and if we characterize one branch by either term, we must characterize the other by its opposite, and not, for example, characterize one branch by a colour, the other by a mode of progression, swimming for instance.

643 a.

Furthermore living beings [cannot be divided] by the functions common to body and soul, by Flying, for instance, and Walking, as we see them divided in the current dichotomies. For some groups, Ants for instance, fall under both divisions, some ants flying while others do not. Similarly the division into Wild and Tame [must be rejected]; as it also would involve the disruption of a species into different groups. For in almost all species in which some members are tame, there are other members that are wild. Such for example is the case with Men, Horses, Oxen, Dogs in India,[3] Pigs, Goats, Sheep; groups which, if double, ought to have what they have not, namely, different appellations; and which, if single, prove that Wildness and Tameness do not amount to specific differences. And whatever single element we take as a basis of division the same difficulty will occur.

The method then that we must adopt is to attempt to recognise the natural groups, following the indications afforded by the instincts of mankind, which led them for instance to form the class of Birds and the class of Fishes, each of which groups combines a multitude of differentiæ, and is not defined by a single one as in dichotomy. The method of dichotomy is either impossible (for it would put a single group under different divisions or dissimilar groups under the same division); or it only furnishes a single ultimate differentia for each species, which either alone or with its series of antecedents has to constitute the whole essence.

If, again, a new differential character be introduced at any stage into the division, the necessary result is that the unity of the whole, and the continuity of the division, become merely a unity and continuity of agglomeration, like the unity and continuity of a series of sentences coupled together by conjunctive particles. For instance, suppose we have the bifurcation Feathered and Featherless, and then divide Feathered into Wild and Tame, or into White and Black. Tame and White have no essential relation to Feathered, but are the commencement of an independent bifurcation, and are foreign to the series at the end of which they are introduced.

As we said then, we must define at the outset by a multiplicity of differentiæ. If we do so, privative terms will be available, which are unavailable to the dichotomist.

643 b.

The impossibility of reaching the definition of any of the ultimate forms by dichotomy of the larger group, as some propose, is manifest also from the following considerations. It is impossible that a single differentia, either by itself or with its antecedents, shall express the whole essence of a species. (In saying a single differentia by itself I mean such an isolated differentia as Cloven-footed; in saying a single differentia with its antecedents I mean such a series as Footed, Two-footed, Cloven-footed. The very continuity of such a series of successive differentiæ in a division is intended to show that it is their combination that expresses the character of the resulting unit, or ultimate group. But one is misled by the usages of language into imagining that it is merely the final term of the series, Cloven-footed for instance, that constitutes the whole differentia, and that the antecedent terms, Footed, Two-footed, are superfluous. Now it is evident that such a series cannot consist of many terms. For if one divides and subdivides, one soon reaches the final differential term; but for all that, one has not got to the ultimate division, that is, to the species.) No single differentia, I repeat, either by itself or with its antecedents, can possibly express the essence of a species. Suppose, for example, Man to be the animal to be defined; the single differentia will be Cloven-footed, either by itself or with its antecedents, Footed and Two-footed. Now if man was nothing more than a Cloven-footed animal, this single differentia would duly represent his essence. But seeing that this is not the case, more differentiæ than this one will necessarily be required to define him; and these cannot come under one division; for each single branch of a dichotomy ends in a single differentia, and cannot possibly include several differentiæ belonging to one and the same animal.

It is impossible then to reach any of the ultimate animal forms by dichotomous division.

(Ch. 4.) It deserves inquiry why a single name denoting a single group was not invented by mankind, as an appellation to comprehend the two groups of Water animals and Winged animals. For there are certain attributes common to the two [1] and [differentiating them from] the rest of the animal kingdom. However, the present nomenclature is just. Groups that only differ in degree, and in the more or less of an identical element that they possess, are aggregated under a single class; groups

644a.

whose attributes are not identical but analogous are separated. For instance bird differs from bird by gradation, or by excess and defect; some birds have long feathers, others short ones, but all are feathered. Bird and Fish are more remote and only agree in having analogous organs; for what in the bird is feather, in the fish is scale. Such analogies can scarcely however serve universally as indications for the formation of groups, for almost all animals present analogies in their corresponding parts.

The individuals comprised within a species, such as Socrates and Coriscus, are the real existences; but inasmuch as these individuals possess one common specific form, it will suffice to state the universal attributes of the species, that is, the attributes common to all its individuals, once for all, as otherwise there will be endless reiteration, as has already been pointed out.

But as regards the larger groups—such as Birds—which comprehend many species, there may be a question. For on the one hand it may be urged that as the ultimate species represent the real existences, it will be well, if practicable, to examine these ultimate species separately, just as we examine the species Man separately; to examine, that is, not the whole class Birds collectively, but the Ostrich, the Crane, and the other indivisible groups or species belonging to the class.

On the other hand, however, this course would involve repeated mention of the same attribute, as the same attribute is common to many species, and so far would be irrational and tedious. Perhaps, then, it will be best to treat generically the universal attributes of the groups that have a common nature and contain closely allied subordinate forms, whether they are groups recognised by a true instinct of mankind, such as Birds and Fishes, or groups not popularly known by a common appellation, but withal composed of closely allied subordinate groups; and only to deal individually with the attributes of a single species, when such species—man, for instance, and any other such, if such there be—stands apart from others, and does not constitute with them a larger natural group.

It is generally similarity in the shape of particular organs, or of the whole body, that has determined the formation of the larger groups. It is in virtue of such a similarity that Birds, Fishes, Cephalopoda, and Testacea have been made to form each a

644 b.

separate class. In their respective subdivisions the organs are not merely analogous, as the bone of man and the spine of fish, but are identical, with the exception of certain corporeal differentiations in respect of largeness smallness, hardness softness, smoothness roughness, and other oppositions of this kind, and, in one word, in respect of degree.

We have now touched upon the canons for criticising the method of natural science, and have considered what is the most systematic and easy course of investigation; we have also dealt with division, and the mode of conducting it so as best to attain the ends of science, and have shown how dichotomy is either impracticable or inefficacious for its professed purposes.

Having laid this foundation, we proceed to the next topic, and by way of introduction we observe, that *(Ch.* 5*)* some members of the universe are ungenerated, imperishable, and eternal, while others are subject to generation and decay. The former are excellent beyond compare and divine, but less accessible to knowledge. The evidence that might throw light on them, and on the problems which we long to solve respecting them, is furnished but scantily by sensation; whereas respecting perishable plants and animals we have abundant information, living as we do in their midst, and ample data may be collected concerning all their various kinds, if only we are willing to take sufficient pains. Both departments, however, have their special charm. The scanty conceptions to which we can attain of celestial things give us, from their excellence, more pleasure than all our knowledge of the world in which we live; just as a half glimpse of persons that we love is more delightful than a leisurely view of other things, whatever their number and dimensions. On the other hand, in certitude and in completeness our knowledge of terrestrial things has the advantage. Moreover, their greater nearness and affinity to us balances somewhat the loftier interest of the heavenly things that are the objects of the higher philosophy. Having already treated of the celestial world, as far as our conjectures could reach, we proceed to treat of animals, without omitting, to the best of our ability, any member of the kingdom, however ignoble. For if some have no graces to charm the sense, yet even these, by disclosing to intellectual perception the artistic spirit that designed them, give immense pleasure to all who can trace links of causation, and are inclined to philosophy. Indeed, it would be strange if mimic

645a.

representations of them were attractive, because they disclose the mimetic skill of the painter or sculptor, and the original realities themselves were not more interesting, to all at any rate who have eyes to discern the reason that presided over their formation. We therefore must not recoil with childish aversion from the examination of the humbler animals. Every realm of nature is marvellous: and as Heraclitus, when the strangers who came to visit him found him warming himself at the furnace in the kitchen, is reported to have bidden them not to be afraid to enter, as even in that kitchen divinities were present, so we should venture on the study of every kind of animal without distaste; for each and all will reveal to us something natural and something beautiful. Absence of hap-hazard and conduciveness of everything to an end are to be found in Nature's works in the highest degree, and the resultant end of her generations and combinations is a form of the beautiful.

If any person thinks the examination of the rest of the animal kingdom an unworthy task, he must hold in like disesteem the study of man. For no one can look at the primordia of the human frame—blood, flesh, bones, vessels, and the like—without much repugnance.[1] Moreover, in every inquiry, the examination of material elements and instruments is not to be regarded as final, but as ancillary to the conception of the total form. Thus the true object of architecture is not bricks mortar or timber, but the house; and so the principal object of natural philosophy is not the material elements, but their composition, and the totality of the form to which they are subservient, and independently of which they have no existence.

The course of exposition must be first to state the attributes common to whole groups of animals, and then to attempt to give their explanation. Many groups, as already noticed, present absolutely common attributes, that is to say, absolutely identical affections, and absolutely identical organs, feet, feathers, scales, and the like; while in other groups the affections and organs are only so far identical as that they are analogous. For instance, some groups have lungs, others have no lung, but an organ analogous to a lung in its place; some have blood, others have no blood, but a fluid analogous to blood, and with the same office. To treat of the common attributes in connexion with each individual group would involve, as already suggested, useless iteration. So much for this topic.

645 b.

As every instrument and every bodily member subserves some partial end, that is to say, some special action, so the whole body must be destined to minister to some plenary sphere of action. Thus the saw is made for sawing, for this is its function, and not sawing for the saw. Similarly the body too must somehow or other be made for the soul, and each part of it for some subordinate function, to which it is adapted.

We have, then, first to describe the common functions, common, that is, to the whole animal kingdom, or to certain large groups, or to the members of a species. In other words, we have to describe the attributes common to all animals, or to assemblages, like the class of Birds, of closely allied groups differentiated by gradation, or to groups like Man not differentiated into subordinate groups. In the first case the common attributes may be called analogous, in the second generic, in the third specific.

When a function is ancillary to another, a like relation manifestly obtains between the organs which discharge these functions; and similarly if one function is the end of another, their respective organs will stand to each other in the same relation. Other phenomena there are that are [neither ancillary to higher ones, nor the end of lower ones, but] the inevitable results of the existing conditions [under which the animal is living].

Instances of what I mean by functions and affections are Reproduction, Growth, Copulation, Waking, Sleep, Locomotion, and other similar vital actions. Instances of what I mean by parts are Nose, Eye, Face, and other so-called members or limbs, and also the more elementary parts of which these are made. So much for the method to be pursued. Let us now try to set forth the causes of all vital phenomena, whether universal or particular, and in so doing let us follow that order of exposition, which conforms, as we have indicated, to the order of nature.

BOOK II.

(Ch. 1.) The nature and the number of the parts of which animals are severally composed are matters which have already been set forth in detail in the book of Researches about Animals.[1] We have now to inquire what are the causes that in each case have determined this composition; a subject reserved by us for separate consideration.

Now there are three degrees of composition; and of these the first in order, as all will allow, is composition out of what some call the elements, such[2] as air, earth, water, fire. Perhaps however it would be more accurate to say composition out of the elementary forces;[3] nor indeed out of all of these, but out of a limited number of them, as defined in previous treatises. For fluid and solid, hot and cold, form the material of all composite substances;[4] and all other differences are secondary to these, such differences, that is, as heaviness or lightness, density or rarity, roughness or smoothness, and any other such properties of matter as there may be. The second degree of composition is that by which the homogeneous parts of animals, such as bone, flesh, and the like, are constituted out of the primary substances. The third and last stage is the composition which forms the heterogeneous parts, such as face, hand, and the rest.[5]

Now the order of actual development and the order of logical existence are always the inverse of each other. For that which is antecedent in the true order of nature is posterior in the order of development, and that is genetically last which is logically first. (That this is so is manifest by induction. For a house does not exist for the sake of bricks and stones, but these materials for the sake of the house; and the same is the case with the materials of other bodies. For generation is a process from a something to a something; that which is generated having a cause in which it originates and a cause in which it ends. The originating cause is the primary efficient cause, which is something already endowed with tangible existence, while the final cause is some definite [and predictable] form; for man generates man, and plant generates plant, and in each case out of the material which environs both.)[6] In order of time then the material and the generative process must necessarily be anterior to the being that is generated; but in logical order the definitive character and form of each being precedes the material. This is evident if one only tries to define the process of formation. For the definition of house-building includes and presupposes that of the house; but the definition of the house does not include nor presuppose that of house-building; and the same is true of all other productions. So that it must necessarily be that the elementary material exists for the sake of the homogeneous parts, seeing that these are genetically posterior to it, just as the heterogeneous parts are posterior genetically to them.[7] For these heterogeneous parts have reached the end and goal, having the third degree of composition, in which degree generation or development often attains its final term.[8]

Animals then are composed of homogeneous parts, and are also composed of heterogeneous parts. The former however exist for the sake of the latter.[9] For the active functions and operations of the body are carried on by these; that is, by the heterogeneous parts, such as the eye, the nostril, the whole face, the fingers, the hand, and the whole arm. But inasmuch as there is a great variety in the functions and motions not only of aggregate animals but also of the individual organs, it is necessary that the substances out of which these are composed shall present a diversity of properties. For some purposes softness is advantageous, for others hardness; some parts must be capable of extension, others of flexion. Such properties then are distributed separately to the different homogeneous parts, one being soft another hard, one fluid another solid, one viscous another brittle; whereas each of the heterogeneous parts presents a combination of multifarious properties. For the hand, to take an example, requires one property to enable it to effect pressure, and another and different

646 b.

property for simple prehension.[10] For this reason the active or executive parts of the body are compounded out of bones, sinews, flesh, and the like, but not these latter out of the former.

So far, then, as has yet been stated, the relations between these two orders of parts are determined by a final cause. We have however to inquire whether necessity may not also have a share in the matter; and it must be admitted that these mutual relations could not from the very beginning have possibly been other than they are. For heterogeneous parts can be made up out of homogeneous parts, either from a plurality of them, or from a single one, as is the case with some of the viscera, which varying in configuration are yet, to speak broadly, formed from a single homogeneous substance; but that homogeneous substances should be formed out of a combination of heterogeneous parts is clearly an impossibility. For these causes, then, some parts of animals are simple and homogeneous, while others are composite and heterogeneous; and dividing the parts into the active or executive and the sensitive, each one of the former is, as before said, heterogeneous, and each one of the latter homogeneous. For it is in homogeneous parts alone that sensation can occur, as the following considerations show.

Each sense is confined to a single kind or order of sensibles, and its organ must therefore be such as to admit the action of that kind, and [of no other. It must therefore have the properties of that kind and of no other; for] that which is endowed with a property *in posse* is acted upon by that which has the like property *in esse*.[11] The one-ness of its sensibles implies then the one-ness or homogeneity of the sense-organ. Thus it is that while no physiologists ever dream of saying of the hand or face or other such part that one is earth, another water, another fire, they couple each separate sense-organ with a separate element, asserting this one to be air and that other to be fire.[12]

Sensation then is confined to the simple or homogeneous parts. But, as might reasonably be expected, the organ of touch, though still homogeneous, is yet the least simple of all the sense-organs. For touch more than any other sense appears to be correlated to several distinct kinds of objects, and to recognise more than one category of contrasts, heat and cold, for instance, solidity and fluidity, and other similar oppositions.[13] Accordingly the organ which deals with these varied objects is of all the sense-organs

647 a.

the most corporeal,[14] being either the flesh, or the substance which in some animals takes the place of flesh.

Now as there cannot possibly be an animal without sensation, it follows as a necessary consequence that every animal must have some homogeneous parts; for these alone are capable of sensation, the heterogeneous parts serving for the active functions. Again as the sensory faculty, the motor faculty, and the nutritive faculty, are all lodged in one and the same part of the body, as was stated in a former treatise,[15] it is necessary that the part which is the primary seat of these principles shall on the one hand, in its character of general sensory recipient, be one of the simple parts; and on the other hand shall, in its motor and active character, be one of the heterogeneous parts. For this reason it is the heart which in sanguineous animals constitutes this central part, and in bloodless animals it is that which takes the place of a heart. For the heart, like the other viscera, is one of the homogeneous parts; for, if cut up, its pieces are homogeneous in substance with each other. But it is at the same time heterogeneous in virtue of its definite configuration.[16] And the same is true of the other so-called viscera, which are indeed formed from the same material as the heart. For all these viscera have a sanguineous character owing to their being situated upon vascular ducts and branches. For just as a stream of water deposits mud, so the various viscera, the heart excepted,[17] are, as it were, deposits from the stream of blood in the vessels. And as to the heart, the very starting-point of the vessels, and the actual seat of the force by which the blood is first fabricated, it is but what one would naturally expect, that out of the selfsame nutriment of which it is the recipient its own proper substance shall be formed.[18] Such then are the reasons why the viscera are of sanguineous aspect; and why in one point of view they are homogeneous, in another heterogeneous.

(Ch. 2.) Of the homogeneous parts of animals, some are soft and fluid, others hard and solid; and of the former some are fluid permanently, others only so long as they are in the living body.

Among the fluids [1] are blood, serum, lard, suet, marrow, semen, bile, milk when present, flesh, and their various analogues. For the parts enumerated are not to be found in all animals, some animals only having parts analogous to them. Of the hard and solid homogeneous parts bone, fish-spine,[2] sinew, blood-vessel, are

647 b.

examples. The last of these points to a sub-division that may be made in the class of homogeneous parts.³ For in some of them the whole and a portion of the whole are synonymous. Thus a portion of vessel is still called vessel. While in others there is not this identity of name; and so far these parts agree with the heterogeneous parts; for a portion of a face is never called face.

The first question to be asked is what are the causes to which these homogeneous parts owe their existence? The causes are various; and this whether the parts be solid or fluid. Thus one set of homogeneous parts represent the material out of which the heterogeneous parts are formed; for each separate organ is constructed of bones, sinews, flesh, and the like; which are either essential elements in its formation, or contribute to the proper discharge of its function. A second set are the nutriment of the first, and are invariably fluid, for all growth occurs at the expense of fluid matter;⁴ while a third set are the residue of the second. Such for instance are the fæces and, in animals that have a bladder, the urine; the former being the dregs of the solid nutriment, the latter of the fluid.

Even the individual homogeneous parts present variations, which are intended in each case to render them more serviceable for their purpose. The variations of the blood may be selected to illustrate this. For different bloods differ in their degrees of thinness or thickness, of clearness or turbidity, of coldness or heat; and this whether we compare the bloods from different parts of the same individual or the bloods of different animals. For, in the individual, all the differences just enumerated distinguish the blood of the upper and of the lower halves of the body; and, dealing with classes, one section of animals is sanguineous, while the other has no blood, but only something resembling it in its place. As regards the results of such differences, the thicker and the hotter blood is, the more conducive is it to strength, while in proportion to its thinness and its coldness is its suitability for sensation and intelligence. A like distinction exists also in the fluids which are analogous to blood. This explains how it is that bees⁵ and other similar creatures are of a more intelligent nature than many sanguineous animals; and that, of sanguineous animals, those are the most intelligent whose blood is thin and cold. Noblest of all are those whose blood is hot, and at the same time thin and clear. For

648a.

such are suited alike for the development of courage and of wisdom. Accordingly the upper parts are superior in these respects to the lower, the male superior to the female, and the right side to the left.[6] As with the blood so also with the other parts, homogeneous and heterogeneous alike. For here also such variations as occur must be held either to be related to the essential constitution and mode of life of the several animals, or, in other cases, to be merely matters of slightly better or slightly worse. Two animals for instance may have eyes. But in one these eyes may be of fluid consistency, while in the other they are hard; and in one there may be eyelids, in the other no such appendages. In such a case, the fluid consistency and the presence of eyelids, which are intended to add to the accuracy of vision, are differences of degree.[7]

As to why all animals must of necessity have blood or something of a similar character, and what the nature of blood may be, these are matters which can only be considered, when we have first discussed hot and cold. For the natural properties of many substances are referable to these two elementary principles; and it is a matter of frequent dispute what animals or what parts of animals are hot and what cold. For some maintain that water animals are hotter than such as live on land,[8] asserting that their natural heat counterbalances the coldness of their medium; and again that bloodless animals are hotter than those with blood, and females than males. Parmenides, for instance, and some others declare that women are hotter than men,[9] and that it is the warmth and abundance of their blood which causes their menstrual flow, while Empedocles maintains the opposite opinion. Again, comparing the blood and the bile, some speak of the former as hot and of the latter as cold, while others invert the description. If there be this endless disputing about hot and cold, which of all things that affect our senses are the most distinct, what are we to think as to our other sensory impressions?

The explanation of the difficulty appears to be that the term "hotter" is used in several senses; so that different statements, though in verbal contradiction with each other, may yet all be more or less true. There ought then to be some clear understanding as to the sense in which natural substances are to be termed hot or cold, solid or fluid. For it appears manifest, that these are properties on which even life and death[10] are largely dependent,

648 b.

and that they are moreover the causes of sleep and waking, of maturity and old age, of health and disease; while no similar influence belongs to roughness and smoothness, to heaviness and lightness, nor in short to any other such properties of matter. That this should be so is but in accordance with rational expectation. For hot and cold, solid and fluid, as was stated in a former treatise,[11] are the foundations of the physical elements.

Is then the term hot used in one sense or in many? To answer this we must ascertain what special effect is attributed to a hotter substance, and if there be several such, how many these may be. A body then is in one sense said to be hotter than another, if it impart a greater amount of heat to an object in contact with it. In a second sense, that is said to be hotter which causes the keener sensation when touched, and especially if the sensation be attended with pain. This criterion however would seem sometimes to be a false one;. for occasionally it is the idiosyncracy of the individual that causes the sensation to be painful.[12] Again, of two masses of one and the same substance, the larger is said to have more heat than the smaller. Again, of two things, that is the hotter, which the more readily melts a fusible substance, or sets on fire an inflammable one. Again, of two bodies, that is said to be the hotter which takes the longer time in cooling, as also we call that which is rapidly heated hotter than that which is long about it; as though the rapidity implied proximity and this again similarity of nature, while the want of rapidity implied distance and this again dissimilarity of nature. The term hotter is used then in all the various senses that have been mentioned, and perhaps in still more. Now it is impossible for one body to be hotter than another in all these different fashions. Boiling water for instance, though it is more scalding than flame, yet has no power of burning or melting combustible or fusible matter, while flame has. So again this boiling water is hotter than a small fire, and yet gets cold much more rapidly and completely. For in fact fire never becomes cold; whereas water invariably does so. Boiling water again is hotter to the touch than oil; yet it gets cold and coagulates more rapidly than this other fluid.[13] Blood again is hotter to the touch than either water or oil, and yet coagulates before them. Iron again and stones and other similar bodies are much longer in getting heated than water, but when once heated burn other substances with

648b.

a much greater intensity. Another distinction is this. In some of the bodies which are called hot the heat is derived from without, while in others it belongs to the bodies themselves; and it makes a most important difference, whether the heat has the former or the latter origin. For to call that one of two bodies the hotter, which is possessed of heat, we may almost say, accidentally and not of its own essence, is very much the same thing as if, finding that some man in a fever was a musician, one were to say musicians are hotter than healthy men. Of that which is hot *per se* and that which is hot *per accidens*, the former is the slower to cool, while not rarely the latter is the hotter to the touch. The former again is the more burning of the two—flame for instance as compared with boiling water—while the latter, as the boiling water, which is hot *per accidens*, is the more heating to the touch. From all this it is clear that it is no simple matter to decide which of two bodies is the hotter. For the first may be the hotter in one sense, the second the hotter in another. Indeed in some of these cases it is impossible to say simply even whether a thing is hot or not. For the actual substratum may not itself be hot, but may be receptive of heat as an attribute; as, supposing hot water or hot iron had single names, would be the case with the substratum of the substances denoted by such names. It is after this manner that blood is hot.[14] In such cases, in those, that is, in which the substratum owes its heat to an external influence, it is plain that cold is not a mere privation, but an actual existence.[15]

There is no knowing but that even fire may be another of these cases. For the substratum of fire may be smoke or charcoal, and, though the former of these is always hot, smoke being an uprising vapour, yet the latter becomes cold when its flame is extinguished, as also would oil and pinewood under similar circumstances. But even substances that have been burnt nearly all possess some heat, cinders, for example, and ashes, the dejections also of animals, and, among the excretions, bile; because some residue of heat has been left in them after their combustion. It is in another sense that pinewood and fat substances are hot; namely, because they rapidly assume the actuality of fire.

Heat appears to cause both coagulation and melting.[16] Now such things as are formed merely of water are solidified by cold, while such as are formed of nothing but earth are solidified by fire. Hot substances again are solidified by cold, and, when they consist chiefly of earth, the process of solidification is rapid, and the resulting substance is insoluble; but, when their main constituent is water, the solid matter is again soluble. What kinds of substances however admit of being solidified, and what are the causes of solidification, are questions that have already been dealt with more precisely in another treatise.[17]

In conclusion, then, seeing that the terms hot and hotter are used in many different senses, and that no one substance can be hotter than others in all these senses, we must, when we attribute this character to an object, add such further statements as that this substance is hotter *per se*, though that other is often hotter *per accidens*; or again that this substance is potentially hot, that other actually so; or again, that this substance is hotter in the sense of causing a greater feeling of heat when touched, while that other is hotter in the sense of producing flame and burning. The term hot being used in all these various senses, it plainly follows that the term cold will also be used with like ambiguity.

So much then as to the signification of the terms hot and cold, hotter and colder.[18]

(Ch. 3.) In natural sequence we have next to treat of solid and fluid. These terms are used in various senses. Sometimes for instance they denote things that are potentially, at other times things that are actually, solid or fluid. Ice for example, or any other solidified fluid, is spoken of as being actually and accidentally solid, while potentially and essentially it is fluid. Similarly earth and ashes and the like, when mixed with water, are actually and accidentally fluid, but potentially and essentially are solid. Now separate the two constituents in this last instance; and you have on the one hand the watery part, capable of passing by imbibition into other substances, and this is both potentially and actually fluid; and on the other hand you have the earthy part, and this is both potentially and actually solid. It is to bodies that are solid in this double manner that the term "solid" is most properly and absolutely applicable. So also the opposite term "fluid" is strictly and absolutely applicable to that only which is both potentially and actually fluid. The same remark applies also to hot bodies and to cold.

These distinctions, then, being laid down, it is plain that blood
649 b.

is essentially hot in so far as that heat is connoted in its name; just as if boiling water were denoted by a single term, boiling would be connoted in that term. But the substratum of blood, that which it is [in substance] while it is blood [in form] is not hot. Blood then in a certain sense is essentially hot, and in another sense is not so. For heat is included in the definition of blood, just as whiteness is included in the definition of a white man, and so far therefore blood is essentially hot. But so far as blood becomes hot from some external influence, it is not hot essentially.[1]

As with hot and cold, so also is it with solid and fluid. We can therefore understand how some substances are hot and fluid so long as they remain in the living body, but become perceptibly cold and coagulate so soon as they are separated from it; while others are hot and consistent while in the body, but when withdrawn undergo a change to the opposite condition, and become cold and fluid. Of the former blood is an example; of the latter bile; for while blood solidifies when thus separated, yellow bile under the same circumstances becomes more fluid.[2] We must attribute to such substances the possession of opposite properties in a greater or less degree.

In what sense, then, the blood is hot and in what sense fluid, and how far it partakes of the opposite properties, has now been fairly explained. Now since everything that grows must take nourishment, and nutriment in all cases consists of fluid and solid substances, and since it is by the force of heat that these are concocted[3] and changed, it follows that all living things, animals and plants alike, must on this account if on no other have a natural source of heat. This natural heat moreover must belong to many parts,[4] seeing that the organs by which the various elaborations of the food are effected are many in number. For first of all there is the mouth and the parts inside the mouth, on which the first share in the duty clearly devolves, in such animals at least as live on food which requires disintegration. The mouth, however, does not actually concoct the food, but merely facilitates concoction;[5] for the subdivision of the food into small bits facilitates the action of heat upon it. After the mouth come the upper and the lower abdominal cavities,[6] and here it is that concoction is effected by the aid of natural heat. Again, just as there is a channel for the admission of the

650 a.

unconcocted food into the stomach, namely the mouth, and in some animals the so-called œsophagus, which is continuous with the mouth and reaches to the stomach, so must there also be other and more numerous channels by which the concocted food or nutriment shall pass out of the stomach and intestines into the body at large, and to which these cavities shall serve as a kind of manger.[7] For plants get their food from the earth by means of their roots; and this food is already elaborated when taken in, which is the reason that plants produce no excrement,[8] the earth and its heat serving them in the stead of a stomach. But animals, with scarcely an exception, and notably all such animals as are capable of locomotion, are provided with a stomachal sac,[9] which is as it were an internal substitute for the earth. They must therefore have some instrument which shall correspond to the roots of plants,[10] with which they may absorb their food from this sac, so that the proper end of the successive stages of concoction may at last be attained. The mouth then, its duty done, passes over the food to the stomach, and there must necessarily be something to receive it in turn from this. This something is furnished by the blood-vessels,[11] which run throughout the whole extent of the mesentery from its lowest part right up to the stomach. A description of these will be found in the treatises on Anatomy and Natural History.[12] Now as there is a receptacle for the entire matter taken as food, and also a receptacle for its excremental residue, and again a third receptacle, namely the vessels, which serve as such for the blood, it is plain that this blood must be the final nutritive material in such animals as have it; while in bloodless animals the same is the case with the fluid which represents the blood.[13] This explains why the blood diminishes in quantity when no food is taken, and increases when much is consumed,[14] and also why it becomes healthy and unhealthy according as the food is of the one or the other character. These facts, then, and others of a like kind, make it quite plain that the purpose of the blood in sanguineous animals is to subserve the nutrition of the body. They also explain why no more sensation is produced by touching the blood, than by touching one of the excretions or the food, whereas when the flesh is touched sensation is produced. For the blood is not continuous nor united by growth with the flesh, but simply lies loose in its receptacle, that is in the heart and
650 b.

vessels.[15] The manner in which the parts grow at the expense of the blood, and indeed the whole question of nutrition, will find a more suitable place for exposition in the treatise on generation and development, and in other writings.[16] For our present purpose all that need be said is that the blood exists for the sake of nutrition, that is the nutrition of the parts; and with this much let us therefore content ourselves.

(Ch. 4.) What are called fibres[1] are found in the blood of some animals but not of all. There are none for instance in the blood of deer and of roes; and for this reason the blood of such animals as these never coagulates.[2] For that portion of the blood which consists mainly of water is not liable to coagulation, this process occurring only in the earthy part, that is in the fibres, during the evaporation of the moisture.

Some at any rate of the animals with watery blood have a keener intellect than those whose blood is of an earthier nature. This is due not so much to the coldness of their blood as to its thinness and purity; neither of which qualities belongs to the earthy matter. For the thinner and purer its fluid is, the more active is an animal's sensibility. Thus it is that some exsanguineous animals, notwithstanding their want of blood, are yet more intelligent than some among the sanguineous kinds. Such for instance, as already said, is the case with bees[3] and ants, and whatever other animals there may be of a like nature. At the same time too great an excess of water makes animals timorous.[4] For fear chills the body; so that in animals whose heart contains so watery a mixture the way is, as it were, prepared for the operation of this emotion. For water is congealed by cold. This also explains why bloodless animals are, as a general rule, more timorous than such as have blood, so that they remain motionless, when frightened, and discharge their excretions, and in some instances change colour.[5] Such animals on the other hand as have thick and abundant fibres in their blood are of a more earthy nature, and of a choleric temperament, and liable to bursts of passion. For anger is productive of heat; and solids when they have been made hot give off more heat than fluids. The fibres therefore, being earthy and solid,[6] are turned into so many hot embers in the blood, like the embers in a vapor-bath, and cause ebullition in the fits of passion.[7]

This explains why bulls and boars are so choleric and so

651a.

passionate. For their blood is exceedingly rich in fibres;[8] and the bull's at any rate coagulates more rapidly than that of any other animal.[9] If these fibres, that is to say if the earthy constituents of which we are speaking, are taken out of the blood, the fluid that remains behind will no longer coagulate; just as the watery residue of mud will not coagulate after removal of the earth. But if the fibres are left the fluid coagulates, as also does mud, under the influence of cold. For when the heat is expelled by the cold, the fluid, as has been already stated, passes off with it by evaporation, and the residue is dried up and solidified, not by heat but by cold.[10] So long however as the blood is in the body, it is kept fluid by animal heat.

The character of the blood affects both the temperament and the sensory faculties of animals in many ways. This is indeed what might reasonably be expected, seeing that the blood is the material of which the whole body is made. For nutriment supplies the material, and the blood is the ultimate nutriment. It makes then a considerable difference whether the blood be hot or cold, thin or thick, turbid or clear.

The watery part of the blood is serum; and it is watery, either owing to its not being yet concocted, or owing to its having become corrupted; so that one part of the serum is the resultant of a necessary process, while another part is material intended to serve for the formation of the blood.[11]

(Ch. 5.) The differences between lard and suet correspond to differences of blood.[1] For both are concocted blood; being that surplus of it, which, though well concocted and highly nutritious, has not been expended in forming the fleshy substance of the animal, but remains over owing to the superabundance of food. That such is the composition of these substances is evident from their sheeny appearance. For a sheeny look in fluids comes from their being compounded of air and of fire.[2] It follows from what has been said that no ex-sanguineous animals have either lard or suet; for they have no blood.[3] Among sanguineous animals those whose blood is dense are likely to have suet rather than lard. For suet is of an earthy nature, that is to say, it contains but a small proportion of water and is chiefly composed of earth; and this it is that makes it coagulate, just as the fibrous matter of blood coagulates, or broths which contain such fibrous matter.[4] Thus it is that in those horned animals that have no front teeth

651a.

in the upper jaw the fat consists of suet. For the very fact that they have horns and huckle-bones[5] shows that their composition is rich in earthy matter; for all such appurtenances are solid and earthy in character. On the other hand in those hornless animals that have front teeth in both jaws, and whose feet are divided into toes, there is no suet, but in its place lard;[6] and this, not being of an earthy character, neither coagulates nor dries up into a friable mass.

Both lard and suet when present in moderate amount are beneficial; for they contribute to health and strength, while they are no hindrance to sensation. But when they are present in great excess, they are injurious and destructive. For were the whole body formed of them it would perish. For an animal is an animal in virtue of its sensory part, that is in virtue of its flesh, or of the substance analogous to flesh.[7] But the blood, as before stated, is not sensitive; as therefore is neither lard nor suet, seeing that they are nothing but concocted blood. Were then the whole body composed of these substances, it would be utterly without sensation. Such animals, again, as are excessively fat age rapidly. For their blood is used up in forming fat, and so they have but little of it left; and when there is but little blood the way is already open for decay.[8] For decay may be said to be deficiency of blood, the scantiness of which renders it liable, like all bodies of small bulk, to be injuriously affected by any chance excess of heat or cold. For the same reason fat animals are less prolific than others. For that part of the blood which should go to form semen and seed, is used up in the production of lard and suet, which are nothing but concocted blood; so that in these animals there is either no reproductive excretion at all, or only a scanty amount.[9]

So much then of blood and serum, and of lard and suet. Each of these has been described, and the purposes told for which they severally exist.

(Ch. 6.) The marrow also is of the nature of blood, and not as some[1] think the germinal force of the semen. That this is the case is quite evident in very young animals. For in the embryo the marrow of the bones has a blood-like appearance, which is but consistent with the fact that the parts are all constructed out of blood, and that it is on blood that the embryo is nourished.[2] But, as the young animal grows up

651b.

and ripens into maturity, the marrow changes its colour, just as do the external parts and the viscera.³ For the viscera also in very young animals have each and all a blood-like look, owing to the large amount of this fluid which they contain.

The consistency of the marrow agrees with that of the fat. For when the fat consists of lard, then the marrow also is oily and lard-like; but when the concocted blood is converted into suet, and does not assume the form of lard, then the marrow also has a suety character. In those animals, therefore, that have horns and are without upper front teeth, the marrow has the character of suet; while it takes the form of lard in those that have front teeth in both jaws, and that also have the foot divided into toes. What has been said hardly applies to the spinal marrow. For it is necessary that this shall be continuous and extend without break through the whole back-bone, inasmuch as this bone consists of separate vertebræ. But were the spinal marrow either of soft fat or of suet, it could not hold together in such a continuous mass as it does, but would either be too fluid or too frangible.⁴

There are some animals that can hardly be said to have any marrow. These are those whose bones are strong and solid, as is the case with the lion. For in this animal the marrow is so utterly insignificant, that the bones look as though they had none at all.⁵ However, as it is necessary that animals shall have bones or something analogous to them, such as the fish-spines of water-animals,⁶ it is also a matter of necessity that some of these bones shall contain marrow; for the substance contained within the bones is the nutriment out of which these are formed. Now the universal nutriment, as already stated, is blood; and the blood within the bone, owing to the heat which is developed in it from its being thus surrounded, undergoes concoction, and self-concocted⁷ blood is suet or lard; so that it is perfectly intelligible how the marrow within the bone comes to have the character of these substances. So also it is easy to understand, why, in those animals that have strong and solid bones, some of these should be entirely void of marrow, while the rest contain but little of it; for here the nutriment is all spent in forming the bones.

Those animals that have fish-spines in place of bones have no other marrow than that of the chine.⁸ For in the first place they have naturally but a small amount of blood; and secondly the only hollow fish-spine is that of the chine. In this then marrow is formed; this being the only spine in which there is space for it, and moreover being the only one which owing to its division into parts requires a connecting bond. This too is the reason why the marrow of the chine, as already mentioned, is somewhat different from that of other bones. For, having to act the part of a clasp, it must be of glue-like tenacity, and at the same time sinewy [9] so as to admit of stretching.

Such then are the reasons for the existence of marrow, in those animals that have any, and such its nature. It is the surplus of the sanguineous nutriment apportioned to the bones and fish-spines, which has undergone concoction owing to its being enclosed within them.

(Ch. 7.) From the marrow we pass on in natural sequence to the brain. For there are some [1] who think that the brain itself consists of marrow, and that it forms the commencement of that substance, because they see that the spinal marrow is continuous with it. In reality the two may be said to be utterly opposite to each other in character. For of all the parts of the body there is none so cold as the brain; whereas the marrow is of a hot nature, as is plainly shown by its sheeny appearance,[2] and by its fatness. Indeed this is the very reason why the brain and spinal marrow are continuous with each other. For, wherever the action of any part is in excess, nature so contrives as to set by it another part with an excess of contrary action, so that the excesses of the two may counterbalance each other. Now that the marrow is hot is clearly shown by many indications. The coldness of the brain is also manifest enough. For in the first place it is cold even to the touch; and, secondly, of all the fluids of the body it is the one that has the least blood; for in fact it has no blood at all in its proper substance.[3] This makes it the most consistent of all the fluids.[4] This brain is not an excretion, nor yet is it one of the parts which are anatomically continuous with each other; but it has a character peculiar to itself, as might indeed be expected. That it has no continuity with the organs of sense is plain from simple inspection, and is still more clearly shown by the fact, that, when it is touched, no sensation is produced;[5] in which respect it resembles the blood of animals and their excrement.[6] The purpose of its

652 b.

presence in animals is no less than the preservation of the whole body. How it effects this will be seen from what follows. Some writers assert that the soul is fire or some such force.[7] This however is but a rough and inaccurate assertion; and it would perhaps be better to say that the soul is incorporate in some substance of a fiery character. The reason for this being so is that of all substances there is none so suitable for ministering to the operations of the soul as that which is possessed of heat. For the functions of the soul are nutrition and motion, and it is by heat that these are most readily effected. To say however that the soul is fire is much the same thing as to confound the auger or the saw with the carpenter or his craft, simply because the work is wrought by the two in conjunction. So far then this much is plain, that all animals must necessarily have a certain amount of heat. But as all influences require to be counterbalanced, so that they may be reduced to moderation and brought to the mean (for in the mean, and not in either extreme, lies the true and rational position), nature has contrived the brain as a counterpoise to the region of the heart with its contained heat, and has given it to animals to moderate the latter, compounding it of earth and water.[8] For this reason it is, that every sanguineous animal has a brain; whereas no bloodless creature has such an organ, unless indeed it be, as the Poulp, by analogy.[9] For where there is no blood, there in consequence there is but little heat. The brain then tempers the heat and seething of the heart. In order, however, that it may not itself be absolutely without heat, but may have a moderate amount, branches run from both blood-vessels, that is to say from the great vessel and from what is called the aorta,[10] and end in the membrane which surrounds the brain;[11] while at the same time, in order to prevent any injury from the heat, these encompassing vessels, instead of being few and large, are numerous and small, and their blood scanty and clear, instead of being abundant and thick.[12] We can now understand why defluxions have their origin in the head, and occur whenever the parts about the brain have more than a due proportion of coldness. For when the nutriment steams upwards through the blood-vessels, its refuse portion is chilled by the influence of this region, and forms defluxions of phlegm and serum. We must suppose, to compare small things with great, that the like happens here as occurs in the production

653 a.

of showers. For when vapor steams up from the earth under the influence of heat and is carried into the upper regions, so soon as it reaches the cold air that is above the earth, it condenses again into water owing to the refrigeration, and falls back to the earth as rain.[13] These however are matters which may be suitably considered in the Principles of Diseases, so far as natural philosophy has anything to say to them.[14]

It is the brain again,—or, in animals that have no brain, the part analogous to it,—which is the cause of sleep. For either by chilling the blood that streams upwards after food, or by some other similar influences, it produces heaviness in the region in which it lies (which is the reason that drowsy persons hang the head), and causes the heat to escape downwards in company with the blood. It is the accumulation of this in excess in the lower part that produces complete sleep, taking away the power of standing upright from such animals as are able to assume that posture; and from the rest the power of holding up the head. These however are matters which have been separately considered in the treatises on Sensation and on Sleep.[15]

That the brain is a compound of earth and water [16] is shown by what occurs when it is boiled. For, when so treated, it turns hard and solid, inasmuch as the water is evaporated by the heat, and leaves the earthy part behind.[17] Just the same occurs when pulse and other fruits are boiled. For these also are hardened by the process, because the water which enters into their composition is driven off and leaves the earth, which is their main constituent, behind.

Of all animals, man has the largest brain in proportion to his size; and it is larger in men than in women.[18] This is because the region of the heart and of the lung is hotter and richer in blood in man than in any other animal; and in men than in women.[19] This again explains why man, alone of animals, stands erect. For the heat, overcoming any opposite inclination, makes growth take its own line of direction, which is from the centre of the body upwards.[20] It is then as a counterpoise to his excessive heat that in man's brain there is this superabundant fluidity and coldness; and it is again owing to this superabundance that the cranial bone which some call the Bregma [21] is the last to become solidified;[22] so long does evaporation continue to occur through it under the influence of heat.[23] Man is the only

653a.

sanguineous animal in which this takes place.[21] Man, again, has more sutures in his skull than any other animal,[25] and the male more than the female.[26] The explanation is again to be found in the greater size of the brain, which demands free ventilation, proportionate to its bulk. For if the brain be either too fluid or too solid, it will not perform its office, but in the one case will freeze the body, and in the other will not cool it at all; and thus will cause disease, madness, and death. For the cardiac heat and the centre of life is most delicate in its sympathies, and is immediately sensitive to the slightest change or affection of the blood on the outer surface of the brain.[27]

The fluids which are present in the animal body at the time of birth have now nearly all been considered. Amongst those that appear only at a later period are the residua of the food, which include the deposits of the belly and also those of the bladder. Besides these there is the semen and the milk, one or the other of which makes its appearance in appropriate animals. Of these fluids, the excremental residua of the food may be suitably discussed by themselves, when we come to examine and consider the subject of nutrition.[28] Then will be the proper time to explain in what animals they are found, and what are the reasons for their presence. Similarly all questions concerning the semen and the milk may be dealt with in the treatise on generation,[29] for the former of these fluids is the very starting-point of the generative process, and the latter has no other ground of existence than generative purposes.

(Ch. 8.) We have now to consider the remaining homogeneous parts, and will begin with flesh, and with the substance that, in animals that have no flesh, takes its place. The reason for so beginning is that flesh forms the very basis of animals, and is the essential constituent of their body. Its right to this precedence can also be demonstrated logically. For an animal is by our definition something that has sensibility, and chief of all that has the primary sensibility, which is that of Touch;[1] and it is the flesh, or analogous substance, which is the organ of this sense. And it is the organ, either in the same way as the eye is the organ of sight, that is it constitutes the primary organ of the sense; or it is the organ and the medium through which the object acts combined, that is it answers to the eye with some or other transparent medium attached to it.[2] Now in the case of

653b.

the other senses it was impossible for nature to unite the medium with the sense-organ, nor would such a junction have served any purpose; but in the case of touch she was compelled by necessity to do so. For of all the sense-organs that of touch is the only one that has a corporeal medium, or at any rate its medium is more corporeal than any other.

Regarding then the flesh in its sensory character, it is plain that all the other parts exist on its account. By the other parts I mean the bones, the skin, the sinews, and the blood-vessels, and, again, the hair and the various kinds of nails, and anything else there may be of a like character. Thus the bones are a contrivance to give security to the soft parts, to which purpose they are adapted by their hardness; and in animals that have no bones the same office is fulfilled by some analogous substance, as by cartilage in some fishes, and by fish-spine in others.

Now in some animals this supporting substance is situated within the body, while in some of the bloodless species it is placed on the outside. The latter is the case in all the Crustacea,[3] as the Carcini and the Carabi; it is the case also in the Testacea, as for instance in the several species known by the general name of oysters. For in all these animals the fleshy substance is within, and the earthy matter, which holds the soft parts together and keeps them from injury, is on the outside. For the shell not only enables the soft parts to hold together, but also, as the animal is bloodless and so has but little natural warmth, surrounds it, as a chaufferette does the embers, and keeps in the smouldering heat. Similar to this seems to be the arrangement in another and distinct genus of animal, namely in the Tortoises, including the Chelone and the several kinds of Emys.[4] But in Insects and in Cephalopods the plan is entirely different, there being moreover a contrast between these two themselves. For in neither of these does there appear to be any bony or earthy part, worthy of notice, distinctly separated from the rest of the body. Thus in the Cephalopods the mass of the body consists of a soft flesh-like substance, or rather of a substance which is intermediate to flesh and sinew, and not so readily destructible as actual flesh. I call this substance intermediate to flesh and sinew, because it is soft like the former, while it admits of stretching like the latter.[5] Its cleavage however is such that it splits not longitudinally, like sinew, but into circular segments,

654 a.

this being the most advantageous condition, so far as strength is concerned. These animals have also a part inside them corresponding to the spinous bones of fishes. For instance in the Cuttle-fishes there is what is known as the os sepiæ, and in the Calamaries there is the so-called gladius. In the Poulps on the other hand there is no such internal part, because the body or, as it is termed in them, the head,[6] forms but a short sac, whereas it is of considerable length in the other two; and it was this length which led nature to assign to them their hard support, so as to ensure their straightness and inflexibility; just as she has assigned to sanguineous animals their bones or their fish-spines as the case may be. To come now to Insects. In these the arrangement is quite different from that of the Cephalopods; quite different also from that which obtains in sanguineous animals, as indeed has been already stated. For in an insect there is no distinction into soft and hard parts, but the whole body is hard, the hardness however being of such a character as to be more flesh-like than bone, and more earthy and bone-like than flesh. The purpose of this is to make the body of the insect less liable to get broken into pieces.[7]

(Ch. 9.) There is a resemblance between the osseous and the vascular systems; for each has a central part in which it begins, and each forms a continuous whole. For no bone in the body exists as a separate individuality in itself, but each is either a portion of what may be considered a continuous whole, or at any rate is linked with the rest by contact and by attachments; so that nature may use adjoining bones either as though they were actually continuous and formed a single bone, or, for purposes of flexure, as though they were two and distinct. And similarly no blood-vessel has in itself a separate individuality; but they all form parts of one whole. For an isolated bone, if such there were, would in the first place be unable to perform the office, for the sake of which bones exist; for, were it discontinuous and separated from the rest by a gap, it would be perfectly unable to produce either flexure or extension; nor only so, but it would actually be injurious, acting like a thorn or an arrow lodged in the flesh. Similarly if a vessel were isolated, and not continuous with the vascular centre, it would be unable to retain the blood within it in a proper state. For it is the warmth

654 b.

derived from this centre that hinders the blood from coagulating;[1] indeed the blood, when withdrawn from its influence, actually becomes putrid. Now the centre or origin of the blood-vessels is the heart, and the centre or origin of the bones, in all animals that have bones, is what is called the chine. With this all the other bones of the body are in continuity; for it is the chine that keeps the body extended and straight. But since it is absolutely necessary that the body of an animal shall bend during locomotion, this chine, while it is one in virtue of the continuity of its parts, yet by its division into vertebræ is made to consist of many segments. It is from this chine that the bones of the limbs proceed, and with it they are continuous, in those animals that have limbs; and these bones form joints at the place where the limbs admit of flexure; being fastened together by sinews, and having their extremities adapted to each other, either by the one being hollowed and the other rounded,[2] or by both being hollowed and including between them a huckle-bone, as a connecting bolt, so as to allow of flexure and extension. For without some such arrangement these movements would be utterly impossible, or at any rate would be performed with great difficulty. There are some joints, again, in which the lower end of the one bone and the upper end of the other are alike in shape. In these cases the bones are bound together by sinews, and cartilaginous pieces are interposed in the joint, to serve as a kind of padding, and to prevent the two extremities from grating against each other.

Round about the bones, and attached to them by thin fibrous bands, grow the fleshy parts, for the sake of which the bones themselves exist. For just as an artist, when he is moulding an animal out of clay or other soft substance, takes first some solid body as a basis, and round this moulds the clay; so also has nature acted in fashioning the animal body out of flesh. Thus we find all the fleshy parts, with one exception, supported by bones, which serve, when the parts are organs of motion, to facilitate flexure, and, when the parts are motionless, act as a protection. The ribs, for example, which enclose the chest are intended to ensure the safety of the heart and neighbouring viscera. The exception of which mention was made is the belly. The walls of this are in all animals devoid of bones; in order that there may be no hindrance to the expansion which necessarily occurs in this

655 a.

part after a meal, nor, in females, any interference with the growth of the embryo, which is lodged here.[3]

Now the bones of viviparous animals, of such that is as are not merely externally but also internally viviparous,[4] vary but very little from each other in point of strength, which in all of them is considerable. For the vivipara in their bodily proportions are far above other animals, and many of them occasionally grow to an enormous size, as is the case in Libya and in hot and dry countries generally. But the greater the bulk of an animal, the stronger, the bigger, and the harder, are the supports which it requires; and comparing the big animals with each other, this requirement will be most marked in those that live a life of rapine. Thus it is that the bones of males are harder than those of females; and the bones of flesh-eaters, that get their food by fighting, are harder than those of herbivora. Of this the Lion is an example; for so hard are its bones, that, when struck, they give off sparks, as though they were flints. It may be mentioned also that the Dolphin, inasmuch as it is viviparous, is provided with bones and not merely with fish-spines.[5]

In those sanguineous animals, on the other hand, that are oviparous, the bones present successive slight variations of character. Thus in Birds there are bones, but these are not so strong as the bones of the Vivipara.[6] Then come the Oviparous fishes, where there is no bone, but merely fish-spine. In the Serpents too the bones have the character of fish-spine, excepting in the very large species,[7] where the solid foundation of the body requires to be stronger, in order that the animal itself may be strong, the same reason prevailing as in the case of the Vivipara. Lastly in the Selachia, as they are called, the fish-spines are replaced by cartilage. For it is necessary that the movements of these animals shall be of an undulating character; and this again requires the solid framework of the body to be pliable, and not rigid in its motions. Moreover in these Selachia[8] nature has used all the earthy matter on the skin; and she is unable to distribute to many different parts one and the same superfluity of material.[9] Even in viviparous animals many of the bones are cartilaginous. This happens in those parts where it is to the advantage of the surrounding flesh that its solid base shall be soft and mucilaginous. Such, for instance, is the case with the ears and nostrils; for in projecting parts, such as these, rigid substances would soon get

655 a.

broken. Cartilage and bone are indeed fundamentally the same thing, the differences between them being merely matters of degree.[10] This is manifested in the fact that neither cartilage nor bone, when once cut off, grows again.[11] Now the cartilages of these land animals are without marrow, that is without any distinctly separate marrow. For the marrow, which in bones is distinctly separate, is here mixed up with the whole mass, and gives a soft and mucilaginous consistence to the cartilage. But in the Selachia the chine, though it is cartilaginous, yet contains marrow; for here it stands in the stead of a bone.

Very nearly resembling the bones to the touch[12] are such parts as nails, hoofs, claws, horns, and the beaks of birds, all of which are intended to serve as means of defence. For the organs which are made out of these substances, and which are called by the same names as the substances themselves, the organ hoof for instance and the organ horn, are contrivances to ensure the preservation of the animals to which they severally belong. In this class too must be reckoned the teeth, which in some animals have but a single function, namely the mastication of the food, while in others they have an additional office, namely to serve as instruments of offence; as is the case with all animals that have sharp interfitting teeth or that have tusks. All these parts are necessarily of a solid and earthy character; for the value of a weapon depends on such properties. Their earthy character explains how it is that all such parts are much more developed in viviparous quadrupeds than in man. For there is always more earth in the composition of these animals than in that of the human body. However, not only all these parts but such others as are nearly connected with them, skin for instance, bladder, membrane, hairs, feathers, and their analogues, and any other similar parts that there may be, will be considered farther on with the heterogeneous parts. There we shall examine into the causes which produce them, and into the objects of their presence severally in the bodies of animals. For, as with the heterogeneous parts, so with these; it is from a consideration of their functions that alone we can derive any knowledge of them. The reason for dealing with them at all in this part of the treatise, and classifying them with the homogeneous parts, is that under one and the same name are confounded the entire organs and the substances of which they are composed.[13] But of all these

655 b.

substances flesh and bone form the basis. Semen and milk were also passed over, when we were considering the homogeneous fluids. For the treatise on generation will afford a more suitable place for their examination, seeing that the former of the two is the very foundation of the thing generated, while the latter is its nourishment.

(Ch. 10.) Let us now[1] make, as it were, a fresh beginning, and consider the heterogeneous parts, taking those first which are the first in importance.[2] For in all animals, at least in all the perfect kinds,[3] there are two parts more essential than the rest, namely the part which serves for the ingestion of food, and the part which serves for the discharge of its residue.[3] For without food growth and even existence is impossible. Intervening again between these two parts there is invariably a third, in which is lodged the vital principle. As for plants, though they also are included by us among things that have life, yet are they without any part for the discharge of residue.[4] For the food which they absorb from the ground is already concocted, and they give off as its equivalent their seeds and fruits. Plants, again, inasmuch as they are without locomotion, present no great variety in their heterogeneous parts. For, where the functions are but few, few also are the organs required to effect them.[5] The configuration of plants is a matter then for separate consideration. Animals, however, that not only live but feel, present a much greater multiformity of parts, and this diversity is greater in some animals than in others, being most varied in those, to whose share has fallen not mere life but life of high degree. Now such an animal is man. For of all living beings with which we are acquainted man alone partakes of the divine, or at any rate partakes of it in a fuller measure than the rest.[6] For this reason, then, and also because his external parts and their forms are more familiar to us than those of other animals, we must speak of man first; and this the more fitly, because in him alone do the natural parts hold their natural position; his upper part being turned towards that which is upper in the universe. For, of all animals, man alone stands erect.[7]

In man, then, the head is destitute of flesh; this being the necessary consequence of what has already been stated concerning the brain. There are, indeed, some[8] who hold that the life of man would be longer than it is, were his head more abundantly furnished with flesh; and they account for the absence of this substance by saying that it is intended to add to the perfection of sensation. For the brain they assert to be the organ of sensation; and sensation, they say, cannot penetrate to parts that are too thickly covered with flesh. But neither part of this statement is true. On the contrary, were the region of the brain thickly covered with flesh, the very purpose for which animals are provided with a brain would be directly contravened. For the brain would itself be heated to excess and so quite unable to cool any other part; and, as to the latter half of their statement, the brain cannot be the cause of any of the sensations, seeing that it is itself as utterly without feeling as any one of the excretions. These writers see that certain of the senses are located in the head, and are unable to discern any reason for this; they see also that the brain is the most peculiar of all the animal organs; and out of these facts they form an argument, by which they link sensation and brain together.[9] It has however already been clearly set forth in the treatise on Sensation, that it is the region of the heart that constitutes the sensory centre. There also it was stated that two of the senses, namely touch and taste, are manifestly directly dependent on the heart;[10] and that as regards the other three, namely hearing, sight, and the centrally placed sense of smell, it is the character of their sense-organs[11] which causes them to be lodged as a rule in the head. Vision is so placed in all animals.[12] But such is not invariably the case with hearing or with smell. For fishes and the like hear and smell, and yet have no visible organs for these senses in the head;[13] a fact which demonstrates the accuracy of the opinion here maintained. Now that vision, whenever it exists, should be in the neighbourhood of the brain is but what one would rationally expect. For the brain is fluid[14] and cold, and vision is of the character of water,[15] water being of all transparent substances the one most easily confined.[16] Moreover it cannot but necessarily be that the more precise senses will have their precision rendered still greater if ministered to by parts that have the purest[17] blood. For the motion of the heat of blood destroys sensory activity. For these reasons the organs of the precise senses are lodged in the head.

It is not only the fore part of the head that is destitute of flesh, but the hind part also. For, in all animals that have a

656b.

head, it is this head which more than any other part requires to be held up. But, were the head heavily laden with flesh, this would be impossible; for nothing so burdened can be held upright. This fact is an additional proof that the absence of flesh from the head has no reference to brain sensation. For there is no brain in the hinder part of the head,[18] and yet this is as much without flesh as is the front.

In some animals hearing as well as vision is lodged in the region of the head. Nor is this without a rational explanation. For what is called the empty space is full of air, and the organ of hearing is, as we say, formed of air. Now there are channels[19] which lead from the eyes to the blood-vessels that surround the brain; and similarly there is a channel which leads back again from each ear and connects it with the hinder part of the head. But no part that is without blood is endowed with sensation, as neither is the blood itself, but only certain parts formed of blood.[20] So that none of the bloodless parts of sanguineous animals are endowed with sensation, nor their blood itself; for no such part is sensitive in any animal.

The brain in all animals that have one is placed in the front part of the head; because the direction in which sensation acts is in front; and because the heart, from which sensation proceeds, is in the front part of the body; and lastly because the instruments of sensation are the blood-containing parts, and the cavity in the posterior part of the skull is destitute of blood-vessels.

As to the position of the sense-organs, they have been arranged by nature in the following suitable manner. The organs of hearing are so placed as to divide the circumference of the head into two equal halves; for they have to hear not only sounds which are directly in a line with themselves, but sounds from all quarters. The organs of vision are placed in front, because sight is exercised only in a straight line, and moving as we do in a forward direction it is necessary that we should see before us, in the direction of our motion. Lastly, the organs of smell are placed with good reason between the eyes. For as the body consists of two parts, a right half and a left, so also each organ of sense is double. In the case of touch this is not apparent, the reason being that the primary organ of this sense is not the flesh or analogous part, but lies internally.[21] In the case of taste, which is merely a modification of touch[22] and which

656 b.

is placed in the tongue, the fact is more apparent than in the case of touch, but still not so manifest as in the case of the other senses. However even in taste the fact is evident enough; for in some animals the tongue is plainly forked.[23] The double character of the sensations is however much more conspicuous in the other organs of sense. For there are two ears and two eyes, and the nostrils, though combined together, are also two. Were these latter otherwise disposed and separated from each other as are the ears, neither they nor the nose in which they are placed would be able to perform their office. For in such animals as have nostrils olfaction is effected by means of inspiration,[24] and the organ of inspiration is placed in front and in the middle line. This is the reason why nature has brought the two nostrils together and placed them as the central of the three sense-organs, setting them symmetrically on either side of a perpendicular line, where they benefit by the inspiratory motion.[25] In other animals than man the arrangement of these sense-organs is also such as is adapted in each case to the special requirements. *(Ch. 11.)* For instance in quadrupeds the ears project from the head and are set to all appearance above the eyes. Not that they are in reality above the eyes; but they seem to be so, because the animal does not stand upright, but has its head hung downwards. This being the usual attitude of the animal when in motion, it is of advantage that its ears shall be high up and very moveable.[1] For they can then be turned in all directions, and readily take in sounds from all quarters. *(Ch. 12.)* In birds, on the other hand, there are no ears, but only the auditory passages.[1] This is because their skin is hard and because they have feathers instead of hairs, so that they have not got the proper material for the formation of ears.[2] Exactly the same is the case with such oviparous quadrupeds as are clad with scaly plates, and the same explanation applies to them. There is also one of the viviparous quadrupeds, namely the seal, that has no ears but only the auditory passages.[3] The explanation of this is that the seal though a quadruped is a quadruped of stunted formation.[4]

(Ch. 13.) Men, and Birds, and Quadrupeds, viviparous and oviparous alike, have their eyes protected by lids. In the vivipara there are two of these; and both are used by these animals not only in closing the eye, but also in the act of blinking; whereas
657a.

the oviparous quadrupeds, and [1] the heavy-bodied birds as well as some others, use only the lower lid to close the eye; [2] while birds blink by means of a membrane connected with the canthus. The reason for the eyes being thus protected is that nature has made them of fluid consistency, in order to ensure keenness of vision. For had they been covered with hard skin, they would, it is true, have been less liable to get injured by anything falling into them from without, but they would not have been sharp-sighted. It is then to ensure keenness of vision that the skin over the pupil is fine and delicate; while the lids are superadded as a protection from injury. It is as a still further safeguard, that all these animals blink, and man most of all; this action (which is not performed from deliberate intention but from a natural instinct) [3] serving to keep objects from falling into the eyes; and being more frequent in man than in the rest of these animals, because of the greater delicacy of his skin. These lids are made of a roll of skin; and it is because they are made of skin and contain no flesh that neither they, nor the similarly constructed prepuce, unite again when once cut.[4]

As to the oviparous quadrupeds, and such birds as resemble them in closing the eye with the lower lid, it is the hardness of the skin of their heads which makes them do so.[5] For such birds as have heavy bodies are not made for flight; and so the materials which would otherwise have gone to increase the size of the feathers are diverted thence, and used to augment the thickness of the skin.[6] Birds therefore of this kind close the eye with the lower lid; whereas pigeons and the like use both upper and lower lids for the purpose. As birds are covered with feathers, so oviparous quadrupeds are covered with scaly plates; and these in all their forms are harder than hairs, so that the skin [7] also to which they belong is harder than the skin of hairy animals. In these animals, then, the skin on the head is hard, and so does not allow of the formation of an upper eyelid,[8] whereas lower down the integument is of a flesh-like character, so that the lower lid can be thin and extensible.

The act of blinking is performed by the heavy-bodied birds [9] by means of the membrane already mentioned, and not by this lower lid. For in blinking rapid motion is required, and such is the motion of this membrane, whereas that of the lower lid is slow. It is from the inner canthus, that is from the one nearest
657 b.

to the nostrils, that the membrane comes. For it is better to have one starting-point for nictitation than two; and in these birds this starting-point is the junction of eye and nostrils, an anterior starting-point being preferable to a lateral one.[10] Oviparous quadrupeds do not blink in like manner as the birds; for, living as they do on the ground, they are free from the necessity of having eyes of fluid consistency and of keen sight, whereas these are essential requisites for such birds as have to use their eyes at long distances. This too explains why birds with talons, that have to search for prey by eye from aloft, and therefore soar to greater heights than other birds, are sharp-sighted; while common fowls and the like, that live on the ground and are not made for flight, have no such keenness of vision. For there is nothing in their mode of life which imperatively requires it.

Fishes and Insects and the hard-skinned Crustacea present certain differences in their eyes, but so far resemble each other as that none of them have eyelids.[11] As for the hard-skinned Crustacea it is utterly out of the question that they should have any; for an eyelid, to be of use, requires the action of the skin to be rapid. These animals then have no eyelids and, in default of this protection, their eyes are hard, just as though the lid were attached to the surface of the eye, and the animal saw through it. Inasmuch however as such hardness must necessarily blunt the sharpness of vision, nature has endowed the eyes of Insects, and still more those of Crustacea,[12] with great mobility (just as she has given some quadrupeds very moveable ears), in order that they may be able to turn to the light and catch its rays, and so see more plainly. Fishes however have eyes of a fluid consistency. For all animals that move much about have to use their vision at considerable distances. If now they live on land, the air in which they move is transparent enough. But the water in which fishes live is a hindrance to sharp sight, though it has this advantage over the air, that it does not contain so many objects to knock against the eyes. The risk of collision being thus small, nature, who makes nothing in vain, has given no eyelids to fishes, while to counterbalance the opacity of the water she has made their eyes of fluid consistency.

(Ch. 14.) All animals that have hairs on the body have lashes on the eyelids; but birds and animals with scale-like plates, being

hairless, have none. The Libyan ostrich, indeed, forms an exception; for, though a bird, it is furnished with eyelashes.[1] This exception, however, will be explained hereafter. Of hairy animals, man alone has lashes on both lids. For in quadrupeds there is a greater abundance of hair on the back than on the under side of the body; whereas in man the contrary is the case, and the hair is more abundant on the front surface than on the back. The reason for this is that hair is intended to serve as a protection to its possessor. Now, in quadrupeds, owing to their inclined attitude, the under or anterior surface does not require so much protection as the back, and is therefore left bald, in spite of its being the nobler of the two sides. But in man, owing to his upright attitude, the anterior and posterior surfaces of the body are on an equality as regards need of protection. Nature therefore has assigned the protective covering to the nobler of the two surfaces;[2] for invariably she brings about the best arrangement of such as are possible. This then is the reason that there is no lower eyelash in any quadruped; though in some a few scattered hairs sprout out under the lower lid.[3] This also is the reason that they never have hair in the axillæ, nor on the pubes, as man has. Their hair, then, instead of being collected in these parts, is either thickly set over the whole dorsal surface, as is the case for instance in dogs, or, sometimes, forms a mane, as in horses and the like, or as in the male lion, where the mane is still more flowing and ample. So, again, whenever there is a tail of any length, nature decks it with hair, with long hair if the stem of the tail be short, as in horses, with short hair if the stem be long, regard also being had to the condition of the rest of the body.[4] For nature invariably distributes her material, by subtracting from one part and giving to another. Thus when she has covered the general surface of an animal's body with an excess of hair, she leaves a deficiency in the region of the back. This for instance is the case with bears.[5]

No animal has so much hair on the head as man. This in the first place is the necessary result of the fluid character of his brain, and of the presence of so many sutures in his skull. For wherever there is the most fluid and the most heat, there also must necessarily occur the greatest outgrowth.[6] But, secondly, the thickness of the hair in this part has a final cause, being intended to protect the head, by preserving it from excess of either heat or cold. And as the brain of man is larger and more fluid than that of any other animal, it requires a proportionately greater amount of protection. For the more fluid a substance is, the more readily does it get excessively heated or excessively chilled, while substances of an opposite character are less liable to such injurious affections.

This however is a digression, into which we have been led by the close connection of hair and eyelashes; the causes to which these latter owe their existence being the real matter in hand. We must therefore put off all further details concerning the hair till the proper occasions arrive and then return to the full consideration of the subject.[7]

(Ch. 15.) Both eyebrows and eyelashes exist for the protection of the eyes; the former that they may shelter them, like the eaves of a house, from any fluids that trickle down the head;[1] the latter to act like the palisades which are sometimes placed in front of enclosures, and to keep out any objects which might otherwise get in. The brows are placed over the junction of two bones,[2] which is the reason that in old age they often become so bushy[3] as to require cutting. The lashes are set at the terminations of small blood-vessels. For the vessels come to an end where the skin itself terminates; and, in all places where these endings occur, the exudation of moisture of a corporeal character necessitates the growth of hairs,[4] unless there be some operation of nature which interferes, by diverting the moisture to another purpose.[5]

(Ch. 16.) In the generality of viviparous quadrupeds, there is no great variety in the forms of the organ of smell. In those of them however whose jaws project forwards and taper to a narrow end, so as to form what is called a snout, the nostrils are placed in this projection, there being no other available plan; while, in the rest, there is a more definite demarcation between nostrils and jaws. But in no animal is this part so peculiar as in the elephant, where it attains an extraordinary size and strength. For the elephant uses its nostril as a hand; this being the instrument with which it conveys food, fluid and solid alike, to its mouth. With it, too, it tears up trees,[1] coiling it round their trunks. In fact it applies it generally to the purposes of a hand. For the elephant has the double character of a land animal, and of one that lives in swamps. Seeing then that it

has to get food in the water,² and yet must necessarily breathe, inasmuch as it is a land animal and has blood; seeing, also, that its excessive weight prevents it from passing rapidly from water to land, as some other sanguineous vivipara that breathe can do, it becomes necessary that it shall be suited alike for life in the water and for life on dry land. Just then as divers are sometimes provided with instruments for respiration, through which they can draw air from above the water, and thus may remain for a long time under the sea,³ so also have elephants been furnished by nature with their lengthened nostril; and, whenever they have to traverse the water, they lift this up above the surface and breathe through it. For the elephant's proboscis, as already said, is a nostril. Now it would have been impossible for this nostril to have the form of a proboscis, had it been hard and incapable of bending. For its very length would then have prevented the animal from supplying itself with food, being as great an impediment as the horns of certain oxen, that are said⁴ to be obliged to walk backwards while they are grazing. It is therefore soft and flexible, and, being such, is made, in addition to its own proper functions, to serve the office of the fore-feet; nature in this following her wonted plan of using one and the same part for several purposes.⁵ For in polydactylous quadrupeds the fore-feet are not intended merely to support the body, but also to serve as hands. But in elephants, though they must be reckoned polydactylous, as their foot has neither cloven nor solid hoof,⁶ the fore-feet, owing to the great size and weight of the body, are reduced to the condition of mere supports; and indeed their slow motion and⁷ unfitness for bending make them useless for any other purpose. A nostril, then, is given to the elephant for respiration, as to every other animal that has a lung, and is lengthened out and endowed with its power of coiling, because the animal has to remain for considerable periods of time in the water, and is unable to pass thence to dry ground with any rapidity. But as the feet are shorn of their full office, this same part is also, as before said, made by nature to supply their place, and give such help as otherwise would be rendered by them.

As to other sanguineous animals, the Birds, the Serpents and the oviparous quadrupeds, in all of them there are the nostril-holes, placed in front of the mouth; but in none are there any distinctly formed nostrils, nothing in fact which can be called nostrils except from a functional point of view. A bird at any rate has nothing which can properly be called a nose. For its so-called beak is a substitute for jaws. The reason for this is to be found in the natural conformation of birds. For they are winged bipeds; and this makes it necessary that their head and neck shall be of light weight; just as it makes it necessary that their breast-bone shall be narrowed. The beak therefore with which they are provided is formed of a bone-like substance, in order that it may serve as a weapon as well as for nutritive purposes, but is made of narrow dimensions to suit the small size of the head. In this beak are placed the olfactory passages. But there are no nostrils; for such could not possibly be placed there.

As for those animals that have no respiration,[8] it has already been explained why it is that they are without nostrils, and perceive odours either through gills, or through a blow-hole,[9] or, if they are insects, by the hypozoma; [10] and how their power of smelling depends, like their motions, upon the innate spirit [11] of their bodies, which in all of them is implanted by nature and not introduced from without.

Under the nostrils are the lips, in such sanguineous animals, that is, as have teeth. For in birds, as already has been said, the purposes of nutrition and defence are fulfilled by a bone-like beak, which forms a compound substitute for teeth and lips. For supposing that one were to cut off a man's lips, unite his upper teeth together, and similarly his under ones, and then were to lengthen out the two separate pieces thus formed, flattening them on either side and making them project forwards, supposing I say this to be done, we should at once have a bird-like beak.

The use of the lips in all animals except man is to preserve and guard the teeth; and thus it is that the distinctness with which the lips are formed is in direct proportion to the degree of nicety and perfection with which the teeth are fashioned. In man the lips are soft and flesh-like and capable of separating from each other. Their purpose, as in other animals, is to guard the teeth, but they are more especially intended to serve a higher office, contributing in common with other parts to man's faculty of speech. For just as nature has made man's tongue unlike

659 b.

that of other animals, and, in accordance with what I have said is her not uncommon practice,[12] has used it for two distinct operations, namely for the perception of savours and for speech, so also has she acted with regard to the lips, and made them serve both for speech and for the protection of the teeth. For vocal speech consists of combinations of the letters, and most of these it would be impossible to pronounce, were the lips not moist, nor the tongue such as it is. For some letters are formed by closures of the lips and others by applications of the tongue. But the differences of these movements, their nature and their number, are questions, the discussion of which belongs to the writers on articulation. It was necessary however for us to follow up the several parts in question at once to the function now assigned to them, and to show that they are of a character well suited for its performance. Therefore it is then that they are made of flesh. And the flesh of man is softer than that of any other animal, the reason [13] for this being, that of all animals man has the most delicate sense of touch.[14]

(Ch. 17.) The tongue is placed under the vaulted roof of the mouth. In land animals it presents but little diversity. But in other[1] animals it is variable, and this whether we compare them as a class with such as live on land, or compare their several species with each other. It is in man that the tongue attains its greatest degree of freedom, of softness, and of breadth; the object of this being to render it suitable for its double function. For its softness fits it for the perception of savours, a sense which is more delicate in man than in any other animal, softness being most impressionable by touch, of which sense taste is but a variety.[2] This same softness again, together with its breadth, adapts it for the articulation of letters and for speech. For these qualities, combined with its freedom from attachment, are those which suit it best for advancing and retiring in every direction. That this is so is plain, if we consider the case of those who are tongue-tied in however slight a degree. For their speech is indistinct and lisping; that is to say they have not got the full power of uttering letters. In being broad is comprised the possibility of becoming narrow; for in the great the small is included, but not the great in the small.

What has been said explains why, even among birds, those that are most capable of pronouncing letters are such as have

660a.

the broadest tongues;[3] and why the viviparous and sanguineous quadrupeds, where the tongue is hard and thick and not free in its motions, have a very limited vocal articulation. Some birds have a considerable variety of notes. These are the smaller kinds.[4] But it is the birds with talons that have the broader tongues and consequently the greater aptitude for speech. All birds use their tongues to communicate with each other. But some do this in a greater degree than the rest; so that in some cases it even seems as though actual instruction were imparted from one to another by its agency.[5] These however are matters which have already been discussed in the Researches concerning Animals.[6]

As to those oviparous and sanguineous animals that live not in the air but on the earth, their tongue in most cases is tied down and hard, and is therefore useless for vocal purposes; in the serpents however and in the lizards it is long and forked, so as to be suited for the perception of savours.[7] So long indeed is this part in serpents, that though small while in the mouth it can be protruded to a great distance. In these same animals it is forked and has a fine and hair-like extremity, because of their extreme liking for dainty food. For by this arrangement they derive a two-fold pleasure from savours, their gustatory sensation being as it were doubled.

Even some bloodless animals have an organ that serves for the perception of savours; and in sanguineous animals such an organ is invariably present. For even in such of these as would seem to an ordinary observer to have nothing of the kind, some of the fishes for example, there is a kind of shabby representative of a tongue,[8] much like what exists in river crocodiles. In most of these cases the apparent absence of the part can be rationally explained on some or other ground. For in the first place the interior of the mouth in animals of this character is invariably spinous. Secondly in water animals there is but short space of time for the perception of savours, and as the use of this sense is thus of short duration, shortened also is the separate part which subserves it. The reason for their food being so rapidly transmitted to the stomach is that they cannot possibly spend any time in sucking out the juices; for were they to attempt to do so, the water would make its way in during the process. Unless therefore one pulls their mouth very widely open indeed,
660 b.

the projection of this part is quite invisible. The region exposed by thus opening the mouth is spinous; for it is formed by the close apposition of the gills, which are of a spinous character.

In crocodiles the immobility of the lower jaw also contributes in some measure to stunt the development of the tongue. For the crocodile's tongue is adherent to the lower jaw;[9] and its upper and lower jaws are as it were inverted, for in other animals it is the upper jaw which is the immoveable one. The tongue, then, of this animal does not adhere to the upper jaw, because that would interfere with the ingestion of food, but adheres to the lower jaw, because this is, as it were, the upper one which has changed its place.[10] Moreover it is the crocodile's lot though a land animal to live the life of a fish, and this again necessarily involves an indistinct formation of the part in question.[11]

The roof of the mouth resembles flesh, even in many of the fishes; and in some of the river species, as for instance in the fishes known as Cyprini,[12] is so very flesh-like and soft as to be taken by careless observers for a tongue. The tongue of fishes, however, though it exists as a separate part, is never distinctly visible like this, as has been already explained. Again, as the gustatory sensibility is intended to serve animals in the selection of food, it is not diffused equally over the whole surface of the tongue-like organ, but is placed chiefly in the tip;[13] and for this reason it is the tip which is the only part of the tongue separated in fishes from the rest of the mouth. As all animals are sensible to the pleasure derivable from food, they all feel a desire for it. For the object of desire is the pleasant. The part however in which food produces the sensation is not precisely alike in all of them, but while in some it is free from attachments, in others, where it is not required for vocal purposes, it is united with the base of the mouth; in some again it is hard, in others soft or flesh-like. Thus even the Crustacea,[14] the Carabi for instance and the like, and the Cephalopods, such as the Sepias and the Poulps, have some such part inside the mouth. As for the Insects, some of them have the part which serves as tongue inside the mouth, as is the case with ants, and as is also the case with many Testacea, while in others it is placed externally. In this latter case it resembles a sting or piercer, and is hollow and spongy, so as to serve at one and the same time for the tasting and for the sucking up of nutriment. This is plainly to be seen in flies and bees and all such animals, and likewise in some of the Testacea. In the Purpuræ,[15] for instance, so strong is this part that it enables them to bore holes through the hard covering of shell-fish, of the spiral snails, for example, that are used as bait to catch them. So also gad-flies and cattle-flies [16] can pierce through the skin of man, and some of them even through the skins of other animals. Such, then, in these animals is the nature of the tongue, which is thus as it were the counterpart of the elephant's nostril. For as in the elephant the nostril is used as a weapon, so in these animals the tongue serves as a piercer or sting.[17]

In all other animals the tongue agrees with the description already given.

BOOK III.

(Ch. 1.) We have next to consider the teeth, and with these the mouth, that is the cavity which they enclose and form. The teeth have one invariable office, namely the reduction of the food; but besides this general function they have other special ones, and these differ in different groups. Thus in some animals the teeth serve as weapons; but this with a distinction. For there are offensive weapons and there are defensive weapons; and while in some animals, as the wild carnivora, the teeth answer both purposes, in many others, both wild and domesticated, they serve only for defence.[1] In man the teeth are admirably constructed for their general function, the front ones being sharp, so as to cut the food into bits, and the hinder ones broad and flat, so as to grind it to a pulp; while between these and separating them are the dog-teeth, which, in accordance with the rule that the mean partakes of both extremes, share in the characters of those on either side, being broad in one part but sharp in another.[2] Similar distinctions of shape are presented by the teeth of other animals, with the exception of those whose teeth are one and all of the sharp kind. In man, however, the number and the character of the teeth have been mainly determined by the requirements of speech. For the front teeth of man contribute in many ways to the formation of letter-sounds.

In some animals, however, the teeth, as already said, serve merely for the reduction of food. When, besides this, they serve as offensive and defensive weapons, they may either be formed into tusks, as for instance is the case in swine, or may be sharp-pointed and interlock with those of the opposite jaw, in which

661 b.

case the animal is said to be saw-toothed. The explanation of this latter arrangement is as follows. The strength of such an animal is in its teeth, and the efficacy of these depends on their sharpness. In order, then, to prevent their getting blunted by mutual friction, such of them as serve for weapons fit into each other's interspaces, and are so kept in proper condition. No animal that is saw-toothed is at the same time furnished with tusks.[3] For nature never makes anything superfluous or in vain. She gives, therefore, tusks to such animals as strike in fighting, and serrated teeth to such as bite. Sows, for instance, have no tusks, and accordingly sows bite instead of striking.

A general principle must here be noted, which will be found applicable not only in this instance but in many others that will occur later on. Nature allots each weapon, offensive or defensive, to those animals alone that can use it; or, if not to them alone, to them in a more marked degree; and she allots it in its most perfect state to those that can use it best; and this whether it be a sting, or a spur, or horns, or tusks, or what it may of a like kind.

Thus as males are stronger and more choleric than females, it is in males alone that such parts as those just mentioned are found, or at any rate it is in males that they are found in the highest degree of perfection.[4] For though females are of course provided with such parts as are no less necessary to them than to males, the parts for instance which subserve nutrition, they have even these in an inferior degree,[5] and the parts which answer no such necessary purpose they do not possess at all. This explains why stags have horns, while does have none; why the horns of cows are different from those of bulls, and, similarly, the horns of ewes from those of rams. It explains also why the females are often without spurs in species where the males are provided with them, and accounts for similar facts relating to other such parts.[6]

All fishes have teeth of the serrated form, with the single exception of the fish known as the Scarus.[7] In many of them there are teeth even on the tongue and on the roof of the mouth.[8] The reason for this is that, living as they do in the water, they cannot but allow this fluid to pass into the mouth with the food. The fluid, thus admitted, they must necessarily discharge again without delay. For were they not to do so, but to retain it for

662a.

a time while triturating the food, the water would run into their digestive cavities. Their teeth therefore are all of the sharp kind, so as to serve for comminution of their food, and at the same time are numerous, and set in many parts, that by their very abundance, in the absence of any grinding faculty, they may mince the food into small bits.[9] Their teeth are also curved, because these are almost the only weapons which they possess.[10]

In all these offices of the teeth the mouth also takes its part; but besides these functions it is subservient to respiration, in all such animals as breathe and are cooled by external agency. For nature, as already said,[11] uses the parts which are common to all animals for many special purposes, and this of her own accord.[12] Thus the mouth has one universal function in all animals alike, namely its alimentary office; but in some, besides this, the special duty of serving as a weapon is attached to it; in others that of ministering to speech; and again in many, though not in all, the office of respiration. All these functions are thrown by nature upon one single organ, the construction of which she varies so as to suit the variations of office. Therefore it is that in some animals the mouth is contracted, while in others it is of wide dimensions. The contracted form belongs to such animals as use the mouth merely for nutritive, respiratory, and vocal purposes; whereas in such as use it as a means of defence it has a wide gape. This is its invariable form in such animals as are sawtoothed. For seeing that their mode of warfare consists in biting, it is advantageous to them that their mouth shall have a wide opening; for the wider it opens, the greater will be the extent of the bite, and the more numerous will be the teeth called into play.

What has just been said applies to fishes as well as to other animals; and thus in such of them as are carnivorous, and made for biting, the mouth has a wide gape; whereas in the rest it is small, being placed at the extremity of a tapering snout. For this form is suited for their purposes, while the other would be useless.

In birds the mouth consists of what is called the beak, which in them is a substitute for lips and teeth. This beak presents variations in harmony with the functions and protective purposes which it serves. Thus in those birds that are called Crookedclawed[13] it is invariably hooked, inasmuch as these birds are carnivorous, and eat no kind of vegetable food whatsoever. For

662 b.

this form renders it serviceable to them in obtaining the mastery over their prey, and is better suited for deeds of violence than any other. Moreover, as their weapons of offence consist of this beak and of their claws, these latter also are more crooked in them than in the generality of birds. Similarly in each other kind of bird the beak is suited to the mode of life. Thus, in woodpeckers[14] it is hard and strong, as also in crows and birds of crowlike habit, while in the smaller birds it is delicate, so as to be of use in collecting seeds and picking up minute animals. In such birds, again, as eat herbage, and such as live on the edges of marshes—those, for example, that swim and have webbed feet—the bill is broad, or adapted in some other way to the mode of life. For a broad bill enables a bird to dig into the ground with ease, just as, among quadrupeds, does the broad snout of the pig, an animal which, like the birds in question, lives on roots. Moreover, in these root-eating birds and in some others of like habits of life, the tips of the bill end in hard points, which gives them additional facility in dealing with herbaceous food.

The several parts which are set on the head have now, pretty nearly all, been considered. In man, however, the part which lies between the head and the neck is called the face, this name (in Greek *prosōpon*) being, it would seem, derived from the function of the part. For as man is the only animal that stands upright, he is also the only one that looks directly in front (in Greek *prosō*); and the only one whose voice is emitted in that direction.[15]

(Ch. 2.) We have now to treat of horns; for these also, when present, are appendages of the head. They exist in none but viviparous animals; though in some ovipara certain parts are metaphorically spoken of as horns, in virtue of a certain resemblance.[1] To none of such parts however does the proper office of a horn belong; for they are never used, as are the horns of vivipara, for purposes which require strength, whether it be in self-protection or in offensive strife. So also no polydactylous animal[2] is furnished with horns. For horns are weapons of strife, and these polydactylous animals possess other means of security. For to some of them nature has given claws, to others teeth suited for combat, and to the rest some or other adequate defensive appliance. There are horns, however, in most of the cloven-hoofed animals, and in some[3] of those that have a solid hoof, serving them as an offensive weapon, and in some cases

also as a defensive one. There are horns also in all animals that have not been provided by nature with some other means of security; such means for instance as speed, which has been given to horses; or excessive bulk of body, which is sufficient in itself to protect an animal from being destroyed by others and which has been given to camels, and in a still greater measure to elephants. Other animals again are protected by the possession of tusks; and among these are the swine, though they have a cloven hoof.[4]

All animals again whose horns are but useless appendages have been provided by nature with some additional means of security. Thus deer are endowed with speed; for the large size and great branching of their horns makes these a source of detriment rather than of profit to their possessors.[5] Similarly endowed are the Bubalus[6] and gazelle;[7] for though these animals will stand up against some enemies and defend themselves with their horns, yet they run away from such as are fierce and valiant. The Bonasus again, whose horns curve inwards towards each other [and are therefore of no use as weapons], is provided with a means of protection in the discharge of its excrement; and of this it avails itself when frightened. There are some other animals besides the Bonasus that have a similar mode of defence.[8] In no case however does nature ever give more than one adequate means of protection to one and the same animal.[9]

Most of the animals that have horns are cloven-hoofed; but the Indian ass, as they call it, is also reported to be horned, though its hoof is solid.[10]

Again as the body, so far as regards its organs of motion,[11] consists of two distinct parts, the right and the left, so also and for like reasons the horns of animals are, in the great majority of cases, two in number. Still there are some that have but a single horn; the Oryx[12] for instance, and the so-called Indian ass; in the former of which the hoof is cloven, while in the latter it is solid. In such animals the horn is set in the centre of the head; for as the middle belongs equally to both extremes, this arrangement is the one that comes nearest to each side having its own horn.

Again, it would appear consistent with reason that the single horn should go with the solid rather than with the cloven hoof. For hoof, as also claw, is of the same nature as horn; so that the two naturally undergo division simultaneously and in the

663 a.

same animals. Again, since the division of the cloven hoof depends on deficiency of material, it is but rationally consistent, that nature when she gave an animal an excess of material for the hoofs, which thus became solid, should have taken away something from the upper parts and so made the animal to have but one horn.[13]

Rightly too did she act when she chose the head whereon to set the horns. And Æsop's Momus[14] is beside the mark, when he finds fault with the bull for not having its horns upon its shoulders. For from this position, says he, they would have delivered their blow with the greatest force, whereas on the head they occupy the weakest part of the whole body. Momus was but dull-sighted in making this hostile criticism. For had the horns been set on the shoulders, or had they been set on any other part than they are, the encumbrance of their weight would have been increased, not only without any compensating gain whatsoever, but with the disadvantage of impeding many bodily operations. For the point whence the blows could be delivered with the greatest force was not the only matter to be considered, but the point also whence they could be delivered with the widest range. But as the bull has no hands and cannot possibly have its horns on its feet or on its knees, where they would prevent flexion, there remains no other site for them but the head; and this therefore they necessarily occupy. In this position, moreover, they are much less in the way of the movements of the body than they would be elsewhere.

Deer are the only animals in which the horns are solid throughout, and are also the only animals that cast them.[15] This casting is not simply advantageous to the deer from the increased lightness which it produces, but, seeing how heavy the horns are, is a matter of actual necessity.

In all other animals the horns are hollow for a certain distance, and the end alone is solid, this being the part of use in a blow. At the same time, to prevent even the hollow part from being weak, the horn does not grow out of the skin, but has a solid piece from the bones fitted into its cavity. For this arrangement is not only that which makes the horns of the greatest service in fighting, but that which causes them to be as little of an impediment as possible in the other actions of life.

Such then are the reasons for which horns exist; and such the reasons why they are present in some animals, absent from others.

663 b.

Let us now consider how the necessary results of the material nature are made available by rational nature for a final cause.[16]

In the first place, then, the larger the bulk of animals, the greater is the amount of corporeal and earthy matter which they contain. Thus no very small animal is known to have horns, the smallest horned animal that we are acquainted with being the gazelle.[17] But in all our speculations concerning nature, what we have to consider is the general rule; for that is natural which applies either universally or generally.[18] And thus when we say that the largest animals have most earthy matter, we say so because such is the general rule. Now this earthy matter is used in the animal body to form bone. But in the larger animals there is an excess of it, and this excess is turned by nature to useful account, being converted into weapons of defence. Part of it necessarily flows to the upper portion of the body, and this is allotted by her in some cases to the formation of tusks and teeth, in others to the formation of horns. Thus it is that no animal that has horns has also front teeth in both jaws, those in the upper jaw being deficient.[19] For nature by subtracting from the teeth adds to the horns; the nutriment which in most animals goes to the former being here spent on the augmentation of the latter. Does, it is true, have no horns and yet are equally deficient with the males as regards the teeth. The reason, however, for this is that they, as much as the males, are naturally horn-bearing animals; but they have been stripped of their horns, because these would not only be useless to them but actually baneful;[20] whereas the greater strength of the males causes these organs, though equally useless, to be much less of an impediment. In other animals, where this material is not secreted from the body in the shape of horns, it is used to increase the size of the teeth; in some cases of all the teeth, in others merely of the tusks, which thus become so long as to resemble horns projecting from the jaws.[21]

(Ch. 3.) So much, then, of the parts which appertain to the head. Below the head lies the neck, in such animals as have one. This is the case only with those that have the parts to which a neck is subservient. These parts are the larynx[1] and what is called the œsophagus. Of these the former, or larynx, exists for the sake of respiration, being the instrument by which such animals as breathe inhale and discharge the air. Therefore it is that, when there is no lung, there is also no neck. Of this

664a.

condition the Fishes are an example. The other part, or œsophagus, is the channel through which food is conveyed to the stomach; so that all animals that are without a neck are also without a distinct œsophagus.[2] Such a part is in fact not required of necessity for nutritive purposes; for it has no action whatsoever on the food. Indeed there is nothing to prevent the stomach from being placed directly after the mouth. This however is quite impossible in the case of the lung. For there must be some sort of tube common to the two divisions of the lung, by which the breath may be apportioned to their respective bronchi, and thence pass into the air pipes; and such an arrangement will be the best for giving perfection to inspiration and respiration. The organ then concerned in respiration must of necessity be of some length; and this again necessitates there being an œsophagus to unite mouth and stomach.[3] This œsophagus is of a flesh-like character, and yet admits of extension like a sinew.[4] This latter property is given to it, that it may stretch when food is introduced; while the flesh-like character is intended to make it soft and yielding, and to prevent it from being rasped by particles as they pass downwards, and so suffering damage. On the other hand the windpipe and the so-called larynx are constructed out of a cartilaginous substance. For they have to serve not only for respiration, but also for vocal purposes; and an instrument that is to produce sounds must necessarily be not only smooth but firm. The windpipe lies in front of the œsophagus, although this position causes it to be some hindrance to the latter in the act of deglutition.[5] For if a morsel of food, fluid or solid, slips into it by accident, choking and difficult breathing and violent cough ensue. This must be a matter of astonishment to any of those who assert that it is by the windpipe that an animal imbibes fluid.[6] For the consequences just mentioned occur invariably, whenever a particle of food slips in, and are quite obvious. Indeed on many grounds it is ridiculous to say that this is the channel through which animals imbibe fluid. For there is no passage leading from the lung to the stomach, such as the œsophagus which we see leading thither from the mouth. Moreover, when any cause produces sickness and vomiting, it is plain enough whence the fluid is discharged. It is manifest also that fluid, when swallowed, does not pass directly into the bladder

664 b.

and collect there, but goes first into the stomach. For, when red wine is taken, the dejections of the stomach are seen to be coloured by its dregs; and such discoloration has been even seen on many occasions inside the stomach itself, in cases where there have been wounds opening into that organ. However it is perhaps silly to be minutely particular in dealing with silly statements such as this.

The windpipe then, owing to its position in front of the œsophagus, is exposed, as we have said, to annoyance from the food. To obviate this, however, nature has contrived the epiglottis. This part is not found in all viviparous animals, but only in such of them as have a lung; nor in all of these, but only in such as at the same time have their skin covered with hairs, and not either with scaly plates or with feathers. In such scaly and feathered animals there is no epiglottis, but its office is supplied by the larynx,[7] which closes and opens, just as in the other case the epiglottis falls down and rises up; rising up during the ingress or egress of breath, and falling down during the ingestion of food, so as to prevent any particle from slipping into the trachea. Should there be the slightest want of accuracy in this movement, or should an inspiration be made during the ingestion of food, choking and coughing ensue, as already has been noticed. So admirably contrived, however, is the movement both of the epiglottis and of the tongue, that, while the food is being ground to a pulp in the mouth, the tongue very rarely gets caught between the teeth; and, while the food is passing over the epiglottis, seldom does a particle of it slip into the windpipe.

The animals which have been mentioned as having no epiglottis owe this deficiency to the dryness of their flesh and to the hardness of their skin. For an epiglottis made of such materials would not admit of easy motion.[8] In fact it would take a longer time to shut down an epiglottis made of the peculiar flesh of these animals, and shaped like that of those with hairy skins, than to bring the edges of the trachea itself into contact with each other.

Thus much then as to the reasons why some animals have an epiglottis while others have none, and thus much also as to its use. It is a contrivance of nature to remedy the vicious position of the windpipe in front of the œsophagus. That position is the result of necessity. For it is in the front and centre of the body that the heart is situated, in which we say is the principle of life and the source of all motion and sensation. (For sensation and motion are exercised in the direction which we term forwards, and it is on this very relation that the distinction of before and behind is founded.) But where the heart is, there and surrounding it is the lung. Now inspiration, which occurs for the sake of the lung and for the sake of the principle which has its seat in the heart, is effected through the windpipe. Since then the heart must of necessity lie in the very front place of all, it follows that the larynx also and the windpipe must of necessity lie in front of the œsophagus. For they lead to the lung and heart,[9] whereas the œsophagus leads to the stomach. And it is an universal law that, as regards above and below, front and back, right and left, the nobler and more honourable part invariably is placed uppermost, in front, and on the right, rather than in the opposite positions, unless some more important object stands in the way.[10]

(Ch. 4.) We have now dealt with the neck, the œsophagus, and the windpipe, and have next to treat of the viscera. These are peculiar to sanguineous animals, some of which have all of them, others only a part, while no bloodless animals have any at all.[1] Democritus then seems to have been mistaken in the notion he formed of the viscera, if he fancied that the reason why none were discoverable in bloodless animals was that these animals were too small to allow them to be seen. For, in sanguineous animals, the heart and liver are visible enough when the body is only just formed, and while it is still extremely small. For these parts are to be seen in the egg sometimes as early as the third day, being then no bigger than a point;[2] and are visible also in aborted[3] embryos, while still excessively minute. Moreover, as the external organs are not precisely alike in all animals, but each creature is provided with such as are suited to its special mode of life and motion, so is it with the internal parts, these also differing in different animals. Viscera, then, are peculiar to sanguineous animals; and this accords with the fact that the viscera are each and all formed from sanguineous material, as is plainly to be seen in the new-born young of these animals. For in such the viscera are more sanguineous, and of greater bulk in proportion to the body, than at any later period of life, because the nature of the material and its abundance are most distinctly marked in objects at the period of their first formation.[4] There is a heart, then, in

665b.

all sanguineous animals, and the reason for this has already been given. For that sanguineous animals must necessarily have blood is self-evident. And, as the blood is fluid, it is also a matter of necessity that there shall be a receptacle for it; and it is clearly to meet this requirement that nature has devised the blood-vessels. These, again, must necessarily have one primary source. For it is preferable that there shall be one such, when possible, rather than several. This primary source of the vessels is the heart.[5] For the vessels clearly are *from* it, and not *through* it.[6] Moreover, being as it is homogeneous, it has the character of a blood-vessel. Again its position is that of a primary or dominating part. For nature, when no other more important purpose stands in her way, places the more honourable part in the more honourable position;[7] and the heart lies about the centre of the body, but rather in its upper than its lower half, and also more in front than behind. This is most evident in the case of man, but even in other animals there is a tendency in the heart to assume a similar position, in the centre of the necessary part of the body, that is to say of the part which terminates in the vent for excrement. For the limbs vary in position in different animals, and are not to be counted with the parts which are necessary for life. For life can be maintained even when they are removed; while it is self-evident that the addition of them to an animal is not destructive of it.

There are some[8] who say that the vessels commence in the head. In this they are clearly mistaken. For in the first place, according to their representation, there would be many sources for the vessels, and these scattered; and secondly these sources would be in a region that is manifestly cold, as is shown by its intolerance of chill, whereas the region of the heart is as manifestly hot.[9] Again, as already said, the vessels extend through all the other viscera, but no vessel extends through the heart.[10] From this it is quite evident that the heart is a part of the vessels and their origin; and for this it is well suited by its structure. For its central[11] part consists of a thick and hollow body, and is moreover full of blood, as though the vessels took thence their origin. It is hollow to serve for the reception of the blood, while its wall is thick, that it may serve to protect the source of heat. For here, and here alone in all the viscera and in fact in all the body, there is blood without blood-vessels, the blood elsewhere being always contained within vessels.[12] Nor is this but con-

666a.

sistent with reason. For the blood is conveyed into the vessels from the heart, but none passes into the heart from without. For in itself it constitutes the origin and fountain, or primary receptacle, of the blood. It is, however, from dissections and from observations on the process of development that the truth of these statements receives its clearest demonstration. For the heart is the first of all the parts to be formed; and no sooner is it formed than it contains blood. Moreover the motions of pain and pleasure,[13] and generally of all sensation, plainly start from the heart, and find in it their ultimate termination. This, indeed, reason would lead us to expect. For the starting-point must, whenever possible, be one; and, of all places, the best suited for a starting-point is the centre. For the centre is one, and is equally or almost equally within reach of every part. Again, as neither the blood itself, nor yet any part which is bloodless, is endowed with sensation, it is plain that that part which first has blood, and which holds it as it were in a receptacle, must be the primary source of sensation.[14] And that this part is the heart is not only a rational inference, but is also evident to the senses. For no sooner is the embryo formed, than its heart is seen in motion like a living creature, and this before any of the other parts, as though it constituted the starting-point of life in all animals that have blood. A further evidence of the truth of what has been stated is the fact that no sanguineous animal is without a heart. For the primary source of blood must of necessity be present in them all. It is true that sanguineous animals not only have a heart but also invariably have a liver. But no one could ever deem the liver to be the primary organ either of the whole body or of the blood.[15] For the position in which it is placed is far from being that of a primary or dominating part; and moreover in the most perfectly finished animals there is another part, the spleen, which as it were counterbalances it.[16] Still further, the liver contains no spacious receptacle in its substance, as does the heart, but has its blood in a vessel like all the other viscera. The vessel moreover extends through it, and no vessel whatsoever originates in it; for it is from the heart that all the vessels take their rise. Since then one or other of these two parts must be the central source, and since it is not the liver which is such, it follows of necessity that it is the heart which is the source of the blood, as also the primary organ in other respects. For the definitive characteristic of an animal is the possession of sensation; and the first sensory part is that which first has blood; that is to say is the heart, which is the source of blood and the first of the parts to contain it.

The apex of the heart is pointed and more solid than the rest of the organ. It lies against the breast, and entirely in the anterior part of the body, in order to prevent that region from getting chilled. For in all animals there is comparatively but little flesh over the breast, whereas there is a more abundant covering of that substance on the posterior surface, so that the heat has in the back a sufficient amount of protection. In all animals but man the heart is placed in the centre of the pectoral region; but in man [17] it inclines a little towards the left, so that it may counterbalance the chilliness of that side. For the left side is colder in man, as compared with the right, than in any other animal.[18] It has already been stated that even in fishes the heart holds the same position as in other animals; and the reasons have been given why it appears not to do so. The apex of the heart, it is true, is in them turned towards the head, but this in fishes is the front aspect, for it is the direction in which their motion occurs.[19]

The heart again is abundantly supplied with sinews,[20] as might reasonably be expected. For the motions of the body commence from the heart, and are brought about by traction and relaxation. The heart therefore, which, as already said, is as it were a living creature inside its possessor, requires some such subservient and strengthening parts.

In no animals does the heart contain a bone, certainly in none of those that we have ourselves inspected,[21] with the exception of the horse and a certain kind of ox. In these exceptional cases the heart, owing to its large bulk, is provided with a bone as a support; just as the bones serve as supports for the body generally.[22]

In animals of great size the heart[23] has three cavities; in smaller animals it has two; and in all has at least one. The reason for this, as already stated, is that there must be some place in the heart to serve as a receptacle for the first blood; which, as has been mentioned more than once, is formed in this organ. But inasmuch as the main blood-vessels are two in number,[24] namely the so-called great vessel and the aorta, each of

666 b.

which is the origin of other vessels; inasmuch, moreover, as these two vessels present differences, hereafter to be discussed, when compared with each other, it is of advantage that they also shall themselves have distinct origins. This advantage will be obtained if each side have its own blood, and the blood of one side be kept separate from that of the other.[25] For this reason the heart, whenever it is possible, has two receptacles. And this possibility exists in the case of large animals, for in them the heart, as the body generally, is of large size. Again it is still better that there shall be three cavities, so that the middle and odd one may serve as a common origin for both sides.[26] But this requires the heart to be of greater magnitude, so that it is only in the largest animals that the heart has three cavities.

Of these three cavities it is the right which has the most abundant and the hottest blood,[27] and this explains why the limbs on the right side of the body are also warmer than those on the left.[28] The left cavity has the least blood of all, and the coldest; while in the middle cavity the blood, as regards quantity and heat, is intermediate to the other two, being however of purer quality than either. For it behoves the supreme part to be as tranquil as possible, and this tranquillity can be ensured by the blood being pure, and of moderate amount and warmth.[29]

In the heart of animals there is also a kind of joint-like division, something like the sutures of the skull.[30] This is not however attributable to the heart being formed by the union of several parts into a compound whole, but is rather, as already said, the result of a joint-like division. These jointings are most distinct in animals of keen sensibility, and less so in those that are of duller feeling, in swine for instance. Different hearts differ also from each other in their sizes, and in their degrees of firmness; and these differences somehow extend their influence to the temperaments of the animals. For in animals of low sensibility the heart is hard and solid, while it is softer in such as are endowed with keener feeling. So also when the heart is of large size the animal is timorous, while it is more courageous if the organ be smaller and of moderate bulk. For in the former the bodily affection which results from terror already pre-exists;[31] for the bulk of the heart is out of all proportion to the animal's heat, which being small is reduced to insignificance in the large space, and thus the blood is made colder than it would otherwise be.

667 a.

The heart is of large size [33] in the hare, the deer, the mouse, the hyæna, the ass, the leopard, the marten, and in pretty nearly all other animals that are either manifestly timorous, or that betray their cowardice by their spitefulness.

What has been said of the heart as a whole is no less true of its cavities and of the blood-vessels; these also if of large size being cold.[33] For just as a fire of equal size gives less heat in a large room than in a small one, so also does the heat in a large cavity or a large blood-vessel, that is in a large receptacle, have less influence than in a small one. The more spacious, moreover, these cavities and vessels are, the greater is the amount of spirit [34] which they contain, and the greater its effect, for all hot substances are cooled by the motion of external objects.[35] Thus it is that no animal that has large cavities in its heart, or large blood-vessels, is ever fat, the vessels being indistinct and the cavities small in all or most fat animals.[36]

The heart again is the only one of the viscera, and indeed the only part of the body, that is unable to tolerate any serious affection.[37] This is but what might reasonably be expected. For, if the primary or dominant part be diseased, there is nothing from which the other parts which depend upon it can derive succour. A proof, that the heart is thus unable to tolerate any morbid affection, is furnished by the fact that never has it been seen diseased in a sacrificial victim, though this is not the case with the other viscera. For the kidneys are frequently found to be full of stones, and growths, and small abscesses, as also is the liver, the lung, and more than all the spleen.[38] There are also many other affections which are seen to occur in these parts, those which are least liable to such being the portion of the lung which is close to the windpipe, and the portion of the liver which lies about the junction with the great blood-vessel. This again admits of a rational explanation. For it is in these parts that the lung and liver are most closely in communion with the heart. On the other hand when animals die not by sacrifice but from disease, they are found on dissection to have morbid affections of the heart.

(Ch. 5.) Thus much of the heart, its nature, and the end and cause of its existence in such animals as have it. In due sequence we have next to discuss the blood-vessels, that is to say the great vessel and the aorta. For it is into these two[1] that the blood first passes when it quits the heart; and all the other vessels
667 b.

are but offshoots from them. Now that these vessels exist on account of the blood has already been stated. For every fluid requires a receptacle, and in the case of the blood the vessels are that receptacle. Let us now explain why these vessels are two, and why they spring from one single source, and extend throughout the whole body.

The reason, then, why these two vessels coalesce into one centre, and spring from one source, is that the sensory soul is in all animals actually one; (in sanguineous animals one not only actually but potentially, but in some bloodless animals one actually only and not potentially;[2]) and this one-ness of the sensory soul determines a corresponding one-ness of the part in which it primarily abides. Where, however, the sensory soul is lodged, there also and in the self-same place must necessarily be the source of heat;[3] and, again, where this is there also must be the source of the blood, seeing that it thence derives its warmth and fluidity. Thus, then, in the oneness of the part in which is lodged the prime source of sensation and of heat is involved the one-ness of the source in which the blood originates; and this, again, explains why the blood-vessels have one common starting-point.

The vessels, again, are two, because the body of every sanguineous animal that is capable of locomotion[4] is bilateral; for in all such animals there is a distinguishable before and behind, a right and left, an above and below. Now as the front is more honourable and of higher supremacy than the hinder aspect, so also and in like degree is the great vessel superior to the aorta. For the great vessel is placed in front, while the aorta is behind; the former again is plainly visible in all sanguineous animals, while the latter is in some indistinct and in some not discernible at all.

Lastly, the reason for the vessels being distributed throughout the entire body is that in them, or in parts analogous to them, is contained the blood, or the fluid which in ex-sanguineous animals takes the place of blood, and that the blood or analogous fluid is the material from which the whole body is made. Now as to the manner in which animals are nourished,[5] and as to the ways and means by which they absorb nutriment from the stomach, these are matters which will be more suitably considered and explained in the treatise on Generation and Development. But inasmuch as the parts are, as already said, formed out of the blood,

668a.

it is but rational that the flow of the blood should extend, as it does, throughout the whole of the body. For since each part is formed of blood, each must have blood through and in its substance.

To give an illustration of this. The water-courses [6] in gardens are so constructed as to distribute water from one single source or fount into numerous channels, which divide and subdivide so as to convey it to all parts; and, again, in house-building stones are thrown down along the whole ground-plan of the foundation walls; because the garden-plants in the one case grow at the expense of the water, and the foundation walls in the other are built out of the stones. Now just after the same fashion has nature laid down channels for the conveyance of the blood throughout the whole body, because this blood is the material out of which the whole fabric is made. This fact becomes very evident in bodies that have undergone great emaciation. For in such there is nothing to be seen but the blood-vessels; just as when fig-leaves or vine-leaves or the like have dried up, there is nothing left of them but their vessels. The explanation of these facts is that the blood, or fluid which takes its place, is potentially body and flesh, or substance analogous to flesh. Now just as in irrigation the larger dykes are permanent, while the smaller ones are soon filled up with mud and disappear, again to become visible when the deposit of mud ceases; so also do the largest blood-vessels remain permanently open, while the smallest ones are converted actually into flesh, though potentially they are no whit less vessels than before.[7] This too explains why, so long as the flesh of an animal is in its integrity, blood will flow from any part of it whatsoever that is cut, though no vessel, however small, be visible in it. Yet there can be no blood, unless there be a blood-vessel. The vessels then are there, but are invisible owing to their being clogged up, just as the dykes for irrigation are invisible until they have been cleared of mud.

As the blood-vessels advance, they become gradually smaller and smaller, until at last their tubes are too fine to admit the thick blood. This fluid can therefore no longer find its way through them, though they still give passage to the moisture which we call sweat; and especially so when the body is heated, and the mouths of the small vessels are dilated. Instances, indeed, are not unknown of persons who in consequence of a cachectic state have secreted sweat that resembled blood,[8] their

668 b.

body having become loose and flabby, and their blood watery, owing to the heat in the small vessels [9] having been too scanty for its concoction. For, as was before said, every mixture of earth and water—and both nutriment and blood are such—becomes thicker from concoction.[10] The inability of the heat to effect concoction may be due either to its being absolutely small in amount, or to its being small in proportion to the quantity of food, when this has been taken in excess. This excess again may be of two kinds, either quantitative or qualitative; for all substances are not equally amenable to concoction.

The larger the channels, the more easily does the blood flow through them. Thus it is that when hæmorrhages occur from the nostrils and gums and fundament, and sometimes also from the mouth, they are of a passive kind, and not violent as are those from the windpipe.[11]

The great vessel and the aorta, which above lie somewhat apart, lower down exchange positions, and by so doing give compactness to the body. For when they reach the point where the legs diverge, they each split into two, and the great vessel passes from the front to the rear, and the aorta from the rear to the front. By this they contribute to the unity of the whole fabric. For as in plaited work the parts hold more firmly together because of the interweaving, so also by the interchange of position between the blood-vessels are the anterior and posterior parts of the body more closely knit together. A similar exchange of position occurs also in the upper part of the body, between the vessels that have issued from the heart.[12] The details however of the mutual relations of the different vessels must be looked for in the treatises on Anatomy and the Researches concerning Animals.

So much, then, as concerns the heart and the blood-vessels. We must now pass on to the other viscera and apply the same method of enquiry to them.

(Ch. 6.) The lung,[1] then, is an organ found in all the animals of a certain class, because they live on land. For there must of necessity be some or other means of cooling down the heat of the body; and in sanguineous animals, as they are of an especially hot nature, the cooling agency must be an external one; whereas in the bloodless kinds the innate spirit is sufficient of itself for the purpose.[2] The external cooling agent must be

669a.

either air or water. In fishes the agent is water. Fishes therefore never have a lung, but have gills in its place, as was stated in the treatise on Respiration. But animals that breathe are cooled by air. These therefore are all provided with a lung.[3]

All land animals breathe, and even some water animals, such as the whale,[4] the dolphin, and all the spouting Cetacea. For many animals lie halfway[5] between terrestrial and aquatic; some that are terrestrial and that inspire air being nevertheless of such a bodily constitution that they abide for the most time in the water; and some that are aquatic partaking so largely of the land character, that respiration constitutes for them the main condition of life.

The organ of respiration is the lung. This derives its motion from the heart; but it is its own large size and spongy texture that affords amplitude of space for the entrance of the breath. For when the lung rises up the breath streams in, and is again expelled when the lung contracts.[6] It has been stated, but incorrectly, that it is to the lung that the beating of the heart is due. That this is not so is shown by the phenomenon of palpitation occurring, so to speak, in man alone; inasmuch as man alone is influenced by hope and expectation.[7] Again in most animals the heart is at a distance from the lung and placed above it;[8] so that its beating can in no degree be brought about by this latter.

The lung differs much in different animals. For in some it is of large size and contains blood; while in others it is smaller and of spongy texture. In the vivipara it is large and rich in blood, because[9] of their natural heat; while in the ovipara it is small and dry but capable of expanding to a vast extent when inflated. Among terrestrial animals, the oviparous quadrupeds, such as lizards, tortoises, and the like, have this kind of lung; and, among inhabitants of the air, the animals known as birds.[10] For in all these the lung is spongy, and like foam. For it is bladdery and collapses from a large bulk to a small one, as does foam when it runs together. In this too lies the explanation of the fact that these animals are little liable to thirst and [11] drink but sparingly, and that they are able to remain for a considerable time under water.[12] For, inasmuch as they have but little heat,[13] the very motion of the lung, airlike and void, suffices by itself to cool them for a considerable period.[14]

669 b.

These animals, speaking generally, are also distinguished from others by their smaller bulk.¹⁵ For heat promotes growth, and abundance of blood is a sure indication of heat. Heat again tends to make the body erect; and thus it is that man is the most erect of animals, and the vivipara more erect than other quadrupeds.¹⁶ For no viviparous animal, be it apodous ¹⁷ or be it possessed of feet, is so given to creep into holes as are the ovipara.

The lung then exists for respiration; and this is its universal office. But the amount of blood it contains, and its structure generally, varies with the requirements of different groups of animals.¹⁸ There is however no one term to denote all animals that have a lung, no designation, that is, like the term Bird, applicable to the whole of a certain class. Yet the possession of a lung is a part of their essence, just as much as the presence of certain characters constitutes the essence of a bird.

(Ch. 7.) Of the viscera some appear to be single, as the heart and lung; others to be double, as the kidneys; while of a third kind it is doubtful in which class they should be reckoned. For the liver and the spleen would seem to lie half-way between the single and the double organs. For they may be regarded either as constituting each a single organ, or as a pair of organs resembling each other in character.¹

In reality however all the organs are double.² The reason for this is that the body itself is double, consisting of two halves, which are however combined together under one supreme centre. For there is an upper and a lower half, a front and a rear, a right side and a left.

This explains why it is that even the brain and the several organs of sense tend in all animals to consist of two parts; and the same explanation applies to the heart with its cavities. The lung again in ovipara is divided to such an extent, that these animals look as though they had actually two lungs.³ As to the kidneys no one can overlook their double character. But when we come to the liver and the spleen, any one might fairly be in doubt. The reason of this is, that, in animals that necessarily have a spleen,⁴ this organ is such that it might be taken for a kind of bastard liver; while in those, in which a spleen is not an actual necessity but is merely present, as it were, by way of token, in an extremely minute form, the liver plainly consists of two parts; of which the larger tends to lie

669 b.

on the right side and the smaller on the left. Not but what there are some ovipara in which this condition is comparatively indistinctly marked; while on the other hand there are some vivipara in which the liver is manifestly divided into two parts.[5] Examples of such division are furnished by the hares of certain regions that have the appearance of having two livers, and by some fishes, especially the cartilaginous kinds.[6]

It is the position of the liver on the right side of the body that is the main cause for the formation of the spleen; the existence of which thus becomes to a certain extent a matter of necessity in all animals, though not of very stringent necessity.

The reason, then, why the viscera are bilateral is, as we have said, that there are two sides to the body, a right and a left.[7] For each of these sides aims at similarity with the other, and so likewise do their several viscera; and as the sides, though dual, are knit together into unity, so also do the viscera tend to be bilateral and yet one by unity of constitution.

Those viscera which lie below the diaphragm exist one and all on account of the blood-vessels;[8] serving as a bond, by which these vessels, while floating freely, are yet held in connection with the body. For the vessels give off branches which run to the body through the out-stretched structures,[9] like so many anchor-lines thrown out from a ship. The great vessel sends such branches to the liver, the spleen, and the kidneys; and these viscera—the liver and spleen on either side and the kidneys behind—attach the great vessel[10] immoveably to the body. The aorta sends similar branches to the kidneys, but none to the liver nor to the spleen.[11]

These viscera, then, contribute in this manner to the compactness of the animal body. The liver and spleen assist moreover in the concoction of the food; for both are rich in blood,[12] and therefore of a hot character. The kidneys on the other hand take part in the separation of the excretion which flows into the bladder.[13]

The heart then and the liver are essential constituents of every animal; the liver that it may effect concoction, the heart that it may lodge the central source of heat. For some or other part there must be which like a hearth shall hold the kindling fire; and this part must be well protected, seeing that it is, as it were, the citadel of the body.

670a.

All sanguineous animals, then, need these two parts; and this explains why these two viscera, and these two alone, are invariably found in them all. In such of them, however, as breathe, there is also as invariably a third, namely the lung. The spleen on the other hand is not invariably present; and, in those animals that have it, is only present of necessity in the same sense as the excretions of the belly and of the bladder are necessary, in the sense that is of being an inevitable concomitant. Therefore it is that in some animals the spleen is but scantily developed as regards size. This for instance is the case in such feathered animals as have a hot stomach. Such are the pigeon, the hawk, and the kite.[14] It is the case also in oviparous quadrupeds, where the spleen is excessively minute, and in many of the scaly fishes. These same animals are also without a bladder, because the loose texture of their flesh allows the residual fluid to pass through and to be converted into feathers and scales. For the spleen attracts the residual humours from the stomach, and owing to its blood-like character is enabled to assist in their concoction.[15] Should however this residual fluid be too abundant, or the heat of the spleen be too scanty, the body becomes sickly from over-repletion with food. Often too, when the spleen is affected by disease, the belly becomes hard[16] owing to the reflux into it of the fluid; just as happens to those who form too much urine, for they also are liable to a similar diversion of the fluids into the belly. But in those animals that have but little superfluous fluid to excrete, such as birds and fishes, the spleen is never large, and in some exists no more than by way of token. So also in the oviparous quadrupeds it is small, compact, and like a kidney. For their lung is spongy,[17] and they drink but little, and such superfluous fluid as they have is diverted to the formation of feathers.

On the other hand in such animals as have a bladder, and whose lung contains blood, the spleen is watery, both for the reason already mentioned, and also because the left side of the body is more watery and colder than the right. For each of two contraries has been so placed as to go together with that which is akin to it in another pair of contraries. Thus right and left, hot and cold, are pairs of contraries; and right is conjoined with hot, after the manner described, and left with cold.

The kidneys when they are present exist not of actual necessity, but as matters of greater finish and perfection. For by their
670 b.

special character they are suited to serve in the excretion of the fluid which collects in the bladder. In animals therefore where this fluid is very abundantly formed, their presence enables the bladder to perform its proper office with greater perfection.[18]

Since then both kidneys and bladder exist in animals for one and the same function, we must next treat of the bladder, though in so doing we disregard the due order of succession [19] in which the parts should be enumerated. For not a word has yet been said of the midriff, which, though not one of the viscera, is yet one of the parts that environ them, and has to be considered with them.

(Ch. 8.) It is not every animal that has a bladder; those only being apparently intended by nature to have one, whose lung contains blood.[1] To such it was but reasonable that she should give this part. For the character of their lung with its abundant blood causes them to be the thirstiest of animals, and makes them require a more than ordinary quantity not merely of solid but also of liquid nutriment. This increased consumption necessarily entails the production of an increased amount of residue; which thus becomes too abundant to be concocted by the stomach and excreted with its own residual matter. The residual fluid must therefore of necessity have a receptacle of its own; and thus it comes to pass that all animals whose lung contains blood are provided with a bladder. Those animals on the other hand that are without a lung of this character, and that either drink but sparingly owing to their lung being of a spongy texture, or that never imbibe fluid at all for drinking's sake but only as nutriment, insects for instance and fishes, and that are moreover clad with feathers or scales or scaly plates [2]—all these animals, owing to the small amount of fluid which they imbibe, and owing also to such residue as there may be being converted into feathers and the like, are invariably without a bladder.[3] The Tortoises,[4] which are comprised among animals with scaly plates, form the only exception; and this is merely due to the imperfect development of their natural conformation; the explanation of the matter being that in the sea-tortoises the lung is flesh-like and contains blood, resembling the lung of the ox, and that in the land-tortoises it is of larger size in comparison with the bulk of the body than in other animals of the same class.[5] Moreover, inasmuch

671a.

as the covering which invests them is dense and shell-like, so that the moisture cannot exhale through the porous flesh, as it does in birds and in snakes and other animals with scaly plates, such an amount of secretion is formed that some special part is required to receive and hold it. This then is the reason why these animals, alone of their kind, have a bladder, the sea-tortoises a large one, the land-tortoises an extremely small one.[6]

(Ch. 9.) What has been said of the bladder is equally true of the kidneys. For these also are wanting in all animals that are clad with feathers or with scales or with plates; the sea and land tortoises[1] forming the only exception. In some of the birds, however, there are flattened kidney-like bodies, as though the flesh allotted to the formation of the kidneys, unable to find one single place of sufficient size, had been distributed over several regions.[2]

The Emys[3] has neither bladder nor kidneys. For the softness of its shell allows of the ready transpiration of fluid; and for this reason neither of the organs mentioned exists in this animal. All other animals, however, whose lung contains blood are, as before said, provided with kidneys. For nature uses these organs for two separate purposes, namely for the excretion of the residual fluid, and to subserve the blood-vessels,[4] a channel leading to them from the great vessel.

In the centre of the kidney is a cavity of variable size. This is the case in all animals, excepting the seal.[5] The kidneys of this animal are more solid than those of any other, and in form resemble the kidneys of the ox. The human kidneys are of similar shape; being as it were made up of numerous small kidneys,[6] and not presenting one unbroken surface like the kidneys of sheep and other quadrupeds.[7] For this reason, should the kidneys of a man be once attacked by disease, the malady is not easily expelled. For it is as though many kidneys were diseased and not merely one; which naturally enhances the difficulties of a cure.

The duct which runs to the kidney from the great vessel does not terminate in the central cavity, but is expended in the substance of the organ, so that there is no blood in the cavity, nor is any coagulum found there after death. A pair of stout ducts, void of blood, run, one from the cavity of each kidney, to the bladder; and other ducts, strong and continuous, lead into the kidneys from the aorta.[8] The purpose of this arrangement is to

671 b.

allow the superfluous fluid to pass from the blood-vessel into the kidney, and the resulting renal excretion to collect, by the percolation of the fluid through the solid substance of the organ, in its centre, where as a general rule there is a cavity. (This by the way explains why the kidney is the most ill-savoured of all the viscera.) From the central cavity the fluid is discharged into the bladder by the ducts just mentioned, having already assumed in great degree the character of residuum.[9] The bladder is as it were moored[10] to the kidneys; for, as already has been mentioned, it is attached to them by strong ducts. These then are the purposes for which the kidneys exist, and such the functions of these organs.

In all animals that have kidneys, that on the right is placed higher than that on the left.[11] For, inasmuch as motion commences from the right, the organs on this side become stronger than those on the left, and must all push forward in advance of their opposite fellows; as may be seen in the fact that men even raise the right eyebrow more than the left, and that the former is more arched than the latter.[12] The right kidney being thus drawn upwards is brought into contact with the liver; for the liver in all animals lies on the right side.

Of all the viscera the kidneys are those that have the most fat.[13] This is in the first place the result of necessity, because the kidneys are the parts through which the residual matters percolate. For the blood which is left behind after this excretion, being of pure quality, is of easy concoction, and the final result of thorough blood-concoction is lard and suet. For just as a certain amount of heat is left in the ashes of solid substances, such as wood, after combustion, so also does a remnant of the heat that has been developed remain in fluids after concoction; and this is the reason why oily matter is light, and floats on the surface of other fluids.[14] The fat is not formed in the kidneys themselves, the density of their substance forbidding this, but is deposited on their external surface. It consists of lard or of suet, according as the animal's fat is of the former or latter character. The difference between these two kinds of fat has already been set forth in other passages.[15] The formation, then, of fat in the kidneys is the result of necessity; being, as explained, a consequence of the necessary conditions which accompany the possession of such organs. But at the same time the fat has a final cause, namely to ensure the safety of the kidneys, and to maintain their natural heat. For placed, as these organs are, close to the surface, they require a greater supply of heat than other parts. For while the back is thickly covered with flesh, so as to form a shield for the heart and neighbouring viscera, the loins, in accordance with a rule that applies to all joints, are destitute of flesh;[16] and fat is therefore formed as a substitute for it, so that the kidneys may not be without protection. The kidneys, moreover, by being fat are the better enabled to secrete and concoct their fluid; for fat is hot, and it is heat that effects concoction.

Such then are the reasons why the kidneys are fat. But in all animals the right kidney is less fat than its fellow.[17] The reason for this is, that the parts on the right side are naturally more solid and more suited for motion than those on the left. But motion is antagonistic to fat, for it tends to melt it.

Animals then, as a general rule, derive advantage from their kidneys being fat; and the fat is often very abundant and extends over the whole of these organs. But, should the like occur in the sheep, death ensues. Be its kidneys however as fat as they may, they are never so fat but that some part, if not in both at any rate in the right one, is left free.[18] The reason why sheep are the only animals that suffer in this manner, or suffer more than others, is that their fat is harder and more abundant than that of other animals. For the soft lard, of which the fat of some animals is composed, is of fluid consistence, so that there is not the same chance in their case of wind getting shut in and causing mischief. But it is to such an enclosure of wind that rot[19] is due. And thus even in men, though it is beneficial to them to have fat kidneys, yet should these organs become over-fat and diseased, deadly pains ensue. As to those animals whose fat consists of suet, their suet is not so dense as that of sheep, neither is it nearly so abundant; for of all animals there is none in which the kidneys become so soon gorged with fat as in the sheep.[20] Rot then is produced by the moisture and the wind getting shut up in the kidneys, and is a malady that carries off sheep with great rapidity. For the disease forthwith reaches the heart, passing thither by the aorta and the great vessel, the ducts which connect these with the kidneys being of unbroken continuity.

(Ch. 10.) We have now dealt with the heart and the lung,
672b.

as also with the liver, spleen, and kidneys. The latter are separated from the former by the midriff or, as some call it, the *Phrenes*. This divides off the heart and lung, and as already said is called *Phrenes* in sanguineous animals, all[1] of which have a midriff, just as they all have a heart and a liver. For they require a midriff to divide the region of the heart from the region of the stomach; so that the centre wherein abides the sensory soul may be undisturbed, and not be overwhelmed, directly food is taken, by its up-steaming vapour[2] and by the abundance of heat then superinduced.[3] For it was to guard against this that nature made a division, constructing the midriff as a kind of partition-wall and fence, and so separated the nobler from the less noble parts, in all cases where a separation of upper from lower was possible.[4] For the upper part is the more[5] honourable, and is that for the sake of which the rest exists; while the lower part exists for the sake of the upper and constitutes the necessary element in the body, inasmuch as it is the recipient of the food.

That part of the midriff which is near the ribs is somewhat fleshy and thick; but the central part has more of a membranous character, for this structure gives it strength and capability of extension. Now that the midriff is as it were a curtain or screen to prevent heat mounting up from below, is shown by what happens, should it, owing to its proximity to the stomach, attract thence the hot and residual fluid. For when this occurs there ensues forthwith a marked disturbance of intellect and of sensation. It is indeed because of this that the midriff is called[6] *Phrenes*, as though it had some share in the process of thinking, for which the Greek term is *Phronein*. In reality however it has no part whatsoever itself in the matter, but, lying in close proximity to organs that have, it brings about the manifest changes of intelligence in question by acting upon them. This too explains why its central part is thin. For though this is in some measure the result of necessity, inasmuch as those portions of the fleshy whole which lie nearest to the ribs must necessarily be fleshier than the rest,[7] yet besides this there is a final cause, namely to give it as small a proportion of moisture as possible; for, had it been made of flesh throughout, it would have been more likely to attract and hold a large amount of fluid. That rapid heating of it affects sensation in a notable manner is shown by the phenomena of laughing. For when men are tickled they are quickly set a laughing, because the motion quickly reaches this region. And, even when the heating is more slowly applied, there is still a manifest affection and motion of the intellect in opposition to the will. That man alone is affected by tickling,[8] is due firstly to the delicacy of his skin, and secondly to the fact that he is the only animal that laughs. For to be tickled is to be set in laughter, the laughter being produced by such a motion as mentioned of the region of the armpit.

It is said also that when men in battle are wounded anywhere near the midriff, they are seen to laugh, owing to the heat produced by the wound.[9] This may possibly be the case. At any rate it is a statement made by much more credible persons than those who tell the story of the human head, how it speaks after it is cut off. For so some assert, and even call in Homer to support them, representing him as alluding to this when he wrote,[10] "His head still speaking rolled into the dust," instead of "The head of the speaker." So fully was the possibility of such an occurrence accepted in Caria, that one of that country was actually brought to trial under the following circumstances. The priest of Zeus Hoplosmios[11] had been murdered; but as yet it had not been ascertained who was the assassin; when certain persons asserted that they had heard the murdered man's head, which had been severed from the body, repeat several times the words, "It was Cercidas that killed the man." Search was thereupon made and a man of those parts who bore the name of Cercidas hunted out and put upon his trial. But it is impossible that any one should utter a word when the windpipe is severed and no motion any longer derived from the lungs. Moreover among the Barbarians, where heads are chopped off with great rapidity, nothing of the kind has ever yet occurred. Why again does not the like occur in the case of other animals than man? For that none of them should laugh, when their midriff is wounded, is but what one would expect; for no animal but man ever laughs. So too there is nothing irrational in supposing that the trunk may run forwards to a certain distance after the head has been cut off; seeing that bloodless animals at any rate can live, and that for a considerable time, after decapitation, as has been set forth and explained in other passages.[12]

673 a.

The purposes then for which the viscera severally exist have now been stated. It is of necessity upon the inner terminations of the vessels that they are developed; for moisture, and that of a bloody character, cannot but exude at these points, and it is of this, solidified and coagulated, that the substance of the viscera is formed.[13] Thus they are of a bloody character, and in substance resemble each other while they differ from other parts.

(Ch. 11.) The viscera are enclosed each in a membrane. For they require some covering to protect them from injury, and require moreover that this covering shall be light. To such requirements membrane is well adapted; for it is close in texture so as to form a good protection, destitute of flesh so as neither to attract nor hold moisture, and thin so as to be light and not add to the weight of the body. Of the membranes those are the stoutest and strongest, which invest the heart and the brain;[1] as is but consistent with reason. For these are the parts which require most protection, seeing that they are the main governing powers of life,[2] and that it is to governing powers that guard is due.

(Ch. 12.) Some animals have all the viscera that have been enumerated; others have only some of them. In what kind of animals this latter is the case, and what is the explanation, has already been stated. Moreover the self-same viscera present differences in different possessors. For the heart is not precisely alike in all animals that have one; nor in fact is any viscus whatsoever. Thus the liver is in some animals split into several parts, while in others it is comparatively undivided.[1] Such differences in its form present themselves even among the viviparous quadrupeds, but are more marked in fishes and in the oviparous quadrupeds, and this whether we compare them with each other or with the vivipara. As for birds, their liver very nearly resembles that of the vivipara; for in them, as in these, it is of a pure and blood-like colour. The reason of this is that the body in both these classes of animals admits of the freest exhalation, so that the amount of foul residual matter within is but small. Hence it is that some of the vivipara are without any gall-bladder[2] at all. For the liver takes a large share in maintaining the purity of composition and the healthiness of the body. For these are conditions that depend finally and in the main upon the blood, and there is more blood in the liver than in any of the other viscera, the heart only excepted.[3] On the other hand the liver

of oviparous quadrupeds and of fishes is, as a rule, of a pale yellow,[4] and there are even some in which its colour is utterly foul,[5] so as to match the foul composition of their bodies. Such, for instance, is the case in the toad, the tortoise, and other similar animals.

The spleen, again, varies in different animals. For in those that have horns and cloven hoofs, such as the goat, the sheep, and the like, it is of a rounded form;[6] excepting when increased growth and size has caused some part of it to be lengthened out, as has happened in the case of the ox.[7] In all polydactylous animals on the other hand it is elongated. Such for instance is the case in the pig,[8] in man, and in the dog. While in animals with solid hoofs it is of a form intermediate to these two, being broad in one part, narrow in another. Such for example is its shape in the horse, the mule, and the ass.

(*Ch.* 13.) The viscera differ from the flesh not only in the turgid aspect of their substance, but also in position; for they lie within the body, whereas the flesh is placed on the outside. The explanation of this is that these parts partake of the character of blood-vessels, and that while the former exist for the sake of the vessels, the latter cannot exist without them.[1]

(*Ch.* 14.) Below the mid-line of the body lies the stomach, placed at the end of the œsophagus, when there is one, and in immediate contiguity with the mouth, when the œsophagus is wanting.[1] Continuous with this stomach is what is called the gut. These parts are present in all animals, for reasons that are self-evident. For it is a matter of necessity that an animal shall receive the incoming food; and necessary also that it shall discharge the same when its goodness is exhausted. This residual matter, again, must not occupy the same place as the yet unconcocted nutriment. For as the ingress of food and the discharge of the residue occur at distinct periods, so also must they necessarily occur in distinct places. Thus there must be one receptacle for the ingoing food and another for the useless residue, and between these, therefore, a part in which the change from one condition to the other may be effected. These however are matters which will be more suitably set forth, when we come to deal with Development and Nutrition.

We must now consider the variations presented by the stomach and its subsidiary parts. For neither in size nor in shape are these parts uniformly alike in all animals. Thus the stomach is single in all such sanguineous and viviparous animals as have teeth in front of both jaws. It is single therefore in all the polydactylous kinds, such as man, dog, lion, and the rest; in all the solid-hoofed animals also, such as horse, mule, ass; and in all those which like the pig, though their hoof is cloven, yet have front teeth in both jaws.² When, however, an animal is of large size, and feeds on substances of so thorny and ligneous a character as to be difficult of concoction, it may in consequence have several stomachs, as for instance is the case with the camel. A similar multiplicity of stomachs exists also in the horned animals; the reason being that horn-bearing animals have no front teeth in the upper jaw. The camel also, though it has no horns, is yet without upper front teeth.³ The explanation of this is that it is more essential for the camel to have a multiple stomach than to have these teeth. Its stomach, then, is shaped like that of animals without upper front teeth, and, its dental arrangements being such as to match its stomach, the teeth in question are wanting.⁴ They would indeed be of no service. Its food, moreover, being of a thorny character, and its tongue necessarily made of a fleshy substance,⁵ nature uses the earthy matter which is saved from the teeth to give hardness to the palate.⁶ The camel ruminates like the horned animals, because its multiple stomach resembles theirs. For all animals that have horns, the sheep for instance, the ox, the goat, the deer, and the like, have several stomachs. For since the mouth, owing to its lack of teeth, fails to perform its due office as regards the food, this multiplicity of stomachs is intended to supply its place; the several cavities receiving the food one from the other in succession; the first taking the unreduced substances, the second the same when somewhat reduced, the third when reduction is complete, and the fourth when the whole has become a smooth pulp. Such is the reason why there is this multiplicity of parts and cavities in animals with such dentition. The names given to the several cavities are the paunch, the honey-comb, the manyplies and the reed. How these parts are related to each other, in position and in shape, must be looked for in the treatises on Anatomy and the Researches concerning Animals.⁷

Birds also present variations in the part which acts as a recipient
674b.

of the food; and the reason for these variations is the same as in the animals just mentioned. For here again it is because the mouth fails to perform its office and fails even more completely;— for birds have no teeth at all, nor any instrument whatsoever with which to comminute or grind down their food—it is, I say, because of this, that in some of them [8] what is called the crop precedes the stomach and does the work of the mouth; while in others the œsophagus either is dilated throughout,[9] or expands just before it enters the stomach, so as to form a preparatory storehouse for the unreduced food;[10] or the stomach itself has a protuberance in some part,[11] or is strong and fleshy,[12] so as to be able to store up the food for a considerable period and to concoct it, in spite of its not having been ground into a pulp. For nature retrieves the inefficiency of the mouth by increasing the efficiency and heat of the stomach. Other birds there are, such, namely, as have long legs and live in marshes, that have none of these provisions, but merely an elongated œsophagus.[13] The explanation of this is to be found in the moist character of their food. For all these birds feed on substances easy of reduction, and their food being moist and not requiring much concoction, their digestive cavities are of a corresponding character.[14]

Fish are provided with teeth, which are almost invariably of the serrated kind. For there is but one small section in which it is otherwise. Of these the fish called Scarus is an example. And this is [15] probably the reason why this fish apparently ruminates, though no other fishes do so. For those horned animals that have no front teeth in the upper jaw also ruminate.

In all fishes the teeth are sharp;[16] so that these animals can divide their food, though imperfectly. For it is impossible for a fish to linger or spend time in the act of mastication,[17] and therefore they have no teeth that are flat or suitable for grinding; for such teeth would be to no purpose.. The œsophagus again in some fishes is entirely wanting, and in the rest is but short.[18] In order however to facilitate the concoction of the food, some of them, as the Cestreus, have a fleshy stomach resembling that of a bird;[19] while most of them have numerous processes close against the stomach, to serve as a sort of antechamber in which the food may be stored up and undergo putrefaction [20] and concoction. There is a contrast between fishes and birds in the position of these processes. For in fishes they are placed close to the stomach; while in birds, if present at all, they are lower down, near the end of the gut.[21] Some of the vivipara also have processes connected with the lower part of the gut which serve the same purpose as that stated above.[22]

The whole tribe of fishes is of gluttonous appetite, owing to the arrangements for the reduction of their food being very imperfect, and much of it, consequently passing through them without undergoing concoction; and, of all, those are the most gluttonous that have a straight intestine. For as the passage of food in such cases is rapid, and the enjoyment derived from it in consequence but brief, it follows of necessity that the return of appetite is also speedy.[23]

It has already been mentioned that in animals with front teeth in both jaws the stomach is of small size.[24] It may be classed pretty nearly always under one or other of two headings, namely as resembling the stomach of the dog, or as resembling the stomach of the pig. In the pig the stomach is larger than in the dog, and presents certain flat projections of moderate size, the purpose of which is to lengthen out the period of concoction; while the stomach of the dog is of small size, not much larger in calibre than the gut, and smooth on the internal surface.[25]

Not much larger, I say, than the gut; for in all animals after the stomach comes the gut. This, like the stomach, presents numerous modifications. For in some animals it is uniform, when uncoiled, and alike throughout, while in others it differs in different portions. Thus in some cases it is wider in the neighbourhood of the stomach, and narrower at the other end. This is the case in dogs, and explains why they have to strain so much in discharging their excrement. While in other animals, and these the majority, it is the upper portion that is the narrower and the lower that is of greater width.[26]

Of larger size than in any of these animals, and much convoluted, are the intestines of those that have horns.[27] The bulgings moreover both of their stomach and of their intestines are more prominent, in accordance with the larger bulk of their bodies generally. For the horned animals are, as a rule, of large bulk, because of the thorough elaboration which their food undergoes.[28] The gut, excepting in those animals where it runs in a straight line, invariably widens out as we get farther from the stomach and come to what is called the colon and to a kind of

675b.

cæcal dilatation. After this it again becomes narrower and convoluted.[29] Then succeeds a straight portion which runs right on to the vent: This vent is known as the fundament, and is in some animals surrounded by fat, in others not so. All these varying parts have been so contrived by nature as to harmonize with the various operations that concern the food and the residue. For, as the residue gets farther on and lower down, the space to contain it becomes ampler. This is suited to the wants of those animals that, owing either to their large size or to the heat of their digestive cavities,[30] require more nutriment and consume more fodder than the rest; for it allows the food to remain stationary and undergo conversion.

Neither is it without a purpose that, just as a narrower gut succeeds to the upper stomach, so also does the residual food, when its goodness is thoroughly exhausted, pass from the colon and the ample space of the lower stomach[31] into a narrower channel and into the spiral coil. For so nature can regulate her expenditure and prevent the residual substances from being discharged all at once.[32]

Now in all such animals as it behoves to be more temperate[33] in the consumption of food than those we have been considering the lower stomach presents no wide and roomy spaces, neither is their gut ever straight, but has numerous convolutions. For amplitude of space causes desire for ample food, and straightness of the intestine causes quick return of appetite.[34] And thus it is that all animals whose food receptacles are either simple or spacious are of gluttonous habits, the latter eating enormously at a meal, the former making many meals at short intervals.

Again, since the food in the upper stomach, having just been swallowed, must of necessity be quite fresh, while that which has reached the lower stomach must have had its juices exhausted and resemble dung, it follows of necessity that there must also be some intermediate part, in which the change may be effected, and where the food will be neither perfectly fresh nor yet dung. And thus it is that, in all such animals as we are now considering, there is found what is called the jejunum;[35] which is a part of the small gut, of the gut, that is, which comes next to the stomach. For this jejunum lies between the upper cavity which contains the yet unconcocted food and the lower cavity which holds the residual matter, which by the time it has got here is

675 b.

quite worthless. There is a jejunum in all animals, but it is only plainly visible in those of larger bulk, and in these only when they have abstained from food for a certain time. For thus alone can one hit on the exact period when the food lies half-way between the upper and lower cavities; a period which is very short, for the time occupied in the transition of food is but brief. In females this jejunum may occupy any part whatsoever of the upper intestine, but in males it comes just before the cæcum and the lower stomach.[36]

(Ch. 15.) The substance called rennet[1] is found in all animals that have a multiple stomach, but only in the hare[2] among animals whose stomach is single. In the former the rennet neither occupies the large paunch, nor yet the reticulum, nor the terminal abomasus, but is found in the cavity which separates this terminal one from the two first, namely in the so-called psalterium.[3] It is the thick character of their milk which causes all these animals to have rennet; whereas in animals with a single stomach the milk is thin, and consequently no rennet is formed. It is this difference in thickness[4] which makes the milk of horned animals coagulate, while that of animals without horns does not. Rennet forms in the hare because it feeds on[5] herbage that has juice like that of the fig. For juice of this kind coagulates the milk in the stomach of the young animal. Why it is in the psalterium that rennet is formed in animals with multiple stomachs has been stated in the Problems.[6]

BOOK IV.

(Ch. 1.) The account which has now been given of the viscera,[1] the stomach, and the other several parts of the vivipara, holds equally good for the oviparous quadrupeds, and also for such apodous animals as the Serpents. These two classes of animals are indeed nearly akin, a serpent resembling a lizard which has been lengthened out and deprived of its feet. Fishes again resemble these two groups in all their parts, excepting that, while these, being land animals, have a lung, fishes have no lung, but gills in its place. Of all these animals, including the Fishes, none excepting the tortoise has an urinary bladder.[2] For, owing to the bloodlessness of their lung, they drink but little; and such moisture as they have is converted into scales, as in birds it is converted into feathers;[3] and so they come to have the same white matter on the surface of their excretions as we see on those of birds. For even in animals that have a bladder, if the excretion when voided be placed in a vessel, it will throw down a deposit of earthy brine.[4] For the sweet and fresh elements, being light, are expended on the flesh.

Among the Serpents, the same peculiarity attaches to vipers, as among the fishes attaches to the Selachia. For both these and vipers are externally viviparous, but previously produce ova internally.[5]

The stomach in all these animals is single, just as it is single in all other animals[6] that have teeth in front of both jaws; and their viscera are excessively small, as always happens when there is no bladder. In serpents these viscera are, moreover, differently shaped from what they are in other animals. For, a serpent's

676 b.

body being long and narrow, its contents are as it were moulded into a similar form, and thus come to be themselves elongated.⁷

All animals that have blood possess an omentum, a mesentery,⁸ an intestine with its appendages, and, moreover, a diaphragm and a heart; and all, excepting fishes, a lung and a trachea. The relative positions, moreover, of the windpipe and the œsophagus are precisely similar in them all; and the reason is the same as has already been given.⁹

(Ch. 2.) Almost all sanguineous animals have a gall-bladder. In some this is attached to the liver, in others separated from that organ¹ and attached to the intestines, being apparently in the latter case no less than in the former an appendage of the lower stomach.² It is in fishes that this is most clearly seen. For all fishes³ have a gall-bladder; and in most of them it is attached to the intestine, being in some, as in the⁴ Amia, united with this, like a border, along its whole length. It is similarly placed in most serpents. There are therefore⁵ no good grounds for the view entertained by some writers, that the use of the gall-bladder is to give rise to certain sensations. They say that its final cause is to affect that part of the soul which is lodged in the neighbourhood of the liver, and that it induces a gloomy or a cheerful disposition, according as it irritates this or leaves it alone. But this cannot be. For in some animals there is absolutely no gall-bladder at all, in the horse for instance, the mule, the ass, the deer, and the roe; and in others, as the camel, there is no distinct bladder, but merely small vessels that bear some resemblance to one.⁶ Again there is no such organ in the seal, nor, of sea-animals, in the dolphin.⁷ Even within the limits of the same genus, some animals appear to have and others to be without it.⁸ Such for instance is the case with mice; such also with man. For in some individuals there is apparently a gall-bladder attached to the liver, and in others none at all. This explains how the existence of this part in the whole genus has been a matter of dispute. For each observer, according as he has found it present or absent in the individual cases he has examined, has supposed it to be present or absent in the whole genus. The same has occurred in the case of sheep and of goats. For these animals usually have a gall-bladder; but, while in some it is so enormously big as to appear a monstrosity, as is the case in Naxos, in other instances

677 a.

it is altogether wanting, as is the case in a certain district of Chalcis in Eubœa.[9] Another fact, which shows that the opinion of these writers is erroneous, is that the gall-bladder in fishes is separated, as already mentioned, by a considerable interval from the liver. No less mistaken seems to be the opinion of Anaxagoras and his followers, that the gall-bladder is the cause of acute diseases, inasmuch as it becomes over-full, and spirts out its excess into the lung, the blood-vessels, and the chest. For, almost invariably, those who suffer from these acute forms of disease are persons who have no gall-bladder at all, and, were they to be dissected, this fact would be quite evident.[10] Moreover there is no kind of correspondence between the amount of bile which is present in these diseases and the amount which is exuded.[11] The most probable opinion is that, as the bile when it exists in any other part of the body is a mere residuum or a product of decay, so also when it exists in the region of the liver it is equally excremental and has no further use; just as is the case with the dejections of the stomach and intestines. For though even the residua are occasionally used [12] by nature for some useful purpose, yet we must not in all cases expect to find such a final cause; for granted the existence in the body of this or that constituent, with such and such properties, many results must ensue merely as necessary consequences of these properties.[13] All animals, then, whose liver is healthy in composition and supplied with none but sweet blood, are either entirely without a gall-bladder, or have merely [14] bile-containing ducts; or are some with and some without such parts. Thus it is that the liver in animals that have no gall-bladder is, as a rule, of good colour and sweet; and that, when there is a gall-bladder, that part of the liver is sweetest, which lies immediately underneath it. But, when animals are formed of blood less pure in composition, the bile serves for the excretion of its impure residue. For the very meaning of residuum is that it is the opposite of nutriment, and of bitter that it is the opposite of sweet; and sweet blood it is which alone is nutritious.[15] So that it is evident that the bile, which is bitter, cannot have any useful end, but must simply be a purifying excretion.[16] It was therefore no bad saying of old writers that the absence of a gall-bladder gave long life. In so saying they had in mind deer and animals with uncloven hoofs. For such have no

677 a.

gall-bladder and live long. But besides these there are other animals that have no gall-bladder, though those old writers were not aware of the fact, such as the camel and the dolphin;[17] and these also are, as it happens, long-lived. Seeing, indeed, that the liver is not only useful, but absolutely necessary, to all animals that have blood, it is but reasonable that on its character should depend the length or the shortness of life. Nor less reasonable is it that this organ and none other should have such an excretion as the bile. For the heart, unable as it is to stand any violent affection,[18] would be utterly intolerant of the proximity of such a fluid ; and, as to the rest of the viscera, none excepting the liver are necessary parts of an animal.[19] In conclusion, wherever we see bile we must take it to be residual or excremental. For to suppose that it has one character in this part, another in that, would be as great an absurdity as to suppose mucus or the dejections of the stomach to vary in character according to locality and not to be excremental wherever found.

(Ch. 3.) So much then of the gall-bladder, and of the reasons why some animals have one, while others have not.[1] We have next to speak of the mesentery and the omentum ; for these are contained in the same cavity as the parts already described. The omentum, then, is a membrane containing fat; the fat being suet or lard according as the fat of the animal generally is of the former or latter description. What kinds of animals are so distinguished has been already set forth in an earlier part of this treatise.[2] This membrane, alike in animals that have a single and in those that have a multiple stomach, grows from the middle of that organ, along a line which is marked on it like a seam. Thus attached, it covers the rest of the stomach and the greater part of the bowels. It is found in all sanguineous animals whether they live on land or in water.[3] Now the development of this part into such a form as has been described is the result of necessity. For, whenever solid and fluid are mixed together and heated, the surface invariably becomes membranous and skin-like.[4] But the region in which the omentum lies is full of nutriment of such a mixed character. Moreover, in consequence of the thickness of the membrane, that portion of the sanguineous nutriment will alone filter into it which is of a greasy character; for this portion is composed of the finest particles; and when it has so

677b.

filtered in, it will be concocted by the heat of the part, and will be converted into suet or lard, and will not acquire a flesh-like or sanguineous constitution. The development, then, of the omentum is simply the result of necessity. But when once formed, it is used by nature for an end, namely, to facilitate and to hasten the concoction of food.[5] For all that is hot aids concoction; and fat is hot, and the omentum is fat. This too explains why it hangs from the middle of the stomach; for the upper part of the stomach has no need of it, being assisted in concoction by the neighbouring liver. Thus much as concerns the omentum.

(Ch. 4.) The so-called mesentery is also a membrane; and stretches from the intestines, in their whole extent, to the great vessel and the aorta. In it are numerous and close-packed vessels, which run from the intestines into the great vessel and into the aorta. The formation of this membrane we shall find to be the result of necessity, as is that of the other parts.[1] What however is the final cause of its existence in sanguineous animals is manifest on reflection. For it is necessary that animals shall get nutriment from without; and, again, that this shall be converted into the ultimate nutriment, which is then distributed as sustenance to the various parts; this ultimate nutriment being, in sanguineous animals, what we call blood, and having, in exsanguineous animals, no definite name. This being so, there must be channels through which the nutriment shall pass, as it were through roots,[2] from the stomach into the blood-vessels. Now the roots of plants are in the ground; for thence their nutriment is derived. But in animals the stomach and intestines represent the ground, from which the nutriment is to be taken. The mesentery, then, is an organ to contain the roots; and these roots are the vessels that traverse it. This then is the final cause of its existence. But how it absorbs nutriment, and how that portion of the food which enters into the vessels is distributed by them to the various parts of the body, are questions which will be considered when we come to deal with the generation and nutrition of animals.[3]

The constitution of sanguineous animals, so far as the parts as yet mentioned are concerned, and the reasons for such constitution, have now been set forth. In natural sequence we should next go on to the organs of generation, as yet undescribed, on which depend the distinctions of male and female. But, inasmuch as we shall have to deal specially with generation and development hereafter, it will be more convenient to defer the consideration of these parts to that occasion.

(Ch. 5.) Very different from the animals we have as yet considered are the Cephalopods, and the Crustacea. For these have absolutely no viscera[1] whatsoever; as indeed is the case with all ex-sanguineous animals, in which are included two other genera, namely the Testacea and the Insects. For in none of them does the material out of which viscera are formed exist. None of them, that is, have blood. The cause of this lies in their essential constitution. For the presence of blood in some animals, its absence from others, will be included in the conception which determines their respective essences.[2] Moreover, in the animals we are now considering, none of those final causes will be found to exist, which, in sanguineous animals, determine the presence of viscera. For[3] they have no blood-vessels nor urinary bladder, nor do they breathe. All, in fact, that it is necessary for them to have is some organ which shall be analogous to a heart; for in all animals there must be some central and commanding part of the body, to lodge the sensory portion of the soul and the source of life. They must of course also all have the organs of nutrition; and a diversity of character exists among them, depending on differences of these receptacles of food.

In the Cephalopods there are two teeth,[4] enclosing what is called the mouth; and inside this mouth is a fleshy substance, which represents a tongue and serves for the discrimination of pleasant and unpleasant food. The Crustacea have teeth corresponding to those of the Cephalopods, namely their anterior teeth,[5] and also have the fleshy representative of a tongue. This latter part is found, moreover, in all Testacea,[6] and serves, as in sanguineous animals, for gustatory sensations. Similarly provided also are the Insects. For some of these, such as the Bees and the Flies, have, as already described, a proboscis protruding from the mouth;[7] while others, that have no such piercing instrument in front, have a part which acts as a tongue inside the mouth.[8] Such for instance is the case in the Ants and the like. As for teeth, some insects have them, the Bees and the Flies for instance, though in a somewhat modified form, while others, that live on fluid nutriment, are without them. For in many insects the teeth are not organs of mastication, but weapons of defence.

678 b.

In some Testacea, as was said in the[9] first treatise, the organ which is called the tongue is of considerable strength; and in one kind, namely the Sea-snails, in addition to the tongue there are two teeth,[10] resembling those of the Crustacea. The mouth in the Cephalopods[11] is succeeded by a long gullet. This leads to a crop, like that of a bird. Directly continuous with this is the stomach, from which a gut runs without windings to the vent. The Sepias and the Poulps resemble each other completely, so far as regards the shape and consistency of these parts. But not so the Calamaries. Here, as in the other groups, there are two stomach-like receptacles; but the first of these cavities has less resemblance to a crop, and in neither is the form or the consistency the same as in the other kinds, the whole animal indeed being made of a softer kind of flesh.

The object of this arrangement of the parts in question is the same in the Cephalopods as in Birds. For in neither of these groups is the mouth suited for mastication; and therefore it is that a crop precedes their stomach.

For purposes of defence, and to enable them to escape from their foes, the Cephalopods have what is called an ink-bag attached to their body. This is a membranous pouch, which is provided with a terminal outlet just at the point where what is termed the funnel gives issue to the residua of the stomach. This funnel is placed on the ventral surface of the animal. All Cephalopods alike have this characteristic ink-bag, but chief of all the sepia, where it is of greater size than in the rest.[12] When the animal is disturbed and frightened it uses the ink to make the surrounding water black and turbid, and so, as it were, puts a shield in front of its body.

In the Calamaries and the Poulps the ink-bag is placed in the upper part of the body, in close proximity to the *mytis*,[13] whereas in the sepia it is much lower down, against the stomach. For the sepia has a larger ink-bag than the rest, owing to its making more use of it. The reasons for this are, firstly, that it lives near the shore, and, secondly, that it has no other means of protection; whereas the poulp has twining feet[14] that it can use in its defence, and is moreover endowed with the power of changing its colour.[15] This changing of colour, like the discharge of ink, occurs as the result of fright. As to the calamary, it lives far out at sea, being the only one of the Cephalopods that
679 a.

does so; and this gives it protection.[16] These then are the reasons why the ink-bag is much larger in the sepia than in the other Cephalopods; and its larger size again explains its lower position. For though this position removes it farther from the funnel, yet the larger size of the bag gives increased force, and so allows the ink to be ejected with ease even from a distance. The ink itself is of an earthy character, in this resembling the white deposit on the surface of a bird's excrement. And the explanation in both cases is the same, namely the absence of an urinary bladder.[17] For, in default of this, it is the ink that serves for the excretion of the earthy matter. And this is more especially the case in the sepia; because there is a greater proportion of earth in its composition than in that of the other Cephalopods. The earthy character of its bone is a clear proof of this. For in the poulp there is no bone at all, and in the calamary it is small and merely cartilaginous.[18] Why this bone should be present in some Cephalopods, and wanting in others, and how its character varies in those that have it, has now been set forth.

These animals, having no blood, are in consequence cold and of a timid character.[19] Now, in some animals, fear causes an evacuation from the bowels, and, in others, a flow of urine from the bladder.[20] Similarly in these it produces a discharge of ink, and though this ink, like the urine, is residual matter, and though its ejection in fright is merely the result of necessity, yet it is used by nature for a purpose,[21] namely the protection and safety of the animal that excretes it.

The Crustacea also, both the Caraboid forms and the Crabs,[22] are provided with teeth, namely the two so-called anterior teeth; and between these they also present the tongue-like piece of flesh, as has indeed been already mentioned.[23] Directly after their mouth comes a gullet, which is very small considering the size of the whole body; and then a stomach, which in the Carabi and some of the Crabs is furnished with a second set of teeth, the anterior set being insufficient for mastication. From the stomach an unconvoluted gut runs in a direct line to the vent.[24]

The parts described are to be found also in all the various Testacea.[25] The degree of distinctness, however, with which they are formed varies much in the different kinds, and the larger the size of the animal the more easily distinguishable are all these parts

679 b.

severally. In the Sea-snails, for example, we find teeth, hard and sharp, as before mentioned,[26] and between them a fleshy substance like the tongue of Crustacea and Cephalopods, and again a proboscis which has already been described as something between a piercing instrument and a tongue.[27] Directly after the mouth comes a kind of bird-like crop,[28] then a gullet, and continuous with this a stomach, in which is the *mecon*, as it is styled; and this *mecon* in turn gives rise to an intestine, starting directly from it.[29] It is the excretion of this *mecon*, which appears in all the Testacea to form the most palatable morsel. Purpuræ,[30] and whelks, and all other Testacea that have turbinated shells, in structure resemble the sea-snail.

The genera and species of Testacea are very numerous. There are those with turbinated shells, of which some have just been mentioned; and, besides these, there are bivalves and univalves. Those with turbinated shells may indeed after a certain fashion be said to resemble bivalves. For they all, from their very birth, have a covering to protect that part of their body which would otherwise be exposed.[31] This is the case with the Purpuræ, with whelks, with the Nerites,[32] and all the like. Were it not for this, the part which is undefended by the shell would be very liable to injury from without. The Univalves also are not without protection. For on their dorsal surface they have a shell, and by the under surface they attach themselves to the rocks, and so after a manner may be said to become bivalved, the rock representing the second valve. Of these the animals known as limpets are an example. The Bivalves, scallops and mussels for instance, are protected by the power they have of closing their valves; and the turbinated genera by the operculum just mentioned, which transforms them, as it were, from univalves into bivalves. But of all there is none so perfectly protected as the Echinus. For here there is a globular shell which encloses the body completely, and which is moreover set with sharp spines. This peculiarity distinguishes the Echinus from all other Testacea, as has already been mentioned.

The structure of the Testacea and of the Crustacea is exactly the reverse of that of the Cephalopods. For in the latter the fleshy substance is on the outside and the earthy substance within, whereas in the former the soft parts are inside and the hard part without. In the Echinus, however, there is no fleshy part whatsoever.

679 b.

All the Testacea, then, those that have not been mentioned as well as those that have, agree as stated in possessing a mouth [33] with the tongue-like body, a stomach, and a vent; but they differ from each other in the positions and proportions of these parts. The details, however, of these differences must be looked for in the Researches concerning Animals and the treatises on Anatomy. For while there are some points which can be made clear by verbal description there are others which are more suited for ocular demonstration.[34]

Peculiar among the Testacea are the Echini and the animals known as Ascidians.[35] The Echini have five teeth,[36] and in the centre of these the fleshy body,[37] which is common to all the animals we have been discussing. Immediately after this comes a gullet, and then a stomach, divided into a number of separate compartments, which look like so many distinct stomachs; for the cavities are separate, and each contains residual matter. They are all however connected with one and the same œsophagus, and they all end in one and the same vent.[38] There is nothing, with the exception of the stomach, of a fleshy character, as has already been stated. All that can be seen are the so-called ova,[39] of which there are several, contained each in a separate membrane, and certain black bodies which have got no name, and which, beginning at the animal's mouth, are scattered round its body here and there profusely.[40] Of these Echini there are many different species, and in all of them the parts mentioned are to be found. It is not however in every kind that the so-called ova are edible. Neither do these attain to any size in any other species than those which are found in shallow water.[41] A similar distinction may be made generally in the case of all Testacea. For there is a great difference in the edible qualities of the flesh of different kinds; and in some, moreover, the residual substance known as the *mecon* [42] is good for food, while in others it is uneatable. This *mecon* in the turbinated genera is lodged in the spiral part of the shell, while in univalves, such as limpets, it occupies the apex, and in bivalves is placed near the hinge. In these bivalves the so-called ovum lies on the right; while on the opposite side is the vent.[43] The former is incorrectly termed ovum,[44] for it merely corresponds to what in well-fed sanguineous animals is fat; and thus it is that it only makes its appearance in Testacea at those seasons of the year when they are in good condition, namely spring

680 a.

and autumn. For no Testacea can abide extremes of temperature, and they are therefore in evil plight in winter and in summer. This is clearly shown by what occurs in the case of the Echini. For though the ova are to be found in these animals even directly they are born, yet they acquire a much greater size than usual at the time of full moon ; not, as some think, because the Echini eat more at that season, but because the nights are then warmer, owing to the moonlight.[45] For these creatures are bloodless, and so are unable to stand cold and require warmth. Therefore it is that they are found in better condition in summer than at any other season; and this all over the world excepting in the Pyrrhean tidal strait. There the Echini flourish as well in winter as in summer. But the reason for this is that they have a greater abundance of food in the winter, because the fish desert the strait at that season.[46]

The number of the ova is the same in all Echini, and is an odd one. There are in fact five ova, just as there are also five teeth and five stomachs; and the explanation of this is to be found in the fact that the so-called ova are not really ova, but merely, as was said before, the result of the animal's well-fed condition. Oysters also have an ovum, corresponding in character to that of the Echini, but existing only on one side of their body.[47] Now inasmuch as the Echinus is of a spherical form, and not merely a single disk like the oyster, and in virtue of its spherical shape is the same from whatever side it be examined, it follows as a necessary consequence that its ovum must be of a corresponding symmetry. For the spherical shape has not the asymmetry of the disk-shaped body of the Oysters. For though the head in all of these is central, yet their ovum is on one side, namely the upper.[48] Now the necessary symmetry would be observed, were the ovum to form a continuous ring. But this may not be. For it would be in opposition to what prevails in the whole tribe of Testacea;[49] for in all the ovum is discontinuous, and in all, excepting the Echini, asymmetrical, being placed only on one side of the body. Owing, then, to this necessary discontinuity of the ovum, which belongs to the Echinus as a member of the class, and owing to the spherical shape of the body, which is its individual peculiarity, this animal cannot possibly have an even number of ova. For were they in even number, they would have to be arranged exactly opposite to each other, in pairs, so

680 b.

as to keep the necessary symmetry; one ovum of each pair being placed at one end, the other ovum at the other end, of a transverse diameter. This again would violate the universal provision in Testacea. For both in the Oysters and in the Scallops we find the ovum only on one side of the circumference. The number then of the ova must be an uneven one, three for instance or five. But if there were only three, they would be much too far apart; while if there were more than five, they would come to form a continuous mass. The former arrangement would be disadvantageous to the animal, the latter an impossibility. There can, therefore, be neither more nor less than five. For the same reason the stomach is divided into five parts, and there is a corresponding number of teeth. For seeing that the ova represent each of them a kind of body for the animal, from which the materials for growth are derived, there must be a conformity between them and the general configuration of the vital organs. Now, if there were only one stomach, this conformity would be wanting. For either the ova would be too far off from the stomach, or the stomach would be so big as to fill up the whole cavity, and the Echinus would have great difficulty in moving about, and finding due nourishment for its repletion. As then there are five intervals between the five ova, so are there of necessity five divisions of the stomach, one for each interval. So also and on like grounds there are five teeth. For by this arrangement nature is enabled to allot to each stomachal compartment and ovum its separate and similar tooth. These then are the reasons why the number of ova in the Echinus is an odd one, and why that odd number is five. In some Echini the ova are excessively small, in others of considerable size, the explanation being that the latter are of a warmer constitution, and so are able to concoct their food more thoroughly; while in the former concoction is less perfect, so that the stomach is found full of residual matter, while the ova are small and uneatable.[50] Those of a warmer constitution are, moreover, in virtue of their warmth more given to motion, so that they make expeditions in search of food, instead of remaining stationary like the rest. In proof of this, it will be found that they always have something or other sticking to their spines, which they use as feet in their frequent ramblings.[51]

The Ascidians differ but slightly from plants and yet have more of an animal nature than the Sponges, which are in

681a.

fact virtually plants and nothing more. For nature passes from lifeless objects to animals in such unbroken sequence, interposing between them beings which live and yet are not animals, that scarcely any difference seems to exist between two neighbouring classes owing to their close proximity.[52]

A sponge[53] then, as already said, in these respects completely resembles a plant, that throughout its life it is attached to a rock, and that when separated from this it dies. Slightly different from the Sponges are the so-called Holothuriæ and the Sea-lungs,[54] as also sundry other sea-animals that resemble them. For these are free and unattached. Yet have they no feeling,[55] and their life is simply that of a plant, separated from the ground. For even among land-plants there are some that are independent of the soil, and that spring up and grow, either parasitically upon other plants,[53] or even entirely free. Such for example is the plant which is found on Parnassus, and which some call the Epipetrum.[57] This you may take up and hang from the rafters, and it will yet live for a considerable time. Sometimes it is a matter of doubt whether a given organism should be classed with plants or with animals. The Ascidians, for instance, and the like so far resemble plants as that they never live free and unattached,[58] but, on the other hand, inasmuch as they have a certain flesh-like substance, they must be supposed to possess some degree of sensibility.[59]

In the Ascidians there are two orifices and a single septum, which latter separates the part into which the animal takes the fluid that ministers to its nutrition from the part by which it again discharges the superfluity of moisture. For it appears to have no distinct residual matter, such as have the other Testacea. This is itself a very strong justification for considering an Ascidian, and any thing else there may be among animals that resembles it, to be of a vegetable character; for plants also never have any residuum.[60] Finally there runs across the middle of the body of these Ascidians a thin partition, and here it is that we may reasonably suppose the part on which life depends to be situated.

The animals which some call Sea-nettles and others Acalephæ[61] are not Testacea at all nor included in their divisions. Their constitution approximates them on the one side to plants, on the other to animals. For seeing that some of them can detach

681b.

themselves and can seize hold of their food, and that they are sensible of objects which come in contact with them, they must be considered to have an animal nature. The like conclusion follows from their using the roughness of their bodies [62] as a protection against their enemies. But on the other hand they are closely allied to plants, firstly by the imperfection of their structure, secondly by their being able to attach themselves to the rocks with great rapidity, and lastly by their having no visible residuum, notwithstanding that they possess a mouth.

Very similar again to the Acalephæ, are the Starfishes. For these also seize hold of their prey, and suck out its juices, and thus destroy a vast number of oysters.[63] At the same time they present a certain resemblance to such animals as the Cephalopods and Crustacea, inasmuch as they are free and unattached. The same may also be said of the Testacea.

Such then is the structure of the parts that minister to nutrition, and which every animal must necessarily possess. But besides these organs it is quite plain that in every animal there must be some part or other which shall be analogous to what in sanguineous animals is the presiding seat of sensation. Whether an animal has or has not blood, it cannot possibly be without this. In the Cephalopods this part consists of a membrane, containing fluid, through which runs the gullet on its way to the stomach. It lies rather towards the dorsal surface of the animal, and is by some called the *mytis*.[64] Just such another organ is found in the Crustacea, and is known in them also by the same name. This part is formed by a combination of fluid and solid, and is, as before said, traversed by the gullet. For had the gullet been placed farther back, between the *mytis* and the dorsal surface of the animal, the hardness of the back would have interfered with its due dilatation in the act of deglutition. On the outer surface of the *mytis* runs the intestine; and in contact with this latter is the ink-bag, which is thus removed as far as possible from the mouth, while a considerable interval divides its irritating fluid from the nobler and sovereign parts.[65] The position of the *mytis* shows that it corresponds to the heart of sanguineous animals; for it occupies the self-same place. The same is proved by the sweetness of its fluid, which has the character of concocted matter and resembles blood.[66]

In the Testacea the presiding seat of sensation is in a cor-
681 b.

responding position, but is less easily made out.[67] It should, however, always be looked for in the following situations. In such Testacea as are stationary, between the gullet and the channel through which either the excrement or the spermatic fluid[68] is voided; but, in those species which are capable of locomotion, invariably in the centre, midway that is between the right and left sides.

In Insects this important organ lies, as was stated in the first treatise,[69] between the head and the cavity which contains the stomach. In most of them it consists of a single part; but in others, for instance in such as have long bodies and resemble the Juli,[70] it is made up of several parts, so that such insects continue to live after they have been cut into pieces.[71] For the aim of nature is to give each animal only one such governing part; and when she is unable to carry out this intention she causes the parts, though potentially many, to work together actually as one.[72] The phenomenon referred to is much more clearly marked in some insects than in others.

The parts concerned in nutrition are not alike in all insects, but show a considerable diversity. Thus some have what is called a piercer in their mouths, which is a kind of compound instrument that combines in itself the character of a tongue and of lips.[73] In others, that have not got this anterior piercer, there is an organ inside the mouth that answers the same sensory purposes. After the mouth comes the intestine, which is never wanting in any insect. This runs in a straight line and without further complication to the vent; occasionally, however, it has a spiral coil. There are, moreover, some insects in which a stomach succeeds to the mouth, and is itself succeeded by a convoluted intestine.[74] By this arrangement the larger and more voracious insects are enabled to take in a more abundant supply of food.[75] More curious than any are the Cicadæ. For here the mouth and the tongue are united so as to form a single part, through which, as through a root, the fluids on which the creature lives are sucked up.[76] Insects are always small eaters, not so much because of their diminutive size as because of their cold temperament. For it is heat which requires sustenance; just as it is heat which speedily concocts it.[77] But cold neither requires sustenance nor concocts it. In no insects is this more evident than in these Cicadæ. For they find enough to live on in the moisture which is deposited from the air.[78] So also do the Ephemera found about the Black Sea.[79] But while these latter only live for a single day, the Cicadæ subsist on such food for several days, though still not many.

We have now done with the internal parts of animals, and must return to the consideration of such external parts as have not yet been described. It will be better to begin with the animals we have just been describing, that is with the bloodless animals, so that we may not be hampered with them hereafter, but may be free to deal leisurely with the more perfect kinds of animals, those namely that have blood.

(Ch. 6.) We will begin with Insects.[1] These animals, though they consist of but few parts, are yet not without diversities when compared with each other. They are all many-footed; the object of this being to compensate their natural slowness and frigidity, and give greater activity to their motions. Accordingly we find that those which, as the[2] Juli, have long bodies, and are therefore the most liable to refrigeration, have also the greatest number of feet. Again in all insects the body is made up of segments— the reason for this being that in these animals there is no one supreme and sovereign part[3] but several—and the number of feet corresponds to the number of segments. Should the feet fall short of this, their deficiency is supplied by the presence of feathers. Of such feathered insects some live a wandering life and are forced to make long expeditions in search of food. These have a body of light weight, and four feathers, two on either side, to support it. Such are bees and other insects akin to them. When, however, such insects are of very small bulk, their feathers are reduced to two, as is the case with flies.[4] Even insects of squarer build and of stationary habits of life yet come to have as many feathers in all as have bees; for they have shards, which protect the acting feathers from injury. Such are the Melalonthæ[5] and the like. For their stationary habits expose them to much greater risks than are run by those insects that are more constantly in flight, and on this account they are provided with this protecting shield. The feather of an insect has neither barbs nor shaft.[6] For, though it is called a feather, it is no feather at all, but merely a skin-like membrane that, owing to its dryness, necessarily becomes detached from the surface of the fleshy body.

682 b.

The body of an insect is made of segments, not only for the reasons already assigned, but also to enable it to bend in such a manner as may protect it from injury. For such insects as have long bodies can roll themselves up,[7] which would have been impossible, had they not been formed of segments; and even those which cannot do this can yet draw their segments closer together, and so increase the hardness of their bodies. This can be felt quite plainly by putting the finger on any of the insects known as Canthari.[8] ' The touch frightens the insect, and it remains perfectly motionless, while its body is felt to become harder than before. The division, then, of the body into segments has this final cause; but it is also a necessary result of there being several supreme organs in place of one; and this again is a part of the essential constitution of insects, and is a character. which approximates them to plants. For as plants, though cut into pieces, still live, so also do insects. There is however this difference between the two cases, that the portions of the divided insect live for a very short space, whereas the portions of the plant live on and attain the perfect form of the whole, so that from one single plant you may obtain two or more.[9]

Some insects are also provided with another means of protection against their enemies, namely a piercer or sting. In some this is in front, connected with the tongue, in others behind and connected with the tail. For just as the organ of smell in elephants[10] answers several uses, serving alike for purposes of nutrition and for purposes of defence, so also does the lingual arrangement in some insects answer more than one end. For it is the instrument through which they derive their sensations of food, as well as that with which they suck it up and bring it to their mouths; and, when no such anterior piercer or sting exists, the mouth is furnished with teeth, which so far supply its place as to serve either for the mastication of food or for its prehension and conveyance to the mouth. They serve this latter use for instance in ants and in all the various kinds of bees.[11]

As for a tail-sting, nature has given it to such insects as are of a fierce disposition, and to no others. Sometimes this instrument is lodged inside the body, as in bees and wasps. This is a necessary consequence of their being made for flight. For, were their piercer or sting external and of delicate make, it would very easily get spoiled. If on the other hand, still being

683a.

external, it were of stouter build, as in scorpions, its weight would interfere with flight. As for scorpions, they never rise from the ground, and their piercer or sting must therefore be arranged in the way it is, as otherwise it would be of no use as a weapon.[12] The Diptera never have a tail-sting.[13] For the very reason of their being dipterous is that they are small and weak, and therefore require no more than two feathers to support their light weight. And the same reason which reduces their feathers to two causes their piercer or sting to be in front; for their strength is not sufficient to allow them to strike efficiently with the hinder part[14] of their body. Polypterous insects on the other hand are of greater bulk—indeed it is this which causes them to have so many feathers—and their greater size makes them much stronger in their hinder parts. These insects therefore have tail-stings. For it is better, when possible, that one and the same instrument shall not be made to serve several dissimilar uses; but that there shall be one organ to serve as a weapon, which can then be very sharp, and a second distinct one to serve as a tongue, which can then be of spongy texture and fit to absorb nutriment. Whenever, therefore, nature is able to provide two separate instruments for two separate uses, without the one hampering the other, she does so, instead of acting like a coppersmith, who for cheapness makes a spit and lampholder in one. It is only when this is impossible, that she uses one organ for several functions.[15]

The anterior legs are in some cases longer[16] than the others, that they may serve to clean off the dust or other matter which may fall into the insect's eyes and obstruct its sight, which already is not very distinct owing to the eyes being made of a hard substance. Flies and bees and the like may be constantly seen thus dressing themselves with crossed fore-legs. Of the other legs, the hinder are bigger than the middle pair, both to aid in running and also that the insect, when it takes flight, may spring more easily from the ground. This difference is still more marked in such insects as leap, in grasshoppers for instance and in the various kinds of fleas.[17] For these first bend and then extend the legs, and, by so doing, are necessarily shot up from the ground. It is only the hind legs of grasshoppers, and never the front ones, that resemble the two long stern oars by which a ship is steered.[18] For it is essential that the joint shall be
683 b.

bent inwards, and this never occurs in the anterior limbs.[19] The whole number of legs, including those used in leaping, is six, in all these insects.

(Ch. 7.) In the Testacea[1] the body consists of but few parts, the reason being that these animals lead a stationary life. For such animals as move much about must of necessity have more numerous parts than such as remain quiet; for, the more diversified the movements, the greater the number of organs required to effect them.[2] Some species of Testacea are absolutely motionless, and others very nearly so. They would thus fall an easy prey to their enemies, were it not for the hardness of the shell with which nature has invested their body as a means of protection. This shell, as already has been said, may have one valve, or two valves, or be turbinated. In the latter case it may either be spiral as in whelks, or merely globular, as in the Echini.[3] When it has two valves, these may be gaping, as in scallops and mussels, where the valves are united together on one side only, so as to open and shut on the other, or they may be united together on both sides, as in razor-fishes.[4] In all cases alike these Testacea have, like plants, their head downwards. The reason for this is that they imbibe their nourishment from below, just as do plants with their roots.[5] Thus the under parts come in them to be above, and the upper parts to be below. The body is enclosed in a membrane, and through this the animal filters suitable fluid and absorbs nutriment. In all there is a head;[6] but none of the other parts, excepting the receptacle for food, has any distinctive name.

(Ch. 8.) All the Crustacea[1] can crawl as well as swim, and accordingly they are provided with numerous feet. There are four main genera, viz. the Carabi, as they are called, the Astaci, the Carides, and the Carcini. In each of these genera, again, there are numerous species, which differ from each other not only as regards shape, but also very considerably as regards size. For, while in some species the individuals are large, in others they are excessively minute. The Carcinoid and Caraboid Crustacea resemble each other in possessing claws. These claws are not for locomotion, but to serve as hands for seizing and holding objects; and they are therefore bent in exactly the opposite direction to the feet, being so twisted as to turn their convexity towards the body, while the feet turn towards it their concavity

For by this position the claws are best suited for laying hold of food and carrying it to the mouth. The distinction between the Carabi and Carcini consists in the former having a tail while the latter have none. For the Carabi swim about, and a tail is therefore of use to them, serving for their propulsion like the blade of an oar. But it would be of no good to the Carcini; for these animals as a rule live close to shore, and creep into holes and corners. In such of them as live out at sea, the feet are much less adapted for crawling than in the rest, because they make but little use of them for this purpose and depend for protection on their shell-like covering. The Maiæ and the crabs known as Heracleotic are examples of this; the legs in the former being very thin, in the latter very short.[2]

The very minute crabs, that are found at the bottom of the net mixed with small fishes, have their posterior legs expanded into the resemblance of fins or oar-blades, so as to help the animal in swimming.[3] The Carides are distinguished from the Carcinoid species by the presence of a tail; and from the Caraboids by the absence of claws. This is explained by their large number of feet, on which has been expended the material for the growth of claws.[4] Their feet again are numerous to suit their mode of progression, which is mainly by swimming.[5]

The parts on the ventral surface and near the head are in some of these animals formed like gills, for the admission and discharge of water. The parts lower down differ in the different sexes. For in the female Carabi the parts are more laminar than in the males,[6] and in the female Crabs the flap is furnished with hairier appendages. This gives ampler space for the disposal of the ova, which the females retain in these parts instead of letting them go free, like fishes and other animals, as soon as they are brought forth.

In the Carabi and in the Carcini the right claw is invariably the larger and the stronger.[7] For it is natural[8] to every animal to use its right side in preference to its left; and nature, in distributing the organs, invariably assigns each, either exclusively or in a more perfect condition, to such animals as can use it. So is it with tusks, and teeth, and horns, and spurs, and all such offensive and defensive weapons.[9]

In the Astaci alone it is a matter of chance which claw is the larger, and this in either sex.[10] Claws they must have, because they belong to a genus in which this is a constant character;[11]

but they have them in this irregular way, owing to imperfect formation and to their not using them for their natural purpose, but for locomotion.

For a detailed account of the several parts of these animals, of their position, and their differences, those parts being also included which distinguish the sexes, reference must be made to the treatises on Anatomy and to the Researches concerning Animals.

(Ch. 9.) We come now to the Cephalopods.[1] Their internal organs have been already described with those of other animals.[2] Externally there is an uniform sac inclosing the body; and in front of this sac a head surrounded by feet, which form a circle about the mouth and teeth, and are set between these and the eyes. Now in all other animals the feet, if there are any, are placed in one of two ways; either before and behind, or along the sides, the latter being the method adopted in those bloodless animals whose feet are numerous. But in the Cephalopods there is a peculiar arrangement, distinct from either of these. For their feet are all placed at what may be called the fore end. The reason for this is that the hind and fore parts of their body have been drawn up close to each other,[3] as is also the case in the turbinated Testacea. For these latter, while in some points they resemble the Crustacea, in others resemble the Cephalopods. Their earthy matter is on the outside, and their fleshy substance within. So far they are like the Crustacea. But the general plan of their body is that of the Cephalopods; and, though this is true in a certain degree of all the Testacea, it is more especially true of those turbinated species, that have a spiral shell.[4] This general plan, common to the two, is as follows. Let us first consider the case of quadrupeds and of man, where the arrangement is that of a straight line. At the upper end of this line, A represents the mouth, then B the gullet, and C the stomach. After this comes the intestine reaching to the vent, which is marked by D.[5] Such is the plan in sanguineous animals; and round this straight line as an axis are disposed the head and trunk; the remaining parts, such as the anterior and posterior limbs, having been super-added by nature, merely to minister to these and for locomotion.

Now in Crustacea and in Insects there is a tendency to a similar arrangement of the internal parts in a straight line; the distinctions between these groups and the sanguineous animals depending on differences of the external organs which minister to locomotion.

684 b.

But the Cephalopods and the turbinated Testacea have in common an arrangement which stands in contrast with this. For here the two extremities are brought together by a curve, as if one were to bend the straight line marked E until D came close to A. Such, then, is the disposition of the internal parts; and round these, in the Cephalopods, is placed the sac (in the Poulps alone called a head),[6] and, in the Testacea, the turbinated shell which corresponds to the sac. There is, in fact, only this difference between them, that the sac of the Cephalopods is soft while the shell of the Testacea is hard, nature having invested the fleshy parts with this hard coating as a protection to the animal, which from its limited power of locomotion is exposed to considerable risk. In both classes, owing to this arrangement of the internal organs, the excrement is voided near the mouth; at a point below this orifice in the Cephalopods, and in the Turbinata somewhat on one side of it.[7]

Such then is the explanation of the position of the feet in the Cephalopods, and of the contrast they present to other animals in this matter. The arrangement, however, in the Sepias and the Calamaries is not precisely the same as in the Poulps, owing to the former having no other mode of progression than by swimming, while the latter not only swim but crawl.[8] Thus the former have six of their feet above the teeth, and of these six the two outer ones are the biggest; while the remaining two, which make up the total eight, are below the mouth and are much the biggest of all, just as the hind limbs in quadrupeds are stronger than the fore limbs. For it is these lower feet and these[9] hind legs that have to support the weight, and to take the main part in locomotion. And the outer pair of the upper six are bigger than the pair which intervene between them and the uppermost of all, because they have to assist the lowermost pair in their office. In the Poulps, on the other hand, the four central feet are the biggest.[10] Again, though the number of feet is the same in all the Cephalopods, namely eight,[11] their length varies in different kinds, being short in the Sepias and the Calamaries, but greater in the Poulps. For in these latter the body with its sac is of small bulk, while in the former it is of considerable size; and so in the one case nature has used the materials subtracted from the body to give length to the feet, while in the other she has acted in precisely the opposite way, and has given to the growth of the body what she has first taken from the feet.[12] The Poulps, then, owing to the length of their feet, can not only swim but crawl, whereas in the other genera the feet are useless for the latter mode of progression, being small while the bulk of the body is considerable. These short feet would not enable their possessors to cling to the rocks and keep themselves from being torn off by the waves in times of storm; neither would they serve to lay hold of objects at all remote and bring them in; but, to supply these defects, the animal is furnished with two [13] proboscides, by which it can moor itself and ride at anchor like a ship in rough weather.[14] The same processes serve also to catch prey even at some distance and to bring it to the mouth. They are so used both by the Sepias and the Calamaries. In the Poulps the feet are themselves able to perform these offices, and there are consequently no proboscides. In all the Cephalopods that have suckers on their feet and [15] twining tentacles, these act in the same way, and have indeed the same structure, as those plaited instruments which were used of old by physicians to reduce dislocations of the fingers.[16] The tentacles, like these, consist of plaited fibres, which act by pulling upon portions of flesh or any substance of a yielding nature. The physician places his instrument in a slackened condition round the finger; and, when it is put on the stretch, it grasps and clings tightly to whatever may be in contact with its inner surface. The tentacles act in the same manner, serving in place of hands for offensive or defensive purposes, the Cephalopods having indeed no other instrument than either feet or proboscides with which to lay hold on anything and bring it to the mouth.

The suckers are set in double line in all the Cephalopods excepting in one kind of poulp, where there is but a single row.[17] The length and the slimness which is part of the nature of this kind of poulp explains the exception. For a narrow space cannot possibly admit of more than a single line of suckers. This exceptional character, then, belongs to them, not because it is the most advantageous arrangement, but because it is the necessary consequence of their essential specific constitution.[18]

In all these animals there is a fin, encircling the sac. In the Poulps and the Sepias this fin is unbroken and continuous, as is also the case in the larger calamaries. But in the smaller kind, called Teuthides, the fin is not only broader than in the Sepias

685 b.

and the Poulps, where it is very narrow, but moreover only begins in the middle of the side, and does not encircle the entire sac. The use of this fin is to enable the animal to swim, and also to direct its course. It acts, that is, like the rump-feathers in birds, or the tail-fin in fishes. In none is it so small as in the Poulps; where it is difficult to make it out.[19] · For in these the body is of small bulk and can be steered by the feet sufficiently well without other assistance.

All the bloodless animals, namely the Insects, the Crustacea, the Testacea, and the Cephalopoda, have now been dealt with in turn; and the parts of all have been described, whether internal or external.

(Ch. 10.) We must now go back to the animals that have blood, and consider such of their parts, already enumerated, as were before passed over. We will take the [1] viviparous animals first, and, when we have done with these, will pass on to the ovipara, and treat of them in like manner.

The parts that border on the head, and on what is known as the neck and throat, have been already taken into consideration. As for the head itself, such a part is found in all animals that have blood; whereas in some bloodless animals, in crabs for instance, there is no head distinctly separable from the trunk. As to the neck, it is present in all the vivipara, but only in some of the ovipara; for while those that have a lung also have a neck, those that do not inhale the outer air have none.[2]

The head exists mainly for the sake of the brain. For every animal that has blood must of necessity have a brain; and must, moreover, for reasons already given, have it placed as far as possible from the heart.[3] But the head has also been chosen by nature as the part in which to set some of the senses; because its blood is mixed in such suitable proportions as to ensure quiet and precision to the sensations, while at the same time it can supply the brain with such warmth as it requires.[4] There is yet a third constituent superadded to the head, namely the part which ministers to the ingestion of food. This has been placed here by nature, because such a situation accords best with the general configuration of the body. For the stomach could not possibly be placed above the heart, seeing that this is the sovereign organ; and if placed below, as in fact it is, then the mouth could not possibly be placed there also. For this would have neces-

686 a.

sitated a great increase in the length of the body; and the stomach moreover would have been removed too far from the source of motion and of concoction.⁵ The head, then, exists for the sake of these three parts.

The neck, again, exists for the sake of the windpipe. For it acts as a defence to this and to the œsophagus, encircling them and keeping them from injury. In all other animals this neck is flexible and contains several vertebræ; but in wolves and lions it contains only a single bone.⁶ For the object of nature was to give these animals an organ which should be serviceable in the way of strength, rather than one that should be useful for any of the other purposes to which necks are subservient.⁷

Continuous with the head and neck is the trunk with the anterior limbs. In man the fore-legs and fore-feet are replaced by arms and by what we call hands. For of all animals man alone stands erect, in accordance with his god-like nature and essence. For it is the function of the god-like to think and to be wise; and no easy task were this under the burden of a heavy body, pressing down from above and obstructing by its weight the motions of the intellect and of the common sense.⁸ When, moreover, the weight and corporeal substance become excessive, the body must of necessity incline towards the ground. In such cases therefore nature, in order to give support to the body, has replaced the arms and hands by fore-feet, and has thus converted the animal into a quadruped. For, as every animal that walks must of necessity have the two hinder feet, such an animal becomes a quadruped, its body inclining downwards in front from the weight which its soul cannot sustain. For all animals, man alone excepted, are dwarf-like in form. For, as in a dwarf, their upper part is large, while that which bears the weight and is used in walking is comparatively small.⁹ This upper part is what we call the trunk, and reaches from the mouth to the vent. In man it is duly proportionate to the part below, and diminishes much in its comparative size as the man attains to full growth. But in his infancy the contrary obtains, and the upper parts are large, the lower small; so that the infant can only crawl, and is unable to walk; nay, at first cannot even crawl, but remains without motion. In fact all children are dwarfs in shape, but cease to be so as they become men, from the growth of their lower portion; whereas in quadrupeds the reverse occurs; their lower parts being largest

686 b.

in youth, and advance of years bringing increased growth above, that is in the trunk, which extends from the buttocks to the head. Thus it is that colts are scarcely, if at all, below full-grown horses in height; and that while quite young they can touch their heads with the hind legs, though this is no longer possible when they are older. Such then is the form of animals that have either a solid or a cloven hoof. But such as are polydactylous and without horns; though they too are of dwarf-like shape, are so in a less degree; nor is the original disproportion between their upper and lower parts increased by aftergrowth.[10]

Dwarf-like again is the race of birds and of fishes; and so in fact, as already has been said, is every animal that has blood. This is the reason that no other animal is so intelligent as man. For even among men themselves if we compare children with adults, or such adults as are of dwarf-like shape with such as are not, we find that, whatever other superiority the former may possess, they are at any rate deficient as compared with the latter in intelligence. The explanation, as already stated, is that their psychical principle is corporeal, and much impeded in its motions. Let now a still further decrease occur in the [11] elevating heat, and a still further increase in the earthy matter, and the animals become smaller in bulk, and their feet more numerous, until at a later stage they become apodous, and extended full length on the ground. Thus, by gradual small successions of change, they come to have their principal organ below; and at last their cephalic part becomes motionless and destitute of sensation. Thus the animal becomes a plant, that has its upper parts downwards and its lower parts above.[12] For in plants the roots are the equivalents of mouth and head, while the seed, which is produced above at the extremities of the twigs, has an opposite significance.[13]

The reasons have now been stated why some animals have many feet, some only two, and others none; why, also, some living things are plants and others animals; and, lastly, why man alone of all animals stands erect. Standing thus erect, man has no need of legs in front, and in their stead has been endowed by nature with arms and hands. Now it is the opinion of Anaxagoras, that the possession of these hands is the cause of man being of all animals the most intelligent. But it is rational to suppose that the possession of hands is the consequence rather than the cause

687 a.

of his superior intelligence. For the hands are instruments or organs, and the invariable plan of nature in distributing the organs is to give each to such animal as can make use of it; nature acting in this matter as any prudent man would do. For to such an one it would seem much more appropriate to take a person who was already a flute-player and give him a flute, than to take one who possessed a flute and teach him the art of flute-playing. For by the former plan something comparatively insignificant would be added to something of much greater importance; while by the latter the more valuable and the more important element would be superadded to the less valuable one. Seeing then that it is a better plan to assign an instrument to a workman than to assign a workman to an instrument, and seeing also that of all available plans nature invariably adopts the best, we must conclude that man does not owe his superior intelligence to his hands, but his hands to his superior intelligence.[14] For the most intelligent of animals is the one which would put the most organs to the best use; and the hand is apparently not a single organ but many in one; for it is an organ that can serve in the place of many. This instrument, then,—the hand—of all instruments the most variously serviceable, has been given by nature to man, the animal of all animals the most capable of acquiring the most varied handicrafts.

Much in error then are they, who say that the construction of man is not only faulty, but inferior to that of all other animals; seeing that he is, as they point out, barefooted, naked, and without weapon of which to avail himself. For other animals have each but one mode of defence, and this they can never change; so that they must perform all the offices of life and even, so to speak, sleep with sandals on, never laying aside whatever serves as a protection to their bodies, nor changing such single weapon as they may chance to possess. But to man numerous modes of defence are open, and these moreover he may change at will; as also he may adopt such weapon as he pleases, and at such times as suit him. For the hand is talon, hoof, and horn, at will. So too is it spear, and sword, and whatsoever other weapon or instrument you please; for all these can it be from its power of grasping and holding them all.[15] In harmony with this varied office is the form which nature has contrived for it. For it is split into several divisions, and these are capable of divergence.

687b.

Such capacity of divergence does not prevent their again converging so as to form a single compact body, whereas had the hand been an undivided mass, divergence would have been impossible. Again these parts may be used singly or together, and in various combinations. The joints, moreover, of the fingers are well constructed for prehension and for pressure. One of the digits also, and this not long like the rest but short and thick, is placed laterally. For were it not so placed all prehension would be as impossible, as were there no hand at all. For the pressure of this lateral digit is applied from below upwards, while the rest act from above downwards; an arrangement which is essential, if the grasp is to be firm and hold like a tight clamp. As for the shortness of this lateral digit, the object is to increase its strength, so that it may be able, though but one, to counterbalance its more numerous opponents. Indeed were it long it would be of no use. This is the explanation of its being sometimes called the great digit, in spite of its small size; for without it all the rest would be practically useless. The finger which stands at the other end of the row is small, while the central one of all is long, like the centre oar in a ship. This is rightly so; for in grasping an object, as a workman grasps his tool, it is the central part of the encircling hold which is of the most importance.

No less skilfully contrived are the nails. For, while in man these serve simply as coverings to protect the ends of the fingers, in other animals they are also used for active purposes; [and their form in each case is suited to their office.][16]

The arms in man and the fore limbs in quadrupeds bend in precisely[17] contrary directions, this difference having reference to the ingestion of food[18] and to the other offices which belong to these parts. For quadrupeds use their anterior limbs as feet in progression, and must therefore have them bent inwards. In such of the quadrupeds indeed as are polydactylous, these fore limbs are at any rate intended not only to serve in locomotion, but also to act as hands. And they are in fact so used, as any one may see. For these animals seize hold of objects, and also repel assailants, with their anterior limbs; whereas quadrupeds with solid hoofs use their hind legs for this latter purpose.[19] For their fore limbs are not analogous to the arms and hands of man.[20]

It is this hand-like office of the anterior limbs which explains
688a.

why in some of the polydactylous quadrupeds, such as wolves, lions, dogs, and leopards, there are five digits on each fore-foot, though there are only four on each hind one. For the fifth digit of the foot corresponds to the fifth digit of the hand, and like it is called the big one. It is true that in the smaller polydactylous quadrupeds the hind feet also have each five toes. But this is because these animals are creepers; and the increased number of nails serves to give them a tighter grip of the ground, and so enables them to creep up steep places, or even to run overhead, with greater facility.[21]

In man between the arms, and in other animals between the fore legs, lies what is called the breast. This in man is broad, as one might expect. For as the arms are set laterally on the body, they offer no impediment to the expansion of this part. But in quadrupeds the breast is narrow, owing to the legs having to be extended in a forward direction in progression and locomotion.

Owing to this narrowness the mammæ of quadrupeds are never placed on the breast. But in the human body there is ample space in this part; moreover the heart and neighbouring organs require such protection as would be afforded by a fleshy covering; and for these reasons the mammæ in man are placed on the breast, side by side. In the male these mammæ are of a fleshy substance and are therefore of use in the way just stated; but, in the female, nature, in accordance[22] with what we say is her frequent practice, makes these organs minister to an additional function, employing them as a store-place of nutriment for the offspring. The human mammæ are two in number, in accordance with the division of the body into two halves, a right and a left. They are somewhat firmer than they would otherwise be, because the ribs[23] in this region are joined together; and they form two distinct masses, because their presence is in no wise burdensome.[24] In other animals[25] than man, it is impossible for the mammæ to be placed on the breast between the fore legs, for they would interfere with locomotion; they are therefore disposed of otherwise, and in a variety of ways. Thus in such animals as produce but few at a birth, whether horned quadrupeds or those with solid hoofs, the mammæ are placed in the groins, and are two in number,[26] while in such as produce litters, or such as are polydactylous, the dugs are

688 a.

either numerous and placed laterally on the belly, as in swine and dogs, or are only two in number and placed in the centre of the abdomen, as is the case in the lion.[27] The explanation of this latter condition is not that the lion produces few at a birth, for sometimes it has more than two cubs at a time, but is to be found in the fact that this animal has no plentiful supply of milk. For, being a flesh-eater, it gets food at but rare intervals, and such nourishment as it obtains is all expended on the growth of its body.

In the elephant also there are but two mammæ, which are placed under the axillæ of the fore limbs. The mammæ are not more than two, because this animal has only a single young one at a birth; and they are not placed in the groins, because they never occupy that position in any polydactylous animal such as this.[28] Lastly they are placed above close to the axillæ, because this is the position of the foremost dugs in all animals whose dugs are numerous, and the dugs so placed give the most milk. A proof of this is furnished by the sow. For she always presents these foremost dugs to the first-born of her litter. A single young one is of course a first-born; and so such animals as only produce a single young one must have these anterior dugs to present to it; that is they must have dugs close to the axillæ. This, then, is the reason why the elephant has but two mammæ, and why they are so placed. But, in such animals as have litters of young, the dugs are disposed about the belly; the reason being that more dugs are required by those that have more young to nourish. Now as there are but two sides to the body, the right and the left, it is impossible that these dugs should be set transversely in rows of more than two. They must therefore be placed lengthways, and the only place where there is sufficient length for this is the region between the front and hind legs. As to the animals that are not polydactylous but produce few at a birth, or have horns, their dugs are placed in the groins. The horse, the ass, the camel are examples; all of which bear but a single young one at a time, and of which the two former have solid hoofs, while in the last the hoof is cloven. As still further examples, may be mentioned the deer, the ox, the goat, and all other similar animals.

The explanation is that in these animals growth takes place
688 b.

in an upward direction;[29] so that there must be an abundant collection of residual matter and of blood in the lower region, that is to say in the neighbourhood of the excremental orifices. Here therefore nature has placed the mammæ. For the part whence they can most easily derive nutriment will clearly be that part in which the nutriment is set in motion. In man there are mammæ in the male as well as in the female; but some of the males of other animals are without them. Such for instance is the case with horses, some stallions being destitute of these parts, while others that resemble their dams have them.[30] Thus much then concerning the mammæ.

Next after the breast comes the region of the belly, which is left unenclosed by the ribs for a reason which has already been given;[31] namely that there may be no impediment to the swelling which necessarily occurs in the food as it gets heated, nor to the expansion of the womb in pregnancy.

At the extreme end of what is called the trunk are the parts concerned in the evacuation of the solid and also of the fluid residues. In all sanguineous animals with some few exceptions,[32] and in all vivipara without any exception at all, the same part which serves for the evacuation of the fluid residue is also made by nature to serve in sexual congress, and this alike in male and female. For the semen is a kind of fluid and a residue. The proof of this will be given hereafter, but for the present let it be taken for granted. The like holds good of the menstrual fluid in women, and of the part by which they give issue to it. This also, however, is a matter of which a more accurate account will be given hereafter. For the present let it be simply stated as a fact, that the catamenia of the female as also the semen of the male are residual matter.[33] The catamenia, then, and the semen are both fluid, and thus it is only reasonable that the same parts which serve for voidance of the urine should give issue to these residues, which have identical or similar characters. Of the internal structure of these parts, and of the differences which exist between the parts concerned with semen and the parts concerned with conception, a clear account is given in the book of Researches concerning Animals and in the treatises on Anatomy. Moreover I shall have to speak of them again when I come to deal with Generation and Development. As regards, however, the external shapes of the parts, it is plain enough that they are adapted to their operations, as indeed of necessity they must be. There are, however, differences in the male organ corresponding to differences in the body generally. For it is not of an equally sinewy character in all animals. This organ, again, is the only one that, independently of any morbid change, admits of augmentation and of diminution of bulk. The former change is of service in copulation, while the other is required for the advantage of the body at large. For, were the organ constantly in a state of erection, it would be an incumbrance. The organ therefore has been formed of such constituents, as will admit of either condition. For it is partly sinewy, partly cartilaginous,[34] and thus is enabled either to contract or to become extended, and is capable of admitting air.[35]

All female quadrupeds void their urine backwards, because the position of the parts which this implies is useful to them in the act of copulation. This is the case with very few males, though there are some exceptions, as the lynx, the lion, the camel, and the hare.[36] No quadruped with a solid hoof is retromingent.

The posterior portion of the body and the parts about the legs are different in man from what they are in quadrupeds. Nearly all these latter have a tail, and this whether they are viviparous or oviparous. For, even if the tail be of no great size, yet they have a kind of scut; as at any rate a small representative of it. But man is tail-less. He has however buttocks, which exist in none of the quadrupeds. His legs also, calves and thighs alike, are fleshy; while in all other animals that have legs, viviparous or not, they are fleshless, being made of sinew and bone and a substance resembling fish-spine.[37] For all these differences there is, so to say, one common explanation, and this is that of all animals man alone stands erect. It was to facilitate the maintenance of this position that nature made his upper parts light, taking away some of their corporeal substance, and using it to increase the weight of the parts below, so that the buttocks, the thighs, and the calves of the legs, all became fleshy. The character which she thus gave to the buttocks renders them at the same time useful in resting the body. For standing causes no fatigue to quadrupeds, and even the long continuance of this posture produces in them no weariness; for they are supported the whole time by four props,

689 b.

which is much as though they were lying down.[38] But to man it is no easy task to remain for any length of time on his feet, his body demanding rest in a sitting position. This, then, is the reason why man has buttocks and fleshy legs; and the presence of these fleshy parts explains why he has no tail. For the nutriment which would otherwise go to the tail is used up in the production of these parts,[39] while at the same time the existence of buttocks does away with the necessity of a tail. But in quadrupeds and other animals the reverse obtains. For they are of dwarf-like form, so that all the pressure of their weight and corporeal substance is on their upper part; and is withdrawn from the parts below.[40] On this account they are without buttocks and have hard legs. In order however to cover and protect that part which serves for the evacuation of excrement, nature has given them a tail or brush, subtracting for the purpose some of the nutriment which would otherwise go to the legs. Half-way in shape between man and quadrupeds is the ape,[41] belonging therefore to neither or to both, and having on this account neither tail nor buttocks; no tail in its character of biped, no buttocks in its character of quadruped. There is a great diversity of so-called tails; and this organ like others[42] is sometimes used by nature for bye-purposes, being made to serve not only as a covering and protection to the fundament, but also for other uses and advantages of its possessor.[43]

There are differences in the feet of quadrupeds. For in some of these animals there is a solid hoof, and in others a hoof cloven into two, and again in others a foot divided into many parts.

The hoof is solid when the body is large and the earthy matter present in great abundance; in which case the earth, instead of forming teeth and horns, is separated in the character of a nail, and being very abundant forms one continuous nail, that is a hoof, in place of several. This consumption of the earthy matter on the hoof explains why these animals, as a rule, have no[44] huckle-bones; a second reason, however, being that the presence of such a bone in the joint of the hind leg somewhat impedes its free motion. For extension and flexion can be made more rapidly in parts that have but one angle than in parts that have many. But the presence of a huckle-bone, as a connecting bolt, is the introduction as it were of a new limb-segment between the two ordinary ones. Such an addition adds to the weight of

690a.

the foot, but renders the act of progression more secure. Thus it is that even in such animals as have a huckle-bone, it is only in the posterior limbs and never in the anterior ones that this bone is found. For the anterior limbs, moving as they do in advance of the others, require to be light and capable of ready flexion, whereas firmness and extension are what is wanted in the hind limbs. Moreover a huckle-bone adds weight to the blow of a limb, and so renders it a suitable weapon of defence; and these animals all use their hind legs to protect themselves, kicking out with their heels against anything which annoys them. In the cloven-hoofed quadrupeds the lighter character of the hind legs admits of there being a huckle-bone; and the presence of the huckle-bone prevents them from having a solid hoof, the bony substance remaining in the joint, and therefore being deficient in the foot. As to the polydactylous quadrupeds, none of them have huckle-bones. For if they had they would not be polydactylous, but the divisions of the foot would only extend to that amount of its breadth which was covered by the huckle-bone.[45] Thus it is that most of the animals that have huckle-bones are cloven-hoofed.

Of all animals man has the largest foot in proportion to the size of the body.[46] This is only what might be expected. For seeing that he is the only animal that stands erect, the two feet which have to bear all the weight of the body must be both long and broad. Equally intelligible is it that the proportion between the size of the fingers and that of the whole hand should be inverted in the case of the toes and feet. For the function of the hands is to take hold of objects and retain them by pressure; so that the fingers require to be long. For it is by its flexed portion that the hand grasps an object. But the function of the feet is to enable us to walk with security; so that here the undivided part is to be looked on as of most importance. However it is better for an extremity to be divided than to be undivided. For in an undivided foot disease of any one part would affect by sympathy the whole; whereas, if the foot be divided into separate digits, there is not an equal liability to such an occurrence.[47] The digits, again, by being short would be less liable to injury. For these reasons the feet in man are many-toed, while the separate digits are of no great length. The toes, finally, are furnished with nails for the same reason as are the

690 b.

fingers, namely because such projecting parts are weak and therefore require especial protection.

(Ch. 11.) We have now done with such sanguineous animals as live on land and bring forth their young alive;[1] and, having dealt with all their main kinds, we may pass on to such sanguineous animals as are oviparous. Of these some have four feet, while others have none. The latter form a single genus, namely the Serpents; and why these are apodous has been already explained in the dissertation on Animal Progression.[2] Irrespective of this, absence of feet, serpents resemble the oviparous quadrupeds in their conformation.[3]

In all these animals there is a head with its component parts; its presence being determined by the same causes[4] as obtain in the case of other sanguineous animals; and in all, with the single exception of the river crocodile, there is a tongue inside the mouth.[5] In this one exception there would seem to be no actual tongue, but merely a space left vacant for it. The reason is that a crocodile is in a way a land-animal and a water-animal combined. In its character of land-animal it has a space for a tongue; but in its character of water-animal it is without the tongue itself. For in fishes, as has already been mentioned, there is either no appearance of a tongue at all, unless the mouth be stretched open very widely indeed; or, if there be a tongue, it is indistinctly separated from the rest of the mouth.[6] The reason for this is that a tongue would be of but little service to such animals, seeing that they are unable to chew their food or to taste it before swallowing, the pleasurable sensations they derive from it being limited to the act of deglutition.[7] For it is in their passage down the gullet that solid edibles cause enjoyment, while it is by the tongue that the savour of fluids is perceived. Thus it is during deglutition that the oiliness, the heat, and other such qualities of food, are recognised; and in fact the satisfaction from solid edibles and dainties in general is derived almost exclusively from the dilatation of the œsophagus during deglutition.[8] This pleasurable sensation, then, belongs to all sanguineous animals, viviparous or not, alike; but, while the rest have in addition the sensations of taste, tongueless animals have no other satisfaction than it. What has now been said explains why intemperance as regards drinks and savoury fluids does not go hand in hand with intemperance as regards eating and solid relishes.[9]

In some oviparous quadrupeds, namely in lizards, the tongue is bifid, as also it is in serpents, and its terminal divisions are of hair-like fineness, as has already been described.[10] (Seals also have a forked tongue.) This it is which accounts for all these animals being so fond of dainty food.[11] The teeth in these oviparous quadrupeds are of the sharp interfitting kind, as also are the teeth of fishes.[12] The organs of all the senses are present; and these resemble those of other animals. Thus there are nostrils for smell, eyes for vision, and ears for hearing. The latter organs, however, do not project from the sides of the head, but consist simply of the duct, as also is the case in birds. This is due in both cases to the hardness[13] of the integument; birds having their bodies covered with feathers, and these oviparous quadrupeds with horny plates. These plates are equivalent to scales, but of a harder character. This is very manifest in tortoises and river crocodiles, and also in the large serpents. For so hard are they in these animals, as to become even stronger than the bones.[14]

These animals have no upper eyelid, but close the eye with the lower lid.[15] In this they resemble birds, and the reason of the peculiarity is the same as was assigned in their case.[16] Among birds there are some that can not only thus close the eye, but can also blink by means of a membrane which comes from its inner corner. But none of the oviparous quadrupeds blink in this manner.[17] For their eyes are harder than those of birds.[18] The reason for this is that sharpsightedness is of very considerable service to birds, flying as they do in the air, whereas it would be of comparatively small use to the oviparous quadrupeds, seeing that they all live in holes.

Of the two separate portions which constitute the head, namely the upper part and the lower jaw, the latter in man and in the viviparous quadrupeds moves not only upwards and downwards, but also from side to side;[19] while in fishes, and birds, and oviparous quadrupeds, the only movement is up and down. The reason is that this latter movement is the one required in biting and dividing food, while the lateral movement serves to reduce substances to a pulp. To such animals, therefore, as have grinder-teeth this lateral motion is of service; but to those animals that have no grinders it would be quite useless, and they are therefore invariably without it. For nature never makes anything that is
691 b.

superfluous. While in all other animals it is the lower jaw that is moveable, in the river crocodile it is exceptionally the upper one.[20] This is because the feet in this creature are so excessively small as to be perfectly useless for seizing and holding prey; on which account nature has given it a mouth that can serve for these purposes in their stead. For clearly that direction of motion, which will give the greater force to a blow, will be the more serviceable one in holding or in seizing prey; and a blow from above is always more forcible than one from below. Seeing, then, that both the prehension and the mastication of food are offices of the mouth, and that the former of these two is the more essential in an animal that has neither hands nor suitably formed feet, these crocodiles will derive greater benefit from a motion of the upper jaw downwards than from a motion of the lower jaw upwards. The same considerations explain why crabs move only the upper division of each claw and not the lower. For their claws are substitutes for hands, and so require to be suitable for the prehension of food, and not for its comminution; for such comminution and mastication is the office of teeth. In crabs, then, and in such other animals as are able to seize their food in a leisurely manner, and are not forced by being constantly in the water to perform this office with the mouth,[21] the two functions are assigned to different parts, prehension to the hands or feet, the division or mastication of food to the mouth. But in crocodiles the mouth has been so framed by nature as to serve both purposes, the jaws being made to move in the manner just described.

All these animals have a neck, which is the necessary consequence of their having a lung. For the windpipe by which the air is admitted to the lung is of some length.[22] If however the definition of a neck be correct, which calls it the portion between the head and the shoulders, a serpent can scarcely be said with the same right as the rest of these animals to have a neck, but only to have something analogous to that part of the body. It is a peculiarity of serpents, as compared with other animals allied to them, that they are able to turn their head backwards without stirring the rest of the body. The reason of this is that a serpent, like an insect, has a body that admits of being curled up, its vertebræ being cartilaginous and easily bent.[23] The faculty in question belongs then to serpents simply as a necessary consequence of this character of their vertebræ; but at the same time it has a final cause, for it tells to their advantage by enabling them to guard against attacks from behind. For their body, owing to its length and its want of feet, is ill-suited for turning round and protecting the hinder parts; and merely to lift the head, without the power of turning it round, would be of no use whatsoever.

The ovipara with which we are dealing have, moreover, a part which corresponds to the breast; but neither here nor elsewhere in their body have they any mammæ, as neither has any bird or fish. This is a consequence of their having no milk; for a mamma is a receptacle for milk and, as it were, a vessel to contain it. This absence of milk is not peculiar to these animals, but is common to all such as are not internally viviparous.[24] For all such produce eggs, and the nutriment which corresponds to the milk is in them formed in the egg. Of all this, however, a clearer account will be given in the treatise on Generation and Development.[25] As to the mode in which the joints bend, a general account, in which all animals are considered, has already been given in the dissertation on Progression. So also the reasons for the presence or absence of a tail have been already stated at large.[26] It suffices therefore to say that these animals always have a tail of some sort, though the size which it attains varies considerably.

Of all the ovipara that live on land there is none so lean as the Chamæleon.[27] For there is none that has so little blood. The explanation of this is to be found in the psychical temperament of the creature. For it is of a timid nature, as the frequent changes it undergoes in its outward aspect testify.[28] But fear is a refrigeration, and results from deficiency of natural heat and scantiness of blood.[29]

We have now done with the sanguineous animals, both such as are quadrupedous and such as are apodous, and have stated with sufficient completeness what external parts they possess, and for what reasons they have them.

(Ch. 12.) The differences of birds[1] compared one with another are differences of magnitude, and of the greater or smaller development of parts. Thus some have long legs, others short legs; some have a broad tongue, others a narrow tongue; and so on with the other parts. There are very few of their parts that present any greater differences than these, taking birds by

themselves.² But, when we compare birds with other animals, we find the parts differing not merely in relative size but in form. Thus birds are invariably feathered, and this is a peculiarity which is characteristic of them. For while other animals are some hairy, some scaly, some covered with scaly plates, birds alone are feathered. Insects it is true are also feathered, but the feathers of a bird are split and different in kind from the undivided feathers of an insect; for the bird's feather is barbed, while the insect's is not; the bird's feather has a shaft, the insect's has none.³

A second strange peculiarity which distinguishes birds from all other animals is their beak. For as in elephants⁴ the nostril serves in place of hands, and as in some insects⁵ the tongue serves in place of mouth, so in birds there is a bony⁶ beak which serves in place of teeth and lips. Their organs of sense have already been considered.

All birds have a neck extending from the body; and the purpose of this neck is the same as in such other animals as have one.⁷ This neck in some birds is long, in others short; its length as a general rule being pretty nearly determined by that of the legs. For long-legged birds have a long neck, short-legged birds a short one, to which rule, however, the web-footed birds form an exception. For to a bird perched up on long legs a short neck would be of no use whatsoever in collecting food from the ground; and equally useless would be a long neck, if the legs were short. Such birds, again, as are carnivorous would find length in this part interfere greatly with their habits of life. For a long neck is a weak one, and it is on their superior strength that carnivorous birds depend for their subsistence. No bird, therefore, that has talons ever has an elongated neck. In web-footed birds, however, and in those other birds that seem to belong to the same genus, inasmuch as their toes though actually separate are yet flattened and expanded into lobes,⁸ the neck is elongated, so as to be suitable for collecting food from the water; while at the same time the legs are short, so as to serve in swimming.

The beaks of birds, as their feet, vary with their modes of life. For in some the beak is straight, in others crooked; straight, in those whose food requires that form; crooked, in those that live on flesh. For a crooked beak is an advantage in fighting;

693 a.

and carnivorous birds must of course get their food from the bodies of other animals, and in most cases by violence. In such birds, again, as live in marshes and are herbivorous the beak is broad, this form being best suited for digging and cropping, and for pulling up plants. In some of these marsh birds, however, the beak is elongated, as also is the neck, the reason for this being that the bird gets its food from some depth below the surface. For most birds that have this conformation, and most of those that are either actually web-footed or web-footed in the partial way already mentioned, live by preying on some of the small animals that are to be found in water. In these the neck acts the part of a fishing-rod, the beak representing the line and hook.

The upper and under sides of the body, that is of what in quadrupeds is called the trunk, present in birds one unbroken surface. For there are no arms nor fore legs attached to it, but in their stead wings, which are a distinctive peculiarity of birds; and, as these wings are substitutes for arms, their terminal segments lie on the back in the place of a shoulder-blade.[9]

The legs are two in number, as in man; not however, as in man, bent outwards, but bent inwards like the hind legs of a quadruped.[10] The wings are bent like the fore legs of a quadruped, having their convexity turned outwards. That the feet should be two in number is a matter of necessity. For a bird is essentially a sanguineous animal, and at the same time essentially a winged animal; and no sanguineous animal has more than four points for motion.[11] In birds, then, as in those other sanguineous animals that live and move upon the ground,[12] the limbs attached to the trunk are four in number. But, while in all the rest these four limbs consist of a pair of arms and a pair of legs, or of four legs as in quadrupeds, in birds alone the arms or fore legs are replaced by a pair of wings, and this is their distinctive character. For it is of the essence of a bird that it shall be able to fly; and it is by the extension of wings that this is made possible. Of all arrangements, then, the only possible, and so the necessary, one is that birds shall have two feet; for this with the wings will give them four points for motion. The breast in all birds is sharp-edged, and fleshy.[13] The sharp edge is of advantage in flight; for broad surfaces move with considerable difficulty, owing to the large quantity of air which they have to displace. The fleshy character acts as a protection to the breast, which owing to its form would be very weak, were it not amply covered.[14]

Below the breast lies the belly, extending, as in quadrupeds and in man, to the vent and to the place where the legs are jointed to the trunk.

Such, then, are the parts which lie between the wings and the legs. Birds like all other animals, whether produced viviparously or from eggs, have an umbilical cord during their development, but, when the bird has attained to fuller growth, no signs of this remain visible. The explanation of this will be set forth in the treatise on Generation and Development, but amounts to this, that in birds the umbilical cord unites with the intestine, and is not a portion of the vascular system, as is the case in the vivipara.[15]

Some birds, again, are well adapted for flight, their wings being large and strong. Such, for instance, are those that have talons and live on flesh. For their mode of life renders the power of flight a necessity, and it is on this account that their feathers are so abundant and their wings so large. Besides these, however, there are also other genera of birds that can fly well; all those, for example, that depend on speed for security, and all those again that are of migratory habits. On the other hand some kinds of birds have heavy bodies and are not constructed for flight. These are birds that are frugivorous and live on the ground, or that are able to swim and gain their livelihood in watery places. In those that have talons the body, when stripped of [its feathers and] wings, is small; for the nutriment is consumed[16] in the production of these weapons and defensive appliances; whereas in birds that do not fly the contrary obtains, and the body is bulky and so of heavy weight. In some of these heavy birds the legs are furnished with what are called spurs, which replace the wings as a means of defence. Spurs and talons never co-exist in the same bird. For nature never makes anything superfluous; and if a bird can fly, and has talons, it has no use for spurs; for these are weapons for fighting on the ground, and on this account are an appanage of certain heavy-bodied birds. These latter, again, would find the possession of talons not only useless but actually injurious; for the claws would stick into the ground and interfere with progression. This is the reason why all birds with talons walk so badly, and why

694 a.

they never settle upon rocks.[17] For the character of their claws is ill-suited for either action.

All this is the necessary consequence of the process of development. For the earthy matter in the body issues from it and is converted into some or other useful kind of weapon. That which flows upwards gives hardness or size to the beak; and, should any flow downwards, it either forms spurs upon the legs or gives size and strength to the talons. But it does not at one and the same time produce both these results, one in the legs, the other in the claws; for such a dispersion of this residual matter would destroy all its efficacy. In other birds this earthy residue furnishes the legs with the material for their elongation; or sometimes, in place of this, fills up the interspaces between the toes. Thus it is simply a matter of necessity,[18] that such birds as swim shall either be actually web-footed, or, if not so, shall at any rate have a kind of broad blade-like margin running along the whole length of each distinct toe.[19] The forms, then, of these feet are simply the necessary results of the causes that have been mentioned. Yet at the same time they are intended for the animal's advantage. For they are in harmony with the mode of life of these birds, who, living on the water, where their wings are useless, require that their feet shall be such as to serve in swimming. For these feet are so developed as to resemble the broad-bladed oars of a boat, or the fins of a fish; and the destruction of the foot-web has precisely the same effect as the destruction of the fin; that is to say, it puts an end to all power of swimming.[20]

In some birds the legs are very long, the cause of this being that they inhabit marshes. I say the cause, because nature makes the organs for the function, and not the function for the organs.[21] It is, then, because these birds are not meant for swimming that their feet are unwebbed, and it is because they live on ground that gives way under the foot that their legs and toes are elongated, and that these latter in most of them have an extra number of joints.[22] Again, seeing that all birds are made of the same substance,[23] and yet are not all constructed alike to fly, the materials which in some are expended on organs of flight can in others be diverted to different purposes; and in these birds the nutriment which would otherwise go to form the tail-feathers is used in increasing the dimensions of the legs. This is the reason why these birds when they fly make use of their legs as a tail, stretching them out behind, and so rendering them serviceable, whereas in any other position they would be simply in the way.[24]

In other birds, where the legs are short, these are held close against the belly during flight. In some cases this is merely to keep the feet out of the way, but in birds that have talons the position has a further purpose, being the one best suited for rapine.[25] Birds that have a long and a thick neck, keep it stretched out during flight; but those whose neck though long is slender fly with it coiled up. For in this position it is protected, and less likely to get broken, should the bird fly against any obstacle.[26]

In all birds there is an ischium, but of such length that it would scarcely be taken for an ischium, but rather for a second thigh-bone; for it extends as far as to the middle of the belly.[27] The reason for this is that the bird is a biped, and yet is unable to stand erect. For if its ischium extended but a short way from the fundament, and then immediately came the leg, as is the case in man and in quadrupeds, the bird would be unable to stand upright at all. For while man stands erect, and while quadrupeds have their heavy bodies propped up in front by the fore legs, birds can neither stand erect owing to their dwarf-like[28] shape, nor have anterior legs to prop them up, these legs being replaced by wings. As a remedy for this nature has given them a long ischium, and brought it to the centre of the body, fixing it firmly; and under this central point she has placed the legs, that the weight on either side may be equally balanced, and standing or progression rendered possible. Such then is the reason why a bird, though it is a biped, does not stand erect. Why its legs are destitute of flesh has also already been stated; for the reasons are the same as in the case of quadrupeds.[29]

In all birds alike, whether web-footed or not, the number of toes in each foot is four.[30] For the Libyan ostrich may be disregarded for the present, and its cloven hoof and other discrepancies of structure as compared with the tribe of birds will be considered farther on. Of these four toes three are in front, while the fourth points backwards, serving, as a heel, to give steadiness. In the long-legged birds this fourth toe is much shorter[31] than the others, as is the case also with the Crex.[32] In no bird is the number of toes more than four. The arrangement of the toes is such

695 a.

as has been described, in all birds with one exception. This exception is the wryneck.[33] Here two of the toes are in front, the other two behind; and the reason for this is that the body of the wryneck is not inclined forwards so much as that of other birds. All birds have testicles; but they are inside the body. The reason for this will be given in the treatise on the Generation and Development of Animals.[34]

(Ch. 13.) Thus then are fashioned the parts of birds. But in fishes[1] a still further stunting has occurred in the external parts. For here, for reasons already given,[2] there are neither arms nor legs nor wings, the whole body from head to tail presenting one unbroken surface. This tail differs in different fishes, in some having a consistency similar to that of the body, while in others, namely in some of the flat kinds, it is spinous and elongated, because the material which should have gone to the tail has been diverted thence and used to increase the breadth of the body. Such for instance is the case with the Torpedos,[3] the Trygons,[4] and whatever other Selachia there may be of like nature. In such fishes, then, the tail is spinous and long; while in some others it is short and fleshy, for the very same reason which makes it spinous and long in the Torpedo. For to be short and fleshy comes to exactly the same thing as to be long and less amply furnished with flesh.

What has occurred in the Fishing-frog,[5] is exactly the reverse of what has occurred in the other instances just given. For here the anterior and broad part of the body is destitute of flesh, and so all the fleshy substance which has been thence diverted has been placed by nature in the tail and hinder portion of the body.

In fishes there are no limbs attached to the body. For in accordance with their essential constitution they are swimming animals; and nature never makes anything superfluous or void of use. Now, seeing that fishes are essentially sanguineous animals, they must have four points of motion; and, seeing that they are meant for swimming, these must be fins and not feet; for feet are attached to the body that they may be of use in walking on dry ground.[6] Moreover it is impossible for fishes, that are sanguineous animals, to have four fins and also at the same time to have feet or in fact any other kind of limb. Tadpoles,[7] it is true, though they have gills, have feet; but then they have no fins, but merely have their tail flattened out and loose in texture.[8]

695 b.

Fishes, unless, like the Batos[9] and the Trygon, they are broad and flat, have four fins, two on the upper and two on the under aspect of the body; and no fish ever has more than these. For, if it had, it would be an ex-sanguineous animal.

The upper pair of fins is present in nearly all fishes, but not so the under pair; for these are wanting in some of those fishes that have long thick bodies, such as the eel, the conger, and the Cestreus which is found in the lake at Siphæ.[10] When the body is still more elongated, and resembles that of a serpent rather than that of a fish, as is the case in the Smyræna,[11] there are absolutely no fins at all; and locomotion[12] is effected by the flexures of the body, the water being put to the same use by these fishes as is the ground by serpents. For in fact serpents swim in water exactly in the same way as they glide on the ground. The reason for these serpent-like fishes being without fins is precisely the same as that which causes serpents to be without feet; and what this is has been already stated in the dissertation on the Progression and the Motion of Animals.[13] The reason was this. If the points of motion were four,[14] motion would be effected under difficulties. For either the two pairs of fins would be near each other, in which case motion would scarcely be possible, or they would be at a very considerable distance apart, in which case the long interval between them would be just as great an evil. On the other hand, to have more than four such motor points is out of the question. For that would convert the fishes into ex-sanguineous animals.[15] A similar explanation applies to the case of those fishes that have only two fins. For here again the body is of great length and like that of a serpent, and its undulations do the office of the two missing fins. It is owing to this that such fishes can even crawl on dry ground, and can live there for a considerable time; and do not, like other fishes, begin to gasp the moment they are taken out of the water; and the less so, the nearer their nature conforms to that of land-animals. In such fishes as have but two fins it is the upper pair that is present,[16] excepting when the flat broad shape of the body prevents this. These fins, moreover, in such cases are placed at the head, because in this region there is no elongation, which might serve in the absence of fins as a means of locomotion; whereas in the direction of the tail there is a considerable lengthening out in fishes of this conformation. As for the Bati and the like, they

696 a.

use the marginal parts of their flattened bodies in place of fins for swimming.[17]

In the Torpedo and the Fishing-frog the breadth and flatness of the anterior part of the body is not so great as to render locomotion by fins impossible. It necessitates, however, the displacement of the upper pair to a point further back, and the advancement of the under pair to the head. At the same time to compensate for this advancement these lower fins are reduced in size so as to be smaller than the upper ones.[18] In the Torpedo the two upper fins are placed on the tail, and the fish uses the broad expansion of its body to supply their place, each lateral half of its circumference serving the office of a fin.[19]

The head, with its several parts, as also the organs of sense, have already come under consideration.[20]

There is one peculiarity which distinguishes fishes from all other sanguineous animals, namely, the possession of gills. Why they have these organs has been explained in the treatise on Respiration.[21] These gills are in most fishes covered by opercula, but in the Selachia, owing to the skeleton being cartilaginous, there are no such coverings. For an operculum requires fish-bone for its formation, and in other fishes the skeleton is made of this substance, whereas in the Selachia it is invariably formed of cartilage. Again, while the motions of bony fishes are rapid, those of the Selachia are but sluggish, owing to the absence of bone and of sinew. But an operculum requires rapidity of motion, seeing that the office of the gills is to minister as it were to expiration.[22] For this reason in Selachia the branchial orifices themselves effect their own closure, and thus there is no need for an operculum to ensure its taking place with due rapidity.[23] In some fishes the gills are numerous, in others few in number; in some again they are double, in others single. The last gill in most cases is single.[24] For a detailed account of all this, reference must be made to that part of the treatises on Anatomy which relates to fishes, and to the book of Researches concerning Animals.[25]

It is the abundance or the deficiency of the cardiac heat which determines the numerical abundance or deficiency of the gills. For, the greater an animal's heat, the more rapid and the more forcible does it require the branchial movement to be;[26] and numerous and double gills act with more force and rapidity than few and single ones. Thus too it is that some fishes that have but few gills, and those of comparatively small efficacy, can live out of water for a considerable time; for in them there is no great demand for refrigeration. Such, for example, are the eel and all other fishes of serpent-like form.[27]

Fishes also present diversities as regards the mouth. In some this is placed in front, at the very extremity of the body, while in others, as the dolphin[28] and such fishes as resemble the Selachia, it is placed on the under surface; so that these fishes have to turn on their backs in order to take their food. The purpose of nature in this was apparently not merely to provide a means of salvation for other animals, by allowing them opportunity of escape during the time lost in the act of turning—for all the fishes with this kind of mouth prey on living animals—but also to prevent these fishes from giving way too much to their gluttonous ravening after food.[29] For had they been able to seize their prey more easily than they do, they would soon have perished from over-repletion. An additional reason for placing their mouth on the under surface is that the projecting extremity of the head is round and small, so that a mouth, if placed there, could not possibly open widely. In such fishes as have the mouth placed at the anterior extremity there are differences in the extent to which that orifice can open. In those that are carnivorous, such as the fishes[30] with sharp interfitting teeth, whose strength lies in their mouth, this orifice can gape widely, whereas it is placed at the point of a small tapering snout in all such as are not carnivorous.

The skin is in some fishes covered with scales, a scale being a shiny film which owing to its thinness becomes detached from the surface of the body. In others it is rough, as for instance in the Rhine,[31] the Batos, and the like. In others again, but in very few, the skin is smooth.[32] The Selachia have no scales, but a rough skin. This is explained by their cartilaginous skeleton. For the earthy material which has been thence diverted is expended by nature upon the skin.[33]

No fish has testicles[34] either externally or internally; as indeed have no apodous animals, among which of course are included the serpents.[35] One and the same orifice serves both for the excrement and for the generative secretions,[36] as is the case also in all other oviparous animals, the quadrupeds as well as the rest, inasmuch as they have no urinary bladder and form no fluid excretion.[37]

Such then are the characters which distinguish fishes from all other animals. But dolphins and whales and all such Cetacea[38] are without gills; and, having a lung, are provided with a blow-hole. By this they discharge the sea-water which has been taken into the mouth.[39] For, feeding as they do in the water, they cannot but let this fluid enter into their mouth, and, having let it in, they must of necessity let it out again. This they cannot do by the aid of gills; for the use of gills, as has been explained in the treatise on Respiration, is limited to such animals as do not breathe; so that no animal can possibly possess gills and at the same time be a respiratory animal.[40] In order, therefore, that these Cetacea may discharge the water, they are provided with a blow-hole. This is placed in front of the brain; for, if placed behind, it would have cut off the brain from the spine.[41] The reason for these animals having a lung and breathing, is that their large size demands an excess of heat, to render motion possible.[42] A lung, therefore, is placed within their body, and is fully supplied with blood-heat. These creatures are after a fashion land and water animals in one. For so far as they are inhalers of air they resemble land-animals, while they resemble water-animals in having no feet and in deriving their food from the sea. So also seals[43] lie half-way between land and water animals, and bats half-way between animals that live on the ground and animals that fly; and so may be said to belong to both kinds or to neither. For seals, if looked on as water-animals, are yet found to have feet; and, if looked on as land-animals, are yet found to have fins. For their hind feet are exactly like the fins of fishes. Their teeth also are all of the sharp and interfitting kind, as in fishes.[44] Bats again, if regarded as winged animals, have feet; and, if regarded as quadrupeds, are without them.[45] So also they have neither the tail of a quadruped nor the tail of a bird; no quadruped's tail, because they are winged animals; no bird's tail, because they live on the ground. This absence of tail is the result of necessity. For bats fly by means of a membrane, not by means of barbed feathers; and no animal unless it has barbed feathers has the tail of a bird; for a bird's tail is composed of such barbed feathers. As for a quadruped's tail, it would be an impediment to an animal that flies.

(*Ch.* 14.) Much the same may be said also of the Libyan ostrich. For it has some of the characters of a bird, some of the characters of a quadruped. It differs from a quadruped, in possessing wings; from a bird in being unable to soar aloft, and in having feathers that resemble hair and are useless for flight.[1] On the other hand it agrees with quadrupeds in having upper eyelashes,[2] which are the more richly supplied with hairs because the parts about the head and the upper portion of the neck are bare;[3] and it agrees with birds in being feathered in all the parts posterior to these. Again it resembles a bird in being a biped, and a quadruped in having a cloven hoof. For it has hoofs and not toes.[4] The explanation of these peculiarities is to be found in its bulk, which is that of a quadruped rather than of a bird. For, speaking generally, a bird must necessarily be of very small size. For a body of heavy bulk can with difficulty be raised into the air.

Thus much then as regards the parts of animals. We have discussed them all, and set forth the cause why each exists; and in so doing we have severally considered each group of animals. We must now pass on, and in due sequence must next deal with the question of their generation and development.

NOTES.

BOOK I.

(Ch. 1.) 1. A similar view of education, as embracing a knowledge of the methods of sciences, and making its possessor a competent judge of the performance of scientific professors as regards method and the degree of precision which may be expected from them in each science, is to be found in several passages (*e.g. Pol.* iii. 11; *N. Eth.* i. 1). In the former of these passages three degrees or kinds of knowledge seem to be recognised in each science. In medicine, for instance, there is the knowledge of practice, which belongs to the empiric; the knowledge of theory or method, which belongs to the man of education; and the knowledge of practice and of theory combined, which belongs to the scientific physician. Besides this distinction as to the quality of knowledge, there is further a distinction as to its extent; for it may be limited to one science or embrace them all.

2. A. employs only two formal terms of classification, species (εἶδος) and genus (γένος). Of these the former is practically defined by him (*H. A.* i. 1, 4) as "an assemblage of individuals in which not only the whole form of any one resembles in all essential points the whole form of any other, but each separate part, internal and external, similarly resembles the corresponding part in any other." This definition scarcely differs from that of Cuvier: "Chaque corps organisé, outre les qualités communes de son tissu, a une forme propre, non seulement en général et à l'extérieur, mais jusque dans le détail de la structure de chacune de ses parties" (*Regne An.* i. 14); and "tous les êtres appartenants à l'une de ces formes constituent ce que l'on appelle une espèce" (*do.* p. 16). A.'s εἶδος may then as a rule be fairly translated *species*. The other term (γένος) is used much more vaguely. It is described by him as "an assemblage of individuals, all of which bear an obvious resemblance to each other, but which do not belong to one and the same species, inasmuch as their corresponding parts are not precisely similar, but differ usually in colour, shape, or proportion. Sometimes even one has some parts that are not represented in another. Thus Birds and Fishes each form a *genus*, containing numerous species" (*H. A.* i. 1, 5—8). Again, "there are other groups of animals, in which the difference between the corresponding parts is still greater; the only resemblance being that of analogy, as between a scale and a feather; a scale being to a fish what a feather is to a bird" (*H. A.* i. 1, 9). Such groups are too wide asunder to be united into one genus (*D. P.* i. 4, 2). Putting these several passages together, we have a tolerably clear definition of genus; and, judging from the examples, it may mean any natural group of animals larger than a species and not larger than a class. The class

"Birds" for instance or the class "Fishes" is a genus, but the larger division or sub-kingdom "Sanguineous animals," *i.e.* Vertebrata, is not a genus. But in fact A. is very far from adhering strictly to this definition of genus. He uses the term in the most lax manner to express any group however large and however small. Thus we have "the genus of plants," "the genus of animals," where genus equals kingdom. "There are many genera of bees," where it is equivalent to species; and yet in another place "the genus of bees." So again "one genus of oxen has a bone in the heart," where genus answers to variety. This vague use of the term makes it impossible to translate it invariably by the same English word. I have therefore rendered it variously—genus—order—tribe—class—natural group—kind, etc., as seemed most convenient in each separate case.

3. Aristotle recognised four causes, or necessary conditions of existence; the Material, Formal, Efficient, and Final. Everything that is made is made of matter; has a definite form; is brought into being by some agency; and brought into being for a purpose (*Phys.* ii. 3). Take a statue for example. Its material cause is marble; its formal cause the shape into which that marble is fashioned; its efficient or motor cause the sculptor's art; its final cause the realisation of the artist's idea. In the text, however, A. speaks as if there were but two causes. For, as he says elsewhere (*Phys.* ii. 7, 2), the formal, efficient, and final causes are often one and the same. This is the case with living beings. The body constitutes their material cause; the soul the remaining three (*D.A.* ii. 4, 5). The soul is the formal cause; for just as the addition of the impression to wax forms the seal, or as the addition of sphericity to the metal forms the copper globe, so is it the addition of the soul to the body that forms the living organism. The soul is the efficient cause; because it is the soul which, imparted in the generative fluid of the father, effects the development of the inert matter furnished by the mother, and is the motor agent in its after activities. Lastly the soul is the final cause of the organism, for the activity of the soul is the purpose aimed at by nature in its construction (*D. P.* i. 5, 12).

4. A. divides the sciences into three groups (*Metaph.* v. 1). Firstly the *Theoretical*, which are purely intellectual and not concerned with action. In this are comprised Metaphysics, Physics, and Mathematics. Secondly the *Practical;* and thirdly the *Constructive or Artistic.* The Practical and the Artistic comprehend action as well as intelligence; but differ from each other, in that the Practical have no other result than the action itself; whereas the Constructive or Artistic, where the action is over, leave as its result a substantial product.

The contrast in the text (from which I omit the τε) is between the theoretical and the constructive sciences; and the points of contrast are as follows. The theoretical philosopher starts from certain eternal facts or verities (τὸ ὄν)—the mathematician for instance from his axioms—and proceeds to deduce from these those consequences which are linked to them by absolute necessity. The artist, on the other hand, or nature, the chief of artists, starts from an ideal conception, not yet existent in matter, but to be realised in the future (τὸ ἐσόμενον). Starting from this, he reasons backwards through the antecedent steps that are necessary, if the conception is to be realised. The realisation of my conception E, he says, requires first the realisation of D; if D is to be produced, there must previously be C; C again requires B for its production; and so farther and farther back, until he reaches a link in the chain of antecedents, let us say A, the material production of which is within his power. Here the ratiocination ceases, and construction begins. He produces A; then by means of A produces B, from B produces C, and so on, retracing his previous steps, until he reaches E, the conception of which was his starting-point, as its material realisation is his end.

5. (Cf. *D.G. et C.* ii. 9 and 10.) The following is a brief abstract of A.'s views. The only motion capable of being eternal is motion in a circle; and the only element endowed with a rotatory motion is the celestial æther (cf. ii. 1, Note 2). The heavenly bodies consist of this; and they alone are individually eternal. The Divinity, however, wishing to give the things of earth as near an approach to eternity as is compatible with their being made of other elements than æther, caused their motions to be so affected by that of the celestial bodies as to simulate rotation in the only way possible, namely by a cyclical arrangement of their serial phenomena. Not only is this manifested in the periodicity of many phenomena (*D.G.* iv. 10); but still more in the successive stages of the evolution of organisms, these stages being so arranged as to form a circle. Germ, fœtus, infant, man, and then germ again, and so on in eternal succession. Thus a simulacrum of eternity is impressed on even perishable things in the only way possible for them (*D.A.* ii. 4, 4; *D.G.* ii. 1, 3); an eternity however which differs from that of the celestial bodies, in that it does not attach to the individual but to the species. For in the cycle—germ, fœtus, man, germ—it is not the same germ, but only a similar one, in which the circle is completed. Each term in such a cycle is at once the antecedent and the consequent of all the rest. Man necessarily presupposes germ, and germ as necessarily presupposes man. Any hypothetical proposition then that states the necessary relation of any two of the terms —*e.g.* if there is to be a man there must necessarily be a germ—is capable of simple conversion —viz. if there is to be a germ there must necessarily be a man.

By the "propositions expressing hypothetical necessity and capable of simple conversion" A. means, then, all those in which two stages in the cyclical evolution of an organism are placed as antecedent and consequent. By the "cause which determines this" he may mean either the action of the heavenly bodies upon terrestrial bodies; or possibly, going a stage farther back, the purpose of the Divinity in the construction of the world.

6. The older physiologists held that the characters of an animal are determined by the physical causes that bring about its evolution, while A. holds that the characters determine the mode of evolution. The older writers therefore placed the evolution in the foreground, while A. places there the characters (cf. i. 1, Note 27).

7. Very similar to this is the explanation proposed by H. Spencer (*Biol.* ii. ch. 15), in which he attributes the segmentation of the vertebral column to the alternate pressures and tensions which would necessarily be produced by the lateral undulations of an animal with an originally uniform notochord.

8. The text is doubtless corrupt in this passage, and the exact meaning difficult to determine. So far as I can decipher it by the light of other passages (*Phys.* ii. 4—6. *Metaph.* vi. 7—9) the general drift is as follows. The teleological position—this is made as intelligent design *would* have made it, and therefore *was* made by such—would clearly be untenable, could it be shown that a similar object was undoubtedly at times produced simply as the result of accident or chance. Now Aristotle admits that such is sometimes the case, and gives the restoration of health as an example.

How is this difficulty to be met? In the first place, says Aristotle, such an occurrence is quite exceptional. No chance could possibly produce a statue, or, to take Paley's instance, a watch. All those results of art, that are produced from a purely inert material, a material that is without any capacity for self-motion (οἷα κινεῖσθαι ὑφ' αὑτῆι), are quite beyond the power of chance. It is only in the case of such bodies as possess certain inherent motor possibilities that chance can do the work of art. We may suppose for instance a mechanical automaton, so constructed that on touching a spring and starting the action, a series of connected motions shall ensue, leading to some prearranged result. Now chance could never make such an automaton as this; but when such has been made by art, we can readily understand how chance might occasionally touch the spring, and the series of motions ensue with their fixed result: ὅταν ἀρχὴ γένηται κινήσεως, ὥσπερ ἐν τοῖς αὐτομάτοις θαύμασι, συνείρεται τὸ ἐφεξῆς (D. G. ii. 5, 9). Now in every living organism analogous sequences of concatenated motions are present; established either by nature or by habit (De Mem. 2, 16), which is but a second nature, in order to ensure certain desirable ends. Such for instance is the sequence of phenomena which constitute the evolution of an organism from the germ (D.G. ii. 5, 9). This series of consecutive motions can only be set going by fecundation. This and this alone possesses the key of the mechanism. Another sequence is that by which the organism is maintained in a state of health; a sequence of which the final terms are health, uniform bodily condition (ὁμαλότης), heat. Each link in this chain must be in constant activity, if the final effect—health—is to be constantly maintained. Should the chain be interrupted, by any cause whatsoever, at any point, the further dependent motions cease; health vanishes, and disease, which is no more than privation of health, makes its appearance. In such a case what is wanted to restore health is that the series of movements that terminate in it shall be again set going. To do this it will be enough to reproduce any one of the antecedent links; for they are all indissolubly connected with each other. The man of art then, i.e. the physician, hunts about for a link in the chain which may be within his range of action. Health, he says, is dependent on uniformity of bodily condition, this again upon due warmth; but heat can be produced by friction of the body. Here, then, he has come to a link over which he has power. He applies friction, and heat, uniformity, health, follow. Art, then, in such a case restores health by using the machinery of nature, and using it moreover with the intention of producing nature's result. But pure accident can plainly set the same sequence in motion, acting blindly and without any intention whatsoever. By pure accident the ailing body may be subjected to friction, and the whole chain of consequents will result as before, and health be restored. The difference is that the physician acted with definite intention, accident without such. The presence or absence however of intention in the immediate agent is a matter of no importance. Both art and accident make use of machinery constructed by nature with intention; nor could they have brought about the result without so doing. In all cases alike then there was intention, though not in all cases intention on the part of the immediate agent. In all cases alike then it is true that the process of production occurred for the sake of the thing produced.

9. A. uses the term Spontaneity in two senses. In a limited sense, as opposed to Chance; and in a wider sense as including both of these (Phys. ii. 4—6). The different ultimate forms of matter are endowed with different inherent properties. When such different kinds of matter are jumbled together indiscriminately, and not so arranged, as in nature's works, as to make their activities converge to one predesigned end, the interaction of their conflicting properties will habitually result in incoordinate random motions, quite beyond human calculation. Such motions are accidental, or spontaneous in its wider sense.

Sometimes however such accidental motions produce results, such as intelligence or nature would have produced, and produce them by the same steps. In such a case accident is either called chance, or is called spontaneity in its limited sense. It is called chance when the accidental agent is an intelligent being acting with intention, though not with the intention of producing the result which actually occurs. It is called spontaneity when the accidental agent has no intention at all. No inanimate thing therefore, no beast, no child, can possibly be the agent of chance, for they are incapable of intention, though they are often the ágents of spontaneity.

Aristotle's *Spontaneity* does not then imply the absence of external agency, but merely the absence of intention in the agent, and would perhaps be more fitly represented, were such permissible, by the word chance; while Aristotle's *Chance*, which implies an agent acting with a certain intention, though not the intention of producing the result that actually occurs, would find a better though still inadequate representative in our word luck. It is this intermixture of semi-intention that gives force to the line

τύχη τέχνην ἔστερξε καὶ τέχνη τύχην.

10. Empedocles attributed the development and destruction of all bodies to the action of two alternate forces, Friendship and Enmity, upon the particles of the four ultimate elements; while Anaxagoras attributed the phenomena to Intelligence or νοῦς (cf. *Metaph.* i. 3—4, and *Grote's Plato*, i. ch. 1).

11. Compare H. Spencer's account of the formation of the vessels (*Pr. of Biol.* § 300).

12. "If asked what is the material cause of any object, we must state what are the proximate and special substances, not what are the ultimate substances such as fire or earth" (*Metaph.* vii. 4, 5). As to homogeneous and heterogeneous parts, cf. ii. 1, Note 5.

13. "Works of art are said to be made by the artist's tools; but it is truer to say that they are made by the motion of these tools, supplied and directed by art. Just in the same way the growth of a plant or animal is said to be due to heat and cold; but it is only due to them in the sense that these are the instruments of which the nutritive soul makes use in its operations" (*D. G.* ii. 4, 43).

14. In rendering ψυχή *soul* I have adhered to common usage, though *Soul* is far from being an equivalent term. But I know of no term that is. *Vital principle* has been proposed and includes much of A.'s conception which *Soul* omits; but on the other hand it omits as much as at *Soul* includes. For ψυχή is the principle to which are due all the phenomena of life, from the highest intellectual process down to the growth of a microscopic fungus. The former is excluded by *Vital Principle*, the latter by *Soul*, which has moreover the further inadequacy that a religious element enters into the ordinary conception of it. The following abridged passage (*D. A.* ii. 2—3) will serve to give A.'s idea pretty fairly. "The faculties of the soul are many; but, though all living things have a soul, all the psychical faculties are not present in every soul. In the soul of some living things only one faculty is present, in that of others several, and in others again all. The faculties are the Nutritive, the Sensory, the Appetitive, the Locomotor, the Intellectual. In the soul of plants the Nutritive faculty alone is present; in the soul of animals not only this but the Sensory, or at least the Tactile, faculty and with this as a necessary consequence the Appetitive. This is the case in all animals; but only in some of them is there in addition the Locomotor faculty. The number is still smaller in whose soul there is yet further the Intellectual faculty, as in man, and in any other being, if such there be, that equals or even surpasses him in honour." The soul then is the principle of vitality; and each main mode in which vitality manifests itself, that is each main group of functions, is ascribed to a different faculty of this soul.

How is this soul engendered in the body? asks A. (*D. G.* ii. 3). Is it derived from the mother? or from the father? or from neither, but from without? The mother furnishes the material for the formation of the body. But the unfecundated germ never ripens into maturity. It never acquires a sensory faculty; never, that is, develops into an animal. Still it is capable of growth up to a certain point, as the wind-eggs of birds testify, so that some share in the nutritive faculty must be allowed to come from the mother (*D. G.* ii. 5, 3). Such an egg then, if regarded as the conception of a plant, is perfect; but, if regarded as the conception of an animal, is imperfect (*D. G.* iii. 7, 8). The other faculties than the nutritive only appear in the fecundated germ. They are imparted, then, to the germ in the fertilising fluid of the male parent. But how does this fecundating fluid come to possess them? Does it get them from the male organism, from which it issues itself, or from some external source? As regards the Sensory, the Motor, and all other faculties than the Intellectual, they must necessarily come from the father; for they are inseparable from bodily matter, there being no such thing as Sensation and Motion without sensory and motor organs, and the matter of the fecundating fluid is evidently all derived from the father's body. But as regards the higher faculty, or Intellect, the case is otherwise. This requires no bodily substance in which to be incorporate. It exists independently of tangible matter; and so may, and in fact does, come into the fecundating fluid not from the father's body but from without, viz. from the divine soul of the Cosmos. Thus the mother furnishes the material of the body and, in some degree at least, the Nutritive faculty. The father contributes the Sensory and the Motor faculties. While the Intellect comes from the soul of the Cosmos, and is only transmitted by the father intermediately.

15. Cf. Note 3.

16. The Soul is the source of vital motion, and the several psychical modes correspond, though not always as the active source, to the several modes of motion. Of these there are three (*Phys.* v. 2, 8). Firstly motion leading to change of bulk, *i.e.* growth and decay (αὔξησις and φθίσις); with this is associated the Nutritive and Genetic faculty, as the active cause. Secondly motion with change of quality (ἀλλοίωσις), of which sensation is a form (*D. A.* ii. 4, 8); with this is associated the Sensory faculty, no longer however as the active source, but as the passive recipient of the motion which starts from the objects of sense. Thirdly motion with change of place (φορά); with this is associated the Motor faculty of the soul, here again not passive but active.

17. Cf. *Metaph.* v. 1, 7. "The natural philosopher has to deal with the soul, so far as it is inseparably united with matter," *i.e.* with all the soul, excepting the active intellect, which is independent of the body and separable from it (*D. G.* ii. 3, 10; *D. A.* ii. 2, 10). The consideration of this element of the soul belongs to "the first philosophy" or metaphysics. It is, I presume, of the separable intellect that A. speaks, when he compares the relation of soul and body to that of rower and boat (*D.A.* ii. 1, 12); and of the inseparable faculties, when he takes for his simile the relation of vision to the eye, or of the impression to wax (*D. A.* ii. 1, 7—9).

18. The argument seems to be as follows: "Moreover that part of the soul which is independent of matter cannot come within the province of natural science; for this deals only with the works of nature, and these are not abstractions but actual bodies, concretions of form and matter, for by such alone can the ends of nature, viz. the activities of life, be fulfilled. [Natural Science then is concerned with that soul only which is incorporate in matter.] For that there is such a soul, or nature, informing the body, and that to it, and not to blind chance, are due the evolution and activities of organisms, is shown by the constancy of the phenomena they present and by the fact that the result of their evolutional processes is predictable with certainty."

19. Both art and nature are concerned with concrete bodies in which form and matter are combined; but in the case of art the form is impressed on the matter from without,

while in the natural object the moulding principle is within; for the soul or principle of life informs the body not as an external independent force, but as an indwelling inseparable influence. It is comparable, not to a physician acting upon another person, but to a physician curing himself (*Phys.* ii. 8, 15). As to hot and cold, cf. ii. 1, Note 3.

20. Compare this with the poetical account of the creation in the Timæus. The secondary Gods are there represented as borrowing portions of the body of the Cosmos to form the bodies of men and animals; while the Demiurgus gives the surplus of what had formed the cosmical soul to form their intellectual soul.

21. The question whether the Heavens were or were not generated is discussed elsewhere and answered in the negative (*De Cælo*, i. 10, ii. 1).

22. Cf. *Phys.* ii. 4 for a similar passage.

23. Potentiality and Actuality are discussed in the Metaphysics (viii. 6—8). The distinction between them, says A., will be better set forth by giving examples than definitions. What, then, an animal awake is to an animal asleep; what an animal gazing is to an animal with its eyes shut; what the perfected work is to the raw material; what the wrought is to the unwrought, that is Actuality to Potentiality; the relation being sometimes that of a body in motion to the same body at rest, sometimes that of form to matter. In the order of thought Actuality is anterior to Potentiality; for we cannot understand nor define the Potential without first understanding and defining the Actual. That which is "able to build" or that which is "capable of sight" presupposes for its comprehension and definition that which does build and that which does see. In order of time or material existence Actuality is in one sense posterior to Potentiality, in another anterior to it. It is posterior, if we only regard the individual; for before an individual man can actually exist in matter, the potential germ must exist, that is to give rise to him. It is however anterior, if we regard not the individual but the species; for before the germ, that is the Potential, came into being, there must have been an actual man, similar to though not identical with the man that is to be produced, to give origin to the germ.

24. As A. has fully explained what he means by Hypothetical Necessity only a few pages back, it is strange that he should now deal with it again in terms that seem to imply that he is stating something quite new. Very possibly the whole of this long paragraph is an interpolation.

25. Elsewhere (*Metaph.* iv. 5) A. speaks of three kinds of necessity, Absolute necessity, Necessity of coercion, as when a weaker agent is constrained by a stronger one, and Hypothetical necessity. There is also another passage (*Phys.* ii. 9) in which he deals with necessity, and distinguishes, as in the text, two kinds, Absolute and Hypothetical. Plainly, however, it can be to neither of these passages that he is now referring. The passage wherever it is, or was, must have been one in which the two modes of necessity distinguished from each other were Absolute and Coercive necessity. It may perhaps have been contained in the lost dialogue on Philosophy; concerning which see *Heitz, Die verlor. Schrift. d. Arist.* 179.

26. "The natural philosopher must deal with both causes; and more especially with the final cause. For this is the cause of the material, and not the material the cause of it" (*Phys.* ii. 9, 5). So also Plato (*Jowett's Tr.* ii. 540, 541); "Now the lover of intellect and knowledge ought to explore causes of intelligent nature first of all; and secondly those which are moved of others and of necessity move others. And this is what we also must do. Both kinds of causes should be considered by us, but a separation should be made of those which are endowed with mind, and are the workers of things fair and good, and those which are deprived of intelligence and accomplish

their several works by chance and without order. . . . . Creation is mixed, and is the result of an union of necessity and mind."

27. "For, as was said on an earlier occasion, each thing made by nature has certain fixed and definite characters; and these it has not because it is developed with them, but rather it is developed with them because it has them; for the essence precedes and determines the development, not the development the essence. Physiologists of old held a contrary view. For they did not perceive how many causes there are; but recognised only the material and the motor causes, and even these confusedly, while the formal and the final cause entirely escaped their notice" (*D. G.* v. 1, 5).

28. As to Aristotle's notions of the mechanism and use of respiration, cf. iii. 6, Notes 3, 6.

(Ch. 2.) 1. Alluding to Plato's method of dividing downwards until by successive bifurcations the infima species is at last reached. Examples of this method, *abscissio infiniti*, will be found in the Sophistes and Politicus. These are apparently the "published dichotomies" of which A. speaks; and it is to them that his criticisms in this and the two next chapters have immediate reference. The great interest of these chapters to the biologist lies in the evidence they give that the idea of natural classification had occurred to Aristotle, their whole drift indeed being to uphold the claims of natural as opposed to artificial systems.

2. Not a well-chosen example. For Cloven-footed does not necessarily imply Two-footed, as many quadrupeds have free toes. But A. is probably thinking only of Birds, which he subdivides into Web-footed and Cloven-footed; using the latter term as it is used in the following passage: "Great variety of water-fowl, both whole and cloven-footed, frequent the waters" (*Ray on Creation*).

3. By the water-animals with many feet are meant the Cephalopoda and certain Annelida confounded by A. with Myriapoda. Cf. iv. 5, Note 70.

(Ch. 3.) 1. What we call the wing of an insect, A. called the feather, which he distinguished from the feather of a bird by its being undivided into barbs (iv. 6, Note 6).

2. The argument is this. If we start with such a dichotomy as A and $Not\ A$, there must be subdivisions of each of these. Let us say B and C are the subdivisions of A, while D and E are the subdivisions of $Not\ A$. A then is a differentia common to B and C, but though common to them it applies really to each in a different manner. $Not\ A$ is a differentia common to D and E, and as there are no possible diversities of $Not\ A$, it belongs to D and to E in exactly the same sense. In other words the groups D and E have a common undifferentiated element, something therefore which cannot be part of their essence.

3. The wild dogs of India were supposed by A. to be a cross between the Dog and the Tiger. Cf. *H. A.* viii. 28, 14; *D. G.* ii. 7, 9.

4. The following appear to be the chief rules recognised by A. in the classification of animals.

α. The groups must be formed by consideration of the sum of the characters, not by a single character arbitrarily selected.

β. Those characters are the most important which have guided mankind in general in forming groups, to each of which they have given a popular name: in other words the external characters.

γ. There are however natural groups, which are founded on other characters, and which have been confounded popularly with alien groups owing to their external similarity, e.g. Cetacea.

δ. When the individuals in a group are precisely alike in all their parts, the group is a species (i. 1, Note 2). A number of species may resemble each other in all their parts excepting in matters of degree; such species together constitute a larger natural group (γένος), still as a rule with a popular name. Some species, however, as man, stand isolated, and cannot be so combined with other species (see next chapter).

ε. These larger natural groups, and these isolated species, may be arranged in still larger groups. But the basis of such arrangement will be merely analogy or distant resemblances of the parts, not identity with differences of degree. And such groups will have no popular names (see next chapter).

ζ. The natural groups may be arranged in a linear series according to the degree of animality they possess; the series extending from those animals which most nearly resemble plants to those which, as man, are most remote from them. Cf. iv. 10, Note 12.

(Ch. 4.) 1. The similarity is in the media in which the two live, the fish in the liquid water, the bird in the liquid air. So in the Sophistes (*Jowett's Transl.* ii. 479) we read: "Of swimming animals one class live on the wing and another in the water." The close resemblance of flight to natation is shown in the fact that there are both birds and insects that use their wings for swimming, while on the other hand there are fishes that can support themselves for a short time in the air.

(Ch. 5.) 1. This passage seems to imply that A. had, in some degree at any rate, studied the flesh, bones, and vessels, of the human body. But it does not necessarily imply that he had dissected them. For his observation may have been limited to such parts as were exposed in operations by the surgeon's knife, or in wounds received accidentally or in battle. When in fact we remember how excessively strong was the religious feeling of the Greeks as to the sanctity of the human body, and when we also see how ignorant A. was of its internal anatomy, an ignorance he fully admits (*H. A.* i. 16, 1), and which is betrayed in numerous statements, we may feel certain that his scalpel had never touched a human subject, or at any rate an adult one. For I am by no means so certain that A. may not have sought to gratify his curiosity by dissection of the human fœtus. In the first place it is quite easy to conceive that the religious feeling which peremptorily forbad all meddling with the body of the adult may have disregarded the aborted embryo; and in fact there is some reason to believe (*Cuvier, Hist. d. Sc. Nat.* i. 39) that in the time of Galen, when the religious obstacle was as strong as in the time of Aristotle, some such distinction between the sanctity of adult and fœtus was actually recognised. Secondly, such a supposition would explain several difficulties. Thus A. says that the heart is visible in the *aborted* embryo while it is still quite small (*D. P.* iii. 4, 2). He does not actually say in the *human* abortion; but, seeing that he was able to procure the embryos of other animals without waiting for the occasional accident of abortion, and in fact did procure them (*D. G.* iv, 1, 10; v. 1, 12), it is most natural to suppose that it is of the human embryo that he is speaking. Again he says that the human kidney is lobulated, like that of the ox; and this is true of the fœtus, not of the adult. Again he says that the heart in man lies diagonally, with the point inclined to the left, and the right ventricle above the rest (iii. 4, Note 17). It is difficult to see how he can have known this without inspection. That in man there is often, though not invariably, no gall-bladder, is, again, a statement which we can understand, if founded on examination of embryos. For the gall-bladder is not developed till the liver is already so large as almost to fill the abdomen. If, again, the description of the heart and vessels (iii. 4, Note 23) be intended for those parts in man, as would seem to follow from the statement that the right ventricle is uppermost, then this description can only have been got by examination of the fœtus, for it includes, as I believe, the ductus arteriosus. The brain, again, in an aborted fœtus would almost certainly be found in a diffluent condition; and thus would be explained the statement (ii. 7, Note 4) that the human brain is more fluid than that of any other animal.

BOOK II.

(**Ch. 1.**) 1. That is, the treatise which by a mistranslation of its title is usually known as the Natural History of Animals; a mistranslation to which our popular term "natural history" is due. The ordinary title is so sanctioned by use, that I have elsewhere occasionally retained it.

2. It will be noticed that A. says "such as air earth fire and water," implying apparently that there are more elements than these. In fact he held that there was a fifth, the *quintessence* of later writers; this fifth however, the æther, not entering into the composition of strictly terrestrial objects, but forming the sole substance of the heavenly bodies. To this belief he was led by his views as to motion. He held that all visible motion could be reduced on analysis to three elements, (1) motion round the centre, or circular motion; (2) rectilinear motion from the centre towards the periphery, or upwards; (3) rectilinear motion from the periphery towards the centre, or downwards. Now there is no such thing as motion without a moving body. There must therefore be elementary bodies corresponding to these elementary motions. To the motion upwards fire and, in a lesser degree, air correspond; to the motion downwards earth and, in a lesser degree, water. There is apparently nothing left to correspond to circular motion, which is yet the most perfect motion of all, seeing that a circle is a perfect line, which a straight line is not. "From this it is evident that there is in nature some essence of body besides the elements which we have here, more divine than these and superior to them. For it is absurd to suppose that motion in a circle can possibly be an unnatural motion, seeing that everything which is unnatural quickly perishes, whereas this motion, alone of all, is continuous and eternal. So that from all this we infer with perfect confidence, that besides the elements which we have here and about us there is another removed far off, and the more excellent in proportion to its distance from the things of earth" (*De Cælo*, i. 2; iii. 3, 5).

3. The so-called elements, says A. elsewhere (*D. G. et C.* ii. 2–3–5), are not simple bodies but compounds, being produced by combinations of the primary forces or active properties of matter. Tangible objects differ from each other in endless ways, as regards colour, taste, smell, etc. (*Meteor.* iv. 10); but they are all either fluid or solid, and all either hot or cold. Everything tangible presents two of these properties; it is either solid or fluid, and either hot or cold. There are then four main elementary properties, and each object possesses two of them. Now among four things there may be six combinations of two and two (συζεύξεις); but the pairing of two directly opposite properties, as of cold and hot, causes them both to disappear; for they neutralise each other. Thus only four combinations remain, and these correspond to the four apparently simple bodies, fire, air, water, earth; solid and hot forming fire; hot and fluid forming air, for air corresponds to vapour; fluid and cold forming water; cold and solid forming earth.

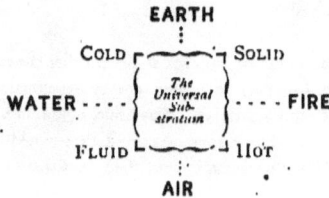

It is evident then why A. holds it more accurate to say composition from the elementary forces rather than from the elements, the former being the components of the latter. It is plain also that when he says "nor out of all of them," he means to exclude all other properties excepting the four main ones, two of which belong to every tangible object. From these four primary properties, he says, all others are derived, and in contrast to them may be called secondary. As to the mode in which the secondary properties are deducible from the primary ones, cf. *D. G. et C.* ii. 2.

It will be noticed that A. uses the adjectival forms, hot, cold, solid, fluid, and not the substantives, heat, fluidity, etc. For he is speaking not of abstract properties, but concrete substances. His views (*D. G. et C.* ii. 1) were as follows. There is one ultimate matter, which forms the universal substratum of all terrestrial things. This matter however has no existence in a condition of isolation, but is invariably combined with some or other of the primary properties, heat, fluidity, etc. Thus we have fluid matter, hot matter, solid matter, cold matter; but there is no such thing as simple matter by itself, any more than there is such a thing as fluidity by itself. By hot, cold, solid, fluid, A. means then the universal substratum in a state of heat, coldness, solidity, or fluidity.

Even hot matter, solid matter, etc., are however not forthcoming as actual existing bodies; for matter, as already explained, is always combined with more than one of the four primary properties. The simplest producible substances would therefore be those formed by matter in combination with two properties, that is the elementary substances, earth, air, fire, water. But even these are not actually forthcoming in absolute purity; for the substances we know as earth, air, water, fire, are not the pure elements themselves, but compounds of all four, in which one element so preponderates as to give its general character and name to the whole. (See next note.)

It is usual to render ὑγρόν and ξηρόν as wet and dry, and not, as I have rendered them, fluid and solid. But A. can never have supposed wetness to be one of the primary properties of matter. The definitions, moreover, given by him (*D.G. et C.* ii. 2) are conclusive. "Wet (διερόν) is that which has extraneous liquid on its surface; Soaked (βεβρεγμένον) is that which has it in its substance. Fluid (ὑγρόν) is that which has no form of its own, but readily accepts one. Solid (ξηρόν) is that which has a distinct form of its own, and resists the imposition of a fresh one."

We know, at the present day, that the physical condition of a substance is distinct from its chemical composition; a substance may be hot or cold, solid, fluid, or gaseous, while all the time its deeper-lying chemical composition remains unchanged. But A. knew of no such distinction. Physical and chemical qualities were to him one and the same thing; substances differed from each other in their composition, because of the different proportions in which the fundamental physical properties were intermixed to constitute them. Water, for instance, in its ordinary fluid condition, consisted of cold matter and fluid matter. When such water became vapour, it changed not merely its physical condition but its composition, hot matter being added to the former constituents; and similarly its composition was altered by another addition when it became ice.

4. By compound substances A. means all substances made by combinations of the elements. "Some substances are simple, others compounds of these. By simple substances I mean those that have natural motions, such as fire, earth, and the like, and their several forms" (*De Cælo*, i. 2, 4). In one sense indeed even the elements are compound (see last note); but it is of compounds out of the elements that A. is here speaking. Every such compound, that is every actually existing substance, contains, says

A. (*D. G. et C.* ii. 8, 1), some proportion of every one of the four elementary substances. The differences between substances depended therefore not on differences in the elements, of which they were made, but on differences in the ever-varying proportions in which these were combined to form them.

A. distinguished clearly enough between chemical combination and mere mixture. In the former, he says (*D. G. et C.* i. 10), the combining substances disappear with their properties, and a new substance with new properties arises from their unification. In the latter the mixed substances remain with all their properties, and it is merely the imperfection of our vision which prevents us from seeing the particles of each lying side by side and separate. Had we the eyes of Lynceus we should do so, however intimate the mixture might be. But though A. thus distinguished chemical combination from mechanical mixture, he had no notion of preferential affinities, nor of course of combination in definite proportions. The elementary bodies combined with each other with perfect indifference, and in any chance proportions. There was thus no such thing as definite composition, and consequently no such thing as definite properties in substances. One piece of matter might resemble another more or less, but that it should be identical with it in composition and therefore in properties was, in the infinity of possibilities, so improbable as to be out of the question.

The compound substances then are formed by combinations of the four elementary substances, and this is A.'s first degree of composition; the study of which has developed, as Frantzius remarks, into modern Chemistry. From these compounds the homogeneous parts or tissues are formed. This is the second degree of composition, and its study corresponds to our Histology. Lastly from the tissues are formed the heterogeneous parts or organs, which are dealt with by Descriptive Anatomy. It is strange that A. should not allude here to the higher grade of composition, namely the formation of the whole body from the organs. Presumably he omits it, as being a stage not reached by all organisms. Cf. ii. 1, Note 8.

5. The division of the parts into Homogeneous and Heterogeneous, which A. puts forward so prominently in this book, corresponds to the more modern division into Tissues and Organs; the main difference being that A. includes among his homogeneous parts not only the tissues but even the secretions. It was the revival of A.'s doctrine in a more perfect form that first made the name of Bichat illustrious.

The heterogeneous parts or organs are formed from the homogeneous parts or tissues. From what are the tissues formed? A. said, directly from the compound substances. Modern histologists as a rule say from cells, fibres and the like, which they interpose between the tissue and its constituent chemical substances. A. knew of nothing answering to these "morphological units," the tissue being to him the last term in the structural analysis. In fact before the microscope was invented the existence of the cell could not be suspected. Theophrastus however, the pupil of A., seems to have tried to resolve the tissue into simpler elements, though still more complex ones than its physical or, as we should now say, its chemical constituents. "Other parts there are," he says, speaking of the organs of plants, "from which these are formed, such as bark, pith, wood, all of which are homogeneous. There are parts again anterior even to these, and from which these are made. Such are juice, fibre, vessel, flesh. These are the primary constituents; there being nothing anterior to them, unless one reckons in the elementary properties of matter, which are the common basis of all substances" (*Hist. Plant.* i. 2).

6. The fact that, with similar material to select from, man generates man and plant plant, shows that it is not the material that determines the process, but the process that determines the material.

7. The final cause must exist in conception before the structures which are made with a view to it. The whole organism therefore exists ideally before the organs, and these again before the tissues, and these latter before their physical constituents. But actually or materially the order is reversed. The physical constituents are the first to be produced; then from these are generated the tissues, and lastly from these the organs. And similar sequences, ideal and actual, occur in the development of other than animal bodies, in plants for instance, in works of art, etc. If, therefore, we have before us the order of genesis, that is of actual evolution, we have merely to invert it to get the order of final causes. The fact, then, that the tissues are evolved after their component substances shows that the latter exist for the sake of the former, and the fact that the organs are evolved after the tissues shows that the tissues are for the sake of the organs.

8. The first degree of composition was that of the compound substances; the second that of the tissues; the third that of the organs. The evolution, then, of an individual organ has reached its final term when this third stage is attained. But in an animal or a plant, as a rule, there is yet a fourth degree of composition. For the entire organism is made up of a multiplicity of organs. This, however, is not the case with all organisms. The simpler kinds (Aristotle would probably have instanced the Sponge, the Actinia, the Medusa and, among plants, Lichens and Fungi) present no such distinction of parts, as allows us to say that they are made up of organs. They are constructed not of organs, but directly out of tissues. Their evolution, therefore, as that of a single organ, ends with the third degree of composition. They are aggregates of the third not of the fourth degree.

9. Having distinguished the homogeneous parts or tissues from the heterogeneous parts or organs, A. proceeds to enquire why these latter are made out of the former, and ascribes it partly to necessity, partly to a final cause. In the first place no other arrangement is possible. The heterogeneous can only result from a combination of homogeneous parts; while the homogeneous cannot possibly be constructed from the heterogeneous. Secondly, an organ is often used for several distinct offices; and therefore requires distinct properties. But its properties are those of the tissues which compose it, and therefore it requires to be made of several tissues, seeing that each tissue has but one main property. A. apparently confuses the properties of an organ with its functions. The *properties* of an organ are doubtless the resultant of the properties of its component tissues; but the *functions* of an organ depend on more than this, namely on the relations and structural connections of the organ as a whole with other parts. The properties of a muscle, for instance, are doubtless the resultant of the properties of the various tissues that enter into the composition of a muscle. The chief of these being muscular tissue, and the main property of this being contractility, the main property of the whole muscle is contractility; and this property attaches to it whatever be its situation. But the function of the muscle is to produce a certain definite motion of some part of the body, and for this are required not merely the property of contractility but certain definite attachments to the bones or other parts that are to be moved.

10. A. had not the slightest suspicion of the contractility of muscle or, as he called it, flesh; the main purpose of this substance being in his opinion to serve as a medium for the sense of touch (cf. ii. 8, Note 2; ii. 10, Note 10). Still less therefore could he have any notion that a limb is flexed or extended, accordingly as this or that part of the fleshy mass about it contracts. He therefore apparently attributes extension and flexion to the presence in the limb of different properties, one extensibility, the other flexibility; these properties being derived by the part, each from a different tissue. But he does not attempt to state what these tissues may be.

11. It was a disputed question whether the passive agent must be similar or dissimilar to the active agent; the former being the opinion of Democritus, the latter the general view. Aristotle says both opinions are partly true, partly false. "The active and the passive agents cannot be absolutely similar; for if so each object would move itself, and everything would be in perpetual motion. Neither can they be utterly dissimilar. For how can two such essentially distinct things as whiteness and a line affect each other? Whiteness indeed and a coloured line can affect each other; but this is in virtue of their generical resemblance, both having colour. So also a savour cannot affect a colour, nor a colour a savour; but one savour affects another savour, one colour another colour. The result then is that the passive and the active agents are generically one, but specifically distinct" (*D. G. et C.* i. 7).

12. The ancients agreed in assigning each separate sense to a separate element, but differed from each other in their distribution, some, as Plato, coupling vision with fire, others, as Democritus, with water. "It is plain that we must attach each one of the sense-organs to one of the elements. The optical part of the eye we must take to be of water. The part of the ear which is sensitive to sound we must take to be of air. Smell we must take to be of fire; for a smell is a kind of smokelike ascent of vapour, and such comes from fire. The organ which is sensitive to touch we must take to be of earth, and taste is but a variety of touch" (*De Sensu*, 2, 18).

From the passage paraphrased in the last note it appears that A. held that nothing could be set in motion excepting by a motor agent homogeneous with itself. Now in sensation "the object of sense sets the medium in motion, and then the motion of the medium is communicated to the sense organ" (*D. A.* ii. 7). In order then for this communication to be possible the medium and the sense organ must be homogeneous with each other. "The medium of sound is clearly air; the ear then must be of this element. The eye must be of water, because to water animals the medium of sight is water, and though to land animals air is the medium, it is so not in its character of air, but in its character of transparent substance. The organ of touch, which lies in or close to the heart, must be of earth, because the flesh which is earthy is the medium of touch (ii. 8, Note 2), and taste goes with touch, being only a variety of it (ii. 10, Note 22). The organ of smell must be of fire," partly because this is the only remaining element, and also "because the medium of smell seems to be of fire, a smell being a kind of smoke-like exhalation which occurs in a fiery medium" (*De Sensu*, 2). There is plainly in the above a difficulty as regards eye and vision. The element air has already been assigned to the ear, and the hypothesis requires each sense organ to be coupled with a distinct element. It is necessary therefore to say the eye is of water, although air is the usual medium of sight; and doubtless the presence of so much fluid in the eye, and the case of water animals, seemed to corroborate this view. But clearly the explanation that air acts as well as water not in its character of element but of transparent substance is inconsistent with the original hypothesis.

The foregoing will serve to show what the ancients meant in connecting each sense with a separate element. But it seems at least doubtful whether A. himself held this doctrine. In the text he speaks only of others holding it, not of himself. It is true the passage quoted above from the De Sensu expressly adopts the doctrine. But there are strong grounds for believing that passage to have been interpolated; seeing that in it smell is said to be "a smokelike exhalation from fire," while very shortly afterwards in the same treatise A. says that this view is held by some but is an error, which he proceeds to refute. His own opinion as to the media, so far as can be gathered from the scanty data forthcoming, seems to have been as follows. Air and water form the medium for sight sound and smell alike, but not in virtue of the same qualities. In sight it is the Transparent (διαφανές) which is effectual. In smell it is a nameless something, which like the Transparent is common to both elements. And similarly there is another nameless something in them both which serves as the medium of sound. These nameless qualities were afterwards called the Trans-olent (δίοσμον) and Trans-sonant (διηχές). Cf. *Torstrik's notes to De Animâ*, ii. 7. Of these several hypothetical media, the sole survivor is the luminiferous æther of modern physicists.

13. "Each sense seems to recognise but one pair of contraries. Vision, for instance, recognizes white and black ; hearing, treble and bass ; taste, bitter and sweet ; (smell ?). But in the tangible object there are many contraries, hot and cold, solid and fluid, hard and soft, and other such oppositions" (*D. A.* ii. 11). This leads A. to enquire whether there may not be several different senses included under touch, and confounded together because they have a common medium, viz. the flesh, which hides from sight their really distinct sense organs, which are placed internally, somewhere in the neighbourhood of the heart. To this question, however, he gives no decided answer. Many modern physiologists hold, as at least probable, that tactile impressions, impressions of pain, and impressions of temperature, though usually referred in common to touch, have in reality their own distinct organs, central and peripheral.

14. And therefore, he intends to imply, the least simple. As to the flesh, cf. ii. 10, Note 10 ; ii. 8, Note 2.

15. Cf. *De Ju. et Sen.* 1.

16. What A. means is this. "Most organs are constructed out of several homogeneous parts or tissues ; but some, as the heart, of only one. Yet in such a case the organ may be considered one of the heterogeneous parts, in virtue of its definite shape." Thus a cartilage or a horn is made of one tissue, cartilaginous or horny tissue, and yet is an organ as much as if it were made of several tissues, because it has a definite shape and size, which suit it to its function. The difference is the same as between silver and a half-crown. The latter has a definite size and form, which makes it equivalent to an organ ; the former is simply material, into the conception of which neither size nor form in any way enter, and answers to the tissue. The one is ἐσχηματισμένον, the other ἀσχημάτιστον.

In short A. divides the parts into three classes, as follows :

α. Parts purely homogeneous, *i.e.* tissues.

β. Parts purely heterogeneous, *i.e.* compound organs.

γ. Parts homogeneous in substance, but heterogeneous as having a definite shape, *i.e.* simple organs.

In the last of these classes A. includes the heart, which he erroneously supposes to be made of a single tissue ; and says it is capable of being the sensory centre in virtue of its homogeneous substance, and capable of being the motor centre in virtue of its heterogeneous form.

17. The heart is excepted, because A. thought that it was formed earlier than the blood, which is true if by blood be meant a red fluid. As to the other viscera, cf. iii. 8, Note 2.

18. A. often (*e.g.* iii. 4 ; *H. A.* iii. 3, 8) contrasts the heart with the other viscera in respect to the relation they severally bear to the vessels. The heart, he says, is like an expanded portion of the vessels, in which the blood is stored as in a reservoir or lake (so Dante, "*nel lago del cor*"); while in the vessels the blood forms a stream. Moreover in the heart no vessel breaks up into branches,' whereas in the other viscera this is invariably the case, the vessel sometimes disappearing in the substance of the viscus, as in the kidney (*D. P.* iii. 9, 5), at other times, as in the liver, passing through. It would

thus appear that A. entirely overlooked the coronary vessels, and so imagined, as stated here, that the nutrition of the heart was effected directly by the blood in its cavities.

(**Ch. 2.**) 1. That fat is fluid, while in the living body, is often stated even in modern books. But the statement would seem to be inaccurate, except in the case of fishes and amphibia (*Todd's Cycl.* i. 58; ii. 232). The heat of the body in man, and in mammalia generally, only suffices to keep the fat in a softish condition.

Why does A. call flesh a fluid? Probably because he thought flesh was a form of blood (iii. 5, Note 7), and so attributed to it the fluidity and coagulability of the latter; which view would have derived support from what he cannot but have noticed, namely the rigidity of the muscles after death. As to the bile, see ii. 3, Note 2; as to serum, ii. 4, Note 6.

2. Cf. ii. 6, Note 6; and, as to sinew, iii. 4, Note 20.

3. The distinction is the same as in last chapter (Note 16), viz. into parts purely homogeneous, *i.e.* tissues, and parts homogeneous in substance but possessed of definite shape. Of the former a piece is synonymous with the whole; for a bit of horny tissue is still horny tissue, a bit of cartilage is still cartilage. Of the latter a bit is not synonymous with the whole; a bit of a heart is not called a heart; because it has not got the size or shape which enters into the conception of a heart. In this respect, then, the latter resembles the compound organs, such as the face, hand, etc.

So far A.'s meaning is clear. But he has chosen so bad an example, in blood-vessel, as to disguise his meaning. For he has carelessly made blood-vessel an instance of the first class of parts, the tissues; whereas it should have been classed by him with simple organs (ἰσχηματισμένα not ἀσχημάτιστα), for the tubular shape is essential to its conception; and it is quite possible to cut a vessel into bits which will no longer be called vessels, if only the bits be such as are no longer tubular.

4. "The food of all animals is mainly fluid; and, even when it is not so originally, it becomes fluid by the excretion of the solid portion" (*D. G.* i. 18, 62).

5. "Bees have a divine element in them, which wasps have not" (*D. G.* iii. 10, 27); that is they have an intelligent soul, incorporate in pure æther. It is to this that Virgil's lines refer:

"His quidem signis, atque hæc exempla secuti,
Esse apibus partem divinæ mentis et haustus
Ætherios dixere."—*Georg.* iv. 219.

Elsewhere A. gives a less flattering account of their intellect, in a passage which may be thus paraphrased: "All animals have sensations; but only some have memory of these. Such are Bees. These therefore have images of the past to guide their life. But, as they cannot hear, their experience is but personal and scanty, for they can neither learn nor teach others; whereas in man the faculty of speech aggregates the memories of many into one common experience, which is the foundation of his art and science. Intermediate to man and bees are those animals that can hear, and that, though speechless, can in some measure communicate with each other by sounds" (*Metaph.* i. 1).

6. A. held, as also did Plato (*Jowett's Transl.* ii. 538), that the right was in nature superior to the left, the upper to the lower, the front to the back. He also held that " Nature, when no more important purpose stands in the way, places the more honourable part in the more honourable position " (iii. 4, 6). This dogma he uses as an axiom beyond dispute, and has recourse to it on numerous occasions in explanation of the relative positions of organs and other phenomena. The stomach, for instance, is placed where it is and not nearer the mouth because otherwise it would be above the heart, a nobler organ than itself (iv. 10, Note 5). Man's nobility is shown by his upper part

being turned towards the upper part of the universe (ii. 10, 5). The front of man is chosen in preference to the back, for the growth of hair (ii. 14, 3). The nictitating membrane comes from the canthus in front, rather than the canthus on the side (ii. 13, 7). The heart, being the noblest part, is in front and in the upper half of the body (iii. 4, 6), and so on.

It is almost entirely as a deduction from this mischievous dogma that he infers that the blood of the upper parts and of the right side is hotter than, or in some way or other superior to, that of the lower parts and left side. I say "almost entirely," because even here A. doubtless thought that his *a priori* statement was confirmed by some actually observed facts. Thus he saw the vena cava and the aorta running side by side down the trunk of the body, both containing blood. The vena cava he noticed was larger than the aorta and lay in its general course on the right of the latter; he also noticed that the blood in the two differed in aspect (iii. 4, Note 24), as also did that of the right and left ventricles. He supposed that the vena cava nourished the right side of the body, on which it was placed, and the aorta the left side. Hence his statement that the blood of the two sides differed in quantity and quality. He found, again, in some animals the blood of the head of a brighter hue than that of the rest of the body (ii. 7, Note 12). Here was evidence of the superiority of the upper parts to the lower. Another observation can hardly have failed to have been made by him, and to have confirmed his previous opinion. When a limb is much exercised, not only is the general temperature of the body raised, but that of the limb itself rises higher than that of the unused parts. The right arm, being the one used preferentially by most men in any action requiring great muscular force, is often so much hotter than the left that the difference is readily perceptible to the touch without any instruments. This may easily have led A. to believe that the blood of the right side was hotter than that of the left, as his previous observations had led him to believe it was more abundant. Still it is not to be denied, that the statement was in the main *a priori*; and that it had, as such dogmas invariably have, the mischievous effect of blinding its acceptor's eyes to facts palpably inconsistent with it.

7. No greater differences that is than occur within the range of a genus (cf. i. 1, Note 2).

8. This was the opinion of Empedocles; it is discussed at length in *De Resp.* 14. The coldness of water-animals is at any rate in part due to the rapid loss of heat to which they are subjected by aquatic life; and thus their temperature often rises when they are taken out of the water and kept in the air, where the conduction is much less rapid. This was observed by Spallanzani to be the case with many fishes, and more recently by Valentin with Aplysiæ.

9. Cf. ii. 7, Note 19. The question whether the catamenia are an indication of greater heat in the female is discussed in *De Gen.* iv. 1, and answered in the negative.

10. A. has left special treatises on Sleeping and Waking, Youth and Old Age, Life and Death; but the treatise on Health and Disease, if ever written, is lost. His general views however, as may be gathered from the first section of the Problemata, were as follows. The characteristics of a living body are that it is hot and contains fluid matter; of the dead body that it is cold and without fluid. The coldness is perceptible to the touch, and the want of fluid to the eye; for not only do the fluids coagulate, but the whole body turns to dust. The heat and moisture of the body are at their maximum in youth. For there is a constant exhalation of fluid and heat going on during life, so that the body gradually becomes colder and its fluid less abundant. The older therefore the body, the more easily is its heat extinguished by any chance cause

of refrigeration, just as a small fire is more easily extinguished than a large one. In other words disease, which consists in an abnormal increase or decrease of the bodily heat and moisture, is the more dangerous the older the body is. Should no disease intervene, the bodily heat and moisture grow less and less by gradual exhalation, until at last they are expended; but so gradual is the process that the departure of the soul occurs imperceptibly and without pain.

11. *D. G. et C.* ii. 2 and 3; cf. ii. 1, Note 3.

12. It is a matter of familiar observation that degrees of heat and cold which affect some persons agreeably are distressing to others; and in disease one sometimes finds a striking contrast in this respect even between different parts of the same person. Thus I once had a patient who presented the following curious phenomenon. A moderately hot substance applied to his right foot caused an agreeable sensation of warmth; but the application of the same to the left foot made him yell, and he said that the sensation he experienced was not of heat but of simple pain.

13. Olive oil can scarcely be meant, as Frantzius supposes; for it coagulates some seven degrees above the freezing-point of water. Ἔλαιον is often used generally for any oil, as (*H. A.* vii. 3, 2) for oil of cedar. Possibly A. is here speaking of fish-oil, with which he was (*H. A.* iii. 17, 3) well acquainted, and which remains fluid at a temperature considerably below the freezing-point of water.

14. Because in A.'s opinion it derives its heat from the heart, or from the celestial heat which has its main seat in the heart.

15. The more obvious phenomena of heat and cold can be explained equally well either by supposing both of these to be actual existences with opposite characters, or by supposing one of them to be merely the absence or privation of the other. Which of these two views was the right one was the subject of early and often-renewed dispute. Plutarch (*De primo frigido*) discusses the question and answers it in the same sense as Aristotle. In stating however the opposite opinion Plutarch incidentally touches on what would I fancy be given by modern physicists as the reason for holding cold to be no more than privation of heat. "Is there," he asks, in beginning his treatise, "such a thing actually existing as cold? or is cold nothing more than privation of heat, as darkness is privation of light and immobility privation of motion? *For in fact cold appears to be quiescent, and heat to be a source of motion.*" (ἐπεὶ καὶ τὸ ψυχρὸν ἔοικε στάσιμον εἶναι, κινητικὸν δὲ τὸ θερμόν).

16. "Limus ut hic durescit, et hæc ut cera liquescit,
Uno eodemque igne."—*Virgil.*

17. Cf. ii. 4, Note 10.

18. Had A. possessed the thermometer or similar instrument he would have seen that in some of his instances the difference is only one of degree. That boiling water for instance acts differently from red-hot iron, because its temperature is enormously inferior. It is worth noticing how well A. has here escaped the popular error, according to which, in all bodies which are ordinarily designated by a common adjective, there must be one common elementary property corresponding to this common title. From this tyranny of an adjective, as Whewell calls it, even Bacon was not free. Among his "instantiæ convenientes in naturam calidi" we find nasturtium which is hot to the tongue, acids which hotly burn the skin, fur and other hot coverings, spirits of wine which, as hot bodies, coagulate white of egg, and so on; the mere verbal link serving to bind together most diverse phenomena.

(Ch. 3.) 1. The external influence is the heat of the heart, to which A. attributes that of the blood (cf. ii. 2, Note 14).

Notes. ii. 3.

2. Bile obtained from the gall-bladder is usually very viscid, owing to the admixture of mucus, derived from the walls of that receptacle, with the slightly alkaline fluid. When this viscid bile is left to stand, the mucus rapidly decomposes, and the fluid becomes acid. This disappearance of the mucus restores to the bile the greater degree of fluidity, which it had before entering the gall-bladder.

3. The opinion that digestion is due to heat appears to have originated with Hippocrates, and was adopted by A. and also by Galen. Digestion according to this view was a process of cooking (see however ii. 6, Note 7), and in Greek the same word ($\pi\acute{\epsilon}\psi\iota\varsigma$) stands for both cooking and digestion. Our words "dyspepsia" and "pepsine" are records of the old belief, which was prevalent for ages after A.'s time, the action of the heat being still called "concoction." The various opinions as to the cause of digestion are thus enumerated by Celsus : "Duce, alii, Erasistrato atteri cibum in ventre contendunt; alii, Pleistonico Praxagoræ discipulo, putrescere; alii credunt Hippocrati, per calorem cibos concoqui; acceduntque Asclepiadis æmuli qui omnia ista vana et supervacua proponunt; nihil enim concoqui, sed crudam materiam, sicut assumpta est, in corpus omne diduci." Although we have now learnt that digestion is due to the action of gastric and other juices, yet it is no less certain that heat is not without considerable influence on the process. A temperature of from 100° to 96° F. is in fact necessary in order to keep up the chemical process, and each successive fall below this standard produces successive retardations of the action; which is completely suspended when the ordinary atmospheric temperature is reached. On the other hand a rise of temperature to about 140° F. causes a decomposition of the gastric juice, and entirely destroys its power.

4. A. looked on the heart as the main but not the exclusive seat of vital heat. "The whole body and all its parts have a certain innate natural heat. But in sanguineous animals the main seat of this heat must be the heart. For, though the other parts by their natural heat can effect the concoction of the food, yet chief and foremost in this office is the heart. The rest of the body then may become cold, and yet life continue; but should the heart cease to be hot, all life is at an end; for no longer does there remain a source whence the rest of the body may derive heat" (*De Juv. et Sen.* 4, 3).

5. A. knew nothing of the salivary glands, or of their action upon starch. He therefore limits the part played by the mouth to mastication, which he truly says is not actually a digestive process, though essential for easy digestion.

6. The upper cavity is of course the stomach. By the lower is meant the large intestine, or rather its cæcal enlargement (cf. iii. 14, Note 35). This is sometimes, as here, spoken of by A. as a seat of digestion, that is as a second stomach, and sometimes merely as a receptacle of residual matter, as though all digestion were over before this part was reached. We may fairly suppose that A. in the different passages is speaking of different animals; for while the cæcum in some animals, as in the horse, really acts as a second stomach, in others, as in man, its contents are almost entirely fœcal.

7. The same simile occurs in the Timæus (*Jowett's Tr.* ii. 564).

8. One term ($\pi\epsilon\rho\acute{\iota}\tau\tau\omega\mu\alpha$) served A. to express several things, viz. (1) The indigestible residue of food, *i.e.* the excreta. This is often distinguished as the "useless residuum" (ii. 10, 2; *D. G.* i. 18, 2). (2) Such part of the food as, though nutritious, is not consumed for the direct benefit of the individual, but for that of the species, as milk, semen, and generally the generative secretions (iv. 10, 47). (3) The parts of the blood which remain after the nobler organs have been supplied, and which are used for the inferior parts, such as sinews, bones, etc. (iii. 5, Note 5). (4) Such inferior parts themselves, *e.g.* hairs (ii. 15, Note 4). (5) Such surplus materials as are not used

immediately, but are stored up in the body, as fat (*D. G.* i. 18, 59). It is in the first sense that plants are said to have no excrement; in the second that seeds are sometimes (iv. 10, 17) regarded as representing the residual matter.

9. A. means sponges. There are numerous microscopical animals capable of active locomotion, and yet without intestinal cavities; but such were of course unknown to Aristotle.

10. The comparison occurs again in iv. 4, 4. Elsewhere A. compares the roots of plants to the mouth of an animal, "being the channel by which they take food from the ground" (*De Juv. et Sen.* 1, 7), and yet again (*D. G.* ii. 7, 1) to the vessels of the umbilical cord.

11. Cf. iii. 5, Note 5. A. knew nothing of the lacteals. But not long after his time, Erasistratus, his pupil, opening a sucking kid (cf. *Galen, An Sanguis in art.* ch. 5), saw many small white vessels in the mesentery. He noticed that these did not, like the blood-vessels, pass to the liver, and also that they were in connection with certain glandular bodies, the mesenteric glands. He supposed rightly enough that the contents of these white vessels were derived from the milk swallowed by the kid; that is he recognised their absorbent character. But Galen (*De Usu part.* iv. 19) held that their office was to nourish the intestines. Erasistratus's observation seems to have led to no further result, and to have been quite forgotten. Thus the discovery had to be made again nearly 2000 years later (A.D. 1622) by Aselli of Cremona.

12. *H. A.* i. 16, iii. 4.

13. The argument is as follows. The entire food, digestible or not, has a receptacle, viz. the stomach; and the indigestible part of it also has a receptacle, viz. the lower abdominal cavity or large gut; the digestible portion must therefore also have a receptacle, inasmuch as it is separated from the indigestible part. But there is no other receptacle than the blood-vessels; which must therefore be the receptacle of the nutritious portion. And as these blood-vessels are seen to contain nothing but blood, the blood and the nutritious matter must be one and the same thing.

14. After a meal the amount of blood is even as much as doubled according to Bernard (*Leçons*, 1859, i. 419).

15. The argument is to the following effect. Neither is the entire food sensitive; nor the excremental part of the food; nor yet the nutritious part of it, even after it has been converted into blood. It is only when the blood has been farther converted into flesh, that it becomes sensitive. Up to that time it is insensible; for though it is in immediate contact with the flesh, yet it has therewith no anatomical continuity whatsoever.

16. A. often refers to a treatise which he was going to write on Nutrition. It has been generally supposed that the De Generatione, in which nutrition is handled to a certain extent, is the treatise thus promised. But this view seems incompatible with the fact that a similar reference to a future treatise "on growth and nutrition" is made in the De Generatione itself (v. 4, 4), in a passage which appears to have been overlooked. The present passage moreover speaks of "other writings" besides the De Generatione. The promised treatise is not extant; perhaps was never written; for no mention of such is to be found in Diogenes Laertius. Heitz (*Die verlor. Schrift. d. Arist.* 61) thinks it probable that a short separate treatise was written, such as those massed together in the Parva Naturalia; and that some portions of it have come down to us merged in the De Generatione. And there is in fact in the De Somno (3, 4) a passage which apparently refers to a treatise on Nutrition as already written.

(**Ch. 4.**) 1. The coagulation of the blood is considered in two other passages (*H. A.* iii. 6; iii. 19). In all of these places A. speaks distinctly of the coagulum as being formed of fibrous matter; thus anticipating the discovery usually said to have been made by Malpighi (cf. *M. Edwards, Leçons*, i. 115). What A. did not discover and what Malpighi did, was that by washing the coagulum the red colour could be discharged, and the fibres shown to be white.

That A. paid much attention to the coagulation of the blood is plain. It will be seen that several of his remarks on the proportion of coagulum and serum in different animals harmonize with modern observations. Elsewhere, moreover, he notices (*Meteor*, iv. 7, 11) that the blood in certain diseased conditions will not coagulate. This is known to be the case in cholera, certain fevers, asphyxia, etc. This fact was probably got from Hippocrates, who bled largely.

2. Elsewhere (*H. A.* iii. 6, 2), besides the deer and roe, the bubalis (antelope) and hare are mentioned as having blood that does not coagulate so fully as that of other animals. All these are animals that are hunted; and it is well known that John Hunter, finding the blood fluid, or only slightly thickened, in two deer that had been hunted to death (*Hunter's Works*, i. 239), formed the opinion that the blood under such circumstances completely loses its power of coagulation. Mr. Gulliver (*Hewson's Works*, p. 25) shows by instances that this is not the case; coagulation sometimes at any rate occurring, though imperfectly. We may fairly suppose that the animals examined by A. had been hunted to death; and though he speaks in this passage of an entire absence of coagulation, in the *Hist. An.* he admits an imperfect degree of it. "In the blood of most animals there are fibres; but none in that of deer, roes, antelopes and some others; so that their blood does not coagulate similarly to that of other animals. The blood of deer however coagulates in about the same measure as that of hares. In both of these coagulation occurs, but the coagulum is not firm as in other animals, but flabby, like the clot in milk when no rennet is used. The blood of the antelope coagulates rather more completely, indeed only a little less fully than that of sheep." In the last clause of this paragraph I followed the MS. in my College library which omits ψυχρόν.

3. Cf. ii. 2, Note 5.

4. Fear and a "blood-frozen heart" have been everlastingly coupled together by writers of all ages. See *Hamlet*, i. 4; *Faery Queen*, i. ix. 25; *Virgil, Æn.* 3, 40, etc. The notion is of course founded on the fact that many of the external signs of fear, as pallor, shivering, erection of hair, are identical with the signs of intense cold. There is an apparent confusion in the passage in the text as to which is cause, and which effect; fear being first said to chill the blood, and then chilled blood to lead to fear. The contradiction is only on the surface. In every emotion, says A. (*D. A.* i. 1), there are two factors, one bodily the other psychical. These two factors are so closely associated with each other, that, when either is in any way evoked, it immediately evokes its fellow, and the emotion is complete. Thus the psychical factor of fear, if excited, will determine the bodily factor, viz. chilling of the blood, etc.; while chilled blood, however produced, will similarly give rise to the psychical factor. Each factor that is may be either cause or consequent of the other.

5. The bloodless animals that remain motionless when frightened are beetles, moths, etc. (iv. 6, Note 8); but the same phenomenon is really observable in some sanguineous animals, *e.g.* in the landrail (*Yarrell's Birds*, iii. 95). Those that discharge their excreta are various insects and cuttle-fishes. Here again however examples can be found among sanguineous animals; snakes for instance (*White's Selborne*, xxv.), hedgehogs, the aurochs as described by Aristotle (iii. 2, 5), and many other animals

(iv. 5, Note 20). Those that change colour are the cephalopods (iv. 5, Note 15); but the sanguineous chamæleon does so as well (iv. 11, Note 28).

6. Though from some of A.'s language it might be supposed that he looked on the whole blood as being fluid while in the living body, and so anticipated Borelli, this passage shows that he really considered the fibrine to exist in the solid form even during life; as also did Plato (*Jowett's Tr.* ii. 578).

7. The hot vapour-bath to which A. alludes was made by getting under an air-tight cloth and throwing aromatic substances upon hot embers. Cf. *Herodot.* iv. 75.

8. Elsewhere (*H. A.* iii. 19; 6) the ass is instanced as well as the bull. Bovine animals (but still more swine and horses) have a larger proportion of fibrine in their blood than man (*Andral, Ann. du Chimie*, 1842, p. 306); and from such scanty observations as exist it would seem that the blood of bulls is richer in fibrine than that of cows or oxen (*ibid.* p. 307). Thackrah seems to have arrived at much the same general conclusion as Aristotle. "Although my experiments are far from evincing a disparity uniform in its reference to the classes of animals, yet it appears probable that a more complete examination would prove *the crassamentum to bear a proportion to the strength and ferocity of the animal*, since I never found the serum in such quantity as in the timid sheep, nor the crassamentum so abundant as in the predatory dog" (*On the Blood*, 1834, p. 154).

That abundant fibrine goes with strength and ferocity appears to be a popularly accepted notion.

"Come you spirits
That tend on mortal thoughts, unsex me here
And fill me from the crown to the toe, top-full
Of direst cruelty! Make thick my blood."—*Macbeth*, i. 5.

9. I cannot find any exact observations as to the period of coagulation of bull's blood. It differs in composition from that of the ox (see last note) and may therefore differ from it in this point also. The blood of an ox, however, commenced coagulating, in Thackrah's experiments, on an average in 6 minutes; the minimum being 2 and the maximum 10; whereas that of the sheep, hog, and rabbit commenced in from ½ to 2 minutes; that of a duck in from 1 to 2 minutes; and that of a mouse, according to Haller, "in a moment." Thackrah says (*On the Blood*, p. 154) that "from my observations the general inference may be drawn that coagulation commences sooner in small and weak animals than in large and strong." This seems in contradiction with A.'s statement.

10. Cf. *Meteor.* iv. ch. 6, 7, 8, where A. discusses at length the questions of coagulation, liquefaction, etc. "Compounds of earth and water," he says, "such, for instance, as blood, in order that they may retain their fluid condition, require a certain amount of water and a certain amount of heat. They can therefore be solidified either by excessive heat or by cold. By heat because it directly causes evaporation of the water. By cold because in the first place it expels the heat, and secondly because the heat in passing off carries with it much of the water in the shape of vapour. Blood when withdrawn from the warm body and exposed to the cold air coagulates owing to the second cause."

11. A. considers the fibrine, or rather the clot, *i.e.* the fibrine with the corpuscles, to be the part of the blood which is ready to serve for nutrition. Besides this, he says, there are in the serum materials derived from the food which after concoction will be converted into this nutritious form (so also *H. A.* iii. 19, 9—12), and others again which are derived from the waste of the body. This accords with the view of those who hold that

Notes. ii. 4—5.

fibrine is a higher elaboration of the albumen of the serum, necessary before this can be put to use; and with the undoubted fact that the blood is not only the channel for nutriment, but also the channel by which such waste as arises from decay is carried off to the excretory organs. That "the necessary process" means the waste of the body caused by its own activity is shown by *De Somno* (3, 10): "Toil produces wasting ; and the product of this waste, unless it be cold, is similar to unconcocted nutriment."

(**Ch. 5.**) 1. A. calls the softer kinds of fat Lard, the harder kinds Suet. This answers to the division of later writers into Pinguedo and Sevum. J. Hunter made four divisions, Oil, Lard, Tallow, Spermaceti, also taking consistency as the basis of distinction.

2. We have here an example of the manner in which the ancient philosophers judged of the composition of a substance. They simply inferred it from a comparison of the superficial qualities with those of the four elements. Oil is shining ; so is fire. Oil is more or less transparent; so is air. Oil then contains fire and air. There was no attempt to reduce bodies to their supposed constituents by actual analysis. "The supposed analysis was, in short," says Whewell, "a decomposition of the body into adjectives not into substances."

3. This is an error. In caterpillars, for instance, there is abundance of fat. A. himself later on (iv. 5, 30) speaks of the Echini as having something like fat, mistaking the nature of their ovaries. He would say, however, that these substances are not true fat, but only something analogous to fat (*D. G.* i. 19, 18), just as he says that the ex-sanguineous animals have no true blood, but only something analogous to blood.

4. The coagulation of broth is due to gelatine and not to fibrine. These substances, however, were of course not distinguished by Aristotle. This may perhaps account in part for his supposing that the fluidity of the blood was due to heat, and its coagulation, when withdrawn from the body, to cold ; for gelatine is thus affected by heat and cold.

5. Cf. iv. 10, Note 44.

6. The fat of Ruminants and Rodents is harder than that of man ; the fat of Carnivora and Pachyderms softer. A.'s statement is therefore correct, excepting as regards the Rodents, which he did not distinguish from the Carnivora. Though he makes no mention of Pachyderms in this place, elsewhere (*H. A.* iii. 17, 1) he correctly says that the horse and the hog have soft fat.

7. Cf. ii. 3, Note 15 ; ii. 10, Note 10.

8. Cf. *Thackrah*, "*On the Blood*," p. 131 : "The state of the general system as to Fatness or Leanness seems to affect the quantity and character of the blood. Fat animals have I believe considerably less blood in proportion to their weight than lean ones ; and in the fat human subject venesection shows the veins to be comparatively small, and the quantity of blood, even when two or three vessels are opened, is less than flows from one vein of a lean person, etc." So also Hippocrates (*Aph.* i. 44) : "Those who are naturally very fat are likely to die earlier than those who are slender ;" which Galen explains by saying that fat men have smaller vessels than lean ones, and so are less plentifully supplied with vital spirit (πνεῦμα). Cf. *Celsus*, ii. 1 ; *Hippocr. Kühn's ed.* iii. 434.

9. Cf. *D. G.* i. 18, 59. That over-fat animals are bad breeders is known to every farmer. So also it is well known that castrated animals grow fat. These and similar facts led Bichat (*Anat. Gén.* i. 55) to express an opinion much the same as that of Aristotle. "On dirait qu'il y a un rapport constant et rigoureux entre la secrétion de la semence et l'exhalation de la graisse ; que ces deux fluides sont en raison inverse l'un de l'autre."

(Ch. 6.) 1. Alluding to Plato, who expresses this view in the Timæus (*Jowett's Transl.* ii. 571).

2. "The bones of the fœtus are void of a distinct medullary canal, and present merely a reddish homogeneous vascular pulp, somewhat consistent but presenting soft portions. This state continues for some time after birth" (*Todd's Cyclop. Anat.* i. 60). So also *Virchow's Cellularpath.* 369.

3. In the fœtus and infant there is less pigment in the body generally than in the adult. The skin, hair, eyes (*D. G.* v. 1, 16), and olfactory region, are all lighter-coloured than in later life. I have tried to show elsewhere (*Med. Chir. Trans.* 1870) that this development of pigment after birth coincides with, and is a necessary condition of, an increased sensory acuteness.

4. That the spinal cord is the marrow of the vertebræ is an error, the memory of which is still preserved in the popular term "spinal marrow." Although A. observed that the cord was in substance quite unlike any other marrow, having indeed no other resemblances to this substance, than its position in a bone cavity and its light colour, and though he knew that it was directly continuous with the brain, which latter he knew was not marrow (see next chapter), yet he held fast to the popular notion, because his theory required the cord to be made of some hot substance, such as he took fat to be. The uses assigned by A. to the spinal cord were, firstly, the mechanical office of holding the vertebræ together, and, secondly, that of tempering the heat of the brain.

5. Cf. *H. A.* iii. 7, 9 : "Some animals, the lion for instance, appear to have no marrow in their bones, because the marrow is excessively small and only present in a few of the bones, as in those of the thighs and fore-legs." Whether the lion (iv. 10, Note 6) has or has not smaller medullary cavities than weaker animals, I cannot say; but it would appear to have bones of more than ordinary density. For the per-centage of hard matter in its bones is 72·3, that of man 68·9, of the ox 69, of the porpoise 64·1 (*Owen's Verteb.* i. 20). So hard are the lion's bones, says Aristotle (ii. 9 ; *H. A.* iii. 7, 9), that they give out sparks when struck.

6. A. distinguishes the substance of which fish-bones are made from that which composes ordinary bone. The difference consists in there being a much smaller amount of heavy inorganic matter in the former than in the latter. It may fairly be supposed that this is of use to the fish by diminishing the specific gravity of its body; and it is in harmony with this view that the proportion of inorganic matter is much higher in the bones of sea-fishes than of such as live in fresh water, the former swimming in a denser medium. The porpoise, though a mammal, has bones in this respect like those of a sea-fish (*Owen's Verteb.* i. 20); and as A. in this place speaks not merely of fishes, but of aquatic animals generally, we might suppose him to mean to include this animal, were it not that elsewhere (ii. 9, 11, and *H. A.* iii. 7, 9) he expressly says, as others had said before him (*Herod.* iv. 53), that the dolphin has true bones, and not fish-spines.

7. This passage is of importance ; for it indicates the answer to the obvious objection, that many of the phenomena attributed by A. to heat are manifestly not so producible. For, in using the term "self-concoction," A. means to draw a distinction between ordinary heat, and the heat of the blood or body. Mere cooking with fire of course does not convert blood into fat, nor digest food, nor the like. But the heat of the body, as the heat of the sun, says A. (*D. G.* ii. 3, 13), is something very different from this. It has a vivifying influence, which simple fire has not, and produces effects far beyond the power of this element. Cf. *Introd.* p. xxiii.

8. No fish has a medullary canal in its bones, though there are some, as the trout, in

which the bony tissue is more or less penetrated by an oily fluid (*Todd's Cyclop.* iii. 958). The same is true of the bones of Cetacea and of seals (*Cuvier, Anat. Comp.* i. 110).

9. Cf. iii. 4, Note 20.

(**Ch. 7.**)   1. As Plato in the Timæus (*Jowett's Transl.* ii. 567).

2. Cf. ii. 5, Note 2.

3. "In its proper substance" as opposed to the vascular membranes that surround it. As to the supposed bloodlessness and coldness of the brain, cf. ii. 10, Note 18.

4. A. uses the term fluid with much latitude. Thus he calls the fæces fluid. This however might be defended, as they sometimes are so, especially in bovine animals. Here he calls the brain fluid, and Galen also calls it "almost fluid." It is true A. says it is the most consistent of all the animal fluids, and also (*D. G.* ii. 6, 35) that it is only actually fluid in the very young, and afterwards gradually becomes more consolidated. But even with these limitations the term gives an exaggerated idea of the softness of the part. Probably A. thought the brain was more fluid during life than after death, reckoning it, with fat and marrow, among the substances which are fluid only so long as they are in the living body (ii. 2, Note 1). It may be objected to this that A. had at any rate seen the brain of the chamæleon during the animal's life (*H. A.* ii. 7), and that he must have known that this was not fluid but solid. But it must be remembered that according to A.'s views the colder the nature of an animal the less fluid should its brain be; for in his opinion it is on the fluidity of the brain that its coldness depends, and this must be proportioned to the animal's heat, which it has to temper. But the chamæleon is cold-blooded; so that the firmness of its brain would be only what A. would expect, and would in no wise lead him to look for like firmness in the brain of a warm-blooded animal.

It will be noticed that the human brain is said to be more fluid than that of any other animal. This is not the case. Doubtless A. had never seen an adult human brain. But I think it not unlikely (i. 5, Note 1) that he may have examined the brain of an aborted fœtus, in which case he would most probably have found the brain diffluent, and that his statement was founded on this.

5. This fact may have been learnt from Hippocrates, or some other surgeon who had exposed the brain in an operation, and noticed its apparent insensibility to mechanical irritation. Or it may have been noticed by A. himself in his vivisection of the chamæleon (*H. A.* ii. 11). Very possibly it may have been an observation made on that same occasion that led him to the hasty generalization that the brain was always cold.

6. I take the meaning to be as follows: "The excrements have of course no anatomical connection with the body, but are isolated substances. The brain, though not an excremental substance, yet so far resembles one that it also is without anatomical connection with the rest of the body, excepting as already stated with the spinal marrow. In this it differs from the other organs, none of which is ever isolated. Thus (ii. 9, 1) every bone is connected with others so as to form an osseous system, and similarly every blood-vessel is connected with the rest so as to form a vascular system. But the brain is isolated. For it is not true as some say that it is anatomically connected with the organs of sense, so as to form with them a sensory system." As to the continuity of brain with sense-organs, cf. ii. 10, Note 9.

7. Democritus (*D. A.* 1, 2).

8. And therefore causing it to be cold; for both earth and water are compounds of cold matter, the former with solid, the latter with fluid matter (cf. ii. 1, Note 3).

9. Elsewhere (*H. A.* i. 16, 2), A. speaks of Cephalopods in general, and not only of the poulp, as having a brain. The cephalic ganglia in these animals are so large

as to rival the brains of vertebrates in size and importance. Thus A., who had made a special study of Cephalopods, could not help seeing their ganglia, whereas those of other invertebrates are so small that, with his want of instruments, it is no wonder they should have escaped his notice.

10. Cf. iii. 4, Note 24.

11. *i.e.* the *pia mater*. A. (*H. A.* i. 16) describes the brain as having two membranes, an outer and stronger one next to the bone (*dura mater*), and an inner one in contact with the brain itself (*pia mater*). This latter is the vascular one, so often mentioned by Aristotle. This membrane consists in great part of a plexus of extremely numerous and very minute vessels, as A. says. The same statement is to be found in *De Somno*, 3, 26: "The small size and narrowness of the vessels on the brain assists in producing refrigeration and in preventing the easy access of the ascending vapour of nutriment." The real use of the peculiar and extreme subdivision of the arteries before they are distributed to the brain seems to be to make the blood-pressure and blood-supply as uniform and equable as possible in all parts of this sensitive organ.

12. Not only in the fœtal mammal, but in the adult batrachian and reptile there are special contrivances by which the head is supplied with purer blood than goes to the rest of the body. The anatomical arrangements by which this is brought about were of course quite unknown to A.; but it is not improbable that he may have noticed the different colour of the blood going to the head and of that going elsewhere, in his vivisections of the tortoise (*De Resp.* 17, 4) and of the chamœleon (*H. A.* ii. 11): What was true of some animals, he supposed to be true of all, because the conclusion chimed in with his *à priori* views (cf. ii. 2, Note 6).

13. The same comparison is to be found in *De Somno*, ch. 3.

14. "As to the causes of health and of disease, these are matters which come not only into the province of the physician, but also to a certain extent into that of the natural philosopher. The two however regard the subject from different points of view, as must not be forgotten. Still it is plain enough that there is no very broad line of demarcation between them. For such physicians, as are boastful and officious, are given to talk of the phenomena of nature, and profess to derive from natural philosophy their principles of practice; while the most accomplished among the natural philosophers rarely fail eventually to touch on the principles of the art of healing" (*De Long. et Br. Vita*, 2). As to the question whether the promised treatise on the Principles of Disease was ever written, see *Heitz, Die verlor. Schrift. d. Arist.* p. 58.

15. A similar account of sleep is given in the special treatise *De Somno*. A. argues that as the main feature of sleep is the abeyance of all the senses, sleep must clearly be due to some condition of the sensorium commune, *i.e.* the heart; and as sleep is notably consequent on a heavy meal, on severe exercise, and the like, it must be due to some effect producible by such influences on the heart. After a meal the dissolved food passes into the blood-vessels, as also after severe exercise does the waste matter resulting from such exercise, and ascends through them in form of vapour. When this reaches the head, it is condensed by the cold brain and falls back to the heart as a cold fluid, consisting after a meal of the coarse and fine elements of the food, and after exercise of coarse matter only. It is this accumulation of cold, coarse, thick fluid in the sensorium commune that suspends its activity. After a time this fluid undergoes concoction, and then the sensorium is relieved and wakens into activity. What happens in sleep, says A., happens also in an epileptic attack, so that sleep is a kind of epilepsy; and in confirmation of this view he cites the perfectly accurate facts, that the night is the most usual time for these fits, and that in most cases the earliest attacks occur during sleep. It is

easy to ridicule A.'s view, and ridicule has not been spared. But to me A.'s theory, erroneous as it was, seems an honest and ingenious attempt to colligate hypothetically and in a presentable form such facts and supposed facts as were known to him or accepted by him. We now know that the brain and not the heart is the sensorium commune; allowing for this fundamental error the view of A. agrees with the modern views, in attributing sleep to an alteration, quantitative and qualitative, in the blood-supply of the sensorium, and in finding a similarity between sleep and epilepsy. A. held that the amount of blood in the sensorium was increased, and until quite recently, when Mr. Durham and others showed by actual inspection that this was not so, but that in reality there was diminished vascularity, physiologists as a rule were of the same opinion. A. thought the qualitative change was due to additional impurity, modern conjecture points to exhausted oxygen. As regards the relation of sleep to epilepsy, "nous pouvons même dire," says Brown Séquard, "que chez beaucoup de personnes non épileptiques le sommeil ressemble à une légère attaque d'épilepsie" (*Leçons sur les nerfs vasomoteurs*, p. 121).

16. Cf. Note 8.

17. Cf. ii. 4, Note 10; ii. 10, Note 18.

18. That man's brain is heavier than that of other animals in proportion to his weight is true with very few exceptions, which are furnished by certain species of small birds, monkeys, and rodents, whose body is lean and therefore light (*Cuvier, An. Comp.* ii. 419). Leuret gives the following general results; in fishes the brain is to body as 1 to 5668; in reptiles as 1 to 1321, in birds as 1 to 212, in mammals as 1 to 186. But in man the brain forms from $\frac{1}{40}$ to $\frac{1}{30}$ of the whole weight.

Whether man or woman has the larger brain in proportion to the body is a question not satisfactorily settled; for observers have arrived at different results. Thus Dr. Peacock in one set of observations (*Monthly Journ. Med. Sc.* vii. 1847) found the encephalon in women in the proportion to the body of 1 : 33·5; that of man 1 : 37·2; that is he found the female brain the heavier in proportion to the whole weight. In another set however (*Path. Tr.* xii.) he found the proportions 1 : 32·73 in the male, and 1 : 39 in the female. The actual weight of the brain of women is, on an average, about 5 ounces less than that of men.

19. The slight differences of temperature between one warm-blooded animal and another cannot be estimated by touch; and as A. had no thermometer his statements in the text are but guesses, and unlucky guesses. (See however ii. 6, Note 7, and Introd. p. xxiii.). For all or most birds, and not a few mammals, are hotter than man. Neither again is man hotter than woman: the differences in this respect being apparently independent of sex; or the balance being in favour of woman. Thus in a long series of observations made by me on a man and woman, the temperature of the latter was notably higher than that of the former (*Diurnal variations of the temperature of the human body in health, St. George's Hospital Reports*, i.). Wunderlich also concludes from such insufficient observations as exist that the temperature in adult women is slightly higher than that of man (*Eigenwärme*, etc. 2nd ed. p. 104).

The reasons why A. considers the male to be hotter than the female are set forth in *De Gen.* iv. 1, 27.

20. The meaning is: heat promotes growth; and as heat mounts upwards from its source, *i.e.* the heart, growth will be promoted in the upward direction in preference to any other. Cf. iv. 10, Note 11. That heat mounts upwards is of course A.'s mode of viewing such facts as the ascent of hot air, and the upward pointing of flame, etc. Cf. ii. 1, Note 2.

21. Elsewhere (*H. A.* iii. 7) A. says there are six bones in the skull. Of these (*H.A.* i. 7) the anterior is the Bregma, which alone covers the brain and is, on this account, the last to ossify. By this he clearly means the anterior fontenelle, which he considers to be a separate bone. The posterior bone, covering the empty space, he calls Inium; clearly meaning the Occipital. Two others are placed above the ears, and are smaller than the rest. By these he doubtless means the Temporals. The other two he does not describe; but they can be nothing else than the Parietals. The Frontal (πρόσωπον) A. reckons as a bone of the face.

22. This is the case with the superior races of man; such as alone would have fallen under A.'s observation. In them the posterior sutures close before the anterior, and both close late. But in the inferior races, according to Gratiolet, the anterior close before the posterior, and both close early (*Soc. Anthropol.* 1861, p. 180).

23. The erroneous notion that the use of the sutures is to ventilate the brain is repeated by Galen (*Organ of Smell*, 2; *De Sanit. tuendā*, i. 13). Their real use is to allow of the growth of the encephalon, which can no longer increase in bulk when the sutures are once closed. The greater development of the anterior lobes in civilized races as compared with the posterior explains the facts given in the last note.

24. I cannot ascertain whether this be so, or not.

25. This is an error. Doubtless A. was led to it by the fact that in numerous animals the sutures become more or less effaced at a very early age. This is notably the case with birds, fishes, and, of mammals, with the cetacea and elephants.

26. "In woman the suture is circular; while in man there are three sutures on the top of the head which run together, in three-cornered fashion. A man's skull has indeed been observed without any suture at all" (*H. A.* iii. 7, 3). The latter statement is borrowed from *Herodotus*, ix. 83. The three sutures meant are the Sagittal and the two divisions of the Lambdoid, which run together and form three angles. The Coronal suture would not be a suture of the cranium in A.'s view, because he makes the frontal bone a bone of the face (cf. Note 21). The account then of the male skull is intelligible enough. Doubtless battle-fields would furnish from time to time specimens for observation, as in the case taken by A. from Herodotus. But it is difficult to account for the statement as to the female skull. The sutures are really identical with those of the male. Of course the opportunities of seeing a female skull would be much fewer than of seeing a male skull; for battle-fields would no longer be of service. Still it is not impossible that A.'s statement may have been founded on some single observation. For it is by no means uncommon for the sutures on the vertex to become more or less effaced in pregnant women; so common indeed is it, that the name "puerperal osteophyte" has been given to the condition by Rokitansky (*Path. Anat.* iii. 208, *Syd. Soc. Transl.*). A woman's skull may have been observed in which the Sagittal suture had thus disappeared; when the Lambdoid, with the lateral sutures, and the Coronal, might fairly be described as forming together a circular suture. It must not be forgotten what great difficulty there was in A.'s time in getting a sight of human bones. Even much later Galen, it is said, went all the way to Egypt for the purpose of seeing merely a bronze representation of the human skeleton (*Cuvier, Hist. d. Sc.* i. 59). A well-known story is told of Democritus, how he was in the habit of wandering about among tombs and was therefore supposed by his fellow-citizens to be mad; and how the great Hippocrates was sent to see him, and, having heard his account, pronounced him not only to be sane, but the sanest of men. Cuvier explains this strange habit of Democritus, by supposing that his object was to find "quelques pièces ostéologiques"!

27. A. is ridiculed by Galen for having made the brain no more than a spongeful of

cold water. It is plain, however, that in reality he assigned to it an office scarcely less important than that he attached to the heart. It is true he made this latter the actual sensory centre, but he represented it as so directly dependent upon the brain for, the discharge of its functions, and as so instantaneously affected by any change which occurs in this organ, that heart and brain came as it were to form one consolidated organ. Seeing that it was impossible for A. to admit the doctrine which made the brain the sensory centre (ii. 10, Note 9), it was necessary for him to devise some other account of the matter; and the ingenious hypothesis he put forth had at least this merit that it apparently covered all the anatomical, physiological, and pathological facts, actual or supposed, with which he was acquainted. It seemed for instance to explain: (1). The supposed absence of any anatomical connection between brain and sense-organs (ii. 10, Note 9). (2). The presence of connecting links between these organs and the heart. For A. imagined that the heart itself was the sense-organ of touch and taste (ii. 10, Note 10), and that the other sense-organs, ear, eye, nostril, were connected by certain ducts or passages (ii. 10, Note 19) with the blood-vessels, and through these of course with the heart (*D. G.* ii. 6, 32). (3). The apparent insensibility of the brain when touched (ii. 7, Note 5). (4). The fact that keenness of sensibility is diminished or annulled in anæmic parts, increased in hyperæmic; and that parts naturally without blood are not sensitive (ii. 10, 14). (5). The supposed bloodlessness of the brain-substance (ii. 10, Note 18). (6). The fact that the heart is the centre of the vascular system. (7). That the heart is the first part to enter into activity and the last to stop work, "*primum vivens, ultimum moriens*" (*D. G.* ii. 5, 11), and therefore probably the seat of the essential characteristic of animal life, viz. sensibility. (8). The augmentation or diminution of the heart's action when intense pleasure or pain is experienced. (9). The loss of sensibility from loss of blood (*H. A.* iii: 19, 8). (10). The loss of sensibility and other psychical effects of brain lesion, as explained in the text. (11). The position of the heart in the centre of the body (ii. 2, Note 6), a dignified and safe position, as of an acropolis (iii. 7, 11), worthy of so high an office. One of the main difficulties which led A. astray in this matter was the apparent want of anatomical connection between brain and sense-organs. A very few years later Erasistratus and Herophilus (whose name still lives in the *torcular Herophili*) showed that such a connection did exist, in the nerves, which they were among the first to separate from tendons, ligaments and the like. Since that day the doctrine which A. repudiated has been universally recognised as true. The unscientific world, however, feeling the heart throb or slacken in joy or grief, still makes this organ the centre of their emotional feelings; and the scientific world still recognises, as an undoubted fact, the intimate connection and rapid sympathy between heart and brain, which A. first pointed out. "En résumé," says Claude Bernard, "chez l'homme le cœur est le plus sensible des organes de la vie végétative; il reçoit le premier de tous l'influence nerveuse cérébrale. Le cerveau est le plus sensible des organes de la vie animale; il reçoit le premier de tous l'influence de la circulation du sang. De là résulte que ces deux organes culminants de la machine vivante soient dans des rapports incessans d'action et de réaction. Le cœur et le cerveau se trouvent dès lors dans une solidarité d'actions réciproques des plus intimes, qui se multiplient et se resservent d'autant plus que l'organisme devient plus développé et plus délicat" (*Revue d. deux Mondes*, 1865, t. lvi. p. 250).

28. Cf. ii. 3, Note 16.

29. *D. G.* i. 17, etc.

(**Ch. 8.**) 1. What does A. mean by saying that Touch is the primary sense? One is tempted at first to attribute to him the view held by modern physiologists, that the higher sensibilities have been evolved by gradual differentiations of parts, originally endowed in common with the rest of the body with sensibility to resistance and to temperature, both of which are included by A. under Touch; in other words, that the remaining special senses are but modifications of Touch or general sensibility. But in the treatise on Sensation (ch. 4) this view, which was held by Democritus, is expressly repudiated. Touch is to A. the primary sense; firstly, because it is the most universally distributed of the senses; no animals being without it, though they may be without any other (*D.A.* iii. 13, 4; ii. 3, 8; *H.A.* i. 3, 3); and, secondly, because it is by touch that we are able to recognise the four primary properties of matter (ii. 1, Note 3; and *D.A.* ii. 11). "Touch," says John Hunter, "is the first sense, because no animal that has a sense (as far as I know) is without it, while there are many animals without the others." And again, "Touch I call the first sense; it is the simplest mode of receiving impressions; for all the other senses have this of touch in common with the peculiar or specific; and most probably there is not any part of the body, but what is susceptible of simple feeling or touch" (*Museum Cat.* iii. 53, 51).

2. This passage seems to have baffled Frantzius, and with him Mr. Lewes. Yet its meaning is clear enough, especially if one compares it with such other passages as those quoted in ch. 10, Note 10. The flesh, A. there argues, is not the organ of touch, in the sense that the eye is the organ of sight, or the ear of hearing, but is simply the medium through which the object affects the sense-organ; and answers therefore to the transparent medium, air or water, through which the visible object acts on the eye, or to the air through which sound acts upon the ear. In the present passage A. says that inasmuch as there is air or water about an animal wherever it may move itself, the requisite medium for sight or for hearing is always at hand, and there is no reason why nature, even if she were able, should so attach the medium of these senses to the sense-organ, as to make it an actual part of the body. But, in the case of touch, a *solid* medium is required for the action of the object upon the sense-organ, and this can only be always at hand, if it be permanently attached to the organ, and carried about by the animal as part of its own body.

3. Cf. iv. 8, Note 1; as to Testacea, cf. iv. 5, Note 25.
4. Cf. iii. 9, Note 3; as to Insects, cf. iv. 6, Note 1; as to Cephalopods, iv. 9, Note 1.
5. Cf. iii. 4, Note 20.
6. Cf. iv. 9, Note 6.
7. Cf. Introd. p. xxix. Note 1.

(**Ch. 9.**) 1. What prevents the blood from coagulating in the living vessels is still unknown; but certainly it is not mere heat, as A. assumes. For moderate heat really favours coagulation, and a temperature about that of the body is found to be most favourable to the process (cf. *Hewson's Works*, Syd. Soc. p. 4).

2. *i.e.* Ball and socket joints, as of hip and shoulder. The next form, containing an astragalus (cf. iv. 10, Note 44), is the ancle joint. The third kind mentioned includes arthrodial joints, *e.g.* the sterno-clavicular, carpal, etc., but probably refers more especially to the knee-joint with its semilunar cartilages.

3. So also iv. 10, 44. To these advantages derived from the absence of abdominal ribs might be added the facility afforded for the motion of the diaphragm during respiration.

4. *i.e.* Of the truly viviparous, not the ovo-viparous such as the Selachia, whose bones are cartilaginous. Cf. iv. 1, Note 5.

5. Cf. ii. 6, Notes 5 and 6.

6. The bones of birds contain a larger proportion of inorganic matter than do those

of other vertebrata. 'This makes them more brittle, which is what A. must mean by calling them weaker.

7. Here A. speaks of the bones of the smaller serpents as made of fish-spine; elsewhere (iv. 11, 17) he says they are cartilaginous. In reality however the proportion of inorganic matter in a snake's bones is very high, nearly as high as in the bones of birds; and this it is which gives so beautiful a whiteness and compact a look to a snake's skeleton. I can find no confirmation of A.'s statement that there is a difference between the bones of small and of large serpents. The only large ophidian he can possibly have seen was the *Coluber elaphis*, which sometimes attains a length of six feet. His information as to other large serpents was simply derived from such "traveller's tales" as that given at *H. A.* viii. 28, 10.

8. Cf. iv. 13, Notes 1 and 33. The skin of the fishes called Selachia by A. is studded with numerous tubercles, granules, or spines, of bony matter; a peculiarity designated as "placoid" by modern ichthyologists.

9. It has been a matter of question, whether the credit of being the first to put forth the law of organic equivalents should be assigned to Geoffrey St. Hilaire or to Goethe; the former of whom spoke of it as "la loi de balancement organique," while the latter expressed it in these terms, "Nature must save in one part in order to spend in another." As a matter of fact, the law, whether true or false, is perfectly recognised by Aristotle, and is used by him over and over again in explanation of morphological phenomena. We have already had in this book one instance of this, when the inverse relation of fat and the generative secretions was mentioned (cf. ii. 5, Note 9), and we shall come to numerous others. Thus, for instance, is explained (ii. 14, Note 4) the coincidence of long hair and short tail; thus also (iii. 2, Note 19) the want of upper front teeth in horned animals; thus again (iv. 9, Note 12) the great length of the arms in cephalopods with a short body, and their comparative shortness when the body is long, etc., etc.

10. Seeing how much attention A. gave to development, it is strange that he should not have noticed that the osseous is preceded by a cartilaginous framework. Had he done so, he would certainly have cited the fact here, in support of his statement of the essential identity of the two substances.

11. See also Hippocrates (*Kühn's ed.* i. 319). When cartilage is fractured, reunion may be effected by fibrous or by calcareous tissue, but never by true cartilage; whereas when bone is fractured, reunion is effected by true osseous tissue. Frantzius and Lewes find in this grounds for attacking the statement in the text. But in reality A. says nothing about reunion of broken parts, and neither he nor Hippocrates can have been ignorant of the common facts of the mending of a broken bone. What is said is that a piece of cartilage or of bone, if once excised, is never regenerated; and though this is not actually true, it is what every physiologist believed to be so till comparatively a short time ago. The statement is founded partly on surgical experience, partly on observations of mutilated animals. When a portion of bone is removed by the surgeon, it is not regenerated unless the periosteum be left. This was unknown till Duhamel's time, though Hippocrates was near it when he said, "An extensive fracture is less formidable if the periosteum be sound" (iii. 369), and A. also when he said, "A bone becomes necrosed, if stripped bare of its membrane" (*H. A.* iii. 13, 2). No effort being made by the ancients to preserve the periosteum, removal of bone was never followed by regeneration. That excised cartilage is never replaced is still the general belief; but Legros and Peyraud have recently shown that regeneration can occur also in this tissue if the perichondrium be preserved (*Virchow's Jahresb.* 1869, p. 143). As to mutilated animals, it was known to A. (*H. A.* ii. 17, 24) that when a lizard's tail is cut off, the

part in time is regenerated. It was believed until very recently that in this case the restoration though externally complete did not extend to the lost vertebræ. But Legros (*Gaz. Médic.* 1869, p. 75) has shown that even these bones are replaced after several years' interval. More rapid restoration of bone had moreover already been observed by Spallanzani to occur after the removal of the limbs of water-newts, and great was the astonishment of physiologists when he announced this fact.

12. It will be noted that A. only likens nails, horns, hoofs, etc., to bone in their tactile properties. In other passages (*D. G.* ii. 6, 50; *H. A.* iii. 9, 2) he says that the former are all developed from the skin, and follow its changes of colour; and he distinguishes the group of dermal parts thus formed from the bones and the teeth; which latter he imagines are not dermal but osseous, because they remain white when the skin is black.

13. An organ or heterogeneous part made from a single tissue or homogeneous part (τα ἰσχηματίσμενα) will have the same name as the tissue. Hoof, nail, cartilage is the name of both organ and tissue. These might therefore be dealt with either among the tissues, or among the organs. The latter plan, says A., is the better; for it is only by studying the purposes subserved by the organ hoof or nail, that we can learn the nature of the tissue hoof or nail. Cf. ii. 1, Note 16.

(Ch. 10.) 1. The discussion of the homogeneous parts, or tissues, is now finished, and A. proceeds to consider the heterogeneous parts or organs.

2. Strangely enough, A. after all does not follow the order here indicated, but begins with the brain and other parts of the head, and then proceeds to the neck, thorax, and abdomen, in succession; following the simple plan of beginning at the top and going downwards.

3. This limitation is introduced because some of the lower animals are without digestive cavities at all (ii. 3, Note 9), and others (*H. A.* i. 2, 2) without excremental orifice. By the latter A. probably means Acalephæ, which have, he says (*D. P.* iv. 5, 49), no visible excretion; though it must be admitted that elsewhere (*H. A.* viii. 2, 15) he speaks of them as having an excremental orifice.

4. Cf. ii. 3, Note 8.

5. A similar recognition of the truth, that simplicity of life and simplicity of structure go hand in hand, will be found at iv. 7, 1.

6. Cf. ii. 2, Note 5, and iv. 10, 8.

7. That man alone is erect is repeatedly mentioned by A. as a proof of his superiority to other animals. Doubtless the erect position, leaving as it does the upper extremities free for skilful manual operations, is an important element in man's structure. But this position is not the exclusive privilege of man; some birds, as the penguin, and some mammals, as the kangaroo, having a vertical attitude.

8. *e.g.* Plato in the Timæus (*Jowett's Trans.* ii. 568), who probably borrowed the opinion, as Galen says he did his physiology generally, from Hippocrates. Democritus also had taught that the sovereign part of the soul was in the head; and Diogenes of Apollonia, more directly, had held that the brain was the seat of sensation, being surrounded by a layer of hot dry air, which was in connection with the sense-organs by means of the blood-vessels, and so sympathised with their motions and affections (cf. *Grote's Plato*, i. 65).

9. How came A. to reject this view of the brain's office in favour of his own apparently less plausible one? The reasons seem to be as follows:

a. Firstly, as he says here, and repeats oftentimes (ii. 7, Note 5; *H. A.* iii. 19, 2), the brain is insensible to external mechanical stimulation. If the brain of a living animal be laid bare, as in A.'s vivisection of the chamæleon (*H. A.* ii. 11), the hemispheres may be cut without any signs of pain whatsoever, and without any struggling on the part of the animal. This difficulty was insuperable to Aristotle. β. He could find no brain, nor anything apparently analogous to a brain, in any of the invertebrata, excepting in the Cephalopods; the cephalic ganglia in other animals having, owing to 'their minute size, escaped his unaided vision. Yet sensation was the special characteristic of an animal. The absence of a brain, then, from numerous sentient creatures was quite imcompatible with the notion that the brain was the sole organ of sensation. γ. The brain he erroneously thought (cf. Note 18) to be bloodless, as also did Hippocrates; and all experience taught him that those parts alone were sensitive that contained blood (cf. Note 20). δ. "It is manifest," he says (ii. 7, 4), "on inspection, that there is no anatomical connection between brain and sense-organs." It has indeed been supposed that he knew of the optic, auditory, and olfactory nerves (cf. Note 19). If he really knew of them, he did not know that they united the sense-organs to the brain itself, but thought that they led to the vascular membrane round it, or to the supposed empty space behind it. They would thus be in connection with the blood, and so with the heart, but not with the actual brain. It is true that in his account of the vivisection of the chamæleon (*H. A.* ii. 11, 9) he says that the eyes are "continuous with the brain," and elsewhere (*De Sensu*, 2, 20) that the eyes are "made out of the brain"; but these passages must be read in connection with others, such as *D. G.* ii. 6, 33, where he says that "the purest part of the fluid which is *about* the brain is separated from it, and passes to the eyes by the channels (πόροι) which visibly connect them with *the membrane that surrounds* the brain." ε. Lastly, he believed that he had good grounds for supposing another part, viz. the heart, to be the sensory centre (cf. ii. 7, Note 27).

10. The heart, according to A., is the sensorium commune; but while three of the five senses have also external organs, viz. the eyes, ears and nostrils, the remaining two, viz. touch and its variety taste, have no such external organs, but are lodged in or close to the heart itself, which is thus their first and also their final organ. "The question," says A., "whether the sense-organ lies internally or not, being on the latter supposition the flesh itself, is not to be answered off-hand by adducing the fact that a sensation is felt the moment the body is touched. For even if one were to stretch a piece of membrane tightly over the surface of the body, a touch would equally call forth immediate signs of sensation; and yet it is plain that the membrane is not the sense-organ. Indeed the fact adduced proves the contrary, for "the direct contact of an object with an organ of sense in no case produces a sensation. Thus if a white body be placed in contact with the eye, there is no sensation of whiteness. This shows plainly that the sense-organ of touch lies deeper than the flesh. For the same must occur in the organ of touch as in the organs of other senses. That is to say it must be, as they are, insensible to objects in direct contact with it. The fact, then, that objects are felt when in contact with the flesh shows that the flesh must be the medium which separates the sense-object from the sense-organ; the flesh and the tongue standing to touch and taste apparently in the same relation as do air and water to sight and hearing" (*D. A.* ii. 11). So, again, "If the coloured body be placed in direct contact with the eye, the eye will not see it. There must be a transparent medium, such as air, which is set in motion by the colour, and which in turn sets in motion the sense-organ, with which it is in continuity. For Democritus was mistaken in supposing that, if the interval between the eye and the object were a vacuum, vision would be so distinct, that we should be able to discern even an ant though it were at the distance of the heaven. . . . In reality, with a vacuum for a medium, there would be no vision at all. The same is true in the case

of hearing or of smelling. A smell or a sound sets the medium in motion, and this in turn sets the organ of sense in motion. But when the substance from which the sound or smell proceeds is placed directly upon the sense-organ, it produces no sensation. The same is true of touch, though it is not so evident for reasons to be given hereafter. The medium in the case of sound is air; in the case of smell it has no designation. For smell is an affection alike of air and of water. Just as any transparent substance is a medium for colour, so smell can occur in either water or air. For even water animals appear to have this sense" (*D. A.* ii. 7).

11. Cf. *De Sensu*, 2. The eye is placed near the brain, because the eye is developed from it (*D. G.* ii. 6, 33); the ear, because it requires to be near the space in the occiput which is full of air; the organ of smell, because smell is of a hot character and so can temper the coldness of the brain (*De Sensu*, 5, 18). All three senses, moreover, derive advantage, as stated further on in this chapter (see also iv. 10, 4), from being in a part where the blood is pure, and heat moderate. Can A. possibly have felt satisfied with this explanation?

12. Not so. In some Annulosa there are ocelli on the gills, on each segment, or even on the tail. Scallops, again, have eye-specks on the edge of the mantle; and star-fishes at the ends of their rays. A. thought that scallops could see (*H. A.* iv. 8, 32), though he had not made out their eye-specks.

13. One might suppose from this passage that the excavations near the anterior part of the snout, which constitute in fishes the external organs of smell, had entirely escaped A.'s notice. But this was not so, as appears from a passage (*H. A.* iv. 8, 9), where he mentions these recesses, and says that some consider them to be organs of sense. This, however, he will not admit, because " the passages (πόροι) do not appear to lead to the brain, but are either blind or lead to the gills." His notion was that in fishes the gills were the external organs of smell (cf. ii. 16, Note 10); and his reason for so thinking appears to have been this. In man the nostrils serve for the admission of air, and at the same time for olfaction. In fishes the gills serve for the admission of water, and so correspond to the nostrils, the water in fishes and the air in man serving one and the same purpose, viz. refrigeration. Finding this correspondence in one point between gills and nostrils, A. assumed that they corresponded in other matters, and so assigned to the gills the olfactory duties of the nostrils. Similarly he supposed that Cetacea smell by the blow-hole, though he did not apparently recognise the fact that this corresponds anatomically to the nostrils; and, again, that in insects the same part served for smell as for cooling the body. That fishes can smell A. inferred from their refusing as a rule to take stinking bait; and that they can hear, from the care which fishermen have to take to avoid making a noise with oars or nets when they approach a shoal (*H. A.* iv. 8, 15). There is no communication in fishes between the internal ear and the outer surface; and the existence of the internal ear entirely escaped Aristotle's notice. He nowhere says how he supposes fishes to hear.

14. Cf. ii. 7, Note 4.

15. Cf. ii. 1, Note 12.

16. "The faculty of sight does not belong to the eye, because it is of water, but because it is transparent, a quality which exists in air no less than in water. But water is less elastic, and more easily kept in place than air, and on this account the eye is made of it. That the eye is made of it, is manifest from the fact, that water runs out of it when it is ruptured " (*De Sensu,* ch. 2, 12).

17. Cf. ii. 7, Note 12.

18. There are in this chapter, as in other passages, three very strange statements

as to the brain: firstly, that it only occupies the front portion of the skull, there being an empty space behind it; secondly, that it is entirely destitute of blood-vessels; and, thirdly, that it is cold to the touch. For the two first of these it is perhaps unfair to hold A. as directly responsible, seeing they are both to be found in Hippocrates (*Kühn's edit.* i. 683, iii. 349), and may have been accepted by A. on his authority without personal examination into the matter. Still A. did undoubtedly himself examine the brains of some animals, and we have to consider how a man who was certainly no utterly mean observer can have reconciled what he learnt from authority with what he saw himself. I suspect that the explanation is to be found in his having only examined, and that imperfectly, the brains of fishes, tortoises, and other cold-blooded animals. For while it is certain that he did examine the brains of such animals, there is no clear sign of his having examined the brains of any warm-blooded animal, at any rate in a fresh condition, though he may very possibly have examined them after cooking, a process to which he seemingly had resort (cf. ii. 7, 16), with the idea of hardening them. Admitting this supposition to be correct, we can see how his errors may have originated. For in Fishes and Reptiles the brain is not large enough to fill the cranial cavity, a character to which Lamarck attached great importance in distinguishing these groups from Mammals and Birds (*Phil. Zool.* i. 276, *Martin's edit.*). In the tortoise, for instance, the area of a vertical section of the brain, according to Desmoulins (*Todd's Cycl.* i. 724), is nearly a third less than the area of the cavity. So also the brain completely fills the brain-case in embryonic fishes, but in the adult only occupies a small part of it, as its growth is by no means proportionate to that of the cranium itself. That A. had noticed this is highly probable from his saying (*D. G.* ii. 6, 35) that the brain of animals is at first of large size, but afterwards falls in and becomes of smaller dimensions. So also in Cephalopods, animals specially studied by A., and with whose so-called brain he was acquainted, the cavity in which the ganglia are lodged is much larger than the ganglia themselves.

So much for the first error. Now for the second. The brain does as a matter of fact receive a very large amount of blood; but by far the greatest part of this goes to the superficial gray matter. All this superficial blood A. reckoned as belonging to the Pia mater, which he describes as highly vascular. Either he did not see that the small vessels were prolonged from this into the superficial brain-substance, or more probably he considered this superficial substance, differing as it does from the mass below in colour and general aspect, to be part of the Pia mater itself, from which in fact he can hardly have learnt to separate it mechanically. That this was really the view of the Pia mater entertained by the ancients of his time is, I think, confirmed by the fact, that when the nerves had afterwards been distinguished from other white structures, Erasistratus still maintained for many years that they ended in the Pia mater. It seems inconceivable that he can have so thought, unless he included in the Pia mater the superficies of the brain itself. There are, however, numerous small vessels in that white mass, which A. regarded as exclusively the brain. These are so small that on section they appear only as bloody puncta, and are so barely visible in the brains of fishes and tortoises, that they might easily escape notice. In the brain of a mammal they are more apparent; but if we imagine, as I have suggested, that A. only examined such brains when cooked, they would have been quite invisible to him. Even had he seen them, I do not think that, considering their minuteness and the general bloodlessness of the part when compared with other organs, he would have attributed any importance to their presence. The contrast in amount in the two cases would have seemed sufficient to warrant him in speaking of the one organ as full of blood, and of the other as having none at all. Similarly, though he knew there was some blood in the lung of oviparous vertebrates, he often speaks of it as bloodless, because the amount was insignificant, as he thought, when compared with that in the lung of a mammal (iii. 6, Note 10).

So also I would explain the third error, that the brain is cold to the touch. He very possibly found the basis for this notion, which was essential for his interpretation of the brain's function, in the brain of a fish or tortoise; for it is extremely unlikely that he even examined the brain of a warm-blooded animal while the warmth of life was still in it. We must remember that the art of dissection was in its infancy, and that even much later, in Galen's time, the mechanical difficulty of removing the calvaria was such, that Galen recommends his readers, because of the imperfection of their instruments, to get from the butcher a head in which the brain was already exposed. Nor must we neglect to make full allowance for the constant results of preconceived theories. Every experimental physiologist must be painfully conscious how they thwart his most honest intentions, and put a film between his eyes and his object. Aristotle would have been more than human to have escaped this source of error.

19. What A. precisely meant by the passages, or channels, or pores ($πόροι$) upon which the sense-organs are placed, is very problematical. Meyer (*Thierkunde;* p. 428) takes him to mean the blood-vessels, mainly because this accords with the statement (*D. G.* v. 2, 2) that all these $πόροι$ pass to the heart. There is no doubt that $πόροι$ is often used by A. to designate blood-vessels; but I think it plain, that A. is here speaking of something which is more distinctive of the sense-organs than the presence of vessels, which they share with the rest of the body. Frantzius, following Schneider, has no doubt that nerves are meant, and thus A. would have to be credited with the anatomical discovery of the nerves of sense, or at any rate of the optic, auditory, and olfactory nerves.' I have little doubt that on several occasions where A. uses the term $πόρος$, the thing he is speaking of is a nerve, as in *D. G.* ii. 6, 33, where he speaks of either the optic nerve, or of some other nerve going to the eye, under this title. And again in this passage: "Cases have occurred, when men have been wounded in battle in the head, in such a way that the $πόροι$ of the eye have been severed; a sudden darkness has then come over them, as though a lamp were extinguished, etc." (*De Sensu*, 2, 17); and perhaps, though I am very doubtful, in the obscure passage in the *Hist. An.* (i. 16, 6). Moreover, that he had seen the optic nerve is certain from his statement (*H. A.* ii. 11, 9) that the eye of the chamæleon is continuous with the brain. Were he then only speaking of the eye, it might fairly be admitted that its $πόροι$ were its nerves; and it may be noted that in after-times $πόροι$ was the term specially applied by Herophilus to the nerves of the eye (*Galen, De Usu part.* iii. 12). But A. uses the same expression for the other sense-organs. "All the sense-organs have $πόροι$ connecting them with the heart" (*D. G.* v. 2, 2). Now it seems to me exceedingly improbable that A. knew of the olfactory or auditory nerves. He clearly looks on the nerve of the eye as something very peculiar, and explains its presence by the eye being made of the same substance as the brain, and therefore requiring a communicating passage by which the cold fluid of this latter may pass into it (*D. G.* ii. 6, 33). This is quite incompatible with the notion that he had seen similar $πόροι$ with similar substance going to the very dissimilar ear and nose. Indeed, he expressly says that the $πόροι$ of these two sense-organs are full of "innate spirit," that is, of something physically like air (ii. 16, Note 11), and that they communicate with the air outside the body. The way moreover in which he speaks of the auditory $πόρος$ in the text shows that he means something of the same character as the external meatus. "There is a $πόρος$ which leads *back again* from the ear to the hinder part of the head," The same notion is apparent in what he says of the olfactory organs of fishes (cf. Note 13).

He refuses to admit that the nasal passages in these animals are organs of smell because they end blindly, and do not lead to the brain. Clearly he knew nothing then of the olfactory nerves of these animals. What he looked for in a sense-organ of sight, hearing, or smell, was not a nerve, but an opening of some kind leading to the inside of the skull.

On the whole I think it most probable that by πόροι in this place A. means no more than openings or foramina by which the sense-organs are in communication with the interior of the skull; in the eye, the optic and other fissures or foramina of the orbit; in the ear, the external and internal meatus; and in the nose, the anterior nares and possibly the ethmoidal foramina, which he may have noticed, small as they are, in a dog's skull; though I am by no means sure he may not have thought the communication was completed by the Eustachian tube, with which he was acquainted. (*H. A.* i. 11, 2), a view which would explain his statement that the olfactory πόροι, no less than the auditory, are full of hot air.

The various foramina or passages place the sense-organ in communication with the vascular membrane that surrounds the brain, and the connection with the heart is completed by means of the blood-vessels that run to it from this membrane. So I interpret the words, "These πόροι lead into the small vessels which extend from the heart to the brain and surround this latter" (*D. G.* ii. 6, 32).

The difficulty of interpreting A.'s exact meaning is probably due to the fact that he was himself not quite certain as to the channels by which he supposed the ear and nostrils to communicate with the inside the skull. For his account of the auditory πόρος differs in each of the three main treatises. In the *Hist. An.* (i. 11, 2) it is positively asserted that there is no πόρος leading to the brain from the inner ear, there being however a blood-vessel which connects the two, and a πόρος (the Eustachian tube) running to the mouth. Here in the *De Partibus* he speaks of a πόρος running from the ear to the empty space in the occiput; while in the *De Generatione* (ii. 6, 32) he says that it runs to the vessels on the surface of the brain.

20. The argument is this: The channels from the eyes end in the blood-vessels outside the brain, and blood itself is insensible. The channels from the ears end in the void space, where there are no blood-vessels; and no part without blood-vessels is sensitive. Neither the sensibility of the eyes nor that of the ears can therefore be explained simply by their connection with the interior of the cranium.

The last sentence in this paragraph with its empty repetition is, I doubt not, an interpolation.

21. Cf. Note 10, and ii. 8, Note 2.

22. The sense of taste "appears to have a greater analogy to touch than any of the others, and appears to be as universal, few animals being endowed with touch, but what are most probably also endowed with taste" (*J. Hunter*). The close connection of touch and taste is shown in the fact that, while the nerves that minister to the other special senses are exclusively channels of their respective special sensations, those which minister to taste are at the same time nerves of ordinary tactile sensibility. This was of course unknown to A., who rests his statement of the similarity of the two senses on the fact that they both require actual contact of the object with the body, whereas the other three senses are affected by distant objects (cf. *D. A.* ii. 10, 1).

23. Alluding to snakes and seals, cf. iv. 11, Note 10.

24. A. explains (*D. A.* ii. 9, 12) the manner in which respiration is essential to smell, in such animals as have lungs, as follows: "Some animals have their eyes bare, and thus see what occurs in the transparent medium directly. Others have their eyes covered with lids, which protect them as the shards protect a beetle's wings, and these

animals only see when this covering is drawn back. So also is it with the organ of smell. In some animals this lies bare and exposed. But in those that have lungs it is covered, and the covering is removed by the act of inspiration; for this dilates the channels and vessels." See also *De Sensu*, 5, 24. By saying that there is a covering he probably only means that there is something analogous to the covering of the eye; this something being the contracted condition of the nasal passages, which are dilated when air enters.

25. A. accounts for the nostrils being where they are by the necessity of their coinciding with the organs for admission of air; but gives no reason why these organs should be central.

(Ch. 11.) 1. "'Man is the only animal with ears that are incapable of motion" (*H. A.* i. 11, 2). As to the use of a large concha, cf. *D. G.* v. 2, 8.

(Ch. 12.) 1. Birds have no concha, neither have Reptiles. But in some birds "which enjoy the locomotive or visual faculties in a less perfect degree than the rest of the class, there is found a peculiar arrangement of the feathers round the external meatus, which serves in some degree the office of an external ear. The Ostrich and Bustard are so provided, and these birds can raise the auditory circle of plumes to catch distinctly any distant sound that may alarm them. The Owls again are furnished with a large crescentic flap, or valve " (*Todd's Cycl.* i. 308).

2. Because ears made of hard skin would not be readily moveable. See what he says in the next chapter as to moveable eyelids.

3. Elsewhere (*D. G.* v. 2, 10) it is said that external ears would not only be useless but prejudicial to seals, as they would allow of the entrance of water. The true teleological explanation of the absence of external ears from these animals, as also from cetacea and birds, is apparently, as Hunter pointed out, that they would be a hindrance to progressive motion.

4. "The seal is as it were a stunted quadruped. For it has feet immediately after its shoulder-blade, and these feet are like hands, just as in the bear. For each foot has five digits, and each digit has three joints and a small nail. The hind-feet also have each five digits, and joints and nails, like the fore-feet, but in shape they resemble the tail of a fish" (*H. A.* ii. 1, 14). Thus it appears that A. thought that the seal had no humerus nor ulna, their shortness disguising their presence in the undissected animal.

(Ch. 13.) 1. The "heavy-bodied" birds are described in various passages as living on the ground, being unsuited for flight, liking to roll in the dust, not constructing regular nests, and frequently having spurs. Partridges, quails, pheasants, common fowls, are mentioned as belonging to the group, which clearly corresponds generally to our Gallinaceæ.

2. In birds, as a rule, as also in chelonia, in crocodiles, and in frogs, the lower lid is much larger and more moveable than the upper one, and it is with it therefore that the eye is closed in sleep. There are, however, some few exceptions. Thus in the nightjar and in the owls the upper lid is the more moveable of the two. This latter exception is noticed by A. elsewhere (*H. A.* ii. 12, 7). In many parrots also the two lids are equally mobile. This is not noticed by A., who probably never saw a living parrot (cf. ii. 17, Note 3). He does, however, a few sentences later, say that pigeons use both lids to close the eye, which also is a correct observation. A. both here and elsewhere speaks erroneously of a nictitating membrane as peculiar to birds. For, though it is especially well developed in birds, yet it is to be found in numerous reptiles, amphibia, and sharks, not to mention some mammals.

3. That is to say, it is an involuntary reflex action.

4. This is an unfortunate statement, borrowed however from Hippocrates (*Kühn's ed.* i. 319; iii. 752). Firstly, the presence of flesh, *i.e.* of muscular tissue, is not essential for reunion after section; secondly, the eyelid does contain muscular tissue; and, lastly, cuts both in it and in the prepuce can be made to unite by proper appliances. It is true, however, as Frantzius points outs, that owing to the looseness of the subcutaneous tissue in these parts, the inflammatory swelling after a wound is very considerable, and keeps the edges of the wound widely apart, so that it requires careful attention to produce reunion. Still such can be brought about when desirable; but in the case of the prepuce it is usually the object of the surgeon to prevent reunion.

5. Because a hard skin, as stated farther on, cannot move with due rapidity. Compare what he says (iii. 3, Note 8) as to the motion of the epiglottis, and (ii. 12, Note 2) of the ears. The mobility of the lid does really stand in direct relation with the delicacy of the integument which forms it. Thus the skin of the lower lid (*Todd's Cycl.* iii. 94) is naked and finer than that of the upper lid in birds and chelonia, and as already noted (Note 2) is the more moveable one.

6. Cf. ii. 9, Note 9.

7. "Upon thick skins, the hair is generally harsh and thick, ... and the case is similar in those animals that are covered with scales or scutes" (*H. A.* iii. 10, 2). The character of the hair seems really to vary with the thickness of the skin, cf. *Low, Domest. Anim.* p. 368.

8. Or rather, of a *moveable* upper eyelid.

9. And by all other birds also (cf. *H. A.* ii. 12, 7).

10. Cf. ii. 2, Note 6.

11. There are exceptions among fishes, particularly in sharks.

12. A.'s knowledge of Crustacea was confined, or nearly so, to Podophthalmata, in which the eyes are supported on moveable peduncles. Insects have, almost invariably, sessile and motionless eyes; and though in a few instances the eyes are on peduncles, these peduncles are not moveable like those of Crustacea. The mobility of the eyes of Crustacea, as compared with Insecta, is to be looked on as an atonement for the smaller mobility of their heads, which are fused with the thorax.

(Ch. 14.) 1. Birds as a rule have no eyelashes. There are however a few exceptions; the ostrich, as here mentioned, and the rhea; some parrots also, owls, and hornbills. But in these "they are rather feathers with short barbs than true eyelashes" (*Owen*). As to the ostrich, cf. iv. 14, Note 2.

2. Cf. ii. 2, Note 6.

3. So far as I can ascertain it is true that man is the only mammal with a distinct marginal lower eyelash, with the exception of some monkeys, an exception elsewhere (*H. A.* ii. 8, 4) recognised by A., and some few antelopes. In very many mammals, especially the smaller kinds, there are no eyelashes at all. In the larger kinds, as a rule, the upper lash is well developed and marginal, while the lower lash is represented, as A. rightly says, by some long straggling hairs set below the lid, not on its margin.

4. In the horse the stump is short and furnished with long hair; while in the ass it is long, and the hair short except at the extremity. It is, however, evident that the rule which A. lays down is far from being of universal application. Still the idea is not so utterly absurd as it appears at first sight. For the tail of an animal, consisting in great part of tegumentary tissues, is in reality liable to vary with other tegumentary structures, such as hair, teeth, horns. The variations however which occur simultaneously in this group of structures are not always such as can be explained by the law of organic

equivalents, according to which excess in one part should be balanced by deficiency in another. This does sometimes occur, as when animals with unusually redundant hair are, as not rarely, deficiently supplied with teeth. Many instances of such an occurrence in the human species are given in *The Field* of Feb. 14, 1874. But more commonly the variations in the allied parts occur in the same direction, excess or deficiency in the one attending excess or deficiency in the other. Thus the well-known Julia Pastrana to a monstrous excess of hair added a doubled set of teeth; and Mr. Darwin quotes an agriculturist as asserting that "pigs with little hair on their bodies are most liable to lose their tails, showing a weakness of the tegumental structure. It may be prevented by crossing with a more hairy breed" (*Dom. An. and Plants*, ii. 327).

5. Cf. ii. 9, Note 9. The tail in the typical bears is remarkably short, and the body usually covered with very long shaggy hair.

6. The moisture of the brain and the heat of the blood on its surface escape, according to A., by the sutures (cf. ii. 7, Note 23). As to fluidity of brain, cf. ii. 7, Note 4.

7. The subject is discussed at length in *D. G.* v. 3.

(Ch. 15.) 1. The explanation and the comparison are borrowed from Xenophon (*Mem.* i. 4, 6), who puts them into the mouth of Socrates. Somewhat similarly we have "my penthouse eyebrows" in Dryden, and "his penthouse lid" in Shakespeare.

2. Cf. ii. 14, Note 6.

3. Cf. *H. A.* iii. 11, 11.

4. In truth the hypertrophy which follows an increased blood-supply is more distinctly marked in the case of hair than of other parts. It is well known that long hairs are developed in the hyperæmic circle round old sores, ulcers, etc. I have several times seen the hair on the hyperæmic ear of a young rabbit, after section of the cervical sympathetic, become longer than that on the opposite side.

It will be remembered that A. was ignorant of the circulation of the blood. He supposed that the blood passed from the heart to the various parts by the vessels, but knew nothing of its returning. Thus when the blood reached the peripheral ends of the vessels, it had to pass out in some form or other; that which escaped internally formed the viscera, that which escaped externally formed hair and the like. Thus the hair was in a certain sense an excretion (cf. ii. 3, Note 8). So also was it regarded by Bacon (*Nat. Hist. cent.* 1, *sect.* 58): "Living creatures put forth (after their period of growth) nothing that is young, but hair and nails, which are excrements and no parts." So also Shakespeare:

"Your bedded hair, like life in excrements,
Start up and stand on end" (*Hamlet*, iii. 4).

Very similar is the view expressed by Sir J. Paget (*Surg. Pathol. Lect.* 2).

5. Such purposes as the growth of feathers, scales, and the like (cf. iii. 7, Note 2).

(Ch. 16.) 1. Cf. *Tennent's Ceylon*, ii. 388.

2. The elephant is very fond of bathing, and often frequents marshy ground. But Aristotle appears to have imagined its habits of life to be much more aquatic than they really are. Elsewhere however (*H. A.* ix. 46, 2) it is said that the elephant lives not in rivers but on their banks, and is unable to swim on account of its heavy weight.

3. From this curious passage it would appear that the ancients were already acquainted with some form of diving apparatus corresponding to the submarine helmet and tubes in use at the present time. It may, however, have been some very simple instrument, such as the reed, by means of which Australian natives are said to be able to swim for a distance under water, so as to approach a flock of ducks without being seen. There is another passage in Aristotle which shows that the diving bell also was known

in his time: "Divers breathe by letting down a metallic vessel. For this does not get filled with water, but retains the air within it" (*Probl.* xxxii.).

The elephant does in fact use its trunk in the way described when crossing a deep river (cf. *Tennent's Ceylon*, ii. 310).

4. This story comes from Herodotus (iv. 183). It is there stated that in a certain part of Africa, inhabited by the Garamantes, there are oxen that walk backwards while grazing, "for their horns are so bent as to render it impossible for them to move forwards while grazing, as the horns would stick into the ground in front of them. These oxen differ in no other respects than this from ordinary oxen, excepting that their hides are thicker and harder." This has been copied by Pliny (*N. Hist.* viii. 45) and others. Heeren finds a foundation for the story in the fact that the horns of cattle among the nomad tribes of Africa are not uncommonly so bent by the herdsmen that one projects forwards, the other backwards; and cattle of this kind are, he says, to be found represented on Nubian monuments.

There is an Egyptian wall-painting in the British Museum (No. 169) which I suppose to be such a representation as Heeren alludes to. One horn is there made to project straight forwards and the other backwards. I attribute the appearance to the artist's inability to deal properly with perspective. Still such a painting may have been the source of the strange account.

5. It is of course true that one single part is often used for several separate purposes, but it is no less true that such an accumulation of functions is a mark of inferiority of organisation, as indeed is fully recognised elsewhere by Aristotle. See for instance iv. 6, Note 15, where he says that nature when it is possible provides separate organs for separate offices, instead of acting like a coppersmith, who for cheapness makes "a spit and lamp-holder" all in one.

6. The foot of the elephant is furnished with five flat hoofs, which correspond to the five toes; these latter being distinct enough in the skeleton, but, in the living animal, concealed within the thick skin, though indicated externally by the divisions of the hoof. A. thus describes it elsewhere: "All animals that have toes have nails, excepting the elephant. For in this animal the toes are not separated nor clearly distinct, and there are no nails whatsoever" (*H. A.* iii. 9, 6). I do not think that A. ever saw an elephant. Had he himself examined the animal, he would hardly have said it had no nails whatsoever, nails of course including hoofs. (Cf. next note, and Introd., pp. xiii–xiv.)

7. It was the general belief of the ancients that the elephant had no joints in its legs and was therefore unable to lie down, but slept leaning against a tree (iv. 10, Note 38). This notion, Sir T. Browne complains (*Vulgar Errors*, iii. 1), was still in his time "alive and epidemicall in England and Italy, although we have had the advantage in England not many years past of an elephant shown in many parts thereof, not only in the posture of standing but kneeling and lying down, whereby although the opinion at present be well suppressed, yet from some strings of tradition and fruitful recurrence of error, it may revive in the next generation again, this being not the first that hath been seen in England." Sir T. Browne's anticipation was realised, and almost up to the present day traces of the old error are to be found in our literature. Aristotle however escaped the mistake; though the inaccuracy of his own account renders it probable that he had never himself seen an elephant, but described it at second-hand. "The elephant," he says, "is not made as some would have it, but is able to bend its legs so as to rest on the ground. Its great weight however renders it impossible for it to bend the legs on both sides at once. It sinks down therefore on one side

or the other, right or left as the case may be, and sleeps in that position. Its hind legs it bends in the same way as a man" (*H. A.* ii. 1, 9). The reader will find an interesting discussion explaining the probable source of the ancient belief in this matter in *Tennent's Ceylon*.

8. In the present day the term "respiration" is commonly used to designate the process by which a gaseous interchange is effected between the blood and the medium, be the organs in which the process is wrought what they may. But A. uses it exclusively for the act of inspiring and expiring air from lungs. The purpose of this was, he thought, to produce cooling. But, though a similar result was obtained by the water acting on the gills, he did not apply the term respiration to this latter process, not crediting the existence of air in water. This was known to Galen, who supposed (*De Usu part.* vi. 9) that the air got into the gills through little holes, which, though large enough to admit air, were yet too small to admit water. As to the reasons why A. supposed fishes to smell by the gills, cf. Note 10.

9. It is of course of the Cetacea that A. is speaking. It must be an accidental slip that makes him include them here amongst animals that do not breathe; for he frequently mentions the fact that they have lungs. The blowhole corresponds anatomically to the nostrils. It is however very doubtful whether any of the Cetacea can smell. Dolphins and porpoises at any rate must be unable to do so; for they have no olfactory nerves.

10. Frantzius gives up the *hypozoma* as unintelligible. There is however no doubt what A. means by it. It is the waist or border-line between thorax and abdomen; which in insects is especially distinct. Nor is there any difficulty in understanding why A. located the sense of smell in this part of an insect's body. He says that the part below this *hypozoma* is that which in insects functionally corresponds to the lungs or gills of higher animals; that is, is the organ through which cooling is produced. This is brought about by there being in this region a portion with a membranous covering, much thinner than the rest of the integument, so as to allow of the escape of heat. The cooling is effected not by the external air, but by the fanning motions of the internal "innate spirit." The motions are visible in the alternate rise and fall of the part of the body in question. Not only is this thin membranous part the organ of refrigeration; but it also corresponds to the lung in another way. It is the organ of sound; and thus it is that there is a special cleft in this part in those Cicadæ that are said to sing, but no such special cleft in those that do not sing (*H. A.* iv. 9, 3; *De Som.* 2, 17).

It is plain that A. is speaking of the so-called drums of the Cicadæ, which are placed on the first segment of the abdomen, that is directly below the *hypozoma*, and which are, as he rightly says, the organs by which these insects produce sounds. Though he describes these rightly as specially belonging to the Cicadæ, yet he seems to think there is something of the same sort in all insects that make buzzing sounds, as bees, wasps, and the like, probably alluding to the thinner portions of integument which lie between the successive segments of the abdomen. That these "drums" serve as the equivalent of the respiratory organs of higher animals is incorrect; yet the notion was by no means an unnatural one. The motions of the abdomen to which A. refers are of course the alternate contractions and dilatations by which air is expelled and inhaled, from and into the tracheal system.

We can now see why A. supposed the olfactory sense of insects to be located in the *hypozoma* or rather in the part below it. It was the same reason as that which made him believe that the gills of fishes (cf. ii. 10, Note, 13) and the blowhole of Cetacea were organs of smell; the reason being that gills, blowhole, hypozoma, corresponded to the

Notes. ii. 16.

nostrils in one respect, viz. as regards the refrigerating process, and therefore probably corresponded to them in others.

That insects perceive odours is unquestionable. But it is still uncertain where their olfactory organs are situated. It is supposed by some writers at any rate that the stigmata which admit air, and which are mostly "below the *hypozoma*," are also the parts which admit olfactory stimulants, "the ultimate ramifications of the tracheæ forming one extensive nose." This view (erroneous as I believe) coincides very fairly with that of Aristotle.

11. A. often speaks of the innate spirit (ἔμφυτον πνεῦμα), and distinguishes it from the spirit or breath that is introduced from without (πνεῦμα ἐπείσακτον). It is however far from clear what his conception of this innate spirit really was.

There is indeed a special treatise *De Spiritu*, but this is most undoubtedly spurious. One sufficient proof of this is that whereas A. in his genuine works gives the same name (φλέβες) to both arteries and veins, and states positively that they both in life contain blood, the author of this treatise has already learnt to apply the term "arteries" to the former, reserving the term φλέβες for the latter; and moreover asserts that the arteries contain air, not blood. The term ἀρτηρία in Aristotle always means trachea, or its larger divisions the right and left bronchus, and is never used for any blood-vessel. So again while A. expressly states, in the passage to which this is a note, that the innate spirit is not introduced from without, the author of the *De Spiritu* says that it varies in amount at different times, and discusses the question whether the increased amount is derived from the food or from the inspired air. Neglecting then this spurious treatise, and putting together the genuine passages in which A. speaks, or seems to speak, of the innate spirit, the following seems to me to be his view.

The "vital heat" which is the immediate agent of the soul in its operations (*D. G.* ii. 4, 43) is not common heat, but something with much greater efficacy. The heat of fire cannot effect digestion, cannot convert blood into fat or the like (ii. 6, Note 7), nor cause the development of the embryo (*D. G.* ii. 3, 13). It is only the vital heat, or the celestial heat of the sun, that can do this. Of this heat, derived from the heavenly bodies, there is a store in the air or spirit which is contained in every fluid; and as everything contains water, "everything is in a sense full of soul" or life (*D. G.* iii. 11, 16). This air or spirit with its stored-up celestial heat is imparted to the embryo in the sperm, of which it forms the active principle; so that "man is produced by man and by the sun" (*Phys.* ii. 2, 11), or, in animals generated spontaneously, is imparted in the fluid from which they originate. Thus in all animals it is innate; and it is on the proportion of this vitalized air or innate spirit that enters into their composition that the greater or less nobility of all animals depends (*D. G.* ii. 3, 11). This innate spirit with its vitalizing heat is comparable to, if not identical with, the heavenly æther of which celestial bodies are made (*D. G.* ii. 3, 12), and becomes the agent of the soul in its operations. Its central seat is the heart, and because it is there, this organ becomes the centre of sensation, motion, and vitality generally.

In short, the innate spirit is the material in which the soul is incorporate, a material akin to, or identical with, the celestial æther.

A.'s views as to the innate spirit, or innate heat, prevailed for many centuries, and are discussed in Harvey's work on Generation (*Exercit.* lxxi).

As regards the mode in which the innate spirit ministers to the soul, the following seems to have been A.'s view. The innate spirit is a suitable agent of the nutritive soul in virtue of its special heat, the use of heat in concoction, growth, development, being evident. It is also a suitable substance to act as the agent of the soul in sensation, because it has physically the character of hot air, and therefore, as air, is capable of receiving the motions, or as we should say the vibrations, of the medium, which are communicated to it through the agency of the several sense-organs; these sense-organs either lying directly in contiguity with the heart, that is with the central seat of the spirit, (as in the case of touch and taste), or communicating with it or its accessory blood-vessels by means of ducts, themselves filled with innate spirit, as in the case of hearing and of smell (*D. G.* ii. 6, 32). So also the innate spirit is a suitable agent for the production of motion. For, as air, it has the faculty of expansion and of contraction by means of changes in its heat; and the motion of parts, which is either a being thrust forward or a being pulled back, can only be brought about by an agent that itself expands and contracts (*De Mot. An.* 10).

A. seems to have pictured to himself the motions of the body as produced in the following way. The spirit in the heart by its changes of bulk acts on the numerous tendinous cords inside that organ (iii. 4, Note 20), and these, being continuous with the sinews which are attached to the various bones, in turn act upon them.

12. Cf. Note 5.

13. Most would say that man has the more delicate sense because he has the more delicate organ. But A. usually inverts the statement; for he insists that nature does not take a man who chances to have a flute and teach him to play on it, but takes a man who can play and gives him a flute (iv. 10, 20). There is however a passage in a later treatise in which A. says that "In each case nature gives organ and function simultaneously; for such is the best plan. The parts in which secretions occur are formed simultaneously with the function of secretion, and with its matter. There is no such thing as vision without an eye, nor perfect eye without vision, etc." (*D. G.* iv. 1, 32).

14. That man is superior to other animals in touch, but inferior to them in the other senses, is often stated by A. (*De Sensu.* 4, 2; *D. A.* ii. 9, 1; *H. A.* i. 15,14). Compare Bichat (*Anat. Gén.* i. 117) and Cuvier (*Anat. Comp.* ii. 538). Elsewhere (*D. G.* v. 2, 8) A. explains that man's inferiority consists merely in his not seeing, hearing, or smelling, objects at so great a distance as other animals, while he surpasses them all in his power of nice discrimination. This however apparently was not the view held by him when he wrote the *De Animâ*, at any rate so far as regards smell. "Man," he says there (ii. 9), "can distinguish pleasant odours from unpleasant ones, and this is all. Here his power of discrimination ends. Just in the same way it is probable that animals with hard eyes (i.e. *Crustacea, and insects*) are unable to discriminate between different colours, excepting so far as that some colours excite terror in them while others do not. . . . The objects that are perceptible by smell seem to be analogous to those that are perceptible by taste; but our sense of taste is more delicate than our sense of smell, inasmuch as taste is a variety of touch, which in man is most acute. For whereas man is far behind other animals in his other senses, in touch he is far superior to them. And this it is that makes him the most intelligent of animals."

(Ch. 17.) 1. That is, in aerial and in aquatic animals.

2. Cf. ii. 10, Note 22.

3. Meaning parrots. In these the tongue is "épaisse, charnue, et arrondie; deux circonstances qui leur donnent la plus grande facilité à imiter la voix humaine" (*Cuvier, R. An.* i. 461). It will be noticed that A. includes parrots among the birds with talons, *i.e.* Raptores. He did not know of the peculiarity of their toes; for he speaks of the wryneck (iv. 12, Note 33) as the only bird that has two of its toes turned backwards.

Notes. ii. 17.

In all probability he had never seen a living parrot; for even as to the fact alluded to in this passage, viz. the peculiar tongue, he plainly (*H. A.* viii. 12, 13) is speaking at second-hand.

4. "Small birds have a greater variety of notes and are more loquacious than large birds" (*H. A.* iv. 9, 14). "It is remarkable that only small birds properly sing. The Australian genus Menura, however, must be excepted; for the Menura Alberti, which is about the size of a half-grown turkey, not only mocks other birds, but its own whistle is exceedingly beautiful and varied" (*Darwin, Descent of Man*, ii. 55).

5. "With birds the voice serves to express various emotions, such as distress, fear, anger, triumph, or mere happiness. It is apparently sometimes used to excite terror. . . . The common domestic cock clucks to the hen, and the hen to the chickens, when a dainty morsel is found. The hen when she has laid an egg repeats the same note very often, and concludes with the sixth above, which she holds for a longer time, and thus expresses her joy. Some social birds apparently call to each other for aid, and as they flit from tree to tree, the flock is kept together by chirp answering chirp. During the nocturnal migrations of geese and other water-fowl, sonorous clangs from the van may be heard in the darkness over-head, answered by clangs in the rear. Certain cries serve as danger-signals, which, as the sportsman knows to his cost, are well understood by the same species and by others. The domestic cock crows, and the humming-bird chirps, in triumph over a defeated rival. The true song however of most birds and various strange cries are chiefly uttered during the breeding season, and serve as a charm, or merely as a call-note to the other sex" (*Darwin, Descent of Man*, ii. 51). Whether the voice of birds, besides expressing emotions and serving to give signals, can also be used by them for the communication of more complex intellectual ideas, is still an open question. "J'incline à croire," however says M. Edwards (*Leçons sur la Phys.* xiv. 118), "que chez quelques-uns de ces animaux, les Hirondelles par exemple, une sorte de conversation peut s'établir entre les différents individus d'une même troupe." In the *Hist. An.* (ix. 31, 2) it is stated that when a battle had occurred in a far-off country, all the crows disappeared from Attica and the Peloponnese, as though information of the banquet had been passed on from crow to crow.

6. Cf. *H. A.* iv. 9.

7. The tongue is not protrusible in Chelonia nor in crocodiles, but highly so in serpents and in lizards. In serpents it is slit into two at the end, and deeply so in lizards. It appears however to be an organ of exploration rather than of taste, for "les serpents, tout en étant fort délicats sur la choix de leur nourriture, ne paraissent pas avoir le sens du goût très developpé; car lorsque ces reptiles ont commencé à ingurgiter leur proie, on peut leur faire avaler d'autres aliments, sans qu'ils s'aperçoivent du changement. Il suffit d'attacher ces corps entre les pattes postérieures de l'animal qu'ils sont en train d'avaler; c'est une opération que l'on pratique souvent dans les ménageries erpétologiques par un motif d'économie" (*M. Edwards*, xi. 451).

8. "There is no tongue in this rudimentary fish (*lancelet*). That organ is often absent or very small in the typical members of the class; its basis, the glossohyal, when it projects at all into the mouth, is rarely covered by integument so organised as to suggest their being endowed with the sense of taste" (*Owen, Vert.* i. 411). See also *Cuvier, An. Comp.* ii. 681.

9. The tongue of the crocodile scarcely projects from the lining membrane in the floor of the mouth. For a drawing of it, see *R. Jones, An. Kingdom*, p. 686. As to the jaw, cf. iv. 11, Note 20.

10. The exact drift of this passage is not very evident. I take it that A. thinks it necessary to explain why the tongue, if it adheres to one jaw, does not adhere to that which in his view is the nobler, namely the upper (ii. 2, Note 6). His explanation is that in reality the tongue does adhere to the upper jaw; but that the upper jaw has been brought into the position of the lower one, as its immobility testifies, lest the adherence of the tongue to it should interfere with deglutition.

11. Cf. iv. 11, Notes 6, 7.

12. In the Cyprinoids the palate is cushioned with a thick soft vascular substance, remarkable for its great irritability. . This is still commonly known in France as "langue de carpe" (*Cuvier, R. An.* ii. 270).

13. This is true.

14. As to the tongue of Crustacea, Cephalopods, Gasteropods, etc., cf. iv. 5, Notes 4, 6, 8.

15. What species of Gasteropod corresponds to Aristotle's Purpura is a matter of doubt. All that we learn from the various passages in which it is mentioned is that it had a spiral shell, an operculum, and a strong tongue, which enabled it to prey on other shell-fish; that it deposited its eggs in honey-like masses; furnished a dye; and that there were numerous species of it, some large, some small. Probably the term includes all the various species of Murex, Buccinum, and Purpura, from which purple dye was obtainable. Of these the more important seem to have been Murex trunculus, and M. brandaris. M. Boblaye found numerous heaps of shells of M. brandaris on the coast of the Morea, close to the ruins of ancient dyeworks. Similar evidence was obtained by Wilde on the Tyrian coast for M. trunculus (cf. *Woodward, Mollusca,* p. 106; *Meyer, Thierkunde,* p. 183). As to the power possessed by the Purpura lapillus of perforating shells by means of its armed tongue, see *Forbes and Hanley, Brit. Mollusca,* iii. 385.

16. The words I have translated vaguely as gad-flies and cattle-flies are in the text Æstri and Myopes. There are not sufficient data to determine what exact species of Diptera are meant. The general statements made about them in various passages seem to point clearly to some or other species of Tabanus such as T. bovinus, and Chrysops cæcutiens (*Aubert and Wimmer*); but the account given of the development of Æstrus (*H. A.* v. 19) is inconsistent with this identification.

17. The similarity consists in the accumulation of distinct functions in one and the same part.

BOOK III.

(Ch. 1.) 1. As a rule the same organs which serve as weapons of defence serve also in offensive warfare; such for example is the case with the long horns of the Oryx. But, as A. says, this is not always the case. Thus the upper branches of the horns are used by some kinds of deer chiefly or exclusively for defence, while the brow antlers are used in attack. In wild boars the skin over the shoulder is specially modified to form a shield, which, like the mane of a lion, is exclusively a weapon of defence. Similar distinctions may be noticed with regard to the teeth. In such carnivora as the lion they serve indifferently for protection and attack; but in the Babirusa pig the lower tusks alone are used for offence, the upper ones being useless except for protection. In the common wild boar exactly the reverse is the case; the upper tusks being here the offensive, and the lower the defensive, weapons. Cf. *Darwin, D. of Man*, ii. ch. 17.

2. That is, "broad below and sharp above" (*H. A.* ii. 3, 1).

3. "Tusks and horns never co-exist in the same animal; nor does any animal that is saw-toothed ever have either of these parts" (*H. A.* ii. 1, 52). Cf. iii. 2, Notes 9 and 19.

4. That the males in any armed species are almost invariably furnished with more formidable weapons than the females is a conspicuous fact, as also is their more pugnacious temperament. The temperament is according to A.'s views the antecedent of the weapons. But it is more probable that both weapons and temperament are attributable to one common cause; and what that cause is Darwin has shown in his work on sexual selection. The males contend with each other for the females, and such males as chance variation has endowed with a slightly stronger weapon or slightly stouter heart will as a rule prevail in the struggle; and, obtaining preferential possession of the females, will leave offspring in greater numbers than their less favoured competitors. Of this offspring some will inherit the physical and moral advantages of their sires. Of these again the best-armed and the most valiant will be most successful in propagating their kind; and so on, generation after generation, the comparatively weakly and cowardly being eliminated at each stage of improvement.

5. The only grounds for saying that the organs of vegetative life are smaller proportionately in females than in males are, so far as I am aware, the smaller size of the gills in female fishes (*Yarrell, Fishes*, i. xxi), and of the respiratory organs in the females of the higher vertebrates; and the alleged smaller proportions of the female heart (*M. Edwards, Leçons*, iii. 483). Perhaps however A. merely means that all the organs of females are smaller than the corresponding parts in males. If so, he must be speaking only of Mammals. For while he recognises the greater size of the males in this group, he also recognizes the contrary in other groups (*H. A.* iv. 11, 9; v. 5, 3; *D. G.* i. 16, 2).

6. It will be noticed how carefully and accurately A. expresses himself in this passage. As he was of course ignorant of the reindeer, his statement that the female deer are without horns is quite correct. As to sheep and cattle he merely says that the horns differ in the two sexes, being stronger in the male (*H. A.* iv. 11, 15). This is also correct. For "in all the wild species of sheep and goats the horns are larger in the male than in the female, and are sometimes quite absent in the latter, as is also the case in several domestic breeds. In most wild bovine animals the bull has longer and thicker horns than the cow. While in the domestic races of cattle, the horns of the bull though thicker than those of the cow are shorter" (*Darwin, Des. of Man.* ii, 245). So also he is correct in simply saying that female birds are *often* without spurs when the males have them. For in some species of Gallinaceæ the hens are without any vestige of spurs; in most they possess them in a rudimentary condition; while in a few exceptional cases they have them fully formed.

Elsewhere (*H. A.* ix. 49, 2) it is remarked that in some pugnacious hens small spurs rise up on the legs; and mention is made (*H. A.* iv. 2, 9) of a crustacean in which the male has much larger spur-like appendages than the female.

7. The Scarus is doubtless the parrot-fish (*Scarus Cretensis*) of the Archipelago. The beak-like jaws of these fishes have a dense covering of four-sided prismatic denticles. With this strong apparatus they scoop off the calcareous lithophytes from the bottom of the sea, on which they browse just as the ruminants crop the herbage of the fields. See *Owen's Vert.* i. 378, for a representation of this dentition. The parrot-fish is by no means the only exception to the general statement that all fishes have serrated dentition. In the wolf-fish for instance most of the teeth are powerful crushers, as in many other

genera that live on Testacea and Crustacea. The rays, again, and skates have the mouth paved with flat teeth, and A. was familiar with these fishes. He speaks more guardedly elsewhere (iv. 13, Note 30).

8. "In the sharks and rays the teeth are supported by the upper and lower jaw; but many other fishes have teeth growing from the roof of the mouth, from the surface of the tongue, from the bony hoops supporting the gills, and some have them developed from the base of the nose and base of the skull" (*Owen*).

9. The mouth in many fishes, *e.g.* the pike, is beset with a countless number of sharp teeth which project from all parts of the internal surface. The object of this is not so much the comminution of the food, as A. supposes, as to enable the fish to retain hold of its slippery prey. Similarly the recurved form of the teeth, noticeable in many predatory species, serves to prevent the prey when once in the mouth from escaping, the points being all directed towards the œsophagus.

10. The other weapons are the dorsal fin, armed with rigid spines and highly developed for defence in such a fish as the perch, where the dentition is "en fin velours" (cf. *Rolleston, Forms of Animal Life*, p. 43); and the still stronger spines on the back of dog-fishes, and the skin of rays, etc.

11. Namely, at ii. 16, 6, when speaking of the elephant's trunk. Similar statements are made (*D. P.* iv. 10, 33, *and* 58) concerning the female mammæ, and the tails of animals.

12. That is to say without any compulsion from the necessary laws of matter. As to the general statement, cf. M. Edwards (*Leçons de Phys. Comp.* i. 21), "En effet, lorsqu'une propriété physiologique commence à se localiser dans une série d'animaux de plus en plus parfaits, elle s'exerce d'abord à l'aide d'une partie qui existait déjà dans l'organisme des espèces inférieures et qui est seulement modifiée dans sa structure pour s'approprier à des fonctions spéciales. Tantôt c'est, pour ainsi dire, un fonds commun qui fournit aux diverses facultés leurs premiers instruments particuliers; d'autres fois c'est à un appareil déjà destiné à des usages spéciaux que la fonction nouvelle emprunte ses organes, et c'est seulement après avoir épuisé les ressources de ce genre, que la puissance créatrice introduit dans la constitution des êtres à organisation plus parfaite un élément nouveau."

13. *i.e.* the Raptores, cf. iv. 12, Note 1.

14. The example is well chosen. For in woodpeckers, especially in the larger species, the beak acquires the density of ivory (cf. *Owen, Vert.* ii. 146). In the raven also, which is the bird usually meant by A. when he speaks of crows, the beak is hard and strong.

15. A. does not make 'the mistake committed by many other writers, of basing man's supremacy on his power of gazing upwards; on the contrary he rightly describes him as looking in front. The error he escaped is ridiculed by Galen (*De Usu part.* iii. 3), who says it can only be entertained by those who had never seen a flat fish, and that every donkey can bend back his neck and look upwards as easily as can man. But that man alone of animals is erect, is repeatedly mentioned by A. as a proof of his superiority. Doubtless the erect position leaving as it does the upper extremities free for skilful manual operations is an important element in man's structure. But this position is not the exclusive privilege of man; some birds, as the penguin, having a vertical attitude, and even some mammals, as the kangaroo. Cf. *Lewes, Arist.* p. 309.

(Ch. 2.) 1. For instance in some male fishes, lizards, and many beetles, where the horns are not weapons but mere ornaments. So A. calls the antennæ of Crustacea horns (*H. A.* iv. 2, 10). He alludes however more especially to the Egyptian snake (*H. A.* ii. 1, 36): "Thus the Egyptians speak of the snakes about Thebes as horned, because they have a kind of projection which as it were simulates a horn." This is a reference to *Herodot.* ii. 74, and the snake in question was doubtless the Cerastes of Egypt.

2. *i.e.* Carnivora, Rodentia, Insectivora, Cheiroptera, as well as man, apes, and elephants; in fact all Mammalia known to A. excepting Ruminantia, Solidungula, and Cetacea.

3. Meaning the Indian Ass. Cf. Note 10.

4. And therefore, he implies, might be expected to have horns, like most cloven-hoofed animals.

5. It is somewhat astounding to find so determined a teleologist suddenly declaring that antlers are not merely useless but actually injurious to stags. A modern writer however (*Bailly, Sur l'usage des cornes, Ann. d. Sc. Nat.* ii. 371) has come to the same conclusion: "Quant aux bois du cerf, du renne, de l'élan, on sait qu'ils sont plus nuisibles qu'utiles." The horns are however not so utterly useless as is here supposed, the upper antlers serving in defence, the brow antlers in attack (*Desc. of Man*, ii. 253). Still, as Darwin points out, the large branching horns do present a difficulty. For a straight point would inflict a much more serious wound than several diverging ones. Their great size and branching serve however as ornaments, and so give an advantage in the sexual struggle.

6. The Bubalus must not be confounded with the Bos Bubalus or Buffalo, which was known to A. under the name of the wild ox of the Arachotæ (*H. A.* i. 21). His Bubalus or Bubalis, as he elsewhere calls it, is always mentioned by him in company with deer, antelopes, and the like. It is mentioned in like association by Herodotus (iv. 192), who enumerates it among the animals of Libya; and by Pliny it is said to be something like a calf or deer (*Nat. Hist.* viii. 15). From these insufficient data it is taken to be the Antelope bubalis, or hartbeeste of Africa.

The Dorcas that had horns like those of the Hippelaphus or nylghau (*H. A.* ii. 1, 22), that was the smallest known animal with horns, and that was an inhabitant of Africa (*Herod.* iv. 192), is probably the gazelle, and I have so rendered it. The gazelles are by no means cowardly. They fly of course from lions and panthers, of which they form the chief prey, but "the flock when brought to bay defend themselves with courage and obstinacy, uniting in a close circle with the females and fawns in the centre, and presenting their horns at all points to the enemy."

7. The Bonasus (*H. A.* ix. 45) is universally admitted to be the aurochs or European bison, the Bison jubatus of Pliny, which in the present day is almost extinct, existing only in Lithuania and in the Caucasus, but which in ancient times abounded in the forests of Europe generally. A. speaks of it (*H. A.* ii. 1, 35) as living in his days in Pæonia and Medica, *i.e.* North Macedonia. There is a fine specimen in the British Museum. The story of the use to which the Bonasus puts its dung is given with more detail elsewhere (*H. A.* ix. 45, 6). The only conjecture I can make as to the foundation of the statement is that it may have been derived from the aurochs, in its flight, kicking up stones and dirt into the face of its pursuers, just as the giraffe is said to do (cf. *Dallas, Animal Kingd.* p. 712), and the ostrich.

8. For instance snakes, hedgehogs, skunks, and, of invertebrata, cuttle-fishes and the beetles known from their habits as Bombardiers. See the account of Brachyurus crepitans given by Kirby and Spence. Mr. Tristram (*The Great Sahara*, p. 64) describes the houbara or bustard as employing a similar singular mode of defence when hunted with falcons: "As the hawk approaches, the houbara ejects both from the mouth and vent a slimy fluid. A well-trained bird eludes this shower by repeated feints, until the quarry's

supply of moisture is exhausted. An impatient one rushes in and gets his whole plumage so bedaubed that his flight is materially impeded, and his swoop when made. is irresolute."

9. This statement, so often made by A., has much truth in it. For example many insects are protected by the dull tints of their colouring, or their resemblance to vegetable or inanimate objects, rendering them practically invisible to birds. But when they are endowed with some more special means of defence, their colouring is often such as to render them very conspicuous. The stinging Hymenoptera, for instance, are as a rule showy and brilliant, and in no single instance are protected by mimicry of vegetable or inanimate objects. The Chrysididæ again, though stingless, can roll themselves into a ball as hard and polished as if of metal, and these are most gorgeously coloured. So also the fœtid Hemiptera, and the ladybirds that emit fluids which are highly distasteful to birds, are in large proportion gay-coloured and conspicuous (cf. *Wallace, Natural Selection*, 2nd ed. p. 69). Facts of similar significance are observable in mammalia. "Very few male quadrupeds," says Darwin (*Descent of Man*, ii. 257), have weapons of two distinct kinds specially adapted for fighting with rival males," a statement which he proceeds to support by the inverse relation which obtains as a rule between the development of horns and of canine teeth.

10. The account of the Indian Ass with a solid hoof, and a single horn, was taken by A. from Ctesias, who apparently did not profess himself to have seen more of the animal than its astragalus. It has been plausibly conjectured that the Indian Rhinoceros (*R. unicornis*) is the animal meant. For, though this animal has three toes, they are so indistinctly separated, that the real character of the foot might easily escape a casual observer, to whom the animal would moreover probably not give much leisure for observation. I may, however, observe that on the obelisk of Nimroud, made long before the time of Ctesias, and very possibly seen by him, there is represented a rhinoceros, with feet distinctly divided into toes. An argument on the side of the supposed identification is furnished by the fact that the horn of the Indian Ass was supposed to have certain magical powers, so that a cup made of it gave the drinker immunity from poison, as is related by Philostratus in his life of Apollonius ; while similar virtues are assigned in the East to rhinoceros horn, even in the present day. Supposing the one-horned ass of India to be the Rhinoceros unicornis, may it not be that "the asses with horns" (οἱ ὄνοι τὰ κέρεα ἔχοντες) which Herodotus (iv. 191) enumerates among the animals of Libya are the two-horned rhinocerotes of Africa ?

11. An apparent recognition of the fact so much insisted on by Bichat, namely the greater symmetry of the organs of animal life, as compared with the organs of vegetative life. Cf. iii. 5, Note 4.

12. The Oryx is probably the Leucoryx of North Africa, which is often represented on Egyptian and Nubian monuments. It is supposed that some individual that had lost a horn in fighting had been seen, and taken for a member of a normally one-horned species. I do not think it necessary to suppose this ; for the Oryx, when seen in profile, has wonderfully the look of having a single horn, and I once actually heard some ladies at the Zoological Gardens when they came to it, cry out, "Why, it has only got one horn " ! The explanation of the appearance is that the horns run straight back from their origin without diverging, save in the very smallest degree, to right and left. Thus when the animal is seen in profile, one horn concealing the other parallel one, the appearance is as though there were a single central horn. When the horns diverge widely from each other, as for instance in the common ox, no such appearance is produced by a side view. So long as 2000 years after Aristotle, we find Sir T. Browne asserting, in opposition

to those who held that the unicorn was a fabulous animal, that there are no less than five kinds; among which he reckons the Oryx and the Indian ass. Cf. *Vulgar Errors*, iii. 23.

13. Cf. ii. 9, Note 9.

14. The fable of Momus, the critic God, is alluded to by Lucian (*Nigrinus*, 32), and told in full by Babius (*Sir C. Lewes's ed.* 59). Their account of the criticism on the bull's structure is not quite the same as Aristotle's. Momus objects that the horns are so placed as to be in the way of the animal's sight when it has its head down to attack its foe.

15. A. knew nothing of the giraffe, except perhaps by name, if the Hippardium, as some think, be that animal. So that he is correct in saying that deer alone have solid horns; and that they alone cast them. The rest of the horned ruminants are all sheath-horned—cavicornia. That is to say, their horns consist each of a conical process of bone, which is covered by a sheath of horny matter, and is not cast periodically like the solid horn of the stag, excepting by the Prong-horned Antelope of North America.

16. Cf. Introduction, p. iv.

17. The gazelle, though small, is by no means the smallest of the horned ruminants; sundry other species of antelope, such as the guevi and the kleenebock, being much more diminutive. Indeed one variety of guevi is said by Adanson to be not much larger than a good-sized Norway rat.

18. Cf. Introd. p. vii.

19. "The inverse relationship between the development of teeth and horns, exemplified by the total absence of canines in the ruminants with persistent frontal weapons, by their first appearance in the periodically hornless deer, and by their larger size in the absolutely hornless musks, is further illustrated by the presence not only of canines but of a pair of laniariform incisors in the upper jaw of Camelidæ" (*Owen*, *Vert.* iii. 348), and to this statement may be added the recently acquired fact that the water-deer of China has no antlers, like other true deer, but has two long projecting canine teeth to serve in their place for defence. It is however very doubtful whether these facts are to be explained as in the text by the law of organic equivalents (ii. 9, Note 9). Still the amount of organic matter consumed in the development of horns is so great, that it is by no means impossible that their presence may necessitate a greater economy in the rest of the body; and this economy will be practised in those parts which are the least necessary, such as the canine teeth which are no longer required as weapons of strife. "Tusks and horns," says Darwin (*Desc. of Man*, ii. 258), "are manifestly of high importance to their possessors, for their development consumes much organised matter. A single tusk of the Asiatic elephant, one of the extinct woolly species, and of an African elephant, have been known to weigh 150, 160, and 180 pounds, and even greater weights have been assigned by some authors. With deer in which the horns are periodically renewed, the drain on the constitution must be greater: the horns for instance of the moose weigh from 50 to 60 pounds, and those of the extinct Irish elk from 60 to 70 pounds, the skull of the latter weighing on an average only 5¼ pounds. With sheep, although the horns are not periodically renewed, yet their development, in the opinion of many agriculturists, entails a sensible loss to the breeder." That such may be the case we may readily suppose when we consider that horns weighing 72 lbs. have been developed in deer in ten weeks (cf. *Huxley*, *Verteb.* 385).

20. Cf. Note 5.

21. Thus in the Babirussa pig the upper tusks "more nearly resemble horns than teeth."

(Ch. 3.) 1. The word I have rendered *larynx* is in the Greek *pharynx*. It is quite clear however that the part which is made of cartilage, serves for vocal and respiratory purposes, lies in front of the œsophagus, etc., can only be what we call larynx, and I have therefore so translated it. Yet the word *larynx* was known to A., and occasionally used by him as by us. It would seem that the two words *pharynx* and *larynx* had not in his day been clearly differentiated from each other, but were used indifferently for one and the same part (*H. A.* iv. 9, 1 *and* 2), namely the larynx. What we call *pharynx* had for A. no distinct name, being nothing more than the first part of the œsophagus; which latter he says, later on in this chapter, is directly continuous with the mouth. This can hardly be called confounding *pharynx* and *larynx*, with which Mr. Lewes charges Aristotle. Galen sometimes uses *pharynx* as equivalent to *larynx*; sometimes in the modern sense, as the common meeting-place of gullet and windpipe (cf. *Darembery's Galen*, i. 381).

2. "In some fishes there is no œsophagus at all; in the rest it is of short length" (*D. P.* iii. 14, 12). As a rule the œsophagus is indistinct in fishes, being scarcely differentiated from the stomach and intestine. In some fishes however, as the rays, it is distinct enough.

3. It would probably be truer to say that there is a long trachea in order that there may be a long neck, so as to facilitate the motions of the head, than to say, as A. does, that there must be a long neck, in order to provide space for a long trachea. Still the length of the trachea is not without use; for the air in its passage down the long canal is filtered of its dust, moistened, and warmed. In some animals the trachea is still further lengthened by being formed into a coil.

4. Cf. iii. 4, Note 20.

5. It is indeed impossible to explain teleologically the strange position occupied by the orifice of the trachea. A supposed explanation has been found in the homologies of the part. The lungs and trachea correspond anatomically to the swim-bladder and pneumatic duct of fishes, and have probably been developed as modifications of these latter organs, whose place they occupy (*Darwin, Or. of Species*, p. 191). But the duct in fishes as a general rule opens on the dorsal, and very exceptionally on the ventral, aspect of the œsophagus; a fact which scarcely harmonizes with this explanation.

6. Alluding to Plato (*Jowett's Transl.* ii. 584). Hippocrates mentions and attacks this same strange notion (*De Morbis*, iv. 30).

7. Mammals alone have an epiglottis. In other vertebrata the opening into the larynx and trachea is closed simply by constrictor muscles.

8. Cf. ii. 13, Note 5.

9. Frantzius, as I think erroneously, infers from this passage that A. supposed the trachea to communicate directly with the heart. Had A. so imagined, he would not have said, as in the text, "leads to the lung and the heart," but merely "to the heart"; for the fact of its also leading to the lung would have had nothing to do with the matter. But, as the trachea only leads to the lung, he is obliged to mention this organ as well as the heart; his argument being as follows. "The heart is in front; but, where the heart is, there and surrounding it must be the lung, in order to perform its due office to the heart. The lung, then, must also be in front; and therefore the windpipe also, which leads to it." There is indeed one vague passage (*H. A.* i. 16, 14) which would at first sight seem to establish Frantzius's view. "The heart also is connected with the windpipe by fatty, cartilaginous, and fibrinous bands. . . . . When the windpipe is inflated, in some animals there is no sign of the air getting into it, but in some of the large animals it plainly does." Allowing that by "it" is meant the heart, which is not

certain, for it may only mean the trachea, the passage still by no means necessarily implies that A. thought there was any communicating channel between trachea and heart. It merely states that the two are connected by bands, and that a passage of air from the windpipe to the heart is somehow possible in some large animals. In order, however, for this to occur, A. by no means supposed it necessary that a direct communicating channel should exist, as is sufficiently shown in his description of the lungs: "When the windpipe," he says, "reaches the lung, it divides and subdivides, each division producing smaller and smaller branches, till the whole lung is permeated by them" (*H. A.* i. 16, 13). "There are also ducts (i.e. *the pulmonary blood-vessels*) which lead from the heart to the lung; and these also divide and subdivide, their branches accompanying the branches from the windpipe. But there is no communication between the two (οὐδεὶς δέ ἐστὶ κοινὸς πόρος). Notwithstanding this, however, air can pass from the former (i.e. *the bronchial tubes*) into the latter (i.e. *the pulmonary vessels*), owing to the close contact in which the two lie (διὰ τὴν σύναψιν), and be transmitted to the heart" (*H. A.* i. 17, 5). This passage shows that A. not only had a fair knowledge of the anatomy of the lung, but also that he believed the air to pass from the air-passages into the blood-vessels through their unbroken walls, just as we hold the oxygen to do. The trachea then was not supposed by him to lead directly to the heart, but merely to the lung. As to his statement, if it be his statement, that mechanical inflation of the trachea sometimes sends air visibly into the heart, it can only be explained by his having ruptured the parts in his experimental manipulations.

10. Cf. ii. 2, Note 6.

(Ch. 4.) 1. It must not be supposed that A. means that the bloodless animals have none of what we call viscera. For he often mentions the stomach, intestines, and other internal organs of cephalopods, insects, etc. He limits the term viscera to such internal parts as are so coloured as to resemble blood, of which in fact he supposes them to be formed (iii. 4, 3; iii. 10, 13). As the bloodless animals have merely a fluid analogous to blood, so they can only have parts analogous to viscera. It is however to be noted that once A. admits of an exception to this, viz. the liver or *mytis* of the Cephalopods (iv. 5, Note 13). This he regards as a viscus, doubtless on account of its dull-red or violet hue.

2. Cf. *H. A.* vi. 3, 2, where it is said that the heart in the bird's egg at its first appearance looks like a bloody spot, and palpitates as though endowed with life; a description which is the origin of the "punctum saliens" of later writers. These minute observations as to the heart in ovum and embryo were made, as we learn from another passage (*De Juv.* 3, 4), by A. himself, and are sufficient to establish his fame as an original observer. The heart is not actually the first part to appear in the embryo, but it is the first to enter actively into its functions, contracting in the bird so early as the second day of incubation, and becoming a few hours later rhythmical in its motions.

3. Cf. i. 5, Note 1.

4. The liver in the mature fœtus forms $\frac{1}{20}$th of the whole body; in the adult it forms only $\frac{1}{37}$th. The heart also is larger proportionately to the whole body in the young embryo ($\frac{1}{50}$th) than in the mature fœtus ($\frac{1}{120}$th), and in the fœtus than in adult man ($\frac{1}{160}$th). In infancy again the lungs are of a brightish colour, "which might be compared to blood froth; but as life advances they become darker, mottled with spots, patches, etc." Cf. *Quain's Anat.* 1145.

5. In calling the heart the origin or centre of the vessels, A. implies two distinct things: firstly, that it is the place where the blood is made; and, secondly, the place whence the blood, when thus made, is propelled into the vessels, blood going from it, but none returning to it.

13

His predecessors (*H. A.* iii. 3, 5) had said that the origin of the vessels was in the head; but it does not appear clearly what they meant by origin, or whether they used the term in the same sense as did Aristotle. This much, however, seems certain: that they regarded the heart as no essential part, if part at all, of the vascular system. Neither Syennesis nor Polybus, who was son-in-law of Hippocrates, so much as mention the heart in their accounts of the vascular system; and though Diogenes speaks of it as receiving two large branches, he clearly regards these branches as of no more importance than the branches to other organs or parts (*H. A.* iii. 2; iii. 3). A. had therefore to show not only that the heart was the centre of the vascular system, but firstly that it was part at all of that system.

His arguments are somewhat confusedly given, but may be thus arranged.

That the heart is part of the vascular system is shown in the first place by dissection; for, when exposed, it is seen in most direct and evident communication with the large vessels. Secondly, the heart resembles the rest of the vascular system in structure; for it is homogeneous in substance, like the blood-vessels (cf. ii. 1_6, Note 16). Thirdly, the heart has no nutrient vessels, which can only be explained on the view that it is nourished by blood, of which it is the receptacle (cf. ii. 1, Note 18). The solidarity of heart and vessels is still further shown by the fact that throbbing occurs simultaneously in them all (*De Resp.* 20, 7). The heart then is part of the vascular system. That it is the centre of the system is shown, firstly, by dissection, for the large vessels seem to radiate from it. Secondly, the heart is the first part formed in the embryo (*D. G.* ii. 4, 33, 36), and, no sooner is it formed, than it is found to contain blood, at a time when there are no blood-vessels as yet to be seen (*De Resp.* 20, 6); that is to say the heart contains blood, at a period when there is no other organ than itself in which the blood can possibly have been fabricated. Thirdly, the seat of the blood formation must be some part where there is much heat, and whence heat cannot readily escape. The region of the heart is such; for the trunk is sensibly hotter than the extremities; and comparing the heart with the rest of the vascular system, its wall, though of similar material, is found to be thicker, so as to keep in the heat. Fourthly, it is probable, and preferable on practical as well as metaphysical grounds, that the source of the blood shall be an unpaired and central organ, so as to be in as equal reach as possible of all parts of the body; and, moreover, seeing of what vital importance such an organ is, that it shall be in some well-protected position. It must also evidently be some part present in all animals that have blood. The heart alone fulfils all these conditions, or fulfils them better than any other organ. Lastly, the heart is shown by independent considerations to be the centre of sensation; and the intimate relation of sensation with blood-supply renders it highly probable that the sensory centre will also be the blood-centre. M. Edwards (*Leçons sur la Phys.* iii. 5) says that A. was the first to show that the blood-vessels communicate with the heart, or arise from it. It must however be noted that Plato in the *Timæus* (§ 45) incidentally speaks of the heart as the meeting-point or knot (ἅμμα) of the vessels and the fountain of the blood.

6. Cf. Note 10.

7. Cf. ii. 2, Note 6.

8. Elsewhere (*H. A.* iii. 3, 5) A. says that not only some, but all his predecessors held this opinion.

9. The temperature of the body sensibly declines, the farther one goes from the centre towards the extremities.

10. The most natural interpretation of this passage and some others would doubtless be that the blood-vessels pass right through the viscera, and come out again on the other

side; in which case A. would have to be credited with the opinion that artery and vein were in direct peripheral communication with each other, and that the surplus blood from a viscus passed away by one or other vessel, and came back in a circle to the heart. But, in spite of the wording of the passages, I cannot believe that this was A.'s opinion. I have no doubt that he thought that the vessels ended in the viscera, and indeed (*D. P.* iii. 9, 5) he expressly says that this is the case in the kidneys. How then is the word διέχουσι, which I have rendered "extend through," to be understood? I think it must mean "spread throughout the substance"; the contrast between heart and viscera being that in the latter the vessel breaks up into nutrient branches which retain the character of vessels, while in the heart there is no such breaking up, but the vessels expand into a reservoir, and lose altogether the character of vessels, while the heart is nourished at the expense of the blood in its own cavities (ii. 1, Note 18). At the same time there are certainly passages in which διέχουσι has the other sense. Such, for instance, is the passage (*H. A.* i. 17, 12) referred to in Note 15. That passage I interpret as meaning that the hepatic vein, when it reaches the portal eminences of the liver, sends branches into it, which terminate in the substance of that organ, while the rest passes on (*Vena portæ*) and terminates on the walls of the intestine.

11. By the central part is meant, as I take it, the main bulk of the heart in opposition to the apical part, which later on is described as being solid. Possibly, however, the whole of what we call heart may be meant, and be called central, because the pericardium is included in the heart by Aristotle.

12. Cf. ii. 1, Note 18.

13. Alluding to the throbbing of the heart on any strong emotion, whether pleasant or painful.

14. Cf. ii. 7, Note 27. Neither the blood, nor yet parts without blood, are sensitive; but only parts which contain blood, and of these that which first contains blood will first be sensitive, that is will be the primary source of sensation.

15. Galen, however, did suppose that the liver was the origin of the vessels, in the sense of being the organ in which the blood was formed. Galen founded his opinion upon a more correct view of the vena portæ than that entertained by Aristotle. A. apparently thought (*H. A.* i. 17, 12) that the vena portæ was simply the continuation on the far side of the liver of the hepatic vein, conveying blood from the heart past the liver to the intestinal parts. The absorbed food passed, as he thought, up the portal vein into the hepatic vein, and so on to the heart without pause in the liver. Galen recognised the fact that the absorbed food was converted into blood on its passage, in the liver.

16. And therefore it is not a single organ, such as a dominating part should be. Cf. iii. 7, Note 1.

17. This correct description of the position of the human heart, though it renders it probable that A. had seen the organ *in situ*, does not actually prove such to have been the case. For, as Lewes says, A. may have been led to his conclusion by merely feeling the impulse of the heart on the left side; and Galen in fact (*De Usu part.* vi. 2) says that the heart is central, but erroneously supposed to be on the left because the impulse is felt there. There is however, I think, another ground for suspecting that A. spoke from actual inspection of the human heart. He describes the right ventricle as being not only on the right side, but *above* the rest of the heart, that is anterior to it (*H. A.* iii. 3, 10). This is true of the human heart, which is so tilted round as to bring the right ventricle to the front, but is not the case in other animals (*cf. Todd's Cycl.* ii. 578).

It is not quite true that man is the only animal in which the heart inclines to the left. A like obliquity exists in the higher quadrumana (*Cuvier, Anat. Comp:* iv. 197), and in the mole.

18. The probable reason why A. supposed the right side to be hotter than the left is pointed out at ii. 2, Note 6 ; and that reason would only apply in the case of man.

19. By the apex of the heart of fishes A. plainly means the point at the anterior extremity of the organ, where the bulbus arteriosus gives off the branchial artery. This however has no anatomical correspondence with the apex of the heart of other vertebrates.

A. makes a similar statement as to the position of the fish's heart elsewhere (*H. A.* ii. 17, 1 ; *De Resp.* 16, 3), and accounts for it by saying that the head in other animals is moved in a vertical plane, from above downwards, whereas in fishes it has no such motion. Forwards then in a fish is in the line from tail to mouth, while in other animals it is in the line from above downwards, that is from the back to the sternum. Strange as this explanation is, it is still stranger when one considers that, in order to supply it, A. had to abandon his usual definition of forwards, as the direction in which sight and sense generally is exercised, and to give a new and inconsistent one.

20. It is important to have a clear understanding of what A. meant by νεῦρα (sinews), as it is one of the words which have led commentators astray. The chief passage concerning the νεῦρα is the following (*H. A.* iii. 5) : "The sinews (νεῦρα) like the blood-vessels have their origin in the heart. For in the largest of the heart's cavities (i.e. *right ventricle*) are found sinews (i.e. *chordæ tendineæ*); and the aorta, as it is called, is a sinewy blood-vessel. Its ultimate branches are indeed completely sinews. For they are solid, and have the same kind of extensibility as those sinews which terminate about the joints (i.e. *the ligaments*). The sinews however do not, like the vessels, form a continuous whole. For the vessels, as in anatomical outlines, give the configuration of the whole body, and this so perfectly, that in very emaciated individuals the whole bulk of the frame appears to consist of one mass of small vessels ; for the very same part which in fat persons is flesh is turned into small vessels when they become thin. The sinews on the other hand form no such continuous system, but are placed separately from each other about the joints and bendings of the bones. For, did they form a continuous whole, their continuity would be apparent in emaciated bodies. The chief sinews are that connected with the hollow of the knee, which is the part of main importance in leaping, the double sinew called the tendon (*Achillis*?), the Epitonus, and the shoulder sinew, which two latter are used in acts requiring great strength. Others there are without names about the joints. For all the bones are connected together by sinews (i.e. *ligaments*) at their points of contact, with the exception of the skull bones, which are connected by sutures. Sinew can be split lengthways ; transversely however it cannot be so split, but admits of considerable extension. The sinews are surrounded by a slimy fluid, which is white and sticky (*synovial fluid?*). If a sinew be cut in two, it never reunites. No numbness ever occurs in a part which is without sinews, etc."
From this it is quite plain that what A. meant by νεῦρον was sinew, ligament, and fibrous tissue generally ; though it is highly probable that he confounded with these such nerves as he may have seen, owing to their white colour. In fact the last clause in the above quotation shows pretty plainly that such was the case. Still it is absurd to say as did Galen, and even in modern time Milne Edwards (*Leçons*, iii. 5), that A. held that the small arteries were converted into nerves ! This is simply a mistranslation of νεῦρον. What A. meant was that they were converted into tendinous fibres, and into this error he was led by his limited means of observation rendering it impossible for him to detect the minute cavity in a small arterial branch, which is indeed reduced to nothing by post-mortem contraction.

'We have now to consider in what manner these fibrous parts came to be, in A.'s scheme, the main instruments of motion. Of the contractility of muscular tissue he knew nothing; though it is impossible to suppose that he did not know that what we call a muscle swelled up, becoming shorter and broader, during action. The changes of shape for instance in the Biceps, perfectly well known to every painter and sculptor, cannot possibly have escaped his notice. Such a muscle however he considered to have two constituents; firstly flesh, that is the true red muscular tissue, which he supposed to be nothing more than an aggregate of small vessels clogged up with inspissated blood (iii. 5, Note 7); and, secondly, tendinous fibres and other fibrous elements such as the muscular sheath, etc., which he supposed to be the ultimate terminations of the arteries, converted into solid strings. The action of the muscle he attributed not to the former of these elements, the red muscular tissue, but to the latter, the really inactive tendinous fibres, which have, he says, a transverse extensibility, that is to say can become broader and shorter.

His idea of the mode in which these tendinous parts were called into play seems to have been as follows. The heart, as it is the centre of the nutritive and the sensory principles, so also is the centre of voluntary motion. By its independent (cf. ii. 16, Note 11) contractions and relaxations (for it is as it were a distinct living being within its possessor) it acts upon the chordæ tendineæ, and either directly or through these upon the fibrous aorta. This in turn acts upon the tendinous fibres of the muscles, which are in fact its terminal branches, and these fibres become transversely extended, and consequently longitudinally shortened; these again act in turn upon the true tendons and ligaments, by which the bones are set in motion.

The want of continuity in the tendinous system of which A. speaks is the gap between the chordæ tendineæ and the true tendons attached to the bones, a gap which he fills up by the tendinous aorta and its branches.

Such I take to be A.'s inadequate conception of the mechanism of motion. That he himself felt how unsatisfactory it was, we may infer from his saying so very little on the subject, notwithstanding its importance. We must remember, moreover, that, while nerves were still undiscovered, no explanation of voluntary motion was possible. A. had to find some anatomical machinery connecting the tendons, which were clearly the immediate agents that acted on the bones, with the volitional centre, which he took as we know to be the heart and not the brain. He could find no other continuous substance between these two, than some or other kind of fibrous tissue, in the form either of tendinous fibre or of arterial wall. This therefore he assumed to be the intermediate agent, no other being apparently forthcoming.

21. This is one of many passages showing that A. himself practised dissection.

22. Cf. *H. A.* ii. 15, 6. It is not uncommon to find in large mammalia, especially in Pachyderms and Ruminants, a cruciform ossification in the heart, below the origin of the aorta. In the ox this is a normal formation, as also in the stag. But in Pachyderms, or at any rate in the horse, it is only found in old individuals, and appears to be the result of pathological degeneration. Galen, in his manual of dissections, tells a curious story of the triumph he obtained over the assembled physicians of Rome by his demonstrating the presence of a bone in the heart of an elephant when they had failed to find it. See also *De Usu part.* vi. 19.

23. A full description of the heart is given in the *Hist. An.* (i. 17, and iii. 3). There, as here, it is stated that it has only three cavities. Aubert and Wimmer (i. 238) suppose that A. took the two auricles to form one cavity, viz. that which he terms the right cavity. Frantzius supposes that the left auricle was overlooked. Both commentators thus make the second and third of A.'s cavities correspond to the right and left ventricles

respectively. Any one who reads A.'s description will see that this view of the matter is utterly untenable, and would turn every sentence in the description into nonsense. There can, I think, be no possible doubt that the three cavities are the right ventricle, the left ventricle, and the left auricle. Why it may be asked did A. omit the right auricle? Simply because he looked on it as a venous sinus, being a part not of the heart but of the great vein (*i.e.* superior and inferior venæ cavæ). That he so regarded it, is plain from his always speaking of the superior and inferior venæ cavæ as forming a single vessel, not as two distinct ones, and he even says in one place (*II. A.* iii. 3, 8) that the heart appears very much like a part of the great vein, being interposed between its upper and lower divisions. Galen held a precisely similar view of the right auricle. "Gàlien," says Daremberg (i. 387), "considére la veine cave supérieure comme une continuation directe de la veine cave inférieure, l'oreillette droite n'étant qu'un diverticulum ou un lieu de passage." Such a view was quite natural; for the right auricle "semble formée par la réunion des veines caves qui s'ouvrent aux deux extrémités supérieure et inférieure de cette oreillette" (*Cuvier, Leçons*, iv. 199). This being understood, A.'s description of the heart becomes fairly intelligible. Here are the main parts of it, as I interpret them. "The heart has three cavities. The largest is placed on the right (*right ventricle*); the smallest on the left (*left auricle*); and the one of middle size (*left ventricle*) lies in the middle. All these cavities—even the two smaller ones—have openings in them which lead to the lung (*pulmonary artery; pulmonary veins; and, for the left ventricle, the fœtal ductus arteriosus*), but it is only in one of them (*right ventricle*) that the communication with the lung is conspicuous (*pulmonary artery*). The largest cavity (*right ventricle*) is connected with the great blood-vessel (*right auricle which is simply dilated junction of venæ cavæ*); and the middle cavity (*left ventricle*) is connected with the aorta. Moreover passages (*pulmonary artery and veins*) lead from the heart to the lungs, and divide after the same pattern as the windpipe, their branches accompanying the branches of this latter throughout the whole lung, and the former being placed above the latter. There is no communicating passage between these two systems of branches, but those which come from the heart receive the breath from the others, in consequence of their close contact with them, and transmit it to the heart. For one of the passages (*pulmonary artery*) leads to the right cavity (*right ventricle*) and the other (*pulmonary veins*) to the left cavity (*left auricle*)" (*H. A.* i. 17). And again, "The heart in the largest animals has three cavities. The largest of these (*right ventricle*) is on the right, and is above the rest; the smallest (*left auricle*) is on the left; and the middle one in size (*left ventricle*) is also the middle one in position. Each of the two latter cavities is much smaller than the largest one (*right ventricle*). All three have openings which lead to the lungs; but these openings are so small as to be scarcely visible, excepting in one cavity (*right ventricle*). The great blood-vessel (*right auricle and venæ cavæ*) is connected with the largest cavity (*right ventricle*), and after passing through the centre of the cavity issues from it again in the form of a blood-vessel (*pulmonary artery*), as though the cavity were a part of the vessel, in which the blood collected as in a reservoir. The aorta issues from the middle cavity (*left ventricle*), having however a much narrower tube [than the pulmonary artery]. The great vessel (*venæ cavæ plus right auricle*) passes through the heart, and after issuing from it (*as pulmonary artery*) extends into the aorta (*by the ductus arteriosus*). The great vessel is membranous and skin-like; but the aorta, which is smaller than the great vessel, is very tendinous, and, as it extends upwards towards the head and downwards towards the lower parts, gets narrower, and assumes altogether the character of sinew (cf. Note 20). The great vessel sends first a branch upwards above the heart, to the lung and the junction with the aorta (*pulmonary artery and ductus arteriosus*), this branch forming a large and unbranching vessel. There are indeed two branches from the great vessel, the one which goes to the lung (*pulmonary artery*), and one which goes to the backbone and last cervical vertebra (*azygos vein*). The one which goes to the lung (*pulmonary artery*) divides into two, as the lung itself consists of two parts; and sends branches which accompany each air-pipe, ... the branches of the vessel being above the branches of the wind-pipe. The vessel which goes to the cervical vertebra and backbone (*v. azygos*) runs back along the backbone, and gives off branches to each rib and vertebra, ultimately dividing into two, opposite the vertebra next above the kidney (*the left and right azygos veins which in man unite somewhat higher up, but also are often united by a cross branch about this point. See Gray's Anat. f.* 241). ' Such are the divisions of these branches of the great vessel. The main trunk of the great vessel, in the part which extends from the heart above these branches (*vena cava superior above point where azygos joins it*), splits in two directions (*venæ innominatæ*). .... Such is the distribution of the vessels above the heart. But the part of the great vessel which is below the heart (*vena cava inferior*) passes down from above through the diaphragm. .... The branches of the smaller vessel which is called the aorta are distributed exactly in the same way as those of the great vessel (*venous system*), and its branches accompany those of the latter, being however much smaller, etc." (*H. A.* iii. 3).

These passages leave no possible doubt as to what A. meant by his three cavities. If any further proof were wanting that the largest cavity is not meant to designate the right auricle but the right ventricle, it is furnished by the following passage : "There are sinews (i.e. *chordæ tendineæ*) inside the largest cavity of the heart"; for there are such in the ventricle, but not in the auricle.

It is almost superfluous to say that the size of an animal does not in any way determine the number of cavities in its heart. Galen (*De Usu part.* vi. 19) points out A.'s mistake, and says that the horse has no more than the sparrow, the ox than the mouse. It is not impossible that the blunder may have arisen from observation, though of very imperfect kind. The largest animals known were of course mammals, with four cavities. The huge crocodile, again, has four, while the other and smaller reptiles have but three. Cetacea again, though A. knew them to be really mammals, were classed by the vulgar with fishes, and have four cavities, while the smaller aquatic animals with which they were usually confounded have two.

24. The passages quoted in the last note show what is meant by the great vessel and the aorta. The former corresponds to the venous system, including the two venæ cavæ, the right auricle, which was considered to be the dilated junction of these, and the pulmonary artery, which is described as a continuation of the great vessel on the other side of the heart. The aorta and its branches are of course the arterial system. The differences noted by A. between the two are that the arteries have much thicker and firmer walls than the veins (*II. A.* iii. 3, 13) ; that the former are of smaller calibre than the latter (*II. A.* iii. 4, 1), and as a rule lie in front of them ; and lastly that the two contain different kinds of blood, that in the aorta and the middle cavity of the heart being purer than that in the great vessel and its cavity, the right ventricle. The difference in purity was shown by difference in colour. "Blood is red ; but that which is of inferior quality, either naturally or from disease, is of a darker tint " (*II. A.* iii. 19, 3).

25. Frantzius translates,. "If the blood be of two kinds and each kind be kept separate," and considers the passage of importance as showing that A. recognized differences between arterial and venous blood. That A. did recognise such differences is certain, but I do not think he alludes to them here. For διφυής is never used in this treatise to express "zweifacher natur," but is invariably applied to organs of similar

nature placed on opposite sides of the body, *e.g.* the kidneys. A. appears to have thought that the great vessel nourished the right side of the body, the aorta the left. Cf. Note 28.

26. A. does not explain in what way the middle cavity is common to the two sides; nor is the statement consistent with the description quoted in Note 23. A similarly unintelligible and even more inconsistent statement is made in the *De Somno* (3, 28). It is there stated that when food is absorbed it is carried up as a vapour to the head, where it is condensed, and falls back, pure and thick materials alike, to the right and left cavities of the heart, reaching the former by the great vessel, the latter by the aorta. The separation of the pure material from the thick is then effected by the central cavity. Thus A. either makes the aorta arise from the left auricle, or he interposes the auricle between the two ventricles; neither of which blunders occurs in his detailed description of the heart and vessels. Either there has been some tampering with the text, or the passage in the *De Somno* was written before A. had made out the structure of the heart as described in the *Hist. Animalium*. The latter hypothesis, however, would still leave the passage, to which this is a note, unexplained.

27. According to Bernard, though the correctness of his statement is not universally accepted, the blood in the left cavities is really somewhat colder than that in the right. But, even if it be so, A. can only be right by accident; for he had no possible means of measuring the difference, which is but a fraction of a degree. Moreover, he also says that the blood of the left auricle is hotter than that of the left ventricle, which is not the case. His statement then seems to be purely *à priori*, and noticeable as such, seeing that almost invariably his statements are based upon observed facts, though often very insufficient ones. Cf. *Introd.* p. xviii.

28. Because, as he supposed, the venæ cavæ nourished the right side of the body, and the aorta, which in its general course lies somewhat to the left of the venæ cavæ, nourished the left side. As to temperature of right and left sides, cf. ii. 2, Note 6.

29. It would thus appear that A. regarded the left ventricle as the supreme part.

30. The allusion is to the transverse and longitudinal grooves which mark out on the surface the limits of auricles and ventricles. A. is quite right in saying that the heart is not formed by the union of distinct parts into a whole. It is at first a body with a single cavity; which cavity is converted into several by the after-development of internal septa.

31. Cf. ii. 4, Note 4.

32. The heart is very large in the hare, nearly twice as heavy in proportion to the body weight as in man. As regards the other animals I can give no accurate figures.

The Pardalis from the description given elsewhere (*Physiog.* 5, 11) is supposed to be the leopard, and I have so rendered it.

Prof. Rolleston (*Journal of Anat.* 1868) identifies the γαλῆ of the ancients, which among the Greeks filled the place of the domestic cat, with the Mustela Foina, or white-breasted marten. The wild species, or ἴκτις, also mentioned by A., he identifies with the yellow-breasted marten or pine-weasel.

33. A. must mean when the cavities of one heart are compared with those of another heart, not when different cavities of one and the same heart are put in comparison. For he has already said that the right cavities and vessels are larger and yet hotter than those on the left.

34. Cf. ii. 16, Note 11.

35. Cf. iii. 6, Note 2.

36. Cf. ii. 5, Note 8.

37. Cf. iv. 2. Note 18. Daremberg (*Galien*, i. 401) represents A. as saying in this

passage that the heart is not liable to disease, or at any rate less liable than other organs; just as Galen said that it was made of hard flesh which could not easily be injured. But in fact A. says nothing of the kind, but merely states what is fairly true, viz. that diseases of the heart are more certainly fatal, and less consistent with apparently good health, than diseases of other parts; so that when a victim, *i.e.* an animal supposed to be of sound health, is sacrificed, its heart is never found diseased, though such is frequently the case when an animal dies of a malady. What would A. have thought of the bull sacrificed by Cæsar, which the soothsayers asserted to have no heart at all! (*Cicero, De Div.* ii. 16).

38. The spleen is liable to tubercle, and is indeed, with the lymphatic glands, its favourite seat in children (*Rokitansky*). It is also extremely liable to embolism; and enlarges in malarious diseases, which were probably very common in A.'s time and country.

(**Ch. 5.**) 1. Cf. iii. 4, Note 24. It is strange that even up to the present day it should be universally stated by writers on the history of physiology that up to the time of Galen all philosophers supposed that the arteries contained nothing but air. Even Cuvier, the great admirer of Aristotle, attributes to him this erroneous notion. Milne Edwards actually considers why it was that Galen attacked Erasistratus rather than Aristotle for holding this doctrine. Nothing can be plainer than that A. knew perfectly well that the arteries contained blood, and this chapter is sufficient by itself to show that he did so. The mistake has, I imagine, arisen from two causes. Firstly, that writers have got into confusion by translating φλέψ into *vein*; whereas it means *blood-vessel*, that is artery or vein alike; and by still more absurdly translating ἀρτηρία into *artery*, whereas it means *trachea*. Secondly, that the treatise *De Spiritu* has been trusted, as a genuine work of Aristotle; whereas it is shown not only by its language but by its statements to be most certainly spurious, and is in flagrant contradiction with the genuine treatises. Cf. ii. 16, Note 11.

2. Cf. iv. 5, Note 71. Alluding to such Invertebrata as insects, myriapods, and annelids, which he frequently mentions as capable of living for a short time when cut into segments; which shows that each segment must have its own centre of animality; the entire animal seemingly consisting of an aggregation of many animals, each with a certain individuality, which ordinarily is merged in the life of the aggregate, but is capable of asserting its existence when the segment is isolated; the only reason, in fact, why such an isolated segment does not live more than a short time, being that it has not got the necessary organs of nutrition. One cannot but be struck with the similarity of this view to that set forth by Herbert Spencer (*Princ. of Biol.* ii. ch. 4 and 5), who considers the Articulata to be "tertiary aggregates." The following passage expresses A.'s view: "Many insects can live when cut into pieces, in this respect resembling plants. This necessarily implies that their nutritive soul, though actually one, is potentially many; and, in the case of the animals, the same must be true of the sensory soul; for each segment plainly retains some sensibility. Such an animal resembles a number of separate animals united by growth into a single mass. There is this difference between such an animal and a plant. The segments of a plant can live for an indefinite time, and each segment can grow into the form of the entire plant of which it was a portion. But, the segments of the animal only live for a very short time. This is because they have not got the organs that are necessary for their maintenance, some of the segments having no mouth, some no stomach, some neither mouth nor stomach, and so on. In animals of the most perfect conformation, no such phenomena as these are observable; because their nature has reached the highest possible

degree of unity. Still even in these some portions of the whole, when isolated, seem to retain a certain small degree of sensibility, that is show the presence of a soul. Tortoises, for example, can still move, when the heart has been removed" (*De Ju. et Sen.* 2; *De Resp.* 17, 4).

3. Because heat, though not the soul itself, is the necessary agent of the soul in all its operations. Cf. iv. 10, Note 11; i. 1, Note 13.

4. As all sanguineous animals, *i.e.* all vertebrates, are capable of locomotion, these words might seem surplusage. But they are not so. For A. holds that the bilateral symmetry of animals belongs to them primarily in virtue of their locomotor organs; and that the symmetrical disposition of these determines an imperfect degree of bilateral symmetry in the organs of vegetative life. Cf. iii. 2, Note 11.

5. A.'s general notions on the subject of nutrition were much as follows. Food, being the material for the formation of the body, must contain the same substances as those of which the body itself is composed (*De G. et C.* ii. 8, 4); and therefore, as the body is complex, so must the food be (*De Sensu*, 5, 30). No one substance therefore forms a sufficient food for any living thing. Even plants which seem to live on water really live on water and earth, as farmers who use manure know. The most nutritive substances are those which are sweet (*De Sensu*, 4, 14), and in all nutritive substances it is the sweet element which is really nutritive, though the sweetness may be disguised by the intermixture of bitter, etc., into the flavour. With sweet substances must be reckoned fat, which is nearly allied to them (*De Longit. Vitæ*, 5, 11).

The food masticated in the mouth, but not otherwise altered (if. 3, Note 5), reaches the stomach, where it is concocted; the heat for this purpose, which is not common heat but a heat with special powers (ii. 6, Note 7), being supplied by the liver and spleen, which are hot organs in close contiguity with the stomach (*D. P.* iii. 7, 10). The solid and indigestible portion passes off by the lower bowel, but the fluid portion, which alone can be serviceable in nutrition (cf. ii. 2, Note 4), is absorbed by the blood-vessels of the stomach and intestine (*D. P.* iv. 4, 3; ii. 3, 11), over the surface of which they are spread like the roots of a plant. These blood-vessels open by very minute and invisible pores into the intestine, pores like those in jars of unbaked clay that let water filter through (*D. G.* ii. 6, 19). The matter thus absorbed passes up to the heart in the form of vapour (ἀναθυμιᾶται), not as yet being blood, but only (ii. 4, Note 11) an imperfect serum (ἰχώρ). In the heart and vessels (*De Somno*, 3, 3) it undergoes a second concoction, these being the hottest parts of the body, and by this second concoction the serum is converted into blood (*H. A.* iii. 19, 9), the ultimate food of all the organs. The amount of blood thus formed is extremely small, as compared with the original materials; for were it not so, the body would grow to an enormous bulk.(*D. G.* i. 18, 46). The blood when made passes from the heart by the vessels (arteries and veins alike), being mingled with air inhaled by the lungs and thence conveyed to the heart (iii. 6, Note 3), and is carried to all parts of the body. Each organ selects from the common stock those materials which it requires. The nobler parts, such as the flesh and the organs of sense, take the choicer elements, while the inferior parts, as bones and sinews, are fed on the inferior elements or leavings (ὑπολείμματα) of the former (*D. G.* ii. 6, 41). This nutrition of the parts goes on most actively at night (*De Somno*, 1, 15).

Thus every part of the blood that can be turned to account is utilised; but such as from its quality is unfit for use, for instance any bitter substance, is excreted as bile, urine, sweat, etc., in company with the matter which results from the decay (σύντηξις) of the parts themselves.

Such surplus of nutritious matter as there may be, after all parts are satisfied, is either converted into fat, or into generative secretions, or escapes at the extremities of the vessels, forming internally the viscera and flesh, and externally the scales, hairs, feathers, etc. Cf. iii. 8, Note 2.

6. The simile is borrowed from the *Timæus* (*Jowett*, ii. 570), and is also used at *H. A.* iii. 4, 15. Galen used a simile not unlike it (*De Nat. Fac.* iii. 15).

7. This passage, with that quoted iii. 4, Note 20, shows clearly what was A.'s idea of the nature of flesh, or muscular tissue. He traced veins and arteries into the muscle, found their branches getting smaller and smaller, until at last he lost sight of most of them. This, he thought, was owing to the small veins being choked up by the thick blood; the thus obstructed tubes constituting the muscular substance. At the same time the small arteries ceased to be tubular and were solidified into tendinous fibres, which being continuous on the one hand with the heart by the aorta and on the other with the tendons and bones were the instruments of motion.

8. Voigtel states that he observed blood to sweat from under the arm of a young man after violent exertion. Such perspiration is also said to have been observed in scurvy and low forms of fever. Landerer observed a red-coloured sweat in the axilla of a patient suffering from fever. Cf. *Todd's Cycl.* iv. 844.

9. The formation of blood was supposed by A. to go on mainly in the heart, but also partially in the blood-vessels. Cf. *De Somno*, 3, 3.

10. Cf. ii. 4, Note 10.

11. If this passage be genuine, the meaning must be that the windpipe being of smaller calibre than the other channels mentioned does not allow blood to flow through it so easily as they do; and therefore that when blood gets into it, it is expelled with force. But I strongly suspect that the whole passage is an interpolation, written at a later date, when ἀρτηρία had acquired the meaning of artery; and that the passage (here without meaning) had reference to the distinction between passive hæmorrhages from veins and active hæmorrhages from arteries. That the writer in fact meant to say this: "The veins are larger than the arteries; and so the blood flows more easily through them than through these. Thus, when bleeding occurs from the veins, the hæmorrhage is passive, as we see in the ordinary bleedings of the nose, etc.; whereas, when bleeding occurs from an artery, the blood is ejected with force and the hæmorrhage is active."

12. The common iliac arteries, formed by the division of the descending aorta, do in fact, as A. says, come forwards and lie in front of the common iliac veins; whereas as a general rule the veins lie in front of the arteries.

What however is meant by saying that a similar interchange of position occurs between veins and arteries above the heart it is difficult to understand. I can but conjecture that the reference is to the pulmonary artery (considered by A. to be a vein; see iii. 4, Notes 23—24), which at its origin is in front of the aorta, and then runs upwards and backwards under the aortic arch, sending moreover its right and larger division behind the ascending aorta. A somewhat similar, but much vaguer, passage occurs in the *Timæus* (*Jowett*, ii. 571).

(Ch. 6.) 1. It will be noticed that A. always speaks of *the lung* of an animal, and not as we do of *the lungs*. He considers the two to be merely subdivisions of a single organ, because they have one common outlet, viz. the trachea. When the right and left bronchi which lead from this to either lung are of more than ordinary length, as in birds, he admits that the lung has the outward appearance of being a double organ, but still considers it really to be a single one for the above reason; though "any one might think that there were two because the ducts from the two divisions unite at a considerable distance from them" (*H. A.* ii. 17, 4; *D. P.* iii. 7; 3). So again (*H. A.* i. 16, 11),

"The lung, in all animals that have one, has a tendency to consist of two parts. But the division is not so apparent in the vivipara as in the ovipara, and is least apparent in man. But in the ovipara, that is in the birds and the oviparous quadrupeds, the two parts are so widely separate that there appear to be two lungs." As to the Ophidia, where often only one lung is developed, he specially mentions (*H. A.* ii. 17, 22) that their lung is simple, *i.e.* undivided.

2. Cf. ii. 16, Notes 10 and 11. It is noticeable that, though A. considers the "innate spirit" to be of a hot nature, he several times speaks of it as producing refrigeration; not, however, by its direct but by its indirect action, in causing fanning motions in the body. See iii. 6, Note 14.

3. A.'s theory of respiration, as expressed in the separate treatise on the subject, is as follows. He rejects the opinion that the purpose of respiration is to keep up the internal heat of the body (*De Resp.* 5; 6, and 4, 8), and holds that it has exactly the contrary object. Heat is being perpetually produced in the heart, and would accumulate in excess, were there no means of reducing it when necessary (*De Resp.* 8, 6). The bloodless animals produce so little heat, that no special arrangements are required to cool them; the simple bathing of their surface with air or water being sufficient as a rule for the purpose (*De Resp.* 9, 1). Yet even in some of these, as in certain insects, there is a provision, in the Hypozoma (ii. 16, Note 10), for the better reduction of the heat. In sanguineous animals, however, that are of a hotter nature, there is always some special provision for keeping the heat within bounds. In fishes the reduction is effected by the water, which bathes the gills into which blood is conveyed from the heart (*De Resp.* 21, 6). It is, says A., the water itself and not, as some would have it, the air contained in the water, which is the agent of refrigeration. In support of this statement he urges several arguments (*De Resp.* 3, 3), of which the chief is that no bubbles are given off by fishes under water, as there would be were air inspired and expired. In other sanguineous animals the internal heat is greater, and refrigeration is effected by the more perfect agency of air (*De Resp.* 15, 2) inspired into a lung, air being a more perfect agent than water because it can permeate the body more rapidly. The lung itself differs in different animals, being more perfect the nobler, that is to say the hotter, the animal is. Thus it is dry and bladder-like in ovipara (cf. Note 10) that are comparatively cool; and full of blood in the vivipara that are of a hotter character (*H. A.* i. 17, 7.; *De Resp.* 3, 2). The cold air, drawn into the lung, reaches the bronchial tubes (σύριγγες), and as the vessels containing hot blood run alongside these tubes and in immediate contact with them (*De Resp.* 21, 4; *H. A.* iii. 3, 15), the air cools it, and carries off the superfluous heat; as is shown by the fact that the air expired is much hotter than the air inspired (*De Resp.* 5, 6). Some of the air which enters the lung gets from the bronchial tubes into the blood-vessels, although there is no direct communication between them, simply owing to the close contiguity in which tubes and vessels lie (iii. 3, Note 9). The air permeates the body rapidly and cools the blood in the vessels throughout the body, as the air in the lung cools the greater heat in the heart.

It appears then that lung and gills have the same function, and, says A., they consequently never co-exist. No animal that has a lung ever has gills. "For it is best to have a single organ for a single purpose; and one method of refrigeration is enough for any animal" (*De Resp.* 10, 6). As regards this last passage, we may remark that A. was of course in complete ignorance of the perennibranchiate amphibia, so that his erroneous statement that gills and lungs never co-exist may be passed over. One cannot, however, but ask, as did Galen, how he reconciles his present statement with his having in fact attributed one and the same function to lung and to brain. He nowhere explains this seeming inconsistency. I imagine, however, that what he would have said was this. The lung provides for the general refrigeration of the heart and body at large. But in order to ensure the perfection of the sense-organs (*D. P.* ii. 10, 11), it is necessary that there shall be a part where the refrigeration shall be much more intense, and this part is the brain.

4. Cf. iv. 13, Note 38.

5. " Of all animals the strangest are the dolphins and those other Cetacea, such as the whale, that have a blow-hole. For one cannot easily class them either simply as water-animals, or simply as land-animals, if we define land-animals as those that take in air, and water-animals as those which take in water. For these animals do partly one, partly the other. For they take in sea-water and discharge it by the blow-hole, and they also have a lung and with it take in air, etc." (*H. A.* viii. 2, 4). From this and similar passages it is plain that A. made a distinct division of Cetacea, separating them on the one hand from the viviparous quadrupeds owing to their living entirely in the water and having no distinct limbs, and on the other hand from the fishes, owing to their having a lung, true bones, and mammæ.

6. The mechanism of respiration is described elsewhere (*De Resp.* 21). The lung is compared, aptly enough, to a pair of forge bellows. When the lung is expanded, air rushes in; when it is contracted, the air is again expelled. The expansion is brought about by the heat derived from the heart; heat always causing expansion in the parts to which it extends. The lung then, heated by the heart, expands; and with it the cavity of the thorax. Cold air rushes in to fill the void, and the heat is reduced. This causes the lung and thorax to collapse, and the air is expelled.

7. The argument seems to be this. If the motion of the heart depended on the lung, then that motion should be precisely similar in all animals that have a lung. But this is not the case; for in man alone, or nearly so, does palpitation occur. A. guards himself somewhat by the words "*so to speak*," which is a usual form with him for "*with some exceptions*." Otherwise he is in error in saying that man is the only animal whose heart is set in violent palpitation by mental emotion, as every experimental physiologist knows. "In a frightened horse," says Darwin, "I have felt through the saddle the beating of the heart so plainly that I could have counted the beats" (*On Expression of Emotions*, p. 77). The distinction between jumping palpitation (πήδησις) and ordinary heart action (ἅλσις and σφύγμος) is elaborated in *De Resp.* 20. A.'s explanation of the heart's action and of the pulse, as there given, was as follows : The food, he says, is without intermission pouring into the heart; here it is heated; and this heating causes it to swell, just as water swells and bubbles up when boiled. The dilatation of the heart is due to this, as also (see last note) is the expansion of the lung and thorax, which leads to the admission of cold air into that cavity. The entrance of air cools not only the lung but also the heart, and in consequence they both contract. This alternate expansion and contraction of the heart extends to the blood-vessels (i.e. *arteries and veins*), as they are continuous with the heart, and the blood within them is affected by the changes of heat in the same way as that in the heart. Thus the blood-vessels throb simultaneously with the heart, and all at the same moment. The internal heat is greater in youth than in after-life (ii. 2, Note 10); consequently the whole process described, which is due to this heat, takes place more rapidly at that period of life; and this explains why the pulse is more rapid in youth than in after-life. Aristotle also compares the beating of the heart to the throbbing felt in a swelling while pus is yet being formed, this throbbing like the pulsation being due to concoction; for, as soon as the pus is concocted and fully formed, the throbbing ceases.

8. In saying that in most animals the heart lies above the lungs, A. means, I imagine, that in birds and reptiles the lung extends far down below the site of the heart; which is in fact the case, if we allow, as A. did, that the air-sacs form part of the bird's lung. Cf. Note 10.

9. Their heat is great, and therefore they require a large lung to temper it.

10. A.'s account suits very well to the lungs of amphibians and reptiles, but as regards birds can only be explained by admitting that the true lungs, owing to their comparatively small size and their being confined to the back of the thorax, had escaped his notice, and that he took the much larger air-sacs for them, or at any rate included these in the lung. A. thought that a bladder-like lung was an inferior organ, because it had but a small amount of blood. It is an inferior organ, because of the small surface for the exposure of blood to the air.

11. "Birds with talons may be said, speaking generally, never to drink at all. Other birds drink, but sparingly" (*H. A.* viii. 18, 3). As to reptiles, cf. iii. 8, Note 4.

12. The real reason why a reptile or amphibian can remain under water for a long time is that its tissues produce, for equal weights, less carbonic acid in a given time than those of other animals, so that there is less rapid need for respiration (cf. *Bert. Leçons sur la Resp.*). As to such birds, as the duck, etc., it is the large amount of blood in their body, which, forming a store of oxygen, enables them to remain so long without breathing.

13. A. always regards birds as cold animals, though their great heat is readily perceptible to touch, and cannot have been unknown to him. It is, however, in vital heat, not in ordinary heat, that he holds them deficient. Cf. Introd. p. xxxi.

14. A. seems to have had some strange notion that a fan cools a body not merely by bringing a continuous current of cold air into contact with it, but directly by its own motion, that is independently of the air. "Every hot body," he says, "is cooled by the motions of bodies external to itself" (*D. P.* iii. 4, 30). So he supposes here that when an animal is under water, its lung will continue in motion, and that, though no air is admitted, yet the motion will itself produce a certain amount of cooling in the neighbouring parts. See also *De Resp.* 9, 6.

15. Cf. ii. 9, 9.

16. "Erect" seems to be used here, not in its ordinary sense of standing on the hind legs, but as having the body removed from the ground, so as to apply to quadrupeds as well as to men.

17. Alluding to the viper.

18. Plato thought that the lung in all animals was bloodless (cf. *Jowett's Tr.* ii. 564). A. holds that the lung of mammals is the organ which of all is most richly supplied with blood, but that the lung of ovipara is "bladder-like and contains but little blood." He alludes elsewhere (*H. A.* i. 17, 7) to Plato's erroneous statement, without naming him.

(Ch. 7.) 1. It seems to have been the universal opinion of the ancients that the spleen was the left homologue of the liver. In modern times the more general view is that of Müller, that there is no such relation between them, each being an azygos organ. The ancient opinion is not, however, without its modern advocates. Dr. Doellinger for instance (*Grundriss der Naturlehre des menschl. Organ.* 1805) supported it; and still more recently Dr. Sylvester (*The Discov. of the Nature of the Spleen*, 1870) has argued with much ingenuity that "the spleen is not a blood-gland in the mesial line of the body, having no homologous relationship with the liver," but that "it is the left lateral homologue of a portion of the liver, the latter being a combination of a sanguiferous gland and a biliary apparatus," and the spleen the homologue of the former portion of it,

2. On the question of the bilateral symmetry of the organs, and especially of the abdominal organs, where alone there is any difficulty, cf. *Sylvester, Disc. of Nature of Spleen*, p. 12.

3. Cf. iii. 6, Note 1.

4. By animals that necessarily have a spleen are meant, as will presently appear, the viviparous quadrupeds, or mammals; by those that have it merely "by way of token" are meant the oviparous vertebrates, *i.e.* birds, reptiles, amphibia and fishes. The spleen is in fact notably larger in the former than in the latter.

There is some foundation for the statement that the size of the spleen and the distinctness with which the liver is divided into lobes are inversely related to each other. Thus it is in Mammalia that the spleen is largest in proportion to the body, and in them also that the liver is least distinctly lobulated. Among Mammalia it is the rodents that have the smallest spleen, and in these also it is that the liver reaches its maximum of subdivision. On the other hand, the spleen is large in ruminants and their liver at the same time presents scarcely any marks of lobulation. In the Ovipara the spleen is much smaller than in Mammalia, and the liver, as a general though not universal rule, is much more decidedly cleft into distinct lobes. In all birds, in all batrachians, and in all reptiles, excepting Ophidia, the liver is distinctly divided into two lobes. In the remaining class, fishes, the spleen varies much in size; sometimes is apparently altogether absent, sometimes excessively small, sometimes almost as large in proportion to the body as that of a mammal, and the liver is sometimes multilobed, sometimes bilobed, sometimes unilobed. In this class, however, I cannot ascertain that there is any such relation as that mentioned in the text between the two conditions.

5. The exceptional ovipara are the Ophidia and many osseous fishes, where the liver is unilobed. The exceptional vivipara are the rodents (see last Note), of which A. specially mentions the hare. "Near the lake Bolbe, and in other parts, a species of hare is found, that might be taken to have two livers, because the ducts unite at a considerable distance from the organ, just as is the case with [the bronchi from the two divisions of] the bird's lung" (*H. A.* ii. 17, 4).

6. In cartilaginous fishes the liver consists of two distinct lobes, whereas in osseous fishes it is often unilobed.

7. Cf. iii. 5, Note 4.

8. Assisting them in the mechanical way immediately mentioned, and also by providing an outlet for their surplus blood. Cf. iii. 13, Note 1; iii. 8, Note 2.

9. The mesentery is meant.

10. What I have translated "immoveably" is literally "like nails." The introduction of nails into the metaphor is however so out of place, that I am strongly tempted to suggest that A. wrote εὐναί not ἧλοι. Εὐναί are the large round stones to which anchor-lines were fastened in old times. The metaphor would then run on all fours. The ship is the main blood-vessel; the anchor-lines are the outstretching branches; the round anchor-stones are the rounded liver, spleen, kidneys.

11. The hepatic and splenic arteries seem to have escaped A.'s notice; probably because they are not given off directly from the aorta.

12. Plato described the spleen as made of bloodless substance. Cf. *Jowett's Trans.* ii. 566.

13. Cf. Note 18.

14. The spleen is small in all birds; but whether specially so in these, or in the owl, which he adds elsewhere (*H. A.* ii. 15, 7) to the list, I cannot say. The stomach, argues A., is so hot in these birds as to be able to concoct food, without the aid of a spleen.

15. A. assigns two main functions to the spleen; one, to assist by its heat in the concoction of the food; the other, to withdraw superfluous humours from the stomach. When these offices can be adequately performed without the aid of a spleen, then this organ is of small size. Thus in birds the stomach is hot enough to effect concoction by itself, and there is an adequate outlet in the skin for the superfluous humours. In birds then the spleen is small. So also with other ovipara. In fact in these animals the spleen exists for no actual use; but simply to fulfil the law of symmetrical development, which requires some counterpart to the liver.

Such was A.'s idea of the spleen. The notion of its serving to attract superfluous humours was taken from Hippocrates, who thus expresses himself, "I say that, when a man drinks a more than-ordinary amount of fluid, both the body and the spleen attract to themselves the water from the stomach" (*De Morbis*, iv. 9). And again, "When a person has fever and violent thirst, and drinks copiously without vomiting, a part of the fluid passes into the bladder and is expelled as urine; but the rest is taken by the spleen, which attracts it from the stomach, being of a porous and spongy texture, and lying close to the stomach" (*De Morb. Mul.* i. 15).

This notion was actually revived by Sir E. Home, who imagined that when fluid was drunk much of it passed from the cardiac end of the stomach by some unknown channel directly to the spleen. This view, however, he afterwards abandoned. See *Phil. Trans.* 1811.

16. "In those that drink marsh-water the spleen always becomes enlarged, and the belly hard."—*Hippocrates*.

17. A bladder-like lung is to A., owing to the small amount of fluid it contains, an indication of scanty fluid in the body generally. See next chapter.

18. A. thought that the bladder was the essential agent in forming the urine, and the kidneys mere adjuncts, though he also admits that when the fluid leaves the kidney, it already has in a measure the characters of an excretion. Cf. iii. 9, 7. A.'s error was corrected by the time of Galen (*De Usu part.* 5, 5).

19. Namely from above downwards; an upper position implying generally superiority in other respects. Cf. ii. 2, Note 6.

(Ch. 8.) 1. *i.e.* the Mammalia (cf. iii. 6, Note 9). As a matter of fact birds have no bladder, and yet highly vascular lungs; but their real lungs escaped A.'s notice. Cf. iii. 6, Note 10.

2. A. distinguishes the scales of fishes from those of reptiles by giving them distinct names, but nowhere discusses their differences; excepting that he says, "these plates are equivalent to scales, but of a harder character." Cf. iv. 11, Note 14.

As regards the formation of scales, and similar parts, his notion was this. The blood passes from the heart to all parts of the body by the vessels. At last it reaches their ultimate twigs. As none of it returns to the heart, it must here be disposed of in some way or other. That in the internal vessels is converted into the substance of the viscera (cf. iii. 7, Note 8); that in the external vessels oozes out as sweat, or is converted into various integumental structures, nails, hairs, scales, feathers. But when there is too much blood for its excess to be thus got rid of, or when the integument is such as not to allow of transpiration, some other means of disposal are required, and these are furnished by the presence of urinary organs. Bacon (*Nat. Hist.* § 680) expresses a similar opinion.

3. Both here and in other passages it is stated that Mammalia alone have an urinary bladder, with the exception of tortoises. The facts are these. All Mammalia have a true bladder developed from the allantois, directly continuous with the ureters (Monotremata excepted), and serving for the reception of urine and for this alone.

In birds there is no bladder whatsoever.

Of reptiles, the Ophidia are without a bladder. So are lizards, crocodiles, and some other Saurians. But many Saurians and all Chelonia (as also Amphibia) have a bladder which appears to be the remains of the allantois, and which if it be so is the homologue of the mammalian bladder. But this bladder is not in direct continuity with the ureters, but opens out from the anterior wall of the cloaca, while the ureters open into the cloaca posteriorly. This bladder, in spite of its position, is supposed to serve as a receptacle of urine, and urinary salts are said to be found in the fluid it contains. Probably, however, its chief function is to serve as a store-house of fluid for the animal's use in times of drought (cf. *Todd's Cycl.* i. 104; *Darwin, Beagle,* p. 383). This bladder acquires its greatest development in the Chelonia, where it is of very large size. Thus is explained the statement in the text.

In fishes there is nothing homologous to the mammalian bladder; nothing that is developed from an allantois, so far as is known. But in most if not all osseous fishes, and in some cartilaginous fishes, the ureters either before or after their junction form a dilatation, which is called a bladder, and doubtless serves as an urinary reservoir. This dilatation is small, and lies behind the intestine, whereas an allantoidean bladder is always in front; so that it is no wonder it should have escaped A.'s notice. Its presence has indeed escaped some distinguished modern anatomists (cf. *M. Edwards, Leçons,* vii. 326). In no invertebrate is there a bladder.

4. A. is mistaken in supposing that tortoises drink but little. On the contrary, they are very fond of water. Darwin describes them as wearing broad and well-beaten paths to the springs in Chatham Island, and adds: "Near the springs it was a curious spectacle to behold many of these huge creatures, one set eagerly travelling onwards with outstretched necks, and another set returning after having drunk their fill. When the tortoise arrives at the spring, quite regardless of any spectator, he buries his head in the water above the eyes, and greedily swallows great mouthfuls at the rate of about ten a minute" (*Voyage of Beagle,* p. 383). Had A. known this, he would most certainly have accounted for the tortoise's bladder by its thirsty habits.

5. The lungs of Chelonia are of much greater size than those of most Saurians and Amphibia, and "s'étendent le long du dos jusqu'au bassin au-dessus de tous les viscères" (*Cuvier, Leçons,* iv. 347). They are moreover not only thus larger, but contain "in correlation with the non-transpirable integument a much greater development of internal parenchyma" (*Rolleston, Forms of An. Life,* lx.). This comparative abundance of parenchyma is more marked in marine than in other tortoises (*Cuvier, Leçons,* iv. 324 and 332). There can then be no doubt that A. had carefully examined the lungs of tortoises and other reptiles. It is however an exaggeration on his part to say that the lung of a sea-tortoise resembles that of an ox. The amount of parenchyma is by no means so great. Probably he was led to make the comparison by his having already found a likeness between the kidney of the ox and that of the sea-tortoise, in its great subdivision. Cf. next chapter, Note 1.

6. According to Perrault exactly the reverse is the case; the bladder being usually much larger in the land-tortoises than in the sea-tortoises. Cf. *M. Edwards, Leçons,* vii. 344.

(Ch. 9.) 1. A similar statement, that no Ovipara save the tortoises have kidneys, is made elsewhere (*H. A.* ii. 16); where also it is said that the kidney of the tortoise consists, like that of the ox, of numerous smaller parts. The chelonian kidney is in fact extremely subdivided on the outer surface; so that there can be no doubt that A. had examined it. But it is difficult to understand how the kidneys of other Ovipara

14

escaped his notice. It is true they are so differently shaped from those of a mammal, or even of a tortoise, that they might appear to a careless observer to be totally different organs. But the probable explanation is that A. argued *à priori* that it was impossible for there to be a kidney if there were no bladder. For the essential organ in the formation of urine was, as he thought, not the kidney, but the bladder; and the kidneys were but adjuncts to this (iii. 7, Note 18). A kidney then in an animal without a bladder was to A. just as absurd a supposition as would be to us an urinary bladder when there was no kidney. That A. was misled by this preconception is shown by the fact that he did see the kidneys in birds, and did recognize their kidney-like aspect; but yet refused to consider them as true kidneys.

2. In birds the kidneys, almost always trilobed, are flattened against the back, and, fitting into the deep interspaces between the bones, retain the impressions of these successive cavities or depressions.

3. The Emys was some freshwater tortoise (*H. A.* v. 33, 3); but what species is uncertain, as there are several in Greece. None is without a bladder, but this is equally true of all known Chelonia. Neither has any animal now known as Emys a soft shell. The *Sphargis. coriacea* or leathery turtle has a soft shell, and is consequently supposed by Frantzius to be the species meant. But the Sphargis is a marine species. Possibly Emys may have been a name common to both freshwater tortoises and to the marine Sphargis.

4. Cf. iii. 7, Note 8.

5. The cavity in the seal's kidney is very small. It is pictured in section by Buffon (*Hist. Nat.* xiii. pl. 48). The kidney consists of numerous distinct lobes, and in this respect resembles that of an ox.

6. This is not true of adult man, excepting as an occasional anomaly. But it is true of the fœtus. This is one of the statements which lead me to fancy that A. may have dissected the human fœtus. Cf. i. 5, Note 1.

7. Not all quadrupeds other than the ox have non-lobulated kidneys, though such is the general rule. The elephant, bear, otter, all have lobulated kidneys. It is a curious fact, not yet explained, that the kidneys are of this character in nearly all water Mammalia.

8. The bloodless ducts are the ureters. The ducts from the aorta and great vessel are the renal arteries and veins respectively. The reason why A. introduces the word "continuous" appears from the last sentence in this chapter.

9. Cf. iii. 7, Note 18.

10. The same fanciful metaphor was used before. Cf. iii. 7, Note 10.

11. This is the general but not universal rule. One of the exceptions is man, where the right kidney is usually slightly lower than the left.

12. As it was an axiom with A. that the right side was naturally superior to the left (cf. ii. 2, Note 6), so also was it another axiom that all locomotion began from the right (*De Cælo*, ii. 2, 4). In fact, his definition of right is the part from which locomotion begins. In the treatise *De An. Incessu* (4, 7; 6, 1) evidence is adduced in support of this axiom. That motion begins on the right is shown, it is said, by men preferentially carrying burdens on the left shoulder, so as to leave the motor side free; as also by their standing on the left leg more easily than on the right, with the same object; by the attitude assumed in fighting, when the left limbs are advanced and the right kept back, so as to serve for motion and defence; and, lastly, by the fact that spiral shells are dextral, that is to say, that the opening whence the motor organ is protruded is on the animal's right.

Whether men carry burdens preferentially on the left shoulder, so as to bring the right and stronger hand into play, or whether they rest preferentially on the left leg, I cannot say. But parrots, as I have shown elsewhere (*Royal Med. Chir. Trans.* 1871), stand as a rule on the right leg. Spiral shells are as a rule dextral.

As to the remark in the text concerning the raising of the eyebrows, the Greeks appear to have had much more mobile features, and to have studied facial expression more closely than ourselves; so that very possibly the statement may be a true one. The only evidence I can find is furnished by a photograph by Duchenne of a young man simulating grief and arching his brows (reproduced in *Darwin on Express.* pl. 11, 2). The right brow is in this case very much more arched than the left.

13. The kidneys of Mammals are imbedded in a *tunica adiposa*.

14. The argument seems to be this. That fat is the result of concoction is shown by the fact that it floats on water, this upward tendency being a proof of the presence of heat in it; and this heat can only be accounted for by supposing it to be that residue of heat which is always left in a fluid after concoction. Cf. ii. 2, 24.

15. Cf. ii. 5, Note 1.

16. "So again the Creator placed only a small quantity of flesh in the joints of the bones, that it might not interfere with the flexion of our bodies."—*Timæus.*

17. Auber and Wimmer say that this is true of rabbits; whether it is also true of other animals I cannot say.

18. The layer of fat is not equally spread over all the surface of the kidney, at any rate in man, but is accumulated especially upon the outer and inner borders.

19. A. is plainly speaking of some disease that is compatible with accumulation of fat, and that also is, at any rate sometimes, rapidly fatal. Such seems to be the case with rot. "In this disease there is no loss of condition, but quite the contrary. For the sheep in the early stages of rot has a great propensity to fatten" (*Youatt, Book of Farm*, ii. 386). Again the rot is sometimes "rapid in its course, and this season a large number of sheep have been killed very quickly by it" (*Gamgee, Pr. Counc. Rep.* v. 240). I need hardly say that A.'s view of the pathology of the rot is erroneous. He was probably led to attribute the disease to the kidneys, from dropsical collections being a common accompaniment of it.

20. The ox and the sheep, says John Hunter, have more fat about the kidneys, the loins, and within the abdomen, than most other animals (*Museum Cat.* iii. 212).

(Ch. 10.) 1. Mammals alone have a perfect diaphragm. "Most of the Vertebrata, however, exhibit something analogous to the diaphragm. Thus in fishes the muscular septum dividing the cavity of the branchial apparatus from the abdomen bears a certain resemblance to a diaphragm" (*Todd's Cycl.* ii. 1). In birds there is an imperfect diaphragm, most fully developed in the ostrich. In reptiles also there is "a rudimentary form of diaphragm which arises as a broader thinner muscle than in birds from the vertebral column and carapace, and is interposed between peritoneum and pleura, without however meeting its fellow in the middle line from the opposite side" (*Carus, Comp. An.* 149).

A.'s statement is then in a certain sense true. The description, however, given farther on applies only to the perfect diaphragm, viz, that of mammals.

2. The absorbed food was supposed to pass upwards from the intestine through the vessels in the form of a vapour. Cf. iii. 5, Note 5.

3. "For the motion of the heat in blood destroys the sensory activity".(ii. 10, 11).

4. A. has plainly in his mind the views expressed in the *Timæus.* Plato held that man had a triple soul; an intellectual soul, seated in the head; a soul endowed with courage and the nobler passions, which had its seat in the thorax; and a third soul, to which

belonged desire and the grosser passions, which was located in the belly. The diaphragm served as a barrier to preserve the thoracic soul from the inroads of the "ravening beast" below.

5. Cf. ii. 2, Note 6.

6. A notion still commemorated in the anatomical terms "phrenic nerves" and "phrenic centre."

7. The central part of the midriff, which is tendinous, is the "cordiform tendon" of modern anatomists. It is not easy to see why A. should say that the parts nearest the ribs must of necessity be fleshier than the centre. I suppose he must mean, that, as the flesh or muscle lies generally on the external aspect of the trunk, the part of the midriff which comes nearest the outside will partake most of the character of that surface; and so be the most muscular.

8. The anthropoid apes are sensitive to tickling, especially about the arm-pits, and may be said to laugh. I have myself witnessed the fact in the case of the chimpanzee.

9. When the diaphragm is suddenly ruptured, instant death usually follows, and the face is said invariably to assume the peculiar expression or grin, called Risus Sardonicus. Cf. *Dict. d. Sci. Médic.* ix. 214.

10. Iliad x. 557; Odyssey xxii. 329. In both places the reading is φθεγγομένου not φθεγγομένη. The works of Homer appear to have assumed in ancient times almost the position of sacred books, and to have been quoted not merely as poetry, but as authoritative in matters of history and science. Lucian is perpetually making fun of this absurdity.

11. Probably meaning "armed" Zeus. So there was a temple of Here Hoplosmia in the Peloponnesus (cf. *Liddell and Scott*).

12. Cf. iii. 5, Note 2.

13. Cf. iii. 7, Note 8.

(Ch. 11.) 1. The pericardium and dura mater.

2. This shows how far A. was from regarding the brain as an organ of no importance, a mere spongeful of water, as Galen says. Cf. ii. 7, Note 27.

(Ch. 12.) 1. Cf. iii. 7, Note 4.

2. Cf. iv. 2, Notes 7, 8; iv. 3, Note 1.

3. And, in mammals, the lung (*H. An.* i. 17, 7).

4. The liver of mammals and birds is as a rule of a brown-red colour. In reptiles it inclines to a yellow hue; and in fishes this yellow tint is often still more decided. Cf. Cuvier, *Leçons*, iv. 14.

5. "Foul," because the degree of yellowness is to A. a measure of the impurity which the liver has to separate from the blood. Perhaps also with some reference to the views of the soothsayers, who seem to have considered a pale liver to be an unfavourable omen, the lucky tint being the normal mottled red, the ποικίλη εὐμορφία of Æschylus; in which case "foul" would correspond to the "turpia exta" of Livy (xxvii. 26).

6. Or perhaps "of a broad oval form;" στρογγύλος being the term applied to a merchant vessel as distinguished from a ship of war.

7. The spleen "is broader at one end in the cow, reindeer, and giraffe than in other ruminants" (*Owen, Verteb.* iii. 561). In the hog it is elongated; so also in Carnivora generally. In the Ungulata it is of proportionately smaller dimensions than in the Carnivora, and in the horse is "elongated, flattened, broadest at the upper end," A.'s account so far therefore fairly tallies with the facts. But as regards man his statement is erroneous. For though the human spleen is very variable in shape as in size, yet it cannot be said to be elongated in comparison with that of other mammalia. I am, however by no means certain that it is not more elongated in the fœtus than in the adult. It appears

to be so in the drawings in *Crisp on the Spleen*. If so, this would be another argument in support of the view that A. had dissected the fœtus. Cf. i. 5, Note 1.

8. A. seems to have been at a loss how to classify the pig. Here he reckons it with the many-toed animals in opposition to the animals with solid or cloven hoofs. In the next chapter he separates it from the many-toed, and puts it into a separate division, consisting of "those that have a cloven hoof, but yet have front teeth in both jaws," of course in contradistinction to the ruminants. In another place (*H. An.* ii. 1, 31) he says the pig lies half-way between the cloven-hoofed and the solidungulates; and in corroboration of this, states that there are sometimes pigs with a solid hoof; an anomaly of which instances do in fact occur not very rarely.

The foot of the pig has in reality four toes; but of these the two middle ones are much longer and stouter than the others, and form a cloven hoof which is used by the animal in walking. The two lateral toes are also furnished with hoofs, but are placed at some distance above the ground, so as not to touch it.

(Ch. 13.) 1. I take the meaning to be this. Wherever there are blood-vessels there must necessarily be either viscera or flesh; for these are the means by which the blood gets rid of its surplus material (cf. iii. 8, Note 2). As there are vessels both inside and outside the trunk, so there must be viscera or flesh inside and outside it; and, the flesh being without, the viscera are within.

It is the viscera that exist "for the sake of the vessels" (cf. iii. 7, Note 8); the flesh that "cannot exist without them." Cf. iii. 5, Note 7.

(Ch. 14.) 1. *i.e.* in fishes. Cf. iii. 3, Note 2.

2. Cf. iii. 12, Note 8.

3. The camel has in fact two incisor teeth in the upper jaw. But these are placed laterally close against the canines, so as to leave a considerable vacant space in the front of the mouth. Had A. known of the existence of these upper incisors, he would not have failed to find in their presence a striking confirmation of his views as to the inverse development of teeth and horns. Cf. iii. 2, Note 19.

4. The argument is this. The presence of a multiple stomach and the absence of upper incisors are inseparably united by correlation; this being apparently one of those laws of type (Cf. *Introd.* p. x) to which nature is obliged to conform her action. Nature then, when she gave a multiple stomach to the camel, as the best instrument for the digestion of hard food, was forced to take away the upper incisors, although the absence of horns left sufficient matter for their production. The earthy matter, thus not disposed of, was utilised by her in the formation of a hard palate, which to a great extent acts as substitute for the wanting teeth.

5. Because flesh is the medium of taste. Cf. ii. 10, Note 10.

6. Not only in camels but in all ruminants the place of the upper incisors is supplied by a hardened gum, against which the lower teeth bite; and, in addition to this, numerous hard papillæ are developed from the buccal membrane. Along the roof of the mouth, these run in parallel lines, being flattened and furnished with retroverted toothed margins. They are very conspicuous in the camel. Cf. *Owen, Vert.* iii. 392.

7. Cf. *H. An.* ii. 17, 8, and iv. 5, Note 34.

8. Elsewhere (*H. An.* ii. 17, 28) fowls, doves, pigeons, and partridges are enumerated as having a crop. That the crop does in fact in part supply the place of a masticating mouth by softening the food is well known to bird-fanciers. If a pigeon be allowed to swallow a number of peas, they will swell inside the crop to such an extent as almost to suffocate the bird.

9. The œsophagus as a general rule is wide and dilatable in birds, "in correspondence

with the imperfection of the oral instruments as comminutors of the food" (*Owen*). It is especially wide in the cormorant and other fishing birds. A. (*H. A.* ii. 17, 30) gives as examples several species of crows, with which he appears (*II. A.* viii. 3, 15) to have classed the cormorant.

10. Alluding to the *proventriculus* or glandular stomach. This exists in all birds, but is much larger and more glandular when there is no crop, than when such is present. Doubtless in such cases it supplies the absence of the crop (*Cuvier, Leçons,* iii. 408), and acts as a storehouse of food.

11. The example given in the *II. A.* (ii. 17, 31) is a bird which Aubert and Wimmer identify with *Falco tinnunculus*. They point out that in all the diurnal birds of prey there is a peculiarity, thus described by Meckel (*Tr. Gén. d'Anat. Comp.* viii. 314): "L'estomac folliculeux d'une ampleur peu considérable forme subitement une saillie allongée, qui est séparée par une étranglement, supérieurement de l'œsophage, et inférieurement de l'estomac musculaire."

12. The gizzard is strong and muscular in graminivorous birds; but thin and membranous in the carnivorous species.

13. In the Greek text, instead of œsophagus (στόμαχος) we have crop (πρόλοβος). This must be an error; for the presence of a crop is one of the very provisions which A. has just enumerated, and which he says are wanting in the long-legged marsh-birds, *i.e.* the Grallatores. I have therefore substituted œsophagus for crop; which is in harmony with the parallel passage in the *Hist. An.* (ii. 17, 32), where it is said that these birds have a long œsophagus to match their long neck...

In the typical waders there is no crop; neither is the stomach fleshy, but has thin walls, as in piscivorous birds generally. The "dilatation of" the œsophagus before it enters the stomach," *i.e.* the *proventriculus*, would also seem to A. to be absent; for it forms one single cavity with the thin-walled gizzard; at least such is the case in the heron (*Cuvier, Leçons,* iii. 410).

14. As A. here points out the direct correspondence between the nature of the food and the structure of the digestive organs in the case of birds, so also does he elsewhere (iv. 5, 59) point it out in the case of insects.

15. Cf. iii. 1, Note 7. Rumination is regarded by A. as an atonement for deficient mastication owing to want of teeth. Whether the parrot-fish ruminates I do not know; but A. is wrong in saying that no other fish does so. There are several species, especially of the carp tribe, in which a sort of rumination occurs. Cf. *Owen, Comp. Anat.* ii. 236.

16. Cf. iii. 1, Note 9.

17. Because, as he says elsewhere (iii. 1, 10), the water constantly required for their gill function enters in at the mouth, and would interfere with the process.

18. Cf. iii. 3, Note 2.

19. The Cestreus is doubtless some species of Mugil, a tribe of which our grey mullet is a familiar example. What species is meant is uncertain; the Mediterranean containing at least five. In all these Mugilidæ the stomach has much the character of a true muscular gizzard. "Of all the fish I have seen the mullet is the most complete instance of this (the grinding) structure; its strong muscular stomach being evidently adapted, like the gizzard of birds, to the two offices of mastication and digestion."—*John Hunter.*

20. A. seems here to admit that digestion is in part due to putrefaction, a doctrine held by Pleistonicus. Cf. ii. 2, Note 3.

*21. In most osseous fishes, though not in all, there are a variable number of cœcal appendages close behind the pylorus, which have been erroneously held to be the homologues of the pancreas. Their use is not known with certainty. The Selachia are

Notes. iii. 14.

rightly stated by A. (*H. A.* ii. 17, 27) to be without these cœca. In birds, as a rule, there are two cœca at the junction of small and large gut; rarely, as in the heron, a single cœcum. Sometimes, however, as A. notices here and elsewhere (*H. A.* ii. 17, 26), the cœca are absent. This is the case for instance in the wryneck, woodpecker, lark, and cormorant, among birds known to Aristotle.

22. Meaning of course the cœcum and vermiform appendix. There is the greatest variety in the different mammalian orders as to the presence or absence of these. Cf. *Cuvier, Leçons*, iii. 465.

23. Fishes, says A., do not digest their food well, because they have a short gut; and so they are ravenous. Similarly in the *Timæus* it is said that a long intestine was given to animals to prevent insatiable gluttony. An abnormally short gut is in fact a sufficient cause for a ravenous appetite (cf. *Schiff, Sur la Digestion*, i. 44). The normally short gut of a fish is, however, probably to be explained by the easy digestibility of their food. Still there are some grounds for believing that the length of a fish's gut is not so great as it might be with advantage. For if we compare one class of vertebrates with another, and in so doing confine our attention to such species as live on similar food, *e.g.* the carnivorous kinds, we find that the length of the gut in proportion to that of the body is less in fishes than in batrachians or reptiles; less again in these than in birds, and in birds than in mammals. There is thus a gradual increase in the length of the gut, independently of the character of the food, as we get higher in the animal scale (cf. *M. Edwards, Leçons*, vi. 356).

24. What he stated before was that they had a single stomach, not a small one. The single stomach is, however, small as compared with the multiple stomach of the ruminants.

25. The stomach of the dog, as of Carnivora generally, is of small size, somewhat elongated, and perfectly smooth within. That of the pig is of larger dimensions owing to the very ample cardiac cul-de-sac, is of globular shape, and presents on its internal surface two transverse folds on either side of the cardia. Cf. *H. An.* iii. 17, 13.

26. As a rule the intestine of mammalia is divisible into two parts, a small gut following the stomach, and a large gut succeeding to this. But in those that are without a cœcum there is no such distinction of size, the whole intestine being of nearly uniform diameter, or occasionally even becoming somewhat narrower as it advances towards the anus (*Cuvier, Leçons*, iii. 467). Though the dog is not one of these animals without a cœcum, yet its large intestine is exceptionally of scarcely larger calibre than its small gut (*ibid.* p. 485). The straining efforts of a dog in defecation are however scarcely attributable to this. They are more probably due to the hard and earthy character of the fæces.

27. The intestines, longer in Herbivora generally than in Carnivora, attain the greatest length in ruminants. In the sheep, for instance, they are 28 times as long as the body; in the equally herbivorous but non-ruminating rabbit ten times; in the carnivorous dog only five times.

28. "Few horned animals are small and none very small," says A. (*H. A.* ii. 17, 15; but cf. iii. 2, Note 17). Having a complex stomach, their digestion, A. supposes, is more thorough, and the material for growth consequently more abundant; and thus they grow to large size. But this is scarcely in accordance with his former statement, namely, that the complexity of the digestive apparatus is merely an atonement for their imperfect mastication, and for the comparatively indigestible character of their food.

29. Referring to the spiral coil of the colon, which forms one of the characteristics of the Artiodactyla (cf. *Owen. Vert.* iii. 474). The colon becomes narrower where it assumes this spiral disposition. Later on A. calls this part the coil or helix (ἕλιξ). The straight terminal part is of course the rectum.

30. Cf. iv. 5, 60; where it is said that heat requires nutriment and that consequently animals of cold nature take but little food.

31. By "lower stomach" is meant the cœcum and first part of the colon, which precedes the spiral coil (ἕλιξ) of the Artiodactyla (see Note 29). This does undoubtedly serve as a second stomach in some animals, and is sometimes (*e.g.* in the hare) many times as large as the true or upper stomach.

32. But if the residue be useless, why should nature be so economical? A. has in his mind those cases in which he has described the residue as not without some use; as for instance in the aurochs. Cf. iii. 2, Notes 7 and 8, and iv. 5, Note 21.

33. That is to say the Carnivora, who, as compared with herbivorous animals, only get food at rare intervals. In the Carnivora the cœcum and colon are not nearly so capacious as in Herbivora. Their intestine also, though still convoluted, is much shorter.

34. Partly because a short gut causes imperfect digestion, so that much food is wasted (see Note 23), and partly because A. assumes that the satisfaction felt from food is due to contact with the surface of the intestinal tube (iv. 11, Note 8), as in a small degree would appear to be the case. For it is possible by swallowing clay or other indigestible substances to allay temporarily the sensation of hunger. But such relief is only of very brief duration. No adequate satisfaction is experienced, until the food is absorbed, and carried to the various organs that need it for their vital activities.

35. A little way back the colon and cœcum, or second stomach, was said to be the place in which the conversion of food occurs; now that part is spoken of as merely a receptacle for the residue, and the metamorphosis is located in the jejunum. We may, however, fairly suppose the different passages to relate to different animals; the former to those that have a largely developed cœcum, as ruminants, rodents, etc.; the latter to such as have either no cœcum or a small one, as most of the Carnivora. In the latter digestion, begun in the stomach, is over by the time the food reaches the cœcum, having been completed in the small intestine; the middle section of which—or jejunum—may therefore be fairly enough called the place of change. While, in the former, digestion is continued for a length of time after the cœcum is reached. This therefore, with the next succeeding part of the colon, must be in the place of metamorphosis.

36. The jejunum (νῆστις) is the name given to the middle section of the small intestine, because it is usually found empty after death. The passage of the contained food through it takes place with great rapidity (cf. *M. Edwards, Leçons*, iii. 130). There is, so far as I know, no ground for the statement that the arrangement of the intestine differs in male and female.

(**Ch. 15.**) 1. By rennet is usually meant the wall of the fourth stomach of a sucking ruminant, which contains a substance that has the property of coagulating milk; but the term is also occasionally used for the milk when thus coagulated, which, owing to the substance mixed with it, has the power of coagulating other milk. It is in this latter sense that A. uses the word. "Rennet is milk endowed with vital heat" (*D. G.* ii. 4, 29).

2. Moses reckoned the hare among "those that chew the cud." A. did not make this mistake; and it is said that on this account the Septuagint translators introduced boldly the word "not" before "chews the cud" into their version (*Stanley, Lect. on Jewish Church*, iii. 261). But A. considered the hare as so far allied to animals that ruminate, as that it is the only other animal besides them that forms rennet. Varro also (*De Re rusticâ*, ii. 11) speaks of the rennet of the hare as highly efficacious. Whether there be any foundation for the asserted superiority of this animal's rennet I do not know; but all mammals furnish rennet, and not only ruminants and the hare.

3. This is erroneous. It is the fourth stomach that gives rennet.

4. The thickness of milk, as explained in H. A. iii. 20, 6, depends on the proportion of cheese it contains as compared with the whey. The milk of ruminants is rightly stated to contain much more cheese, *i.e.* caseine, than that of other animals.

5. Hares "préferent les plantes, dont la sève est laiteuse."—*Buffon*. The leaves of the common Pinguicula contain a juice which has the power of coagulating milk, and is said by Linnæus to be used by the Laplanders in the fabrication of cheese. The juice of the fig-tree is often mentioned as having this property, *e.g. Iliad*, v. 902; *Columella*, vii. 8.

6. There is no passage in the Problemata suiting this reference; and the same may be said of sundry other references made by A. to that treatise. The Problems, if indeed they be the genuine work of A. at all, have plainly come down to us in a very mutilated condition. Cf. *Heitz, Die Verlor. Schrift. d. Arist.* p. 103.

BOOK IV.

(Ch. 1.) 1. The stomach is not one of the viscera in A.'s sense. Cf. iii, 4, Note 1.

2. Cf. iii. 8, Note 3.

3. Cf. iii. 8, Note 2.

4. Cf. iv. 5, Note 17. The argument is this. In animals that have urinary organs, the urine is the channel through which not only superfluous water but earthy matter is excreted, as is shown by the deposits which occur in urine after standing. When there is no urine, as in birds, the earthy matter is voided with the fæces, and forms the white superficial substance seen on them. I suspect that the last clause in the paragraph is an interpolation.

5. A. includes under Selachia all cartilaginous fishes, among which he erroneously classes the Lophius (cf. iv. 13, Note 5). All these, he often says, with the exception of Lophius, are ovoviviparous; that is, they retain their ova within the body till hatched. In some of these ovovivipara the embryo throughout remains free from all anatomical connection with the mother, but in some, when the nutriment supplied by the yelk is exhausted, the embryo forms a connection with the parent's body (*D. G.* ii. 4, 4; iii. 3, 9). The latter part of this statement applies to certain sharks, which do in fact present a rudimentary placenta. The former part of his statement is too wide a generalisation; for the oviparous dog-fishes and the rays present exceptions to the statement that all A.'s Selachia are, as he says, ovoviviparous. Yet A. (*H. An.* vi. 10, 9) was well acquainted with the eggs of the dog-fishes and the rays. The explanation seems to be that he imagined that the young fish was fully developed in the ovum at the time when this was first laid. It is however very doubtful whether this is the case, unless as an exception. Cf. *Meyer, Thierkunde*, p. 281.

The osseous fishes A. states to be all oviparous. This rule, however, is not without exception; *e.g.* the viviparous blenny.

6. The multiple stomachs of ruminants were supposed by Aristotle to atone for the deficient mastication due to the want of upper incisors. Cf. iii, 14, 7.

7. This is perfectly true. As regards the kidneys, cf. *Rymer Jones, An. Kingd.* p. 709; as regards the liver and lung, cf. *M. Edwards, Leçons*, vi. 427; ii. 309.

8. All vertebrata have a mesentery, with the exception of the lamprey, the carp, and some other fishes, and even these have it in their embryonic stage. As to the omentum; cf. iv. 3, Note 3; as to diaphragm, cf. iii. 10, Note 1.

9. Cf. iii. 3, Note 5.

(Ch. 2.) 1. In certain Ophidia the gall-bladder is in fact completely separated from the liver and lies close to the pylorus. This is so in all the serpents that have the tongue enclosed in a sheath (*Duvernoy, Ann. d. Sc. Nat.* xxx. 127). A similar condition is found in some fishes (*Owen, Lect. on Comp. An.* ii. 243), among others in the Lophius; the Swordfish and the Muræna; all of which are elsewhere (*H. A.* ii. 15, 14) enumerated as examples of this structure. Probably this peculiar arrangement has reference to the long narrow shape of the animals, and exists for convenience of packing.

2. As to lower stomach, cf. ii. 3, Note 6; iii. 14, Note 31. The exact meaning of this passage is doubtful. I understand, however, A. to mean that the bile is in all cases discharged into the intestine at a point below the upper or true stomach.

3. Fishes are very rarely without a gall-bladder, though there are some few exceptions, *e.g.* sawfish, lamprey, and basking-shark.

4. The Amia appears to be the Scomber Sarda of Cuvier. This fish abounds in the Mediterranean. Like the tunny, bonito, and sundry other Scombridæ, it is remarkable for the extreme length and slenderness of its gall-bladder. *Cuvier, Reg. Anim.* ii. 199, and *Owen, Lect.* ii. 244.

5. "Therefore," *i.e.* inasmuch as the bile is always discharged into the intestine as an excrement. The writer alluded to is Plato in the *Timæus*. Cf. *Jowett's Transl.* ii. 564.

6. Elsewhere (*H. A.* ii. 15, 11) the elephant is said to present this structure; and correctly so stated (cf. *Owen, Vert.* iii. 480). Whether a similar structure exists in the camel I do not know. It has, however, no gall-bladder; and the under surface of its liver is marked by numerous irregular and intersecting fissures (*Flower's Lect., Med. Times,* 1872, p. 371). Possibly it may have been these fissures that were taken by Aristotle, or his informant, to be dilated bile-vessels.

7. A. is correct in this enumeration of animals that have no gall-bladder, with the exception of the seal. The Phoca vitulina has a gall-bladder; but it may possibly, though improbably, be that the Phoca monachus, which was the species best known to the ancients (*Cuvier, Regne An.* i. 169), is without one, as Frantzius suggests.

8. The gall-bladder is sometimes present, sometimes absent in giraffes (*Owen, Joly*); in the apteryx and bittern (*Owen*); in the guinea-fowl, etc. It is especially variable, as A. rightly says, in the different species of Mus (*Cuvier, Leçons,* iv. 36). In man a congenital absence of the gall-bladder has been noticed in rare instances (*Rokitansky,* ii. 155; *Phil. Trans.* 1749). This however could not be known to A., who says moreover (*H. A.* i. 17, 10) that *most* men are without a gall-bladder. If, as I have suggested (i. 5, Note 1), A. examined aborted human embryos, he might easily have been led to this erroneous opinion. For the gall-bladder is not developed at all until the third month, at a time when the liver almost entirely fills the abdominal cavity.

9. A similar statement is made in the *Hist. An.* (i. 17, 11); where also we learn that the knowledge of the facts was obtained by observation of sacrificial victims, a source of anatomical information elsewhere referred to (cf. iii. 4, Note 37). Chalcis was, it may be noted, the place to which A. retired when he quitted Athens, and where he finished his life.

10. This clearly professes to be no more than an *à priori* notion, and not to be founded on actual dissection.

11. When an animal's body is opened some time after death, the parts near the gall-

bladder are often found to be stained yellow from an exudation of bile. It is, I imagine, to this overflow that reference is made, as being excessively small in comparison with the amount of bile which is apparent in the human body in cases of jaundice.

12. Residua include for A. not only excretions, but sundry useful secretions (cf. ii. 3, Note 8). But some excretions are also utilised; as in the case of the aurochs (iii. 2, Note 7), the cuttlefish (iv. 5, Note 21); and other animals (iii. 2, Note 8).

13. Cf. Introd. p. iv.

14. Cf. Note 6.

15. Nutritious substances are always sweet, and never bitter (cf. iii. 5, Note 5).

16. There are good reasons for believing that the bile does subserve an useful end, by. facilitating the absorption of fat.

17. The camel is said by A. (*H. A.* viii. 9, 2) to live for 30 years, and exceptionally for 100 years. Burckhart gives it a life of 40 years. As to the dolphin it is stated (*H. A.* vi. 12, 6) that some had been marked by fishermen and let go; and that by their recapture it had been ascertained that they live at least 30 years. There are, I believe, no modern observations on the matter. Horses are said (*H. A.* vi. 22, 8) to live as a rule from 18 to 20 years, and occasionally, if well tended, for 50 years; mares being somewhat longer-lived than stallions. Modern authorities give much the same figures. Stags are said by Flourens to live 30—40 years. It is strange that A. should here speak of stags as long-lived; for elsewhere (*H. A.* vi. 29, 4) he rejects the statements as to their length of life as being mere fable, and says that the gestation and growth of a young stag indicate the contrary.

18. Cf. iii. 4, Note 37.

19. Cf. iii. 7.

(Ch. 3.) 1. His explanation is given in iii. 12. Why some animals have a gall-bladder, while others have none, is still unexplained in any satisfactory manner. It is rarely wanting in Carnivora, very often wanting in Herbivora. Still there are so many exceptions to the general rule that it cannot be said that there is any direct relation between the presence or absence of this organ and the nature of the food. Otherwise we might have accepted the explanation (*Duvernoy, Ann. des Sc. Nat.* xxx, 127) that Carnivora have a gall-bladder because they eat at comparatively long intervals, and so require the bile to be stored up for those occasions; and that it is wanting in Herbivora, because they eat almost continually, and so require a continuous flow of bile into the intestine. S. v. der Kolk thinks that in animals without a gall-bladder the deficiency is compensated, as in the elephant, by the greater width of the bile ducts (cf: *Med. Chir. Review*, 1862, p. 113).

2. Cf. ii. 5, Note 6.

3. A similar statement is made elsewhere (iv. 1, 6; *H. A.* iii. 14). It is, however, erroneous. Mammalia alone have an omentum.

4. A. is apparently thinking of the formation of scum on the surface of boiled milk and the like.

5. Cf. Introd. p. iv.

(Ch. 4.) 1. That is of Hypothetical, not of Absolute, necessity. Cf. Introd. p. iii.

2. Cf. ii. 3, Note 10; iii. 5, Note 5.

3. Cf. ii. 3, Note 16.

(Ch. 5.) 1. Cf. iii. 4, Note 1.

2. Here, as often (*e.g.* iv. 9, 15; iv. 10, 38), A. seems to speak of nature as being in some way or other constrained to construct her works in conformity with set types. Cf. *Introd.* p. x, and iii. 14, Note 4.

3. Urinary bladder and lung (iii. 8, 1) were to A. signs of abundant blood; and

viscera (iii. 7, Note 8) were one of the channels by which superfluous blood was eliminated.

4. By the teeth are meant the two halves of the parrot-like beak; by the tongue is meant the odontophore, of which the anterior part is free from spines and soft, and probably serves as an organ of taste.

5. The "anterior teeth" are the strong shear-like mandibles; which are called anterior to distinguish them from the stomachal teeth presently to be mentioned. By the tongue is meant the bifid lower lip, which has been called a tongue by other writers than A., but is not properly comparable to such an organ. Cf. *Todd, Cycl.* i. 773.

6. The tongue or odontophore forms a very remarkable organ in the Gasteropoda, but there is none in the Conchifera or bivalves of Aristotle.

7. Though there is a "proboscis" in bees and flies alike, yet it has not exactly the same origin in the two cases. In bees it is a development of the labium and maxillæ, the mandibles and upper lip taking no part in the formation and the former serving as biting instruments. But in the Diptera it is a development of the labium, the remaining oral elements being converted into setæ, lancets, etc. These latter are the "*modified teeth*" of flies, as the mandibles are "*the modified teeth*" of bees. The insects that live on fluid nutriment and have no teeth are the Lepidoptera, in which the maxillæ are converted into a long proboscis, while the mandibles are quite rudimentary.

8. The so-called "tongue" of insects is the upper portion of the labium, and is very distinct in some species. In bees and flies the labium with this tongue goes to form what A. calls their proboscis; so that it is only in other insects, that have no such proboscis, that there is a tongue inside the mouth, corresponding to that instrument.

It is evident that A. must have examined with much care the oral arrangements of insects; and when we consider how difficult it is, without magnifying glasses to make them out, we cannot but be struck with admiration at his considerable success in the matter.

9. The words I have rendered "first treatise" are rendered "first book" by Frantzius. He thinks that A. refers to a passage in what is usually reckoned as the second book of the *De Partibus* (ii. 17, 16), and argues from this that that second book is really the first, the book ordinarily called the first being misplaced and transplanted from the *Historia Animalium*. I cannot but think, however, that this view is erroneous, and that A. is referring here to the *Historia Animalium* (iv. 4, 15), which is called the first treatise, as forming the initial portion of his three great connected works on Biology. For A. uses a similar expression later on in this chapter (cf. Note 69), where the reference can only be to the *Historia*, inasmuch as there is no passage in the second book of the *De Partibus* bearing on the matter of which he is then speaking, viz. the position of the mainspring of life in insects.

Perhaps "our earlier, or our initial discussions" would have been a better rendering than "first treatise." For it is impossible to say with certainty whether these biological treatises were regarded by A. himself as distinct treatises, or whether they were not considered by him merely as successive parts of a single work.

10. *i.e.* the horny jaws. I imagine that "Cochli" is used as a general term for most marine gasteropods with spiral shells, and I have therefore rendered it by the vague term "sea-snails." Some have thought that Planorbis and Limnæus are meant. But it is expressly stated (*H, A.* iv. 4, 2) that Cochli are marine, not freshwater, animals.

11. A.'s account of the anatomy and habits of the Cephalopods has received a tribute of praise from many writers. "Respecting the living habits of the Cephalopods," says Owen, "Aristotle is more rich in details than any other zoological author, and Cuvier

has justly observed that his knowledge of this class, both zoological and anatomical, is truly astonishing."

As to the various species known to him, see iv. 9, Note 1; and, as to their external parts, consult the other notes to that chapter. Here we are concerned only with their internal parts. The digestive organs are thus described (*H. A.* iv. 1): "After the mouth there is a long and narrow œsophagus. Continuous with this is a large round crop resembling that of a bird. Then comes the stomach like a rennet. The form of this is spiral, like the shell of a whelk. From this a thin intestine runs back towards the mouth; the intestine is however thicker than the stomach."

It is I think clear that A. did not mean by the crop (προλόβος) what moderns call the crop, which is found in no other dibranchiate cephalopod than the poulp; for he expressly says that the poulp and the sepia are precisely alike so far as these parts are concerned. The crop of the poulp had escaped his observation. The crop of which A. speaks is what we call the stomach. This is, as he says, of softer consistency in the calamary than in the sepia or the poulp, where it is more muscular. What A. calls the stomach is what we look on as the commencement of the gut, which communicates with a membranous dilatation or sac, that is more or less spirally twisted, and is found in calamary, sepia, and poulp alike, though more developed in the first of the three, where it may be not inaptly compared to the spiral body of the whelk. The œsophagus is, as he justly says, long and narrow. Thus his description is accurate, with the exception, that he does not notice the crop of the poulp; while he gives different names to the cavities from those we use.

12. The account of the ink-bag, and of the differences of size and position it presents in the different species, is accurate; it being of course understood that the tetrabranchiate cephalopods, that have no ink-bag, were unknown to Aristotle.

13. The *mytis* is identical with the *mecon*, which exists in all Crustacea (*H. A.* iv. 2, 22); is a bag containing excretory matter (*H. A.* iv. 4, 24); placed near the hinge in bivalves, and in the spiral part of the shell in Turbinata (*H. A.* iv. 4, 22), being spiral itself, in the whelk for instance (*H. A.* iv. 4, 18). This can be nothing else than the liver; and Köhler's notion that the glandular appendages of the veins are meant (*Todd's Cycl.* i. 539) is out of the question. Though A. often states that bloodless animals have no proper viscera, he makes an exception in the case of the mytis (*H. A.* iv. 1, 19). It was doubtless the dull red or violet colour of this organ which gained it this distinction; the viscera being, as he supposed, formed of coagulated blood (cf. iii. 8, Note 2). In fact he speaks later on in this chapter of the mytis as "resembling blood," and believed it to represent the heart.

14. That is to say, have longer tentacles or arms than the rest (cf. iv. 9, Note 15).

15. In reality all these Cephalopods have the faculty of changing colour; but the phenomenon is most conspicuous in the poulps (cf. *Cuvier, R. An.* iii. 10).

16. The Sepiadæ, and still more the calamaries, are pelagic; the poulps are littoral.

17. Cf. iv. 1, Note 4.

18. The internal shell of the sepia consists of a broad spongy calcareous plate, the well-known cuttlefish-bone of the shops. That of the calamary is a thin horny plate, called, from its shape, "the pen." In the poulp there is no internal shell at all.

19. Cf. ii. 4, Note 4.

20. That fear does thus affect the bowels and the bladder is a fact well known to physiologists. To the examples given at ii. 4, Note 5, may be added not only men, but cattle, dogs, cats, and monkeys; in all of which Mr. Darwin has noticed the phenomenon (*Expr. of Emot.* p. 77).

21. Cf. iii. 2, Notes 7 and 8; iii. 14, Note 32.
22. Cf. iv. 8, Note 1.
23. Cf. Note 5.
24. The œsophagus in Crustacea is, as stated in the text, very short. The stomach-teeth are present in all Decapoda, and not only "in the Carabi and some of the crabs.". The intestine is remarkably straight.
25. A.'s Ostracoderma, or Testacea, include all such bloodless animals as have their soft parts within, and their hard part without; the hard part being brittle, and not flexible as in Crustacea (*H. A.* iv. 1, 4). Of their internal structure A. had made out little or nothing. He divides the group, as do modern naturalists, by the character of the shell.

1. Those with a single spiral shell, the Turbinata.
2. Those with a single non-spiral shell, or the Univalves, *e.g.* limpets.
3. Those with a double shell, the Bivalves; which are again subdivided into those whose valves can open, as the mussels, and those whose valves are always closed, as the razor-fishes.
4. Those that are completely enclosed in a hard globular shell, *i.e.* the Echini.
5. Those that are completely enclosed in a shell, of the consistency of leather, *i.e.* the Ascidians (cf. Note 35). To this group, though included among Testacea, the general definition of the Testacea, that they have a brittle and not a flexible shell, is inapplicable.

26. Bronn (*Malacozoa*, part ii. 950), and Lebert (*Müller's Archiv.* 1846, p. 463), believe that A. means the lingual teeth. But these are almost too small to be seen with the naked eye. So Lebert boldly asserts that A. must have used a lens of glass or crystal, or some magnifying instrument! Clearly, however, the jaws are meant, not the lingual teeth: for they are said to be only two in number. Cf. Note 10.

27. In many gasteropods, *e.g.* the whelk, there is a long retractile proboscis. Aristotle gives a much fuller account of the anatomy of the Mollusca in the *II. A.* iv. 4. Neither there nor here, however, is it possible to identify with certainty the various organs which he describes; because there are considerable differences between different species; and we do not know which species was taken by A. as the basis of his account. Probably, however, he had examined the whelk, as he so frequently mentions it.

28. The crop, which comes directly after the mouth, is probably the "buccal mass"; for the dilatation which we call crop in many gasteropods (*e.g.* Dolium, Cypræa, Voluta) is as a rule removed from the mouth by half the length of the œsophagus, though exceptionally (*e.g.* Turbo) it may be much nearer. Cf. *Bronn, Malacozoa,* part ii. 954.

29. The *mecon* (cf. Note 13) is the liver, which in all Gasteropoda is of great size, and fills a large portion of the visceral cavity. It is of a dark brown colour, as also is poppy-juice; which fact is supposed to explain its name; *mecon* being the Greek word for that juice. *Meconium* is still the name given to the bile accumulated in the intestine of the new-born child.

The stomach is here said to contain the *mecon*, and the gut to start not from the stomach, but from this latter. A. seems to have taken the thin membrane which encloses the visceral mass for the stomach. Inside this membrane is the liver, hiding the true stomach, and appearing to give origin to the gut which issues from it.

30. Cf. ii. 17, Note 15.
31. That all Turbinata have opercula is of course an error. In many genera, especially those with larger apertures, it is quite rudimentary or obsolete (*Woodward's Manual,*

102). So also a considerable division of air-breathing gasteropods is inoperculate. The land-snails, however, close their aperture during hybernation by a layer of hardened mucus sometimes strengthened by carbonate of lime. This A. had noticed. For he speaks (*H. A.* viii. 13, 15) of the land-snails as having a *superficial* operculum during hybernation. The operculum when present is so "from the very birth," and the use of the expression shows that A. had attended to the development of the gasteropods.

The operculum of a gasteropod can scarcely be considered to be the homologue of the second valve of a lamellibranchiate mollusc, for it is developed from the foot, not from the mantle. Adanson, however, and more recently Mr. Gray, thought such to be the case (*Woodward's Manual*, p. 47). Though not homologous to the valve, it is however analogous to it; that is, it serves the same purpose, namely, to protect the animal when retracted into the shell.

32. There does not seem sufficient evidence to decide what molluscs exactly are meant. This is the short description given (*H. A.* iv. 4): "The Nerites has a large smooth round shell, in form like that of the whelk. But its mecon is red, not black as is that of the whelk."

33. The Bivalves in reality have no odontophore or tongue.

34. This passage with others shows that the *Hist. Animalium* and the lost treatises on Anatomy were illustrated. Cuvier indeed (*Hist. d. Sc.* i. 141) says the latter contained *coloured* illustrations. I can find no authority for this statement. There is none in the 28 passages referring to the ἀνατομαί collected by Heitz (*Verlor. Schr. des Arist.* p. 70).

35. By Tethya are undoubtedly meant Ascidians, as the description here, and in the *Hist. An.* (iv. 6) shows, and I have therefore so rendered it. A. includes both Echini and Ascidia among the Testacea; though they are, as he says, very different from the three main groups of these animals. That he should so have classed Echini was but natural; for they would appear to him to have all the characters which distinguish his Testacea, viz. a hard brittle covering (which however is not really external), a mouth turned downwards, a stomach, intestine, vent, mecon, and so forth. But that he should have so classed the Ascidians, that have no hard shell, is more remarkable. He had, however, perceived that the external covering of the Ascidians is in reality a. shell. "Their whole body, he says, is hidden in a shell. This shell is something intermediate between skin and shell proper, so that it cuts like hard leather." In the Museum Catalogue (Coll. of Surg. i. 266) it is said that, "Mr. Hunter, who perceived the relations subsisting between Ascidia and Salpa, and knew the true analogy of their external covering, proposed to distinguish them as a distinct group of Mollusks under the term 'soft-shelled,' which more truly accords with their real nature than 'shell-less,' as they have subsequently been designated by Cuvier."

36. The jaws of Echinus with the five teeth form a conical mass, which is still described by writers as "the lantern of Aristotle," in reference to a comparison made in *H. A.* iv. 5, 8.

37. The flesh-like piece is said in the *Hist. An.* (iv. 5, 5,) to be in place of a tongue, and to occupy the centre of the cavity formed by the teeth. As the Echinus has no tongue, the pharyngeal portion of the œsophagus must be meant.

38. The œsophagus of Echinus terminates in a much wider tube, which is continued to the anus without any distinct separation into stomach and intestine. This gastro-intestinal tube is attached, by what may be called a mesentery, to the inner surface of the shell, in such a manner as to form loops or festoons, five in each of its two coils; and it is to this appearance of subdivision that A. alludes. This is plain not only from the careful way in which he here guards himself from saying that there are actually a number of

distinct stomachs, but still more from his language in *Hist. An.* (iv. 5, 6,), where he says that all the *loops* (κόλποι) of the stomach run together to the anus; and where also he makes no mention of an intestine as distinct from the stomach.

39. The "so-called ova" which A. thought to be masses of fat, or of something analogous to the fat of sanguineous animals, are the ovaries, which are five in number, and arranged symmetrically round the upper interior of the shell. These vary in size in proportion to the maturity of the ova within them, and thus are much larger at some seasons of the year than others. It is when the ova are mature that "the roe of the sea-egg" is used for food along the coasts of the Mediterranean, divers being employed to collect these animals. They may be seen in abundance in the market at Marseilles. According to Pennant they are also eaten by the poor in many parts of England.

40. These black bodies are also mentioned at *H. A.* iv. 5, 7, and are there said to be bitter, uneatable, and connected with the origin of the teeth.' They are also said to converge towards the aperture of the test, though separate from each other, and to divide this into segments. The best conjecture I can offer is that A. alludes to the rows of ambulacral vesicles, though I do not know of any species in which these are black. The word "profusely" would accord with this conjecture; for the vesicles are present in hundreds. But less consistent is the statement that similar bodies, though of different colour, are found in Batrachia, Chelonia, and Turbinata.

41. Frantzius and also Meyer (*Thierkunde*, p. 175) translate ἐπιπολάζοντα "floating on the surface." But no Echini float; and seeing that the large esculent species were common articles of diet, A. could scarcely have been so ignorant of their habits as to suppose them to do so. I have little doubt that A. means "that live in shallow water"; and this view is confirmed by a passage (*De Gen.* v. 3, 21) in which he says that those Echini that live in deep water have big spines but small bodies; so that they would not be suitable for eating.

42. Cf. Note 13.

43. Cf. *H. A.* iv. 4. What A. meant by the right and left of a bivalve I cannot say; certainly, however, not what we mean. The bivalve which he seems to have chosen for examination was the scallop, because of its large size (*H. A.* iv. 4, 24); and he is correct in saying that the "ovum" is on one side, and the vent on the opposite side of the circumference of the disk-shaped body. The "ovum" is on the anterior convexity, the vent on the posterior convexity; and for some reason or other the anterior is considered by A. to be the right side. Can it be that he had made out the foot, which is also anterior? If so his notion that motion specially attaches to the right side (cf. iii. 9, Note 12) would make him identify the anterior aspect with the right side.

44. That the ovary of Testacea was miscalled, A. seems to have thought was shown by its having no orifice. "The so-called ovum (*ovary*) never has a duct, and is merely a swollen part of the flesh" (*H. A.* iv. 4, 25). He believed that Bivalves were developed spontaneously or by gemmation.

45. Cicero (*De Divin.* 2, 14) mentions, among other instances of some natural connection existing between things apparently remote and incongruous, "that oysters and other shell-fish increase and decrease with the growth and waning of the moon." So also Lucilius says, "Luna alit ostrea et implet echinos;" and again Manilius, "Si submersa fretis, concharum et carcere clausa, Ad lunæ motum variant animalia corpus." The two last quotations I borrow from Mead (*Influence of Sun and Moon*, etc. 1748, p. 65), who accepts the statement as true.

46. So that the Echini have no competitors for the food.

47. The ovary of Bivalves is really bilateral. But it is not bilateral in A.'s sense

(cf. Note 43) ; for it is on one side only of the circumference, when the body is viewed from above as it lies in either valve.

48. This passage is unintelligible, and the text probably corrupt. As it stands, we should have to suppose that A. took the central muscular mass of the oyster to be a head. This is very improbable, and has no support from other passages. It is true that in ch. 7 it is said that all Testacea have a head, and that in the *Hist. An.* (iv. 4, 21) A., lumping univalves with bivalves, says they all have a head, as also horns and mouth, without specifying its position. But he adds that some of their parts can only be seen "in living specimens, and whilst they are in motion ; " that is to say, he could not find a head in the oyster, which is motionless, though he found one in the locomotive univalves, as the limpet. Probably, as he only says that "some of these parts" are not to be found in the motionless kinds, he may have found the mouth of the bivalves, and perhaps may have taken the labial tentacles for horns. This view is confirmed by a passage (*H. A.* viii. 2, 16) where, after describing the headless sea-anemone as having a mouth, he says it resembles an oyster taken out of its shell. The ovary in this passage is said to be on the upper side ; a little farther back it was said to be on the right side ; an inconsistency, which also seems to point to some corruption of the text.

49. Cf. Note 2.

50. The Echini with small ova are those that live in deep water ; the species with large ova are those that live in shallower places. Cf. Note 41.

51. The spines are really instruments of locomotion, and Agassiz said were the only ones ; but their main function is probably protective, the chief organs of locomotion being the tube-feet, which A. had not noticed either in Echini or star-fishes.

52. The same idea is elaborated more fully in an admirable passage in the *Hist. An.* (viii. 1).

53. Having considered the Testacea, A. now passes on to those animals that are intermediate between these and plants, to such that is as in aftertime were termed zoophytes. In these, he says, locomotion is feeble at best, and often absent, some of them being actually rooted in the soil. Sensibility is also dull, and sometimes scarce a sign of it is detectable. In both of these characters, as also in the absence of any distinct excretory organs, these animals are closely akin to plants. In this group A. reckons Sponges, Holothurias, Sea-lungs, Acalephæ, Star-fishes, and "other similar marine creatures." These latter are probably those mentioned in the *Hist. An.* (iv. 7, 14) ; of which he says he had gathered an imperfect account from fishermen. Among these is one which naturalists have supposed, not improbably, to correspond with *Pinnatula;* and another which I take most probably to be *Holothuria tremula*, which abounds in the Mediterranean.

At the bottom of the group are the sponges. Ever since A.'s time it has been a disputed question whether these should be reckoned as belonging to the animal or the vegetable kingdom. Physiologists now admit their claim to be considered animals ; but they would reject the evidence which led A. to the same conclusion. "The sponge exhibits some signs of sensation ; for they say there is considerable difficulty in detaching it from the rocks, unless the attempt is made stealthily" (*H. A.* i. 1, 18), and again, "It is said that the sponge possesses sensation. This is a proof of it ; it contracts if it perceives any intention of pulling it off from the rocks, and so renders the task more difficult. It does the same, if the wind and waves are violent, in order that it may not lose its attachment. There are some persons who doubt this, as the natives of Torona " (*H. A.* v. 16, 5). Modern naturalists seem to be of the same opinion as these natives of Torona.

54. There are not sufficient data to determine with certainty what animals correspond to the Holothurias and Sea-lungs of Aristotle. They are above the sponges, inasmuch as they are unattached to the ground; but resemble them in the want of locomotion (*H. A.* i. 1) and of sensibility. Very probably, however, A.'s Holothurias are some of the animals still so named. The only difficulty in accepting this is that the Holothurias are most manifestly sensitive; for when irritated they actually often eject their viscera, or fall into pieces; neither are they incapable of locomotion. We may, however, suppose that A. was only acquainted with such dead specimens as fishermen brought to him, or as he found stranded on the shore.

Pliny is so servile a follower of Aristotle, that there can, I think, be no doubt that his *pulmones marini* are the latter's Sea-lungs. Probably some of the larger kinds of Medusæ are meant, the smaller kinds being included with Actiniæ under the name Acalephæ (cf. Note 61). There are a very large number of species of Medusæ in the Mediterranean. I cannot understand why Strack should take the Sea-lung to be the Sea-hare (*Aplysia depilans*). That Medusæ of some kind are meant is rendered probable by the name Sea-lung, which is an apposite title for animals that move by alternate expansions and contractions of the body; a mode of progression still known as Pulmonigrade, and applied to these animals. Secondly, the Medusæ not only float on the surface of the sea, but are often phosphorescent, especially when irritated, and these are characters assigned by Pliny to the Pulmones (*Nat. Hist.* xxxii. 52).

55. If they have absolutely no feeling why does A. not only consider them to be animals but even put them above the sponges, to which he ascribes a rudimentary sensibility? I take it that he does not mean that they are absolutely without feeling; but that they have very little of it.

56. A. thought that parasitical plants, such as mistletoe (*D. G.* i. 1, 11), were engendered out of the decay of some part of the tree on which they grew. Bacon (*Nat. Hist.*§ 656, 643) held a very similar opinion. Mistletoe, he says, is an exudation of something "that the tree doth excern and cannot assimilate."

57. Very probably some kind of Sedum; and, according to Fraas, Sedum rupestre or amplexicaule. There is an English species, S. Telephium, which has gained the popular name "Livelong" from its persistent vitality after being pulled up from the ground.

58. Aristotle's Tethya, or Ascidians, are not Tunicata generally, but only the simple solitary Ascidians, which are always sessile.

59. A. seems here half inclined to remove the Ascidians, which he had before classed with the Echini as peculiar kinds of Testacea, from these latter, and to place them with the Zoophytes, leaving the Echini behind and making them form part of the Turbinata. Similarly he says later on: "Of the Turbinata some have a spiral shell, as the whelks, and some are simply spherical, as the Echini" (iv. 7, 2). A somewhat fuller account of the double-walled sac, with its two orifices, which forms the covering of the Ascidian, is given elsewhere (*H. A.* iv. 6).

By the "septum" I understand the perforated wall that intervenes between the cavity of the pharynx and the atrium; by the "median partition" I understand the reflection of the lining membrane, or atrial tunic, over the viscera. A. supposes the heart to be here, because the heart should be in a central position (iii. 4, 13), but he does not profess to have made it out by dissection. The "flesh-like substance" is the real body of the animal. As to the statement that the presence of this substance implies sensibility, cf. ii. 8, Note 2; ii. 10, Note 10. A. was so convinced that the heart, or whatever corresponded to the heart as the centre of life, must be in a central position, that he attempted to make out a similar condition in plants: "In all seeds there are two valves, and the development starts from the centre, that is from the point where the valves unite, a point which is common to the two sides. For thence grows the stem and thence grows the root, and the *principium vitæ* (ἀρχή) is between these two" (*De Juvent.* 3, 1).

60. The residuum of plants, that is their superfluous food, is, says A. elsewhere, represented by their seeds. Cf. ii. 3, Note 8.

61. Schneider, Strack, Camus, Frantzius, (cf. *Meyer*, *Thierk.* p. 165) all agree in taking A.'s sea-nettles or Acalephæ to mean exclusively the Actiniæ or sea-anemones; and there can be no doubt that the description given here, as also the more detailed one in the *Hist. An.* (iv. 6), is the description of an Actinia. At the same time I cannot but think that A. also included some of the modern Acalephæ in the same group, confounding them with the sea-anemones and imagining them to be free-living species of these latter (*H. A.* v. 16, -1). For though the sea-anemones do in fact possess urticating organs, yet their power of stinging is insufficient, unless in very exceptional cases, to cause any irritation to the fingers, even when the skin has been previously softened by soaking in water (*Proc. Royal Soc.* ix. 723). On the other hand the power of stinging is such a prominent fact in the Medusæ that their name in almost all languages is founded upon it.

62. That is their power of stinging which belongs "to all the surface of their bodies" (*H. A.* ix. 37, 8).

63. "Star-fishes are not unfrequently found feeding on shell-fish. In such cases they enfold their prey within their arms, and seem to suck it out of its shell with their mouths, pouting out the lobes of the stomach" (*Forbes, Brit. Star-fishes*, p. 86). The damage done to oyster-beds by these animals has always been, and still is, a matter of complaint by fishermen. "Bishop Sprat informs us, in his history of the Royal Society, that great penalties are laid by the Admiralty Court upon those engaged in the oyster-fishery who do not tread under their feet or throw upon the shore a fish which they call a Five-finger, resembling a spur-rowel, because that fish gets into the oysters when they gape and sucks them out" (*Todd's Cycl.* ii. 38).

64. The mytis, which in cephalopods is traversed by the œsophagus, is the liver (cf. Note 13), not the heart. The real heart of cephalopods, as of all other Invertebrata, escaped Aristotle.

65. Cf. iv. 2, 13.

66. Cf. Note 13.

67. A. does not profess to have seen the heart of Mollusca, but only to say where it is likely to be found on *à priori* grounds. Cf. Note 59.

68. I suspect that the words "or the spermatic fluid" are an interpolation. For A. (*D. G.* iii. 11, 11) denied the existence of any generative secretions in bivalves. See *Introd.* p. xxviii, foot-note 6.

69. *H. A.* iv. 7. Cf. Note 9. The heart is represented in insects by the dorsal vessel. A. failed to make it out, and concluded on purely *à priori* grounds that it was in the middle of the body (cf. Note 59).

70. A. elsewhere (*H. A.* iv. 1, 6) speaks of Julus and Scolopendra as wingless insects; and (iv. 6, 1) as having many feet. There can be no doubt that, speaking generally, they correspond to our Myriapoda. But A. gives no accurate account of the differences between Julus and Scolopendra; so that we have no actual certainty that the two divisions of Myriapoda to which these names are now given were those meant by him. Probably, however, such was the case. As, however, A. divides (*H. A.* ii. 14, 2) the Scolopendras into land species and water species, we must suppose that he confounded

some or other Annelid with Scolopendra; very probably, a Nereis or Aphrodite, as Müller suggests, an animal still called sea-centipede from its external resemblance to the Myriapoda.

71. Cf. iii. 5, Note 2. "They stir," says Lord Verulam, "a good while after their heads are off, or that they be cut in pieces; which is caused also for that their vital spirits are more diffused throughout all their parts and less confined to organs than in perfect creatures" (*Sylv. Sylvarum, Cent.* vii. § 697).

72. There seems here an inkling of the truth that vegetative repetition is a mark of inferiority.

73. Cf. Note 8.

74. A. includes the Myriapoda among Insecta. In most of these the alimentary canal is a simple intestiniform tube, running in a straight line from mouth to anus. But in some (*e.g.* Glomeris) the tube, though still simple, is convoluted. In many insects the canal is a long convoluted organ, thick and muscular, and divided into a varying number of distinct compartments.

75. The stomach is very minute in such insects as the butterflies, that scarcely eat at all; but in those that live on coarse and indigestible materials it is proportionately elongated and capacious (*Rymer Jones, An. Kingd.* p. 363). As to the intestine, its length and convolutions are greatest in those insects that have a thick and largely developed abdomen, especially if they are herbivorous (do. p. 362).

76. Alluding to the so-called "rostrum" of Hemipterous insects. This is a suctorial tube formed by the upper and lower lips, within which are the mandibles and maxillæ converted into lancet-shaped needles.

77. Most of our food does in fact go to maintain the heat of the body.

78. The Cicadæ really live on the juices of plants. But A. adopts the general belief of the ancients. So Virgil, "Dumque thymo pascentur apes, dum rore cicadæ." See also *Anacreon, Ode* 43; *Theocr.* 4, 16; *Pliny,* xi. 32.

79. The Ephemera of A. are usually supposed to be the insects still so named. There are however no data for the determination. They are said (*H. A.* i. 5, 16) to have only four legs, which is neither true of Ephemera nor of any other insects. Neither does the account of their development (*H. A.* v. 19, 26) altogether suit the modern Ephemera.

(**Ch. 6.**) 1. The following are the characters A. ascribes to his Insecta. 1. They are bloodless. 2. They show segmentation either on the dorsal or ventral surface or on both (*H. A.* i. 1, 16). 3. They have a distinct head, thorax, and abdomen; the thorax however being in some (*Myriapoda*) formed of a number of separate segments, not fused together (*H. A.* iv. 7, 3). 4. Their legs are numerous and in number proportionate to the segments, excepting when the insect has wings (iv. 6, 2). 5. They present no distinct differentiation of their substance into bonelike and fleshlike parts, but consist throughout of an uniformly hard substance intermediate to bone and flesh (*H. A.* iv. 1, 5). 6. They are either without special organs for refrigeration, or have such below the junction of thorax and abdomen (iii. 6, Note 4). 7. They are almost invariably land animals, though with some exceptions; and some are aquatic, when young, but terrestrial, when adult (*H. A.* i. 1, 17). 8. The females are larger than the males (*H. A.* iv. 11, 9). 9. Their primary generative product is not an ovum but a scolex (*Introd.* p. xxvii).

The 5th, 6th, and 7th characters exclude Crustacea; for these have the soft parts within and a harder part without, are aquatic, and sometimes have gill-like apparatus for refrigeration in the thoracic or cephalic region (iv. 8, 7). Although A. thus distinctly separated Crustacea from Insecta, the two were confounded again by after writers. Even Lamarck at first included both under Insecta; though later on (in 1799) he separated them. Crustacea, then, are outside the group. It includes, however, not only insects proper, which are A.'s Hexapodous insects, but also Myriapoda, which are his Polypodous and Wingless insects (iv. 5, Note 70). The third of the above-named characters should exclude the spiders, scorpions, etc. But nevertheless these also are included in the group by A., as indeed they were by modern naturalists until Lamarck separated them in 1800. The fourth character, again, should exclude the parasitic worms. Yet A. includes in the group both the flat and the round parasites ($H. A.$ v. 19, 3), which he calls by the general name of Helminthes. In fact, the only character on which he practically insists is the presence of segmentation; and he even in one place ($H. A.$ i. 1, 16) thus expresses himself: "I call all those animals insects, that show segmentation either on the dorsal or the ventral surface, or on both." This passage must of course be read with the limitations introduced in other places. Still it shows that segmentation was the main character of the group in A.'s estimation. Probably therefore he included Annelida in the group, led to this not only by their manifest segmentation, but by their retention of life when cut into pieces, a character often mentioned by him as specially belonging to insects. Some water annelids were certainly so included by him, being confounded with Myriapoda. Cf. iv. 5, Note 70.

2. Cf. iv. 5, Note 70.
3. Cf. iv. 5, Note 71, and iii. 5, Note 2.
4. The Diptera are as a rule of small size. Still the direct relation here stated to obtain between the bulk of an insect and the number of the wings can hardly be said to exist. There is however some relation between the size of the wings and the weight of the body. "There are three classes of flies in this order (*Diptera*), the form of whose bodies, as well as the shape and circumstances of their wings, is different. First are the slender flies—the gnats, gnatlike flies, and craneflies. The bodies of these are light, their wings narrow, and their legs long, and they have no winglets. Next are those whose bodies, though slender, are more weighty—the Asilidæ, etc.; these have larger wings, shorter legs, and very minute and sometimes even obsolete winglets. Lastly come the flies, Muscidæ, etc., whose bodies, being short, thick, and often very heavy, are furnished not only with proportionate wings, and shorter legs, but also with conspicuous winglets" (*Kirby and Spence*, 7th ed. p. 476). So also there is a connection between the weight of the body and the presence of wings. For while in most insects the tracheæ dilate into air-vesicles "which are subservient to the diminution of the weight of the insect, in the Apterous insects, and especially in the Myriapoda, there is no trace of these" (*Owen's Lectures*, i. 225).

5. The Melolontha of A. is certainly not the beetle now known by that name, viz. the cockchaffer. For A. describes it ($H. A.$ v. 19, 18) as coming from a worm that lives in the dung of cattle and of asses. Very probably some such beetles as the Geotrupidæ are meant. These are stationary during the day; and though they fly in the evening "rasent la terre d'un vol court, lourd et sinueux."

6. Frantzius translates thus: "Their wings also are not divided. For it is not a wing at all, etc." But the word which A. uses for the wing of an insect (πτερόν) is the word used for the feather of a bird, not for its wing (πτέρυξ); and the comparison is not between the wings of an insect and the wings of a bird, which A. knew to be perfectly distinct parts though analogous in function, but between the wings of an insect and the feathers of a bird, which do so far anatomically correspond to each other, as that both are derivations from the common integument. (Cf. iv. 12, 3.) When, then, A. calls insects dipterous and tetrapterous he has an eye to homologies; when we call them two-winged or four-winged we are thinking of analogies.

7. The Juli when alarmed coil themselves up in a spiral form, with the feet entirely concealed. The Glomeridæ roll themselves into a perfect ball. Not only long-bodied insects, but some others, roll themselves up. For instance, the ant known as Myrm. Latreillii is said by Sir J. Lubbock to do so.

8. The description of the Canthari in the *Hist. An.* (v. 19, 18), where they are said to roll dung into balls, in which they deposit their progeny, seems to identify them with the sacred Scarabei of Egypt (*Atruchus sacer*). Many beetles when touched assume attitudes more or less such as here described. "The common dungchaffer, when touched or in fear, sets out its legs as stiff as if they were made of iron wire; which is their posture when dead; and, remaining perfectly motionless, thus deceives," etc., etc. The pill-beetles "pack their legs so close to the body, and lie so entirely without motion when alarmed, that they look like a dead body." Still nearer to A.'s description is the action of certain caterpillars. "The body is kept stiff and immoveable with the separation of the segments scarcely visible" (*Kirby and Spence*).

9. Cf. iii. 5, Note 2.

10. Cf. ii. 16, 5; iv. 12, 4.

11. Ants, bees, and Hymenoptera of all kinds, have biting jaws or mandibles. It is these that A. calls their "modified" teeth (iv. 5, Note 7). These mandibles, however, are not used merely or principally for the prehension of food, as stated in the text, but "comme instruments de sculpture dans les travaux architecturaux de ces animaux" (*M. Edwards, Leçons*, v. 520).

12. The terminal segment of the scorpion is so shaped as to form a sharp uncinated sting, under which are orifices giving issue to the secretion of a poison-gland. The scorpion runs swiftly, arching its tail over its back, and turning it in all directions.

13. This generalisation especially excited the admiration of Cuvier, who says that it implies "un examen presque universel de toutes les espèces." Mr. Lewes is more sober in his estimate, and thinks that, though the generalisation is true, it was made after examination of but few species, and that A. was thus right almost by accident. That A. examined the greater number of species of Diptera, or indeed any considerable part of them, is hardly consistent with his only mentioning in all his writings five kinds, and giving such scanty account of these, that naturalists are unable to identify them with certainty.

14. The text gives τοῖς ἔμπροσθεν, i.e. "with the front part." The sense seems, however, to require τοῖς ὄπισθεν, and I have ventured so to alter it. If this alteration be thought inadmissible, the passage must be rendered, "Weak as they are, they have little power of striking *even* with the front part," implying that they would have still less power to strike from behind.

15. Here we have a distinct statement of the advantage of division of labour in the animal body; a truth which Milne Edwards thought he was the first to enunciate. "Dans les créations de la Nature, de même que dans l'industrie des hommes, c'est surtout par la division du travail, que ce perfectionnement s'obtient," and in a note he adds, "Ce principe de physiologie générale qui aujourd'hui est adopté par presque tous les zoologistes a été formulé pour la première fois dans un article que j'ai publié en 1827" (*M. Edwards, Leçons*, i. 16).

"Spit and lampholder in one," or, as perhaps it would better have been rendered, "spit and candlestick in one," is in the Greek a single word, and so more forcible. This strange implement with a double purpose is also mentioned in the *Politics* (iv. 15, 8), where A. likens to it a board of magistrates, charged with a multitude of distinct functions; such a body as our Boards of Guardians, with their poor-law, sanitary, educational, and other functions. A. has another term of comparison for such a body, viz. "the Delphian knife" (*Polit.* i. 2, 3), an implement apparently used for many distinct purposes in the sacrificial rite.

16. The anterior pair of legs are remarkably long in some insects (*Kirby, Bridg. Tr.* ii. 180); with what use it is difficult to say. Sometimes at any rate it seems to be a provision to enable the male to secure the female, the peculiarity being confined to, or most marked in, the former sex. The explanation given by A. can hardly be the correct one; for the anterior pair are not specially elongated in ants or bees, though these are insects that use their legs to dress themselves.

17. In such insects as are slow walkers all the legs are, as a rule, of much the same length; in those that run quickly all the legs are elongated, the hinder pair being the largest; in swimming insects, and still more in leapers, the hind legs are much longer than the rest. In fleas the difference is not so marked as in grasshoppers; nor do fleas jump, like the latter, exclusively from the hind legs, for, having placed one in a glass tube under a microscope, I have seen it hop with the anterior legs.

18. Literally "resemble a rudder," but I have slightly paraphrased the expression to render it intelligible to those who may not know how a Greek ship was steered. In place of a single rudder, as in a modern ship, there were usually two, one on either side of the stern, resembling large oars, and moved in the same way as the other oars. The size and position of these rudder-oars render, therefore, the comparison to the posterior legs of the locust or grasshopper a very apt one. The resemblance, moreover, extends to the functions. "Whoever," says Kirby, "has seen any grasshopper take flight or leap from the ground will find that they stretch out their legs, and like certain birds use them as a rudder" (*Bridg. Treat.* ii. 162).

19. Cf. iv. 12, Note 10. A.'s meaning is expressed more intelligibly elsewhere (*H. A.* iv. 7, 9), "In some jumping insects the hind legs are simply larger than the rest, while in others they resemble rudder-oars, being bent backwards like the [hind] legs of quadrupeds."

(Ch. 7.) 1. Cf. iv. 5, Note 25.

2. Cf. ii. 10, Note 5.

3. Cf. iv. 5, 22—41.

4. "Aristotle in his Hist. of Animals mentions more than once a shell-fish under the name of Solen in such expressive terms that we can scarcely doubt its identity with the razor-fish, in all probability the Solen marginatus. He states that it buries itself in the sand, perpendicularly, even to the depth of two feet, and can rise and sink in it, but does not leave its hole; that it does not spin a byssus like other Testacea; that it is alarmed by noise, and buries itself rapidly when frightened; that the valves of the shell are connected together at both sides, and that their surface is smooth. Such an enumeration of characters indicates how carefully the great philosopher studied razor-fishes, and with what interest he watched their doings and chronicled their fears" (*Forbes and Hanley, Brit. Mollusca,* i. 240).

5. The ordinary position of most living bivalves is not on their side but vertical, with the opening between the valves downwards. This probably led A. to the conclusion that the head, or what answered to it, was downwards, so as to take in food from below. As to roots of plants, cf. ii. 3, Note 10.

6. Cf. iv. 5, Note 48.

(Ch. 8.) 1. The Crustacea are called by A. Malacostraca, *i.e.* soft-shelled, or sometimes Scleroderma, *i.e.* hard-skinned, and are defined by him as bloodless animals that have their hard matter on the outside and their soft parts within; the hard part,

moreover, though readily bruised or crushed, not being brittle like that of Testacea
(*H. A.* iv. 1, 3; iv. 2). There are, he says, four main genera: 1. Carcini; 2. Carabi;
3. Astaci; 4. Carides. The first three are decapodous; the Carcini having no tail but
a flap, while the remaining two have long tails. This identifies the Carcini with our
Brachyura, or crabs. The Astaci are said to have the anterior pair of feet converted
into strong claws, of unequal size and differently toothed; the second and third pairs
of feet being also chelate. Their shell is smooth, and some of them live in freshwater.
There is no difficulty in recognising in this description the lobster (*Astacus marinus*) and
the river crayfish (*Astacus fluviatilis*). The Carabi differ from the Astaci in having
a rougher shell, larger eyes, longer and stouter antennæ, a narrower thorax, and a harder
and less fleshy body. They differ also in the character of the first pair of feet. In the
Astaci these are chelate in both sexes; but in the Carabi only in the female. On this
last point, however, A.'s language is not always quite consistent. For in the text he
speaks of the Carabi as always having claws like the crabs. This description leaves no
doubt that the animals meant are the spiny lobsters (*Palinurus vulgaris*). Although
the anterior feet of these animals never form such perfect claws as those of Astacus,
yet the terminal joint bends over and meets a process from the penultimate joint, so as
to make a nipper. This process is developed in very different degrees of perfection in
different individuals, as I have myself noticed, and thus it is easy to understand how
at one time they might be described as having claws, at another as without them.
Whether there is any difference in this respect dependent upon sex, I do not know.
There remain the Carides. These are said to have a tail, like that of the Carabi, no
claws, and more than five pairs of feet. The name would thus appear to designate
some of the Amphipoda, and Stomapoda. A. describes two kinds; his account in
one case suiting the sea-mantis (*Squilla mantis*), but in the other being insufficient for
positive identification. As to the separation of Crustacea from Insecta, see iv. 6, Note 1.

2. The Maia is said (*H. A.* iv. 2, 3) to be the largest of the crabs, the next in size being
the Paguri and the Heracleotic crabs, and to have a hard shell (*H. A.* viii. 17, 11).
Again (*H. A.* iv. 3, 3) the Maia and the Heracleotic crabs are said to have their eyes
placed close together, near the median line. Here we are told that the Maiæ have thin
legs, the Heracleotic crabs short ones, and that both live out at sea. From these passages
Cuvier and most writers have concluded with great probability that the Maia answers
to the Maia Squinado or spiny spider-crab, the largest of the crabs common in the
Mediterranean. There are no data to determine what are meant by the "Heracleotic
crabs."

3. In most crabs the four hinder pairs of feet are formed exclusively for running; but
in some few they are flattened out so as to serve in swimming. These swimming crabs
are all small. Rondelet mentions several species as found in the Mediterranean.

4. Cf. ii. 9, Note 9.

5. A. does not explain why an animal that swims should want more legs than one that
has any other mode of progression; and the statement that it does so is somewhat in
opposition with his previous remarks about Myriapoda. Probably he has in his eye the
image of a ship with its numerous oars on either side.

6. "In the Podophthalma, the lamelliform ciliated appendages of the abdominal
segments include similar marsupial or incubatory recesses for the ova. The female lobster
and other Macrura are distinguished from the male by the greater development of these
appendages" (*Owen's Lect.* i. 185). Similarly Cuvier (*Reg. An.* iv. 28), speaking of the
flap or tail of the Brachyura, says, "Triangulaire dans les mâles et garnie seulement
à sa base de quatre ou deux appendices, elle s'arrondit, s'élargit et devient bombée

dans les femelles. Son dessous offre quatre paires de doubles filets velus, destinés à porter les œufs. Plusieurs de ces filets existent dans les mâles, mais dans un état rudimentaire."

7. This is too absolute a statement; and elsewhere (*H. A.* iv. 3, 2) A. speaking more carefully says that the rule is general but not universal. There are some grounds for his statement. "In many species (of the higher Crustacea) the chelæ on the opposite sides of the body are of unequal size, the right-handed one being, as I am informed by Mr. C. Spence Bate, generally though not invariably the largest. This inequality is often much greater in the male than in the female" (*Darwin, Desc. of Man,* i. 330). There are however some small Crustacea in which the right claw appears to be invariably the bigger. Thus I found no exception to this rule in 100 common hermit crabs that I examined in succession. In Alpheus villosus also the right claw is always the larger; and in Nika the right anterior foot is chelate, but not so the left.

8. Cf. iii. 9, 14, and ii. 2, Note 6.

9. Cf. iii. 1, 7.

10. It has been stated recently (*Land and Water,* Aug. 20, 1870) that in lobsters the right claw is the larger in one sex, the left in the other. This however was afterwards contradicted by Mr. H. Lee; and I have myself found it to be erroneous on examination. So far then the statement in the text is correct. But there is no ground for the further statement that the Astaci use their claws only for locomotion and not for prehension.

11. Cf. iv. 5, Note 2, and *Introd.* p. x.

(Ch. 9.) 1. The Cephalopods are called by A. Malacia, *i.e.* Mollusca or soft animals, and are defined by him (*H. A.* iv. 1, 2) as bloodless animals that have their fleshy parts outside, and their hard part, when there is any, within. They all have eight legs, with suckers on them, in front of the head. The head itself is provided with two jaws or teeth, large eyes, and a small brain enclosed in cartilage. These, and the presence of an ink-bag, are the chief characters assigned to them by A., who mentions, however, two other notable peculiarities, namely the adherence of the yelk-bag to the head of the embryo (*D. G.* iii. 8, 7) and the modification of one of the feet in the male poulp to form an instrument of generation (*H. A.* v. 6, 3; v. 12, 3; *D. G.* i. 15, 4). The latter statement, repeated by Pliny (*Nat. Hist.* ix. 74), refers of course to the now re-discovered Hectocotylus.

Aristotle divides his Malacia into two groups. (i.) Those that have a short body and long feet, no "proboscides," and no internal bones; a division corresponding to our Octopoda. (ii.) Those that have a long body and short feet, but in addition have two long "proboscides," with suckers on them. They also have an internal bonelike support. These are our Decapoda.

Of the first group (*Octopoda*) there are, he says, numerous genera. (a) Those that have a shell (*Argonautidæ*). Of these he mentions two species; the Nautilus, doubtless Argonauta argo; and another not determinable. (β) Those that are without a shell (*Octopodidæ*). Of these he mentions the Poulps; the Eledone, and the Bolitæna. (Cf. Note 17.)

Of the second group (*Decapoda*) he mentions three kinds. The Sepias, the Teuthides, and the Teuthi. The Sepia has a broad and strong "os sepiæ," of a texture between bone and fish-spine, and spongy within. Its body is broad rather than long, though of good length in comparison with the feet. It has a narrow fin encircling the whole body. Its ink-bag is large and placed low down in the body cavity. This can only be the modern Sepia; probably Sepia officinalis, and perhaps some others, as A. speaks of "the genus of Sepias" (*H. A.* iv. 1, 2). The Teuthi and the Teuthides have a larger body than Sepia; a smaller ink-bag, placed higher up; and a cartilaginous internal support, shaped like a sword. The modern Teuthidæ, comprising the calamaries or. squids, are thus clearly indicated. It is doubtful, however, what species answer to Teuthi and Teuthides respectively. The Teuthi are said to be bigger than Teuthides; to have a blunter apex; and to be encircled by a continuous fin; whereas the fin only partially encircles the body in the Teuthides. The Teuthus is ordinarily supposed to be Loligo vulgaris, and Teuthis to be Loligo media : a view accepted by Owen (*Todd's Cycl.* i. 561). The description of the fins, however, hardly tallies with this opinion (*M. Edwards, Mollusca*, pl. vii. f. 1). Frantzius is confident that by Teuthis is meant Sepiola or Rossia. This would suit the account given of the fin. But on the other hand the apex of the body is remarkably obtuse in Sepiola or Rossia (*M. Edwards, Moll.* pl. viii. f. 3); whereas A. says that the apex of Teuthis is sharper pointed than that of Teuthus. We must, I think, be content to speak of Teuthi and Teuthides as large and small calamaries without affecting further precision.

2. Cf. iv. 5.

3. A similar idea concerning the cuttlefish, viz. that it was comparable to a vertebrate animal bent double, with the approximated arms and legs extending forwards, was advanced in a paper read before the Academy of Sciences in 1830. This paper was referred to Geoffroy St.-Hilaire and Latreille; was reported on most favourably, and its position in fact almost entirely adopted, by them. This was the starting-point in the famous controversy between G. St.-Hilaire and Cuvier as to unity of type; the controversy which excited Goethe more than the revolution of 1830 (see *Lewes' Goethe*, ii. 436).

4. Excluding, that is, the Echini, which he reckons among the Turbinata, notwithstanding that they have no spiral shell.

5. It thus appears that this treatise was illustrated, as also were those on Anatomy. Cf. iv. 5, Note 33; cf. ii. 8, 8.

6. The head and body in the Octopodidæ are connected by a broad cervical band. This, and the comparatively small size of the body, doubtless caused the entire mass to be looked on as a head by the vulgar.

7. In Gasteropoda the mouth and anus are near each other, but never in the same median plane.

8. The ordinary mode of progression of Octopodidæ is by crawling.

9. A. is not quite correct in his view of the part taken by the posterior limbs, at least in Mammalia. For though these take the chief part in the propulsion of the body, it is on the fore limbs that devolves the greater share in its support; and it is this difference in function that explains the different conformation of *manus* and *pes*. Cf. Owen, *Nature of Limbs*, p. 26, and *Archet. of the Skeleton*, p. 167.

10. There does not seem any very certain rule as to the comparative lengths of the different arms in Sepia and Loligo. The general rule, however, is that there is a gradual increase in length from the dorsal to the ventral pair; and the statement in the text that the ventral pair are the biggest, and the third pair the next in size, accords with this. Neither does there seem to be any certain rule in this matter in Octopodidæ. Cuvier (*Reg. An.* iii. 11) says that their arms are all much of the same length. Owen (*Lect. on Comp. Anat.* i. 344) says that in most of them the dorsal pair are the longest.

11. A. does not reckon the two retractile tentacles or "proboscides" as feet; so that he is correct in saying that all Cephalopoda are octopodous.

12. Cf. ii. 9, Note 9. "The development of the eight external arms bears an inverse proportion to that of the body; they are therefore longer in the short round-bodied Octopi, and shortest in the lengthened Calamaries and Cuttlefishes, in which

the two elongated retractile tentacles are superadded by way of compensation" (*Owen, Lect.* i. 344).

13. As A. speaks of the retractile tentacles of the Decapoda as "proboscides," so Owen (*Lect.* i. 319) calls the proboscis of the elephant a "brobdignagian tentacle," and states that the mechanical arrangement is very similar in the two cases.

14. The Sepias in the Crystal Palace Aquarium have never been seen by Mr. Lloyd (*Field*, Sept. 1, 1876) to anchor themselves in the way described by Aristotle and by most later naturalists. They use their "proboscides" to catch distant prey, darting them out with great rapidity and precision.

15. The "twining tentacles" are the long snake-like arms of the poulp; not the retractile tentacles of the Decapoda. Cf. iv. 5, Note 14.

16. These plaited instruments are mentioned by Hippocrates in his treatise on joints (*Kühn's ed.* iii. 266). They are called "Sauræ" by him; are said to be plaited from some portions of the palm-tree; and are recommended for use in dislocations of the fingers. It was this same "Saura" that made its appearance in London a few years back, and was sold as a toy under the name of the Siamese link.

17. The poulp with a single row of suckers is some species of Eledone; E. moschata according to Frantzius, E. cirrhosa according to Owen, who takes the Bolitæna to be the E. moschata on the ground that it is also called Ozolis by Aristotle (*H. A.* iv. 1, 27), which name seems to allude to its strong odour. The poulps with double rows of suckers include the Octopus vulgaris, which is excessively abundant in the Mediterranean. This is the species which A. speaks of (*H. A.* iv. 1, 26) as the largest and the most littoral. Besides it he speaks of other smaller spotted kinds, which are not edible, without giving enough data for their identification.

18. Cf. iv. 5, Note 5; *Introd.* p. x.

19. The Octopodidæ have in fact no body-fin at all.

(Ch. 10.) 1. The viviparous animals, with blood, are of course our Mammalia. The main characters noted by A. as belonging to them were these. They are sanguineous animals, that produce their young viviparously, and without a previous internal ovum; the sexes are always distinct, and the offspring is attached to the inside of the mother until its birth (*De Gen.* ii. 4, 2), and afterwards is suckled by her (*De Gen.* ii. 1, 28). The male parent has testes, which are sometimes internal, sometimes external (*De Gen.* i. 3, 4). They breathe air by a lung, the entrance to which is guarded by an epiglottis (iii. 3, 10). They have neither feathers nor scales, nor scaly plates, but hairs in their place (*H. A.* ii. 1, 17).

The groups recognised by A. appear to have been these:

1. Bipeds, *i.e.* man.
2. Animals intermediate to man and quadrupeds, *i.e.* apes (*H. A.* ii. 8, 1).
3. Quadrupeds; again divisible into sub-groups.
   - α. Fissipedous animals with teeth in front of both jaws, *i.e.* Carnivora, Rodentia, Insectivora, which are not distinguished by Aristotle; Dermoptera, or bats, which are sometimes spoken of by him as a distinct group, intermediate to these and birds; elephants (ii. 16, 7); and seals, which are "stunted quadrupeds" (ii. 12).
   - β. Cloven-hoofed animals, without upper front teeth, and with horns, *i.e.* Ruminantia, in general.
   - γ. Cloven-hoofed animals, without either upper front teeth or horns, *i.e.* camels.
   - δ. Cloven-hoofed animals, with upper front teeth, and tusks, *i.e.* swine and hippopotamus; which latter animal Aristotle, who doubtless had never seen

it, erroneously supposed, on the authority of Herodotus (cf. *Introd.* p. xvi, foot-note 1), to have only two hoofed toes to its foot.

ϵ. Solid-hoofed animals, *i.e.* Solidungula.

4. Apoda, *i.e.* Cetacea.

2. *i.e.* Fishes. Cf. iii. 2. Serpents, though they have a lung, have no neck. This exception, though not noted here, is dealt with in the next chapter.

3. Cf. ii. 7, 7.

4. Cf. ii. 10, Note 11. The brain requires (ii. 7, 9) a moderate degree of warmth, as do all living parts; but this must not be more than moderate, for "the motion of the heat of blood destroys sensory activity."

5. The argument is this. "The stomach cannot be placed above the heart, for such a position would be inconsistent with the dignity of the chief organ (cf. ii. 2, Note 6); it must therefore be placed below it. But if the mouth were also placed below the heart, the stomach, owing to the length of the œsophagus, would be removed so far from the heart, that digestion, which is due to heat derived from the heart, would not be possible." A. forgets that elsewhere (iii. 3, 2) he has said that the œsophagus is only necessary, because there is a neck, and that, but for this, the stomach might come immediately after the mouth.

6. Cf. *Intr.* pp. xiv, xv. It is plain that A. was not himself acquainted with the lion; for nearly all his statements about its structure are erroneous. Here he says that it has but one cervical vertebra; a little later on he says it has but two dugs; elsewhere that its bones are without medullary cavity, etc. Moreover in one place (*H. A.* ii. 1, 33) he uses the expression "the lion, *as he is represented*." Yet there were lions in his day in Macedonia and North Greece, as we learn from Xenophon (*De Venat.* ch. xi.), and also from Herodotus (vii. 124-6). They were, however, rare (*H. A.* vi. 31, 2), and confined to a small locality, so that the capture of one formed a notable event, as would appear from the following passage: "The lame lion that was caught had many of its teeth broken, from which some persons inferred that a lion lives for many years" (*H. A.* ix. 44, 6); where it would seem that the writer is referring to some occurrence so remarkable, that every one would understand his allusion. It will be observed, however, that the author does not speak as though he had himself seen the captured lion. Probably A. got such facts as he gives about lions from hunters by hearsay. Such clearly was the source of the account in the *Hist. An.* (ix. 44). As to the question of the existence of lions in Greece in old times, see papers by Sir G. C. Lewis in *Notes and Queries*, vol. viii.

7. Such uses, for instance, as turning round quickly to guard the hinder part against a foe (iv. 11, 18); picking up food from the bottom of the water, as do web-footed and other water birds (iv. 12, 8); or catching prey at a distance, the long neck serving as a fishing rod (iv. 12, 11).

8. There are some perceptions, says A., that are peculiar to one sense, *e.g.* colour to vision, hardness and temperature to touch, etc. But there are others not peculiar to one sense, but appreciable by several, or at any rate by vision and by touch. Such are motion, rest, number, figure, magnitude. These, then, are common sensibles, and that which perceives them is the one common or general sense, of which the five senses are special forms. Cf. *D. A.* iii. 1 and 2; *De Som.* 2; *De Sens.* 4, 20.

9. Cf. iv. 9, Note 9.

10. Cf. *H. A.* ii. 1, 47-49. This statement as to the alteration that occurs in the human body in the relative proportions of the upper and lower parts is correct. "After birth, the proportions of the body alter in consequence of the legs growing faster than the

rest of the body. In consequence the middle point of the height of the body—which at birth is situated about the umbilicus—becomes gradually lower until, in the adult male, it is as low as the symphysis pubis" (*Huxley's Verteb.* p. 488). On the other hand, every one is familiar with the preponderate length of a colt's legs as compared with that of its body. Lastly, if one compares a kitten with a cat, one finds no such contrast of proportions.

11. Two of the mundane elements, earth and water, tend to fall downwards, the remaining two, air and fire, to mount upwards. Cf. ii. 1, Note 1. Taking the passage in the text by itself, it might be inferred that A. supposed the soul or vital principle to be identical with heat, as did Democritus. But it was not so. Heat is elsewhere (ii. 7, 6) said to be necessary for the operations of the soul, as its chief instrument, but not to be the soul itself. So also fire (*D. A.* ii. 4, 12) is said not to be the true cause of growth or nutrition, but only an assistant cause. Cf. i. 1, Note 13, and ii. 6, Note 7.

12. A. here takes man as the starting-point, and descends from him to inferior creatures by a succession of small degradations. Elsewhere, however (iv. 5, and *H. A.* viii. 1), he follows the other course, and starting from the simplest organisms mounts upwards, until a succession of superadded improvements brings him to man. In the absence of any notion of the evolution of the more complex from the simpler species, one mode of viewing the series was as good as the other. Lamarck, however, is not quite accurate in stating (*Phil. Zool.* i. 8) that his predecessors, including Aristotle, had invariably in their serial classifications inverted what he insisted was the natural order.

13. Answers, that is to say, to the excretions of animals. Cf. ii. 3, Note 8; iv. 5, Note 60.

14. Cf. ii. 16, Note 13. That the function is superadded to the organ is A.'s usual statement. Somewhat inconsistently, however, he says in one place (*D. A.* ii. 9, 3), "Man has a far more accurate sense of touch than other animals. *For which reason* he is also far more intelligent than they." Lastly, in another passage (*D. G.* iv. 1, 32) he adopts the more tenable position that organ and function are given together.

15. The seeming impotence of man as compared with other animals has always been a favourite topic. See for instance *Shaftesbury, Moralists,* 2, 4. The following passage quoted by Sir C. Bell (*Bridgewater Treat.* p. 106) from Ray, is clearly an imitation of Aristotle: "Some animals have horns, some hoofs, some teeth, some talons, some claws, some spurs and beaks. Man hath none of these, but is weak and feeble and sent unarmed into the world. Why, a hand with reason to use it supplies the use of all these."

16. I have introduced the short clause in brackets to give logical sequence. Plato represents the nails as useless to man, but as given to him by the Creator, because he foresaw that human beings would be degraded into beasts, to whom nails would be of use. Galen (*De Usu part.* i. 8) rejects both Plato's and Aristotle's explanations; and, in answer to A.'s view, objects, that the nails in men are clearly incapable of affording any protection either against changes of temperature or against injuries. His own opinion was that the nails were designed to support the yielding tips of the fingers and to render them more serviceable in the prehension of small objects, which would otherwise slip from them. The modern view is either somewhat similar to this, namely, that they serve by their solidity to give a certain degree of firmness to the tips of the fingers, and so enable them to perceive slight degrees of pressure more perfectly, so far agreeing in function with the phalangeal bones and the tactile corpuscles (*Kölliker, Hum. Micr. Anat.* p. 85); or is something like the view of Plato, inverted, namely that man has them in a rudimentary condition, because he has inherited them from predecessors in byegone ages, to whom they were of use.

17. Cf. iv. 12, Note 10.

18. "L'homme porte les aliments à la bouche au moyen du membre supérieur. Les diverses pièces dont se compose ce membre sont disposées de telle sorte, que leur mouvement de flexion dirige naturellement la main vers la bouche" (*Béclard, Phys.* p. 42).

19. Horses, when fighting together, use their fore-legs for striking, much more than they do their hind-legs for kicking backwards. Cf. *Darwin, Exp. of Emot.* p. 112. The main statement in the text is, however, correct. The anterior limbs in Ungulata are quite useless for prehension, and only subserve locomotion. Hence the absence of clavicles. Whereas in Unguiculate animals, speaking generally, the anterior limbs serve more or less as prehensile organs, and are furnished as a rule with more or less perfect clavicles.

20. Analogous is here used in the modern sense, *i.e.* having similar functions, and not as equivalent to homologous. For A. has already said that the fore-limbs of quadrupeds correspond anatomically to the arms of man.

21. In Canidæ and Felidæ, from which A.'s examples are taken, there are only four toes to the hind-foot, while the fore-feet have each five, as in most Unguiculata. The smaller quadrupeds, that are described as having five hind-toes and as creeping or even running over-head, are such animals as rats, squirrels, moles, martens, weasels. It is, however, not only small quadrupeds and creepers that have five hind-toes; for the same is the case with elephants and bears.

22. Cf. ii. 16, Note 5. "Is not this one of the most admirable things in the works of nature, that she should take some part that has been developed in an animal for some special function, and utilise it for some additional office?" (*Galen, De U. part.* vii. 22). Cf. iii. 1, Note 12.

23. The upper or true ribs which are united to the sternum, in opposition to the false ribs below. Thus there is firmness given to the mammæ by the firm substratum.

24. As the arms are not used for locomotion, the mammæ are not in the way, and so there is no disadvantage in there being two of them; otherwise they would be made to form a single mass.

25. Elsewhere (*H. A.* ii. 8, 4), apes, as well as man, are excepted. Pectoral mammæ are by no means confined, however, to man and apes. In bats, for instance, the two mammæ are pectoral; so also in elephants, as indeed is presently mentioned.

26. The horned animals which produce few at a birth and have only two mammæ are sheep and goats. For in other horned animals, *e.g.* the cow, there are four, as A. elsewhere (*H. A.* ii. 1, 40) mentions. Even in sheep and goats there are really four; but two of these are usually rudimentary. The Solidungula have, as correctly stated, only two mammæ and these inguinal.

There is, as stated in the text, a very close correspondence between the number of mammæ and the number of young produced at a time. The larger uniparous mammals have but two mammæ, *e.g.* elephant, rhinoceros, hippopotamus, horse, etc. The Ruminantia often produce two, and some of the larger Carnivora two or more, at a birth; and these have as a rule four mammæ. Most smaller Carnivora, Insectivora, Rodentia are multiparous, and also have numerous mammæ. Thus the cat has three to six young at a time and eight mammæ. The dog has litters of four to nine, and seven to ten mammæ. The hedgehog has six to seven young and ten mammæ. Rabbits, hares, marmots, black rats, all multiparous, have each ten or more mammæ. So far then A.'s statement is correct. But he seems to fancy that there is also some relation between the number of mammæ and the number of toes. Of course no such direct relation exists. Still it is true that the one-toed Solipedes have but two mammæ; the cloven-hoofed

Ruminants four; and a very large proportion of the polydactylous quadrupeds, as already mentioned, numerous mammæ.

27. The number and position of the mammæ are given correctly by A. in the other instances; but as usual (cf. Note 6) he is in error as regards the lion; for though its mammæ are, as stated, abdominal, they are four, not two, in number. The lion produces not unfrequently four, and occasionally even five or six, at a birth (cf. *D. G.* iii. 10, 24).

28. Cf. iv. 5, Note 2.

29. *i.e.* in the direction from tail to head. This upward growth implies, he says, the accumulation of nutriment in the part from which the growth proceeds, for otherwise there would be no material for the growth; and it is in this land of plenty that the mammæ are placed. In the human body the growth takes place in the contrary direction (cf. Note 10); and the seat of plenty and location of the mammæ is accordingly at the opposite or pectoral end.

30. Linnæus counted the horse among those exceptional quadrupeds in which the male has no teats; but John Hunter discovered vestiges of them in the stallion. Possibly what A. says may be true, and thus the discrepancy between these two modern authorities explained.

31. Cf. ii. 9, Note 3.

32. Frantzius supposes that the exceptions meant are those groups of fishes, such as the Teleostei, in which alone among vertebrates the external urinary and generative apertures are perfectly distinct. I also suppose these to be the exceptions. I would, however, point out, that it cannot be to the distinctness of these two apertures that A. refers. For he expressly and repeatedly denies the existence of urinary organs, and of course of urinary apertures, in fishes, and indeed in all ovipara excepting tortoises (iii. 8, Note 3; iii. 9, Note 1; and iv. 13, Note 36). The whole passage is written carelessly, and must be corrected by the light of other passages, such as the following: "The generative fluid is discharged by the same opening as the residual matter; when an animal has residua of both kinds, fluid as well as solid, by the opening which gives issue to the fluid kind; for the semen is itself a fluid residuum; but when there is no fluid residue, by the opening which gives issue to the solid residue" (*D. G.* i. 18, 62). See also the passage in iv. 13, Note 37. The exceptional condition, then, in these fishes, to which I understand A. to refer, is the distinctness of the generative and anal apertures. And I would take the passage to be as follows: "In all animals, with the exception of the bony fishes, the generative fluid is discharged by the same aperture as the fluid or the solid excrement; in the vivipara by the aperture for fluid excrement; in the ovipara, where there is no fluid excrement, by the anus."

33. Hippocrates (*Kühn's ed.* i. 551) had said, in partial anticipation of Darwin's doctrine of pangenesis, that the semen was formed by contributions from all parts of the parent's body; and he explained on this hypothesis the resemblance of the offspring to the parent, which extended occasionally even to accidental or acquired peculiarities of structure. This opinion is combated by A. (*D. G.* i. 17-18), who insists, among other arguments, that it would imply that the semen was a product of dissolution or decay (σύντηξις), which is clearly inadmissible. He argues that the semen can be nothing else in substance than the surplus or residue of sound nutriment, which, after conversion into blood, has not been required for growth. This, he says, explains why no semen is formed either when the growth is active, as in childhood, or when the power of concocting nutriment is small, as in old age or sickness; and also why those animals, whose surplus nutriment is turned into fat, are not prolific (ii. 5, Note 9).

The semen, then, instead of being, as Hippocrates would have it, something which comes from each and every part of the parent, is something which might have gone to each and every part of the parent.

To the semen of the male corresponds the menstrual discharge of the female; but, in accordance with the colder nature of females, their generative secretion is less concocted (*D. G.* iv. 5, 8), and therefore retains a greater resemblance to blood.

34. Elsewhere (*H. A.* ii. 1, 46) sundry Carnivora are correctly stated to have a bone in the penis; the camel and stag to have no such bone, but a sinewy organ, also correctly; and man to have cartilage in the part, which chances to be true of some negroes. In no other case however does the penis contain cartilage. As to the presence of sinew conferring the power of contraction, cf. iii. 4, Note 20.

35. A. erroneously held erection to be due to air, and not to blood (*Probl.* xxx. 1, 13). To air also was due the force of emission, "for nothing can be thrown to a distance without pneumatic force" (*H. A.* vii. 7, 1).

36. The camel, the cats, and many rodents including the hare, are retromingent.

37. Alluding probably, as Frantzius suggests, to the ossified tendons that occur in old specimens of gallinaceous birds.

38. True of all quadrupeds, this is especially true of elephants. "The structure of his legs affords such support in a standing position, that reclining scarcely adds to his enjoyment of repose; and elephants in a state of captivity have been known for months together to sleep without lying down. . . . Captain Dawson shot an elephant on the banks of the Kalany Ganga. It remained on its feet, but so motionless, that after discharging a few more balls he was induced to go close to it, and found it dead" (*Tennent, Ceylon,* p. 106). Hence in all probability the erroneous belief that the elephant could not lie down, but rested by leaning against a tree (ii. 16, Note 7).

39. Cf. ii. 9, Note 8.

40. The parts below mean here the hind-legs.

41. A good description of the general characters of monkeys is given in the *Hist. An.* (ii. 8). Three kinds are there distinguished: (1) the Pithecus, which has no tail, or only a rudimentary one; (2) the Cebus, which only differs from the Pithecus in having a tail; (3) the Cynocephalus, which is a larger, stronger, and more ferocious, species, with bigger teeth and a face like that of a dog. These data are insufficient for exact identification. Aubert and Wimmer however conjecture that the three species meant are Simia sylvanus; some or other Cercopithecus; and Cynocephalus Hamadryas; all inhabitants of North Africa.

42. Cf. ii. 16, Note 5.

43. For instance as an organ of prehension, as in monkeys; a fly-flapper, as in cattle; an aid in turning, as in dogs; "though the aid must be slight, for the hare, with hardly any tail, can double quickly enough" (*Darwin, Or. of Sp.* p. 196).

44. The bone by which the leg articulates with the ancle is known as the astragalus. This varies much in shape in different animals. In the ruminants it is symmetrical and biconvex, whereas in other animals it is of irregular form and convex only at the upper end. It was only when it had the symmetrical biconvex shape that it was suitable for use as a die; and then only that A., who knew nothing of its homologies, recognised it as an astragalus, just as it is only then that boys recognise it as a hucklebone.

In the British Museum are several ancient Greek dice, or astragali. They are all astragali of ruminants, either the bone itself or copies of the bone in various stones. So in the marble group called "Astragalizontes" it is with the astragali of some ruminant that the boy is playing. Amongst the Greek vases again is one representing the astragalus of a ruminant. The astragali of sheep furnish the hucklebones with which children play at the present day. "There is a game also," says an old writer, "that is played with the pasterne bone in the hynder foote of a sheepe, oxe, gote, fallowe or redde dere, which in Latin is called Talus" (*Brand, Pop. Ant.* ii. 288). A. describes the astragalus as a short biconvex bone adapted to the concavities of the bones above and below, found only in the hind-leg; and this only of animals with cloven hoofs, with the exception of the Indian ass, the hippopotamus, the lynx, and, according to some, the lion. The bone, he says, stands upright in the joint, and has certain projections above. Of the four faces marked in dice with figures, the face which takes the highest figure is turned inwards, so as to front the corresponding face in the other astragalus, while that marked ace is turned outwards. Cf. *H. A.* ii. 1, 34.

45. I suppose he means that, if there were an astragalus, there would be much earthy matter; and, if much earthy matter, then the hoof would be a solid mass; excepting in that part of its breadth, where the earthy matter was used up in making the astragalus.

46. "L'homme a les pieds plus larges, et il peut les écarter l'un de l'autre plus que les autres animaux . . . . La grandeur de la surface du pied de l'homme tient à ce qu'il appuye le tarse, le métatarse et tous les doigts à terre, ce qu'aucun animal ne fait aussi parfaitement" (*Cuvier, Leçons,* i. 474).

47. Cf. iii. 9, 4, where the same is said as to kidneys.

(Ch. 11.) 1. That is all the Mammalia known to him, with the exception of Cetacea.

2. *De Anim. Incessu,* 8, 1. See also iv. 13, 10, where the explanation is repeated.

3. Reptiles and Amphibia are comprised by A. in one group. The main characters ascribed by him to them are these. They are sanguineous animals, and, with the exception of the apodous serpents, four-footed and polydactylous (*H. A.* ii. 10, 2); they are also oviparous, with the exception of the viper, which is ovoviviparous (*H. A.* iii. 1, 28). In virtue of these characters they are called "oviparous quadrupeds."

The sexes are always separate. The ovum is perfect, *i.e.* does not increase in size after deposition (*D. G.* ii. 1, 18; iii. 5, 6; *Introd.* p. xxvii), and has distinct yelk and white (*D. G.* iii. 2, 12). The embryo has two foetal appendages (iv. 12, Note 15), viz. umbilical vesicle and allantois. The testes, when present, are internal, but are absent in the apodous kinds (*H. A.* v. 5, 7; *D. G.* i. 3, 2). The generative outlet is one with the anus (*H. A.* v. 5, 8). The females are usually larger than the males (*D. G.* i. 16, 3). Refrigeration is effected by a lung, of bladder-like character (iii. 5, 6), the entrance to which is not guarded by an epiglottis (iii. 3, 10). In all these characters they resemble birds.

The body is neither feathered nor hairy, but covered with scales, which are harder than those of fishes (iv. 11, 7). A tongue is always present (see Note 5) and often is bifid. The teeth are always of the serrate form (iv. 11, 6). The stomach is single (iv. 1, 4).

Such exceptions as the absence of scales from frogs and other Amphibia, or of teeth from Chelonia, etc., though not mentioned by A., can hardly have been unknown to him. The only distinct subdivision of the group recognised by him appears to be into Tetrapoda and Apoda.

4. Cf. iv. 10, 3-5.

5. There are, as a matter of fact, some oviparous quadrupeds without a tongue; but these are species which were unknown to Aristotle, such as the Carinthian Proteus, the Surinam Pipa, and the Dactylethra of South Africa. The crocodile really has a tongue; but it is flat, destitute of papillæ, and united by its whole extent to the floor of the mouth. This seems to be recognized in other passages (*H. A.* ii. 10, 2; *D. P.* ii. 17, 7). Cf. ii. 17, Note 9.

6. Cf. ii. 17, 7. So also in speaking of fishes elsewhere (*H. A.* ii. 13, 11) A. says, "They have a hard and spinous tongue, which is so attached to the other parts, that sometimes its presence would not be suspected."

7. That the sense of taste must be very dull in fishes is admitted by all naturalists (cf. *Yarrell, Brit. Fishes,* i. xvii); for, as A. justly observes, they do not chew their food, and thus the juices, which alone can excite true taste, are not expressed. Moreover the inside of the mouth is being constantly washed over with water, which must of itself interfere with the possibility of any delicate gustation. Still they are probably not entirely without this sense, as is elsewhere (*H. A.* iv. 8, 8) admitted; for, as there pointed out, they manifest certain preferences for one food rather than another.

8. "On which account a certain gourmandiser wished that his throat were longer than a crane's, implying that his pleasure was derived from the sense of touch" (*Ethics,* iii. 13, 10). The same notion led Spenser, in describing Gluttony, to say, "And like a crane, his neck was long and fyne" (*Faëry Queen,* i. 4, 21).

A. did not fail to observe a fact which some later writers have passed over, viz. that many sensations called Tastes are in reality compound sensations. True tastes have for their almost exclusive organ the tongue, and are only produced by fluids. So far A. is accurate. But into most so-called Tastes enters a tactile element. By touch, which is not limited to the mouth and tongue, but extends to the gullet, we recognise the temperature, the hardness, the oiliness, etc., of substances. So far also A. is fairly correct; though the distension of the œsophagus, of which he speaks, would be rather a muscular than a tactile sensation (compare iii. 14, Note 34). But in most so-called Tastes there is still a larger part due to smell, as any one will find if he roll a high-flavoured wine in his mouth while his nose is held closed. This part of the compound taste A., like many modern writers, does not distinguish from true simple taste, which is limited to the perception of acid, sweet, salt, bitter. Still the interlacing of Smell with Taste, in the popular acceptation of the term, could not, and as a matter of fact did not, escape his notice. The same savoury substances, he says (*De Sensu,* 5, 10), which, when dissolved in fluid and applied to the tongue, cause taste, will, when they act upon the nose through a nameless something (ii. 1, Note 12) that is common to air and water, cause smell. Moreover, he recognises the fact (*De Sensu,* 5, 14) that a smell and a taste, when often experienced simultaneously, become so blended by habitual association that the dual sensation becomes a single one. For a discussion of the relations of Taste with Smell, see a paper contributed by me to the *Royal Med. Chir. Transact.* 1870.

9. That drunkards are small eaters is a well-known fact. The explanation is however more probably injured digestion than deficient sensibility to flavour. The statement is taken from Hippocrates (*Kühn's ed.* i. 528).

10. Cf. *H. A.* ii. 17, 21. The tongue in Ophidia is bifid, as also it is in one great division of Sauria (hence called Fissilinguia or Leptiglossa), but not in all; not, for instance, in the chamæleon nor in the wall gecko, or scarcely so, among species known to Aristotle. In the seal the tongue is deeply notched. See *Buffon, Nat. Hist.* xiii. pl. 50.

11. Cf. ii. 17, Note 7.

12. Cf. iii. 1, Note 7. The teeth of Saurian reptiles are usually acutely conical and slightly hooked. In some cases they are blade-like, and occasionally dentated on the edges. Rarely, as in Cyclodus, they have broad crushing crowns. In Chelonia there are no teeth at all.

13. Cf. ii. 12, Note 2; and ii. 13, Note 5.

14. All reptiles have horny epidermal scales, but not so such Amphibia as the frog and

toad, which A. included in the same group. In the Chelonia and the crocodiles these scales are combined with bony scutes, and these animals are therefore known as Loricata. But nothing of the kind occurs in the large serpents, none of which were actually known to Aristotle (ii. 9, Note 7), but of which he had probably heard fabulous accounts from some of Alexander's companions; from Nearchus, for instance, whose statement as to the existence of monstrous serpents in the East is quoted by Arrian in his *Indica*.

15. Most reptiles have an upper eyelid, though they use the lower lid exclusively or preferentially (cf. ii. 13, Note 2). In Ophidia, however, and some Lacertilia, there are no lids at all, or rather the two lids are transparent and continuous with each other in front of the eye; a condition of things which A. supposed (ii. 13, 10) to exist in Crustacea.

16. Cf. ii. 13, Note 5.

17. This is an error (cf. ii. 13, Note 2).

18. And therefore, he implies, do not require so much protection.

19. The Carnivora are an exception, their teeth being adapted for cutting and not for grinding. This exception, though not mentioned here, is recognised presently, when it is said that lateral motion goes with grinding teeth only, and therefore not with the serrated dentition of Carnivora.

20. This was the common belief of the ancients (cf. *Herodotus*, ii. 68). Cuvier thus accounts for the error: "Les mâchoires inférieures se prolongeant derrière le crâne, il semble que la supérieure soit mobile, et les anciens l'ont écrit ainsi; mais il ne se meut qu'avec la tête toute entière" (*Reg. An.* ii. 18).

21. I suppose A. means that when an animal takes its prey in the water it must generally do so with its mouth, because the anterior limbs are occupied in the act of swimming.

22. Cf. iii. 3, Note 3.

23. The vertebræ of Ophidia are not cartilaginous but osseous. The great flexibility of the spine is due to its division into excessively numerous segments, and to the existence of a perfect ball and socket joint between each of these and that which precedes and follows it.

24. "Internally viviparous" is equivalent to Mammalia, whose ovum was unknown to Aristotle; it excludes ovoviparous animals, which A. called "externally viviparous but internally oviparous." Cf. iv. 1, Note 5.

25. Cf. *D. G.* iii. 2, 9.

26. Cf. iv. 10, Note 43.

27. There is an admirable account of the chamæleon in the *Hist. An.* (ii. 11), and in it occurs a passage of great interest, as showing that A. made vivisections. The chamæleon, though found in Spain, is not found in Greece. It is, however, easy of transport alive; and may have come into A.'s hands either from Africa or Asia Minor. It is, I believe, the only *foreign* animal, concerning which there is satisfactory evidence that it was seen alive by Aristotle (cf. *Introd.* p. xiii).

28. Alluding of course to the well-known changes of colour which occur in this animal (cf. *Owen, Verteb.* i. 556), and which are apparently determined not only by variations in the temperature, the amount of light, and the tints of surrounding objects, but also by emotions, as fear, anger, and the like.

29. Cf. ii. 4, Note 4.

(Ch. 12.) 1. The main characters noted by A. as belonging to birds are as follows. They are sanguineous ovipara, resembling reptiles (iv. 11, Note 3) in having the sexes separate; in having a perfect ovum, and an embryo with two umbilical appendages; a lung so deeply divided as to appear double, of bladderlike character, poor in blood, and without epiglottis; a common orifice for excrement and for generative products; and lastly in closing the eye, with some few exceptions, with the lower lid (ii. 13, 1), the lids being without lashes excepting in the ostrich (ii. 14, 1).

On the other hand, they differ from reptiles and from all other sanguineous animals in having feathers in place of hairs or scales, a beak in place of lips and teeth, and wings in place of arms or fore-legs. The "ischium" is extremely long (Note 27); the legs turn their convexity backwards (Note 10; *De Inc.* 15; *H. A.* ii. 1, 13); the toes, excepting in the ostrich (iv. 14, Note 4), are four in number (Note 30). The bones are brittle (ii. 9, Note 6), and the breast-bone sharp-edged and thickly covered with flesh, especially in birds of rapid flight (*De Inc.* 10, 9). The testes are internal. There is no bladder, though there are flat kidney-like organs (iii. 9, Notes 1 and 2). There is invariably a tongue (*H. A.* ii. 12, 9); there are no teeth, their office being discharged by variable arrangements of the stomach and intestines (iii. 14, 9–10); there is always a gall-bladder (*H. A.* ii. 15, 12); and usually there are one or two cæcal appendages to the gut low down (*H. A.* ii. 17, 34). The ears and nostrils are represented by simple orifices. The eyes are provided with a nictitating membrane (ii. 13, Note 2).

A. makes no exhaustive division of birds. The following groups are, however, distinctly recognised by him.

(*a*) Birds of prey, with talons and hooked beak, fleshy breast and stout thighs (*H. A.* ii. 12, 3), small bodies, powerful wings, abundant feathers, keen sight (*De Inc.* 10, 8–10). These are clearly our Raptores; with which, however, A. also classes the parrot (ii. 17, Note 3).

(*b*) Heavy-bodied birds, ill-suited for flight, of terrestrial habits, fond of dusting themselves, often with spurs (cf. ii. 13, Note 1). These answer generally to our Gallinaceæ.

(*c*) Dovelike birds, laying two white eggs, etc.; clearly Columbidæ.

(*d*) Swimming birds, wholly or partially webfooted (Note 8), with long neck, short legs and tail; our Natatores.

(*e*) Marsh birds, with long legs and neck, the front toes elongated, the hind toe short; our Grallatores.

(*f*) The ostrich, which stands alone (iv. 14), represents our Ratitæ or Cursores.

These are the only groups distinctly recognised by Aristotle; for such terms as "insect-eaters," "grub-eaters," "thistle-eaters," etc., are hardly meant to represent definite subdivisions.

2. The class Aves is remarkably homogeneous. "The structural modifications which they present are of comparatively little importance" (*Huxley*).

3. Cf. iv. 6, Note 6.

4. Cf. ii. 16, Note 5.

5. Cf. iv. 5, Note 8.

6. Not actually bony, but resembling bone in being hard. Cf. ii. 9. 16.

7. Cf. iii. 3, Note 3, and iv. 10, Note 7.

8. The birds alluded to are the Grebes, the Phalaropes, the Coots, in which the toes are bordered with broad membranous lobes, which led Temminck to arrange them in one order to which he gave the name of Pinnatipedes. A. describes this arrangement in more distinct language farther on in the chapter. The word which he uses here to describe the toes, and which I have rendered "flattened and expanded into lobes," is literally "snubnosed." Liddell and Scott, referring to this passage, interpret the term as "with turned-up feet, like some waders." But clearly it is not the turned-up character of a snubnose, but its flat and broad aspect which forms the ground of the

comparison; the main stem of the toe answering to the ridge of the nose, the lobes on either side to the flattened nostrils.

9. The scapula in birds is a simple elongated bone, not flattened out into a plate or blade, and so was not recognised by A. as a "blade-bone," just as he did not recognise the astragalus unless it had the form suiting it for use as a "hucklebone." Cf. iv. 10, Note 44.

10. A. uses two sets of terms to describe the bendings of the limbs (1) Forwards and backwards, (2) Inwards and outwards. A limb is said to be bent forwards or backwards, when its convexity is turned forwards or backwards; *e.g.* the leg of a man is bent forwards; so is the fore-leg of a horse. But the hind-leg of a horse is bent backwards; the arm of a man is bent backwards with a slight inclination to the side. A limb is bent inwards, when its concavity is turned in the direction in which the main bulk of the body lies; outwards when the concavity is turned away from this. Thus both the fore and the hind legs of a horse are bent inwards. So also the leg of a bird is bent inwards; but the leg of a man is bent outwards.

It must be remembered that A. knows nothing of the homologies of the various joints. He simply takes the limbs as wholes, and compares the general direction of their main curvature in different animals.

11. A. rightly says that no sanguineous animal has more than four organs of locomotion, that is, more than four limbs. There are passages from which it might be inferred that he imagined, less correctly, that they never have less than four (cf. iv. 13. Note 6). But in the *De Incessu* (10, 1) he expressly repudiates such a statement.

12. That is not, as whales and fishes, in the water; nor, as birds, in the air.

13. A. had clearly neither dissected, nor seen the skeleton of, an ostrich. In all other birds known to him the sternum is provided with a keel, which he compares (*De Incessu*, 10, 9) to the sharp prow of a felucca, reminding one of the term "Carinatæ" now given to birds with a keeled sternum.

14. The mass of muscles that move the wings is of course meant. It must be remembered that A. knew nothing of muscular contraction (cf. iii. 4, Note 20).

15. It might be supposed from this passage that A. imagined a bird to be developed without an allantois and merely with an umbilical vesicle. But from other passages (*D. G.* iii. 3, 4; *D. G.* iii. 2, 22—28; *H. A.* vi. 3, 8) it is plain that this was not the case. He describes the fœtal bird and reptile as differing from fishes in having two umbilical appendages, one going to the membrane surrounding the yelk, and serving to introduce the nutriment thence derived, the other (*allantois*) to the membranous expansion which lines the inner surface of the shell. This latter appendage, he says, collapses as the embryonic bird enlarges; while the former with the yelk is drawn back into the abdominal cavity, the walls of which unite together behind it. He had not observed the umbilical vesicle of mammals, which is comparatively small, and shrivels up at an early period of fœtal life, and erroneously supposed their allantois to correspond to the umbilical vesicle of birds and reptiles. This error was not corrected till 1667, when Needham discovered the umbilical vesicle of mammals, and recognized its correspondence to that of birds. Neither had A. observed that Amphibia in this matter resemble fishes and not reptiles, with which latter he grouped them.

16. Cf. ii. 9, Note 9.

17. Birds of prey are awkward movers on the ground or other flat surface, because of their talons, and help themselves along by flapping their wings. But the statement made here and elsewhere (*H. A.* ix. 32, 12) that they very seldom or never settle on rocks is erroneous; they often do so, and indeed rocks are the usual resting-place of many.

A writer in the *Penny Cycl.* (x. 163) makes the following remarks, how far accurately I cannot say, concerning the Falconidæ. "The nails or claws to be available must be sharp; and in order that they may be kept in this state and fit for duty, there is a provision to enable the bird to prevent them from coming in contact with the ground or other foreign hard bodies. For the claws are retractile, not indeed in the same manner as those of the cats, which have the power of withdrawing or sheathing theirs within the integuments, but by a conformation which gives the bird of prey the power of elevating its claws at pleasure. The claws of falcons, when sitting on stones or large branches of trees, have often a cramped appearance. But this arises in most instances from the care of the bird so to arrange its talons that their points may not be blunted against the perch."

18. Because the earthy matter has not been used in any other manner, and must be disposed of in some way or other.

19. Cf. Note 8.

20. Cf. iv. 13, Note 12.

21. Cf. iv. 10, Note 14.

22. This is erroneous. The number of phalanges is the same in the several toes of Waders as in other birds, though the toes are as a rule longer.

23. Cf. *Introd.* p. x.

24. "These water birds fly with their legs stretched out behind, using them in place of a tail to steer their course." In the heron, for instance, the tail is short, and the long legs, stretched out in flight, "seem, like the longer tails of some birds, to serve as a rudder" (*Bewick's Birds*, p. 11).

25. Any one who has watched a hawk swoop down on a pigeon will recognise the truth of this description of the position in which it holds its legs.

26. The heron in flight rests its very slender neck and head on the back, so that the bill appears to issue from the chest; while the stork, the ibis, the goose, etc., fly with the comparatively stout neck outstretched.

27. The term "ischia" is used by A. sometimes for the fleshy part of the buttocks, sometimes for the bones which we know as "ossa innominata." It is owing to this double meaning that in some places he speaks of birds as having no ischia, *i.e.* no buttocks; while in others, as here, he says that they have peculiarly long ischia, *i.e.* pelvic bones. The pelvis of a bird is remarkable for its great elongation, both anteriorly and posteriorly. It is thus described elsewhere (*H. A.* ii. 12, 2): "Birds, moreover, have an ischium which is long and resembles a thigh-bone, and is united (*with the vertebral column*) as far as the middle of the belly, so that when it is separated from its connections it looks like a thigh-bone." See also *De Incessu*, xi. 5.

28. Cf. iv. 10, 10—15.

29. Cf. iv. 10, 53.

30. This is a general but not universal rule. In some birds, as the great bustard, the Otis of Aristotle, the toes are reduced to three by suppression of the hallux, as in the ostrich they are reduced to two by suppression of both hallux and second digit.

31. The hind toe varies very much in its development in Waders. Usually it is short, as A. correctly says, but sometimes it is as long as, or even longer than, the others.

32. The Crex was doubtless some bird that derived its name, as does our corn-crake, from its note. But it is uncertain what exact species was thus designated. It was a pugnacious bird (*H. A.* ix. 17, 1), much of the same size as the Ibis (*Herod.* ii. 76); with a sharp and notched beak (*Schol. to Aristoph. Aves*, 1060); and, as this passage shows, it had a stunted hind toe.

33. Although A. speaks here of the wryneck (*Yunx torquilla*) as the only bird that turns two toes backwards, elsewhere (*H. A.* ii. 12, 4) he says there are several in which this is the case. Probably he there refers to cuckoos or woodpeckers or owls, which latter, as also the osprey, can turn the outer toe backwards at will; for he had apparently never himself seen a parrot. (Cf. ii. 17, Note 3.)

34. *D. G.* i. 12.

(**Ch. 13.**) 1. The main characters assigned by A. to Fishes were as follows. They are sanguineous ovipara, with sexes almost, though not quite, invariably distinct (*D. G.* ii. 5, 7); producing either a perfect ovum (*selachia*), which is hatched internally, the embryo in such case becoming exceptionally (*mustelus*) attached to its mother's uterus (*D. G.* iii. 3, 10), or an imperfect ovum, one that is that grows after deposition (*D. G.* iii. 5, 6; Introd. p. xxvii). In either case the ovum differs from that of Birds and Reptiles in presenting no distinction of white and yelk (*D. G.* iii. 3, 8-11), and in giving rise to an embryo with only one umbilical appendage (*D. G.* iii. 3, 4; *H. A.* vi. 10, 3). The skeleton is formed not of true bone, but of a spinous substance or of cartilage, and small spinous bones are to be found isolated in the flesh (*H. A.* iii. 7, 11). There are usually, though not always, scales externally, never hairs nor feathers. The place of limbs is supplied by fins, of which the ventral pair are often missing, and occasionally both pairs (Notes 10, 11). There are gills in place of lung; no bladder nor kidneys. The seminal organs are hollow tubes, and there are no solid ovoid bodies like the testes of Viviparous Quadrupeds and Birds (cf. Note 34). The generative outlet is one with the fæcal (cf. Note 36), with apparently some exceptions (cf. iv. 10, Note 32). The teeth are sharp, but not adapted for mastication; the œsophagus is absent or short; processes, often numerous, are usually given off from the intestine close to the stomach (iii. 14, 14; *H. A.* ii. 17, 26); there is always a gall-bladder (iv. 2, 1).

They are divided into two great groups: (1). Those with a cartilaginous skeleton; which with one exception (cf. Note 5) are ovoviparous. This group is subdivided into the Elongated species, *i.e.* sharks and dog-fishes, and the Flattened species, *i.e.* rays and skates, with which A. classes the oviparous fishing-frog (cf. Note 5). (2). Those with a spinous skeleton, and oviparous.

The former group he calls Selachia; to the latter he gives no special name.

2. I cannot say to what passage A. refers. But his explanation of the substitution of fins for limbs is given a little farther on in this chapter.

3. The electric rays or Torpedos are found abundantly in the Mediterranean, and must have been well known to A., who frequently speaks of them. Yet in these the tail is far from being spinous and elongated, as compared, that is, with other rays. Frantzius suggests therefore that some error has got into the text, and that perhaps Batos should be read instead of Torpedo. A similar correction would have to be made a few lines farther on.

4. The Trygon is doubtless the Trygon Pastinaca or sting-ray, which is abundant in the Mediterranean.

5. The Batrachus or fishing-frog is the Lophius piscatorius, often mentioned by A., and erroneously classed by him with Selachia. Into this error he was doubtless led by the somewhat ray-like form of this fish, by the semi-cartilaginous character of its skeleton (*Cuvier, R. An.* ii. 250), and by its naked skin, rough with warts and tubercles. A. did not fail to observe that the Batrachus differed in many important points from the rest of the group; in being, for instance, oviparous (*De Gen.* iii. 3, 1); and in having an operculum for its gills, and the gills themselves placed laterally (*H. A.* ii. 13, 7). A. had clearly examined the fish with some care; for he notices (cf. iv. 2, Note 1) the

exceptional position of its gall-bladder; but probably he had not examined it often, for he speaks of it as being rare (*H. A.* vi. 17, 9).

6. Cf. iv. 12, Note 11. At first one is struck with admiration at the prescience of A. in identifying the pectoral and ventral fins with the anterior and posterior limbs of other Vertebrata; and one is inclined to credit him with a much more accurate conception of homologies than he really possessed. Not a single word, however, is said of any anatomical correspondence of fin and limb. The identification is based on similarity of function, not on similarity of formation; that is to say, it is founded on analogies, and not on homologies. It is true that the other fins, which are not homologous to limbs, are passed over by A. notwithstanding their analogous office; but this is only owing to the fact that they are single, that is unpaired. How little comparative anatomy had to do with A.'s statement is shown by his overlooking the real pectorals in the rays, and imagining their dorsals, which are merely cutaneous appendages, to be the pectorals misplaced. So also he speaks of the serpents, which have no limbs at all, as still resembling the other sanguineous animals, *i.e.* in having four points of motion. "For," says he, "their flexures are four," while in such fishes as have only two fins "the flexures are two, to replace the missing pair" (cf. *H. A.* i. 5, 15).

7. It is strange and yet, as it appears to me, indisputably true, that A. was perfectly ignorant of the fact that tadpoles are the larval forms of frogs and newts. For it is impossible that he can have known it, and yet made no mention of what would have seemed to him, as indeed it is, a most extraordinary phenomenon. He appears to have looked on tadpoles as aberrant kinds of fishes, and on frogs of course as reptiles.

8. Destitute, that is, of fin-rays, such as exist in the caudal fin of fishes. Elsewhere (*H. A.* i, 5, 10) A. compares the tadpole's tail to that of Silurus glanis, referring, as I suppose, to the fact that in Silurus the anal fin is of great length, extending along the whole belly, and joins, or nearly joins, with the caudal fin, so as to resemble the ventral part of the continuous fin of the tadpole.

9. The Batos is described as a flat cartilaginous fish, with rough skin, and long rough tail (*H. A.* vi. 10, 17); as hiding itself under the sand and then, by means of certain oral processes, attracting small fishes on which it preys (*H. A.* ix. 37, 5). Lastly, it is said to copulate with a different species of fish, called Rhine, and thus to give origin to a mongrel, the Rhinobatus (*H. A.* vi. 11, 7).

The Rhine is said to be a cartilaginous fish, whether flat or elongated is not expressly stated, with a thick tail; producing young twice a year (*H. A.* v. 10, 1), and resembling the Batos in hiding under sand and in its method of attracting prey by means of its oral processes (*H. A.* ix. 37, 5). It has moreover the power of changing its colour, in adaptation to the stones, etc., about it; and is the only fish that can do this (*H. A.* ix. 37, 22).

These data are insufficient for exact determination of the species meant. It is usual, however, to identify Rhine with the angel-fish, and Batos with some or other ray. Numerous rays, as also the angel-fish, hide themselves as described under sand or stones. The angel-fish has also some small processes in front, which might be those which A. supposes to be used to allure small fishes (*Yarrell's Fishes*, ii. 407). But I know of nothing similar in a ray, to suit the statement as to Batos. As regards the power of changing colour, the angel-fish, says Yarrell, "is probably liable to some variation in colour depending on the nature of the ground in the locality in which it is found." This tallies well with A.'s account of Rhine. But it must be remembered that a similar faculty of adapting the colour of the skin to that of the ground belongs to many other fishes. I have frequently, for instance, watched its operation in the plaice; which fish changes its hue very completely and very quickly.

10. The pectoral fins are, as rightly stated in the text, much more constant than the ventral pair. Even in those elongated eels in which no pectorals are visible externally, rudiments of them are to be found on dissection; whereas not only are the ventral fins more often externally wanting than the pectorals, but their absence is often complete, no rudiment of them appearing on dissection, *e.g.* in Muræna, Murænophis, Gymnotus, etc. There are pectoral, but no ventral, fins in the eel, the conger, and the rest of the so-called Apodal Physostomatous fishes. As to the Cestreus, it is impossible to say what fish is here meant. Certainly it is not one of the Mugilidæ, though these are the fishes usually called Cestreus by Aristotle.

11. The Smuræna and the Muræna of A. are in all probability one and the same fish. It is described as elongated; without either ventral or pectoral fins (see last note); marked with different colours; having its branchiæ less distinct than most fishes; depositing numerous ova; living on flesh; hiding itself under the ground in cold weather; occasionally leaving the water. It is moreover often mentioned in association with the eel and conger. It seems most probable that the Muræna Helena is the species meant. This is very common in the Greek seas, where, according to Erhard, it still bears the name Smurna or Sphurna.

12. The pectoral and ventral fins are not, as a rule, such important agents in the propulsion of the fish as A. seems to think. Their chief uses are to give direction to the motion generated by the lateral strokes of the tail, to check the progress when required, to enable the fish to maintain its equilibrium and to keep itself at any level in the water. They have also secondary uses as organs of touch, etc.

In the elongated fishes the undulations of the body take a part in locomotion, but the chief part still devolves, as in other fish, on the lateral strokes of the tail. These, however, were apparently considered by A. as part of the undulatory movement.

13. Cf. *De Incessu*, 8, 1. The treatise on the Motion of Animals is unquestionably spurious. Either therefore the words "and the motion" have been introduced by some after-writer into the text; or Aristotle uses a longer title than usual to designate his treatise "on the progression of animals."

At ii. 16, Note 11, the treatise on the Motion of Animals has been inadvertently quoted as genuine.

14. In the *Hist. Anim.* (i. 5, 15) it is said that serpents and finless fishes are yet moved by four points of motion like other sanguineous animals, for "their flexures are four." The only basis for this seems to have been the desire to bring all sanguineous animals under one general law.

15. That sanguineous animals can never have more than four motor organs is stated over and over again by Aristotle. If it be asked why, the answer is that it is one of those laws of type to which nature for some reason or other is bound to adhere. Cf. *Introd.* p. x.

16. See Note 10.

17. A. correctly enough describes the manner of swimming of the rays; but clearly he had not the faintest suspicion that the lateral expansions which serve the office of propulsion are in reality the pectoral fins themselves. Had his notion of the correspondence of fins and limbs been founded on anatomical knowledge derived from dissection, he would scarcely have made this oversight. As it is, not recognising the true pectorals, he imagines that the dorsal fins, which in many rays are two in number and placed on the tail, are the pectorals, placed far behind their normal position.

18. In the fishing-frog the ventral fins are as stated in advance of the pectorals, and are much smaller than the latter. It is quite true that when the ventral fins are advanced

forwards, so as to become jugular, they are as a rule, if not invariably, reduced in size; and they are also, as a rule, modified in such a way as to serve new purposes, to act for instance as instruments of touch. Cf. *Ann. d. Sci. Nat.*, 1872, t. xvi. p. 93.

19. Cf. Note 17.

20. Namely, in the latter part of the second book and beginning of the third book.

21. *De Resp.* ch. 4.

22. A. says, minister "as it were" to expiration; for expiration is limited by him to the expulsion of air from a lung after inspiration. The expulsion of water through gills is analogous to this, but not the same thing. Cf. ii. 16, Note 8.

23. In these cartilaginous fishes there is no gill-cover; the gills being placed in a series of distinct sacs or pouches, each of which has its own separate slit-like aperture, which is closed during inhalation by its own muscular sphincter. Compare what is said about the epiglottis (iii. 3, 14; ii. 13, Note 5).

24. In the Elasmobranchii or cartilaginous fishes there are five, and in osseous fishes four, gills on either side, as a rule. But the number is subject to some variations. For instance in Lophius, Cotylis, Diodon, there are but three pairs; and in Cuchia only two, one being almost rudimentary. On the other hand in some fishes there is a kind of accessory gill, as in Sturgeon, Chimæra; and in many there is a small vascular apparatus, something like a gill, though without its function, at the top of the respiratory chamber. Each gill consists as a rule of a double row of leaflets. But it is by no means uncommon for the last, that is the fourth, gill in an osseous fish to be, as A. says, furnished with only a single row, *e.g.* Scarus, Scorpæna, Cottus, most Labroids, etc. So far then the statement in the text is perfectly intelligible. But A. also speaks of the other gills, besides this last one, as being sometimes uniserial. The eel for instance has, he says (*H. A.* ii. 13, 8), four uniserial gills; as also the sturgeon (ἔλλοψ) and sundry other fishes. The explanation of this statement is, I imagine, as follows. In some fishes the two series of leaflets that constitute a single gill are quite distinct and free from each other throughout. But in most they are united together at their basal ends for a smaller or larger proportion of their depth. In the eel, for instance, this fusion extends one-third of the whole depth; in the sturgeon two-thirds or more of the whole depth; in the salmon one-half, and so on. When the opposite rows of leaflets are thus partially united for a considerable proportion of their depth, so as to form a single bifurcated plate, they are considered by A. to form only a single row or an uniserial gill; just as he considers the two lungs to be really one bifid organ, because they coalesce into a single trachea. Cf. iii. 6, Note 1.

25. Cf. *H. A.* ii. 13, 7—9.

26. Because the hotter an animal is, the more perfect must be the arrangements for its refrigeration.

27. Why can eels and some other fishes live so long out of water? It is usually said that it is owing to the small size of their branchial apertures, which hinders the drying up of their gills. But Bert has shown that this is not the true cause; the real explanation being that these fishes produce, in a given time, ounce for ounce of body weight, less carbonic acid and therefore require less oxygen than other species.

28. Seeing that dolphins abound in the Mediterranean, and that the main points in their structure, and their habits of life, are accurately enough described by Aristotle, it seems to me quite impossible either that he can have imagined their mouth to be underneath their body, or, as has been suggested, confounded them with the larger sharks. I agree therefore with Frantzius that the word dolphins in the text is an interpolation; and this notwithstanding the objection to that view taken by Meyer, namely,

the fact that the same false statement occurs elsewhere (*H. A.* viii. 2, 32). The same ignorant transcriber who made the addition to the text in the one place may very probably have made it in the other. Cf. *Introd.* pp. xii—xiii.

29. This is, so far as I know, the only place where A. speaks of the structure of an animal as intended for the advantage of other animals than itself. Elsewhere he always speaks of the organs as given to animals to be of service to themselves. "Nature never gives an organ to an animal except when it is able to make use of it." Even here he considers the habit in question to be of use to its possessor, and only speaks doubtfully of its being intended as a means of salvation to others.

30. Sometimes A. speaks of all fishes as having this kind of dentition (cf. iii. 1, Note 7). Here he more correctly limits the statement considerably.

31. Cf. Note 9. Rhine in Greek means "file." The skin of the monk-fish or angel-fish is still used for polishing cabinwork, furnishing a fine sort of shagreen.

32. Cf. *H. A.* ii. 13, 10, where the same statement is made, and certain Selachia, eels, and tunnies mentioned as smooth fishes. The Selachian referred to is doubtless the Mustelus lævis, of which he speaks (*D. G.* iii. 3, 10) as the smooth galeus, and which is still known as the smooth-hound from the comparative softness of its skin. In the eels the scales are so deeply sunk in the skin as to be scarcely apparent, and the smooth and slippery character of these fishes is proverbial.

33. Cf. ii. 9, Notes 8, 9.

34. That is to say they have no solid organs of the globular or ovoid shape which characterises the testes of Mammalia, birds, and most reptiles. This is all that A. can mean ; for he was perfectly aware that the milt was an organ from which the male fish secreted sperm ; and he states, in opposition to those who held that there were no males among osseous fishes, that the ova of the female fish come to nothing unless the male voids the secretion of this milt upon them (*D. G.* iii. 1, 20 ; *H. A.* vi. 14, 6). He refuses however to call these saccular organs "testes," because of their shape and of their being hollow, and styles them spermatic tubes (πόροι) or roe (θορικὰ). He supposed (*D. G.* i. 4) that these saccular spermatic tubes or roe, as also the elongated testes of serpents, corresponded not to the solid globular or ovoid organs of birds, reptiles, and mammals, but to the tubular *vasa deferentia* ; and it was to these latter that he erroneously ascribed the seminal secretion. The ovoid or globular bodies he thought were merely parts superadded, when the secreting spermatic tubes became very long and complicated, for certain mechanical purposes, which are set forth by him. His account of the seminal organs of fishes seems to have been taken from osseous fishes ; for in the rays and sharks, that is to say in his Selachia, the testes are compact oval bodies (cf. *Huxley's Vert.* p. 135). Even, however, if A. had noticed this, it would not have led him to abandon his view, that such bodies were merely mechanical additions, required when the ducts became very long and complicated. For in these fishes the vas deferens is very much contorted and provided with an epididymis.

35. In the Ophidia the testes are excessively elongated and narrow, differing altogether in form from the ovoid organs of such other reptiles as the Chelonia. The form, however, is determined not by the absence of feet, but by the elongation of the whole body ; a cause which elsewhere is cited by A. himself as an explanation of the elongation of the internal organs. It must, however, be remembered that elongation of the body and absence of limbs are according to A. correlated conditions (cf. iv. 11, Note 2).

36. In birds, reptiles, amphibians, there is a cloaca, *i.e.* a common chamber into which open the rectum and the genital organs, as also the urinary, though the latter escaped A.'s

notice. Thus in these animals the fæces and the generative products are voided by one and the same orifice. There is also a cloaca in the Plagiostomous fishes, or Selachia of Aristotle. But though the statement in the text so far is true, it is erroneous as regards other fishes. For in these the anus is distinct from the generative opening; and this fact is, I think, elsewhere recognised by A. (cf. iv. 10, Note 32).

37. The meaning must be: "If there were urinary organs and an external urinary orifice, the genital secretions would be discharged by this. But as there is none, these secretions are discharged by the anus." As to absence of bladder, cf. iii. 8, Note 3.

38. The term "cete" was used prior to Aristotle for any sea-animals of large size, whales, dolphins, sharks, tunnies, etc., and was merely equivalent to "sea-monsters." But A. confines it to the spouting Cetacea. These are made by him to form a distinct group, intermediate between the viviparous quadrupeds and the fishes. They are, he says (*H. A.* viii. 2, 4), the strangest of animals, and it is difficult to determine how they should be classified (cf. iii. 6, Note 5). It is one of A.'s triumphs as a zoologist to have separated the Cetacea from fishes. Here he tells us that they have lungs; elsewhere (*H. A.* i. 5, 1) that they are viviparous, have mammæ, the concealed position of which he accurately describes (*H. A.* ii. 13, 2), and suckle their young. He states also (*D. G.* i. 12, 4) that they have testes, which no fish had in his sense of the word (cf. Note 34); and lastly he points out (ii. 9, 11) that they have true bones and not merely fish-spines— a fact which *possibly* was known to Herodotus, but not so certainly as was assumed at ii. 6, Note 6. A. mentions only four kinds, Delphis, Phocæna, Phalæna, Mysticetus. Of these the first is supposed to be Delphinus Delphis, the common dolphin, which is abundant in the Mediterranean. The Phocæna (*H. A.* vi. 12, 3) is doubtless the Phocæna communis or common porpoise. The Phalæna can hardly be anything else than the sperm-whale or Physeter; for in the sperm-whales the blow-hole is placed much more forwards than in the dolphin, which accords with the only special character mentioned by A. (*H. A.* i. 5, 2), and Physeters moreover are found not uncommonly in the Mediterranean. The Mysticetus, described (*H. A.* iii. 12, 5) as having bristles in the mouth in place of teeth, is the only true whale mentioned. This is probably the Balænopterus musculus or wrinkle-throated whale of the Mediterranean (*Cuvier, R. An.* i. 297).

The Greeks in Aristotle's time could not have been very familiar with spouting whales; for an amusing story is told, in Arrian's *Res Indicæ*, by Nearchus, Alexander's Admiral, of the fright caused to his sailors by the spectacle of a shoal of them. Afterwards he came across one thrown up on the shore and found it measured 50 cubits.

39. The like statement is often enough made now-a-days, but is incorrect. The sea-water taken into the mouth has no access to the respiratory passages and blow-hole, owing to the peculiar arrangement by which the elongated trachea and larynx are continuous with the tubular prolongation of the nasal passage formed by the soft palate. The "spouting" is due to the sudden condensation of expired vapour, and to spray driven up by the force of the expiration, when this commences before the animal has quite reached the surface.

40. A. knew nothing of the characters of Amphibia as distinct from Reptilia. "Of animals that have feet the only one we have ever seen that has a gill is the animal known as the tadpole. No animal has ever yet been seen possessing at once a lung and gills. The reason is this. The purpose of the lung is to produce refrigeration by means of air; and the purpose of the gills is to produce refrigeration by means of water. But a single organ for a single purpose is the best arrangement, and a single mode of refrigeration is in every case sufficient" (*De Resp.* 10, 6). As to the limitation of the term "respiration," cf. ii. 16, Note 8.

41. As to continuity of brain and spinal cord, and its supposed purpose, cf. ii. 7, 11.

42. Heat is the instrument of the soul in motion, as in all operations (i. 1, Note 13). Cetacea therefore that move actively must have much heat; and this again necessitates a perfect organ to regulate heat, and such is the lung.

43. Cf. ii. 12, Note 4.

44. Cf. iii. 1. Note 7; *H. A.* ii. 1, 52. In the seals, says Owen (*Odontog.* i. 506), "the coadaptation of the crowns of the upper and lower teeth is more completely alternate than in any of the terrestrial Carnivora, the lower teeth always passing into the interspace anterior to its fellow in the upper jaw."

45. A. means that the anterior limbs of bats though they are wings yet have claws, and so resemble feet and are unlike the wings of a bird; but at the same time they do not so closely resemble the fore-limbs of a quadruped as to make the bat strictly quadrupedous. A. knew that bats are viviparous and suckle their young; for he speaks of these animals as having cotyledons in their uterus (*H. A.* iii. 1, 31), and groups them with the hare and the rat among viviparous animals with teeth in both jaws.

(**Ch. 14.**) 1. In the ostrich and other Ratitæ the barbs of the feathers are disconnected, so that they come to resemble long hairs, and, owing to their want of firmness, are useless for flight.

2. Cf. ii. 14, Note 1.

3. The head and neck are naked, or covered with only a short downy plumage. Cf. ii. 9, Note 9.

4. The foot of the ostrich has two stout toes, connected at the base by a strong membrane. Of these toes the internal is much the larger, and is furnished with a thick hoof-like claw, but the external and smaller toe is clawless. Aristotle had probably never himself seen an ostrich; for, had he done so, he would scarcely have spoken of its foot as having two hoofs. That the ostrich is a kind of link, uniting birds with mammals, is not a fancy confined to Aristotle. The vulgar opinion in Arabia still makes it the product of a camel and a bird, as in the days when it got the name, already used for it by Pliny, of Struthio-camelus. The height of the bird, its long neck, its bifid foot, its frequentation of the desert, its patient endurance of thirst, and possibly the comparative complexity of its digestive organs, were doubtless the grounds of this strange notion.

ERRATA.

Page 142—i. 1, Note 4, last line but one ; *for* " where " *read* " when."

Page 176—line 7 ; *for* " even " *read* " ever."

Page 177—ii. 10, Note 19, third line of last paragraph ; *for* " inside the skull " *read* " inside of the skull."

Page 237—iv. 10, Note 14, first line ; *for* " the function is superadded to the organ " *read* " the organ is superadded to the function."

255

INDEX TO NOTES.

Note.—The References in this Index are to Book, Chapter, and Note.

A priori statements, iii. 4. 25.
Abdomen, why without ribs, ii. 9. 3.
Absorption, A.'s account of, iii. 5. 5.
Acalephæ, what animals meant, iv. 5. 61;
   no excretions, ii. 10. 3.
Accident, i. 1. 9.
Actiniæ, iv. 5. 61.
Active and passive, ii. 1. 11.
Actuality and potentiality, i. 1. 23.
Æther, i. 1. 6, ii. 1. 2.
Allantois, iv. 12. 15.
Amia, iv. 2. 4.
Amphibia, confounded with reptiles, iv.
   13. 40; development unknown, iv.
   13. 7.
Anatomy, A.'s ignorance of human, i. 5.
   1; treatise on, iv. 5. 34.
Anaxagoras, i. 1. 10.
Angel-fish, iv. 13. 9.
Annelida, confused with myriapoda, i. 2.
   2; classed with insects, iv. 5. 20, iv. 6. 1.
Aorta and great vessel, iii. 4. 24.
Art, and nature, i. 1. 8, i. 1. 19; its instruments, i. 1, 13.
Arteries and Veins, differences of, iii. 4. 24;
   terminations, iii. 4. 20, iii. 5, 7; relative
   positions, iii. 5. 12; parts nourished by
   each, iii. 4. 25, iii. 4. 28; known both
   to contain blood, iii. 5. 1; small in fat
   animals, ii. 5. 8; hepatic and splenic,
   iii. 7. 11; renal, iii. 9. 8; pulmonary,
   iii. 4, 23 and 24; iliac, iii. 5. 12;
   formation of, i. 1. 11; relation to viscera,
   iii. 4. 10.
Ascidians, iv. 5. 35; structure and classification, iv. 5. 59.
Aselli, rediscovered lacteals, ii. 3. 11.
Astaci, iv. 8. 1; claws, iv. 8. 10.
Astragalus, iv. 10. 44.
Aurochs, iii. 2. 7; how it protects itself,
   ii. 4. 5.

Balancement organique, ii. 9. 8.
Batos, iv. 13. 9.
Bats, iv. 13. 45.
Bees, intelligence of, ii. 2. 5.
Bile, its fluidity, ii. 3. 2; its use, iv. 2. 16;
   exudation of, iv. 2. 11.
Bilateral symmetry, iii. 5. 4, iii. 7. 2.
Birds, characters and divisions, iv. 12. 1;
   a homogeneous group, iv. 12. 2; cold
   animals, iii. 6. 13; their development,
   iv. 12. 15; power of intercommunication,
   ii. 17. 5; small are best songsters, ii. 17.
   4; drink but little, iii. 6. 11; the heavy-
   bodied kinds, ii. 13. 1; pinnatipede, iv.
   12. 8; of prey, settling on rocks, iv. 12.
   17; position of legs in flight, iv. 12. 24
   and 25; neck in flight, iv. 12. 26; beak,
   iii. 1. 14; bones, ii. 9. 6; scapula, iv.
   12. 9; sternum, iv. 12. 13; ischia, iv.
   12. 27; pectoral muscles, iv. 12. 14;
   excreta, iv. 1. 4; ear, ii. 12. 1; eyelids,
   ii. 13. 2; eyelashes, ii. 14. 1; spurs, iii.
   1. 6; number of toes, ii. 17. 3, iv. 12.
   30; direction of toes, iv. 12. 33;
   phalanges of toes, iv. 12. 22; hind toe
   of waders, iv. 12. 31; œsophagus, iii.
   14. 9, iii. 14. 13; crop, iii. 14. 8;
   proventriculus, iii 14. 10; gizzard, iii.
   14. 12; cæca, iii. 14. 21; cloaca, iv.
   13. 36; liver and spleen, iii. 7. 4,
   iii. 7. 14, iii. 7. 15; kidneys, iii. 9.
   1 and 2; lung and airsacs, iii. 6. 10.
Bivalves, structure, iv. 5. 43 and 48;
   mouth, iv. 5. 33; ovary, iv. 5. 47;
   generation, iv. 5. 68; second valve, iv.
   5. 31; position, iv. 7. 5. *See* Testacea.
Bladder, iii. 8. 3; of ovipara, iii. 9. 1; of
   tortoises, iii. 8. 6; use, iii. 7. 18.
Blood, how formed, iii. 5. 5; where formed,
   iii. 5. 9; formed after heart, ii. 1. 17;
   increased after food, ii. 3. 14; is the

nutritious part of the food, ii. 3. 13; its fibres the nutritive part, ii. 4. 11; nature of its serum, ii. 4. 11; how far fluid in life, ii. 4. 6, iii. 5. 7; its coagulation ii. 4. 1; cause of its coagulation, ii 4. 10; coagulation more rapid in some animals than others, ii. 4. 9; coagulation imperfect in hunted animals, ii. 4. 2; relation of coagulum to strength and ferocity of animal, ii. 4. 8; arterial and venous, iii. 4. 25; that of head of brighter tint, ii. 7. 12; is not essentially hot, ii. 2. 14, ii. 3. 1; hotter in right cavities than in left, iii. 4. 27; hotter on right side, ii. 2. 6; cold blood goes with fear, ii. 4. 4; is insensible, ii. 3. 15; its relation to heart and viscera, ii. 1. 18; its relation to the flesh, iii. 5. 7; its relation to integumental structures, iii. 8. 2.

Blood vessels. *See* Arteries and Veins.
Bonasus. *See* Aurochs.
Bones, regeneration of, ii. 9. 11; and cartilage, ii. 9. 10; of lion, ii. 6. 5; of fishes, ii. 6. 6; of birds, ii. 9. 6; of serpents, ii. 9. 7; of skull, ii. 7. 21; in heart, iii. 4. 22.
Brain, is fluid, ii. 7. 4; is made of cold elements, ii. 7. 8; its supposed bloodlessness, ii. 10. 18, ii. 7. 3; its blood, ii. 7. 12; its blood-vessels and membranes, ii. 7. 11; its insensibility, ii. 7. 5; its isolation from other parts, ii. 7. 6; is not connected with sense organs, ii. 10. 9; erroneous notions concerning it, ii. 10. 18; its supposed use and its importance, ii. 7. 27, iii. 11. 2; its action similar to that of lungs, iii. 6. 3; reasons for A.'s view, ii. 7. 27; of man, the heaviest, ii. 7. 18; of cephalopods, ii. 7. 9.
Bubalus, and buffalo, iii. 2. 6.
Bustard, mode of defence, iii. 2. 8.

Cæca, of birds and fishes, iii. 14. 21.
Cæcum, called lower stomach, iii. 14. 31; use of, iii. 14. 35, ii. 3. 6; of mammals, iii. 14. 22; of carnivora, iii. 14. 33.
Canthari, iv. 6. 8.
Camel, mouth, iii. 14. 6; stomach and palate, iii. 14. 4; teeth, iii. 14. 3; bilevessels, iv. 2. 6; length of life, iv. 2. 17; retromingent, iv. 10. 36.
Carabi, Carides, Carcini, iv. 8. 1.
Cartilage, and bone, ii. 9. 10; regeneration of, ii. 9. 11.
Catamenia, iv. 10. 33; supposed indication of heat, ii. 2. 9.
Causes, the four, i. 1. 3; relative importance of material and final, i. 1. 26.
Celestial bodies, influence on terrestrial, i. 1. 5.
Celsus, as to digestion, ii. 3. 3; as to fat persons, ii. 5. 8.
Cestreus, iii. 14. 19.
Cephalopods, characters and divisions, iv. 9. 1; internal structure, iv. 5. 11;

internal shell, iv. 5. 18; brain, ii. 7, 9, ii. 10. 18; teeth, iv. 5. 4; liver, iv. 5. 64; ink-bag, iv. 5. 12; external forth, iv. 9. 3; length of tentacles, iv. 9. 10, 11 and 12; action of tentacles, iv. 9. 16; change of colour, iv. 5. 15, ii. 4. 5.
Cetacea, characters and species, iv. 13. 38; their intermediate nature, iii. 6. 5; have lungs, iv. 13. 42; their blowhole, ii. 16. 9 and 10, ii. 10. 13; their spouting, iv. 13. 39.
Chamæleon, changing colour, iv. 11. 28, ii. 4. 5; vivisected by A., iv. 11. 27, ii. 7. 4 and 5.
Chance, relation to design, i. 1. 8; and to spontaneity, i. 1. 9.
Chemical combination, A.'s notion of, ii. 1. 4; not distinguished from physical condition, ii. 1. 3.
Chordæ tendineæ, iii. 4. 20.
Cicadæ, drums, ii. 16. 10; food, iv. 5. 78.
Classification, terms used by A., i. 1. 2; order adopted by A, iv. 10. 12; chief rules recognised by A., i. 3. 4; natural system partly recognised, i. 2. 1.
Cloaca. of ovipara, iv. 13. 36.
Coagulation, causes of, ii. 4. 10; of oil, ii. 2. 13; of blood, *see* Blood.
Cold, whether more than privation of heat, ii. 2. 15.
Composition, three degrees of, ii. 1. 8; chemical, ii. 1. 4.
Concoction. *See* Digestion.
Constructive sciences, i. 1. 4.
Coot, foot of, iv. 12. 8.
Crabs, iv. 8. 2; legs, iv. 8, 3; tail, iv. 8. 6.
Crex, iv. 12. 32.
Crocodile, jaws, iv. 11. 20; tongue, ii. 17. 7, 9 and 10, iv. 11. 5.
Crustacea, characters and divisions, iv. 8. 1; claws, iv. 8. 7 and 10; tail, iv. 8. 6; eyes, ii. 13. 12; teeth and tongue, iv. 5. 5; digestive organs, iv. 5. 24.
Ctesias, iii. 2. 10.
Cyprinoids, palate, ii. 17. 12.

De Spiritu, not genuine treatise, ii. 16. 11, iii. 5. 1.
De Partibus, treatise was illustrated, iv. 9. 5.
Decapoda, tentacles, iv. 9. 13; compared to Sauræ, iv. 9. 16; how used, iv. 9. 14.
Deer, duration of life, iv. 2. 17.
Delphian knife, iv. 6. 15.
Design, relation to chance, i. 1. 8.
Democritus, coupled vision with water, ii. 1. 12; said soul was fire, ii. 7. 7, iv. 10. 11; placed soul in head, ii. 10. 8; said other special senses were developed from touch, ii. 8. 1.
Diaphragm, iii. 10. 1; structure, iii. 10. 7; rupture, iii. 10. 9; why called phrenes, iii. 10. 6; use according to Plato, iii. 10. 4.
Dichotomy, i. 2. 1.

Digestion, ancient explanations of, ii. 3. 3; attributed partly to putrefaction, iii. 14. 20; not due to ordinary heat, ii. 6. 7; its organs correspond to food, iii. 14. 14.
Diogenes, located sensation in brain, ii. 10. 8.
Diptera, size, iv. 6. 4; no sting, iv. 6. 13.
Disease, nature of, ii. 2. 10.
Dislocation, ancient instrument for reducing, iv. 9. 16.
Dissection, practised by A., iii. 4. 21; whether human practised by him, i. 5. 1.
Diving apparatus, known to ancients, ii. 16. 3.
Dogs of India, i. 3. 3.
Dolphin, mouth, iv. 12. 28; duration of life, iv. 2. 17.
Drunkards, small eaters, iv. 11. 9.
Duck, power of remaining under water, iii. 6. 12.

Ear, of man, ii. 11. 1; of birds, ii. 12. 1 and 2; of seal, ii. 12. 3.
Earthworms, iv. 6. 1.
Echini, classed with Testacea, iv. 5. 35; with Turbinata, iv. 9. 4; teeth, iv. 5. 36; mouth, iv. 5. 37; digestive organs, iv. 5. 38; ovaries, iv. 5. 39; black bodies, iv. 5. 40; shallow and deepwater species, iv. 5. 41; use of spines, iv. 5. 51.
Education, should embrace knowledge of methods, i. 1. 1.
Eels, living out of water, iv. 13. 27; gills, iv. 13. 24; fins, iv. 13. 10; scales, iv. 13. 32.
Electric rays, iv. 13. 3.
Eledone, iv. 9. 17.
Elementary, forces, ii. 1. 3; motions, ii. 1. 2.
Elements, number of, ii. 1. 2; their compound nature, ii. 1. 3.
Elephant, whether seen by A., ii. 16. 6; ancient errors concerning it, ii. 16. 7; trunk, ii. 16. 3; tusks, iii. 2. 19; liver, iv. 2. 6; foot, ii. 16. 6; heart, iii. 4. 22; aquatic habits, ii. 16. 2; rests in standing position, iv. 10. 38.
Emotion, physical accompaniments of, ii. 4. 4; iii. 6. 7.
Empedocles, i. 1. 10, ii. 2. 8.
Emys, iii. 9. 3.
Ephemera, iv. 5. 79.
Epiglottis, iii. 3. 7.
Epilepsy, relation to sleep, ii. 7. 15.
Erasistratus, views as to digestion, ii. 3. 3; as to arteries, iii. 5. 1; as to nerves, ii. 10. 18; discovered lacteals, ii. 3. 11.
Erect position, of man, iii. 1. 15; different meanings of, iii. 6. 16.
Erection, iv. 10. 35.
Eternal motion, i. 1. 5.
Evolution, and characters, how related, i. 1. 6, i. 1. 27.
Eyes, why of water, ii. 10. 16; connection with brain, ii. 10. 9; their nerves, ii. 10. 19; of invertebrates, ii. 10. 12.
Eyebrows, use, ii. 15. 1.

Eyelashes, of birds, ii. 14. 1; of mammals, ii. 14. 3.
Eyelids, comparative mobility of upper and lower, ii. 13. 2 and 5; involuntary movement, ii. 13. 3; of reptiles, iv. 11. 15.
Excretions, ii. 3. 8; discharged in fright, ii. 4. 5, iv. 5. 20; used in defence, iii. 2. 7 and 8, iii. 14. 32.

Fanning, production of cold by, iii. 6. 14.
Fat, fluidity of, ii. 2. 1; various kinds, ii. 5. 1; of different animals, ii. 5. 6; of bloodless animals, ii. 5. 3; result of concoction, iii. 9. 14; inversely related to semen, ii. 5. 9; abundance of fat goes with small vessels, ii. 5. 8; absent from joints, iii. 9. 16; of kidneys, iii. 9. 18. 19 and 20.
Father, share in generation of soul, i. 1. 14.
Fear, external symptoms, ii. 4. 4; physical effects, ii. 4. 5.
Feathers, i. 3. 1, iv. 6. 6; of ostrich, iv. 14. 1.
Female, size as compared with male, iii. 1. 5; comparative heat, ii. 2. 9; often unarmed, iii. 1. 6.
Fibres of blood, ii. 4. 1; thought to be solid during life, ii. 4. 6; thought to be the nutritive part, ii. 4. 11; not distinguished from gelatine, ii. 4. 5; more abundant in some animals than others, ii. 4. 8.
Fins, homologies of, iv. 13. 6 and 17; uses of, iv. 13. 12; greater constancy of pectoral, iv. 13. 10; modification of jugular, iv. 13. 18; of tadpole, iv. 13. 8.
Fishermen, information from, iv. 5. 53.
Fishes, characters and divisions, iv. 13. 1; development, iv. 12. 15; how protected, iii. 1. 10; cannot chew food, iii. 14. 17; sense of taste, iv. 11. 7; sense of smell and hearing, ii. 10. 13; changing colour, iv. 13. 9; living out of water, iv. 13. 27; ruminating, iii. 14. 15; oviparous and ovoviviparous, iv. 1. 5; scales, iii. 8. 2, iv. 13. 32; fins, iv. 13. 6, 10, 12, 17 and 18; olfactory organs, ii. 10. 13; bones, ii. 6. 6; no medullary canals, ii. 6. 8; dentition, iii. 1. 7, 8 and 9, iv. 13. 30; tongue, ii. 17. 8, iv. 11. 6; palate, ii. 17. 12; œsophagus, iii. 3. 2; pyloric cæca, iii. 14. 21; short intestine, iii. 14. 23; liver, iii. 7. 6; gall-bladder, iv. 2. 1 and 3; spleen, iii. 7. 4; heart, iii. 4. 19; brain, iii. 10. 18; gills, iv. 13. 23 and 24, ii. 10. 13; respiration, ii. 10. 8, iii. 6. 3, iv. 13. 22; gill-cover, iv. 13. 23; bladder, iii. 8. 3; roe, iv. 13. 34; generative outlet, iv. 10. 32, iv. 13. 36; temperature, ii. 2. 8.
Fishing-frog. *See* Lophius.
Flesh, nature of, iii. 4. 20, iii. 5, 7; called fluid, ii. 2. 1; the medium of touch and taste, ii. 8. 2, ii. 10. 10; its contractility not known to A., ii. 1. 10, iii. 4. 20.
Flexures, of limbs, iv. 12. 10; of arm, iv. 10. 18.
Fluid, and solid, definitions of, ii. 1. 3.

17

Fluids, of body, ii. 7. 4, ii. 2. 1.
Flying, resemblance to swimming, i. 4. 1.
Fœtus, perhaps dissected by A., i. 5. 1; heart visible on third day, iii. 4. 2; viscera, iii. 4. 4; marrow, ii. 6. 2; brain, ii. 7. 4; deficient pigment, ii. 6. 3.
Functions, and properties, ii. 1. 9; have separate organs when possible, iv. 6. 15; sometimes accumulated in single organ, ii. 16. 5 and 12; precede organs, ii. 16. 13, iv. 10. 14.
Food, iii. 5. 5; is fluid, ii. 2, 4.
Foot, large in man, iv. 10. 46.

Galen, as to lacteals, ii. 3. 11; calls brain almost fluid, ii. 7. 4; says vessels are small in fat men, ii. 5. 8; ridicules A.'s view of the brain, iii. 6. 3; and of sinews, iii. 4. 20; and of the heart's cavities, iii. 4. 23; on heart of elephant, iii. 4. 22; on gills of fishes, ii. 16. 8; on position of heart, iii. 4. 17; on its hard flesh, iii. 4. 37; on sutures of skull, ii. 7. 23; locates blood formation in liver, iii. 4. 15; said to have visited Egypt, ii. 7. 26.
Gall-bladder, wanting in some animals, iv. 2. 7; variable, iv. 2. 8; reasons for absence, iv. 3. 1; of serpents, iv. 2. 1; of fishes, iv. 2. 3 and 4; of seal, iv. 2. 7; of sheep in Naxos, iv. 2. 9.
Gallinaceæ, ii. 13. 1.
Gasteropods, position of mouth and anus, iv. 9. 7; proboscis, iv. 5. 27; crop, iv. 5. 28; liver, iv. 5. 29; operculum, iv. 5. 31. *See* Testacea.
Gazelle, iii. 2. 6 and 17.
General sense, iv. 10. 8.
Genus, and species, i. 1. 2.
Gills, do not co-exist with lung, iv. 13. 40. *See* Fishes.
Giraffe, not known to A., iii. 2. 15.
Grasshopper, legs of, iv. 6. 18.
Great vessel, iii. 4. 24.
Grebe, foot of, iv. 12. 8.

Hæmorrhage, active and passive, iii. 5. 11.
Hair, how formed, ii. 15. 4; of head, ii. 14. 6; correlated with teeth, etc., ii. 14. 4; correlated with skin, ii. 13. 7.
Hand, in place of many organs, iv. 10. 15.
Hare, its rennet, iii. 15. 2; its food, iii. 15. 5.
Hartbeeste, iii. 2. 6.
Hawk, legs in flight, iv. 12. 25.
Health, and Disease, how far part of natural philosophy, ii. 7. 14; causes of, ii. 2. 10.
Hearing, medium of, ii. 1. 12, ii. 10. 10.
Heart, is homogeneous and also heterogeneous, ii. 1. 16; how nourished, ii. 1. 18; early formation of, iii. 4. 2; formed before blood, ii. 1. 17; its cavities and anatomy, iii. 4. 23; inconsistent statements about, iii. 4. 26; at first unilocular, iii. 4. 30; left ventricle the supreme part, iii. 4. 29; its chordæ tendineæ, iii. 4. 20; bone in, iii. 4. 22; position of in man, iii. 4. 17; of hare, iii. 4. 32; of fishes, iii. 4. 19; of testacea, iv. 5. 67; of insects, iv. 5. 69; its central position; iv. 5. 59; relation to lung and windpipe, iii. 3. 9; disease of, iii. 4. 37; its action, iii. 6. 7; is centre of vascular system and seat of blood formation, iii. 4. 5; main but not sole seat of vital heat, ii. 3. 4; the source of motion, iii. 4. 20; why held to be the sensorium commune, ii. 7. 27; connection with sense-organs, ii. 10. 19, ii. 10 9; special relation to touch and taste, ii. 10. 10; sympathy with brain, ii. 7. 27; throbs in emotion, iii. 4. 13; ignored by A.'s predecessors, iii. 4. 5.
Heat, and cold, ii. 2. 15; vital distinct from ordinary, ii. 6. 7; vital is chiefly in heart, ii. 3. 4; mounts upwards, ii. 7. 20; of male and female, ii. 2. 9, ii. 7. 19; affects different persons differently, ii. 2. 12; is instrument of soul, i. 1. 13, iii. 5. 3, iv. 10: 11; is cause of digestion, ii. 3. 3; promotes growth, ii. 7. 20; is cause of blood's fluidity, ii. 9. 1; how regulated, iii. 6. 3.
Heavens, not generated, i. 1. 21.
Hemiptera, rostrum of, iv. 5. 76.
Hepatic vessels, iii. 7. 11.
Heracleotic crabs, iv. 8. 2.
Herodotus, ii. 6. 6, ii. 7. 26, ii. 16. 4, iii. 2. 1.
Heron, tail, iv. 12. 24; neck, iv. 12. 26.
Hippardium, iii. 2. 15.
Hippocrates, source of Plato's physiology, ii. 10. 8; on digestion, ii. 3. 3; on brain, ii. 10. 18; on periosteum, ii. 9. 11; on use of spleen, iii. 7. 15; on duration of life in fat persons, ii. 5. 8; on small appetite of drunkards, iv. 11. 9; on trachea, iii. 3. 6; on prepuce, ii. 13. 4; on semen, iv. 10. 33; on "sauræ," iv. 9. 16.
Historia animalium, its title, ii. 1. 1; called first treatise, iv. 5. 9 and 69; was illustrated, iv. 5. 34, iv. 9. 5.
Holothuriæ, iv. 5. 53 and 54.
Homogeneous and Heterogeneous, distinction of, ii. 1. 5, ii. 2. 3, ii. 9, 13; mutual relations, ii. 1. 9.
Homer, respect for his authority, iii. 10. 10,
Homology, of fins and limbs, iv. 13. 6 and 17; of limbs, iv. 12. 10.
Hoofs, are integumental structures, ii 9. 12.
Horns, are integumental structures, ii. 9. 12; not coexistent with tusks, iii. 1. 3; inversely related to teeth, iii. 2. 19; differ in males and females, iii. 1. 6; wanting in polydactylous animals, iii. 2. 2; of Indian ass, iii. 2. 10; of oryx, iii. 2. 12, iii. 1. 1; of ruminants, iii. 2. 15; of bull, iii. 2. 14; for defence or offence, iii. 1. 1; sometimes an encumbrance, ii. 16. 4, iii. 2. 5; simulated in some animals, iii. 2. 1.
Horse, duration of life, iv. 2. 17; mode of fighting, iv. 10. 19; mammæ of male, iv. 10. 30.

Hot, various meanings of, ii. 2. 18.
Hucklebone, iv. 10. 44.
Human body, whether dissected by A., i. 5. 1; proportions of, iv. 10. 10; erect attitude of, iii. 1. 15.
Hunger, allayed by contact of food, iii. 14. 34.
Hymenoptera, their oral instruments, iv. 6. 11.
Hypozoma, ii. 16. 10.

Indian, dogs, i. 3. 3; ass, iii. 2. 10.
Innate Spirit, ii. 16. 11, iii. 6. 2.
Insects, characters and divisions, iv. 6. 1; their wings called feathers, iv. 6. 6, i. 3. 1; bulk and wings, iv. 6. 4; oral organs, iv. 5. 7, iv. 6. 11; tongue, iv. 5. 8; digestive organs, iv. 5. 74 and 75; eyes, ii. 13. 12; olfactory organs, ii. 16. 10; heart, iv. 5. 69; hypozoma, ii. 16. 10; anterior legs, iv. 6. 16; hinder legs, iv. 6. 17, 18 and 19; live when cut in pieces, iii. 5. 2, iv. 5. 71; how protected, iii. 2. 9, iv. 6. 8; defend themselves by excretions, ii. 4. 5, iii. 2. 8; feign death, iv. 6. 8; roll themselves up, iv. 6. 7.
Integumental structures, ii. 9. 12.
Intellectual faculty, separable from matter, i. 1. 14 and 17; outside province of natural science, i. 1. 18.
Intestinal canal, of mammalia, iii. 4. 26; of herbivora, iii. 14. 27; of carnivora, iii. 14. 33; of artiodactyla, iii. 14. 29; effects of shortness, iii. 14. 23 and 34.
Ischia, iv. 12. 27.

Jaw, motion of in carnivora, iv. 11. 19; in crocodile, iv. 11. 20.
Jejunum, iii. 14. 36.
Joints, kinds of, ii. 9. 2.
Juli, iv. 5. 70, iv. 6, 7.

Kidneys, use of, iii. 7. 18, iii. 9. 1; their vessels, iii. 9. 8; lobulation, iii. 9. 6 and 7; position of right and left, iii. 9. 11; tunica adiposa, iii. 9. 13; right not so fat as left, iii. 9. 17; fat not equably disposed, iii. 9. 18; especially fat in sheep and ox, iii. 9. 20; of man and fœtus, iii. 9. 6; of seal, iii. 9. 5; of birds, iii. 9. 2; of chelonia, iii. 9. 1.

Lacteals, discovery of, ii. 3. 11.
Lard, and suet, ii. 5. 1. *See* Fat.
Larynx, called pharynx, iii. 3. 1.
Leopard, iii. 4. 32.
Ligaments, iii. 4. 20.
Limbs, number of, iv. 12. 11, iv. 13. 15; flexures of, iv. 12. 10, iv. 10. 18; part taken by posterior, iv. 9. 9.
Lion, not seen by A., iv. 10. 6; bones and marrow, ii. 6. 5; mammæ, iv. 10. 27; errors concerning it, iv. 10. 6.

Liver, variable colour, iii. 12. 4 and 5; lobulation of, iii. 7. 4, 5 and 6; relation to spleen, iii. 7. 1 and 4.
Lizards, tongue of, ii. 17. 7.
Lobster, claws of, iv. 8. 10.
Locomotion, begins from right, iii. 9. 12.
Lophius, iv. 1. 5; errors concerning, iv. 13. 5; gall-bladder, iv. 2. 1; fins, iv. 13. 18.
Lung, its air-passages and blood-vessels, iii. 3. 9; why called single by A., iii. 6. 1; its action, iii. 6. 6; not source of heart's action, iii. 6. 7; variable amount of blood, iii. 6. 18; bladder-like kind inferior, iii. 6. 3 and 10, iii. 7. 17; of birds and reptiles, iii. 6. 8, 10 and 18; of chelonia, iii. 8. 5 and 6.

Maia, iv. 8. 2.
Malacia. *See* Cephalopods.
Malacostraca. *See* Crustacea.
Male, hotter than female, ii. 7. 19; better armed than female, iii. 1. 4 and 6; size of organs compared with those of females, iii. 1. 5; mammæ of, iv. 10. 30.
Mammæ, position of, iv. 10, 23, 24, 25 and 29; number of, iv. 10. 26 and 27; of males, iv. 10. 30; of lion, iv. 10. 27.
Mammalia, characters and divisions, iv. 10. 1; equivalent to "internally viviparous," iv. 11. 24; umbilical vesicle, iv. 12. 15.
Man, erect position, ii. 10. 7, iii. 1. 15; bodily proportions, iv. 10. 10; senses compared with those of other animals, ii. 16. 14; impotence as compared with other animals, iv. 10. 15; brain, ii. 7. 18; skull, ii. 7. 21; sutures, ii. 7. 26; ears, ii. 11. 1; eye-lashes, ii. 14. 3; kidneys, iii. 9. 6 and 11; spleen, iii. 12. 7; gall-bladder, iv. 2. 8; foot, iv. 10. 46; hand, iv. 10. 15; nails, iv. 10. 16; place in serial classification, iv. 10. 12.
Marrow, not seminal, ii. 6. 1; not in all bones, nor all animals, ii. 6. 5 and 8; and spinal cord, ii. 6. 4; of fœtus, ii. 6. 2.
Marten, iii. 4. 32.
Mastication, ii. 3. 5.
Mecon. *See* Mytis.
Medicine, how far a branch of natural philosophy, ii. 7. 14.
Media, of senses, ii. 1. 12, ii. 10. 10.
Medusæ, iv. 5. 54.
Melolontha, iv. 6. 5.
Memory, not possessed by all animals, ii. 2. 5.
Mesentery, iv. 1. 8.
Methods, of science, part of education, i. 1. 1.
Milk, its composition, iii. 15. 4; its coagulation, iii. 15. 1 and 5.
Mollusca. *See* Testacea.
Momus, fable of, iii. 2. 14.
Monkeys, kinds recognised by A., iv. 10. 41.
Monk-fish. *See* Rhine.
Moon, supposed influence on animals, iv. 5. 45.

Mother, her share in generation of soul, i. 1. 14.
Motion, modes of, i. 1. 16; elementary forms of, ii. 1. 2; rotatory and eternal, i. 1. 5; cooling action of, iii. 6. 14; mechanism of in animals, iii. 4. 20, ii. 16. 11; spurious treatise on, iv. 13. 13.
Mullet, stomach of, iii. 14. 19.
Muræna, iv. 13. 11.
Muscle. *See* Flesh.
Mustelus, its placenta known to A., iv. 13. 1.
Myriapoda, iv. 5. 70, i. 2. 3; intestinal canal of, iv. 5. 74.
Mytis, iv. 5. 13, 29 and 64, iii. 4. 1.

Nails, part of skin, ii. 9. 12; use of, iv. 10. 16.
Natural philosophy, how far concerned with the soul, i. 1. 17 and 18; should deal with final rather than material cause, i. 1. 26; may deal with principles of medicine, ii. 7. 14.
Nature, and art, i. 1. 8 and 19; her order general, not universal, iii. 2. 18; acts under some constraint, iv. 5. 2; avails herself of necessary conditions, iii. 2. 16; usually gives separate organs for separate functions, iv. 6. 15; sometimes uses one organ for several functions, iii. 1. 11 and 12, iv. 10. 22; saves in one part to spend in another, ii. 9. 9; gives animals a structure useful to themselves, iv. 13. 29.
Necessity, various kinds of, i. 1. 23, 24 and 25.
Neck, uses of, iv. 10. 7; use of long one, iii. 3. 3.
Nereis, confounded with centipede, iv. 5. 70.
Nerites, iv. 5. 32.
Nerves, confounded with sinews, iii. 4. 20; whether any were known to A., ii. 10. 9 and 19.
Nictitating membrane, ii. 13. 2, iv. 11. 17.
Nostrils, position of. ii. 10. 25.
Nutrition, A.'s account of, iii. 5. 5; treatise on, ii. 3. 16.
Nylghau, iii. 2. 15.

Occiput, empty space in, ii. 10. 18.
Octopoda, species of, iv. 9. 17; shape, iv. 9. 6; mode of progression, iv. 9. 8; littoral habits, iv. 5. 16; absence of fins, iv. 9. 19.
Œsophagus, whether necessary, iv. 10. 5; of fishes, iii. 3. 2; relation to taste, iv. 11. 8.
Œstrus, ii. 17. 16.
Oils, coagulation of, ii. 2. 13.
Omentum, iv. 3. 3.
Operculum, of gasteropods, iv. 5. 31.
Ophidia, iv. 11. 3; tongue, ii. 17. 7; elongated viscera, iv. 1. 7; gall-bladder, iv. 2. 1; scales, iv. 11. 14; bones, ii. 9. 7; vertebræ, iv. 11. 23; testes, iv. 13. 35; absence of eyelids, iv. 11. 15;
locomotion, iv. 13. 6 and 14; horned species, iii. 2. 1.
Organic equivalents, law of, ii. 9. 9, ii. 14: 4, iii. 2. 13 and 19, iv. 12. 18.
Organs, relation to tissues, ii. 1. 5, 7, 8 and 9; functions and properties, ii. 1. 9; simple and compound, ii. 1. 16; separate for separate functions, iv. 6. 15; sometimes one for diverse functions, iii. 1. 11, ii. 16. 5, ii. 17. 17; whether prior or posterior to functions, ii.'16. 13, iv. 10. 14; pre-existing are modified for new functions, iii. 1. 12, iv. 10. 22; of animal life are symmetrical, iii. 2. 11.
Oryx, iii. 2. 12, iii. 1. 1.
Ostracoderma. *See* Testacea.
Ostrich, not seen by A., iv. 14. 4; nor its skeleton, iv. 12. 13; imperfect diaphragm, iii. 10. 1; eyelashes, ii. 14. 1; feathers, iv. 14. 1; naked head and neck, iv. 14. 3; foot, iv. 14. 4.
Oviparous quadrupeds. *See* Reptiles.
Ovo-vivipara, iv. 11. 24, iv. 1. 5.
Ovum, perfect in birds and reptiles, iv. 11. 3, iv. 12. 1; perfect in selachia, not in other fishes, iv. 13. 1; of mammalia unknown to A., iv. 11. 24; of echini, iv. 5. 39, iv. 5. 50; of testacea, iv. 5. 44.
Oysters, discovery of generative fluids, iv. 5. 68.
Oxen, grazing backwards, ii. 16. 4.

Palate, of Cyprinoids, ii. 17. 12.
Palpitation, distinct from normal heart's action, iii. 6. 7.
Pangenesis, partly anticipated by Hippocrates, iv. 10. 33.
Pardalis, iii. 4. 32.
Parrot, probably never seen by A., ii. 17. 3, ii. 13. 2; tongue, ii. 17. 3.
Parrot-fish. *See* Scarus.
Parts, homogeneous and heterogeneous, ii. 1. 5 and 9; division of, ii. 1. 16, ii. 2. 3.
Passive, and active, ii. 1. 11.
Penis, bone in, iv. 10. 34; erection, iv. 10. 35.
Periodicity, due to influence of celestial bodies, i. 1. 5.
Pharynx, and larynx, iii. 3. 1.
Pia mater, ii. 10. 18.
Pig, its classification, iii. 12. 8.
Pigment, deficient in fœtus, ii. 6. 3.
Pinnatipedes, iv. 12. 8.
Placental fishes, iv. 1. 5.
Plants, no excretions, ii. 3. 8; seeds their residue, iv. 5. 60, iv. 10. 13; their roots, ii. 3. 10; their vital centre, iv. 5. 59; parasitical kinds, iv. 5. 56; some coagulate milk, iii. 15. 5.
Plato, system of dichotomy, i. 2. 1; took his physiology from Hippocrates, ii. 10. 8; coupled vision with fire, ii. 1. 12; thought right superior to left, ii. 2. 6; thought blood fibres were solid during life, ii. 4. 6; thought marrow was generative, ii. 6. 1; thought spinal cord and brain were identical in substance, ii.

7. 1; thought fluid passed by windpipe, iii. 3. 6; said heart was meeting point of vessels, iii. 4. 5.; thought lung was bloodless, iii. 6. 18; described spleen as bloodless, iii. 7. 12; on the triple soul, iii. 10. 4; compared stomach to manger, ii. 3. 7; on use of bile, iv. 2. 5; on use of long intestine, iii. 14. 23; on use of diaphragm, iii. 10. 4; on use of nails, iv. 10. 16; as to absence of fat from joints, iii. 9. 16.
Plutarch, on cold, ii. 2. 15.
Porpoise, bones, ii. 6. 6; deficient marrow, ii. 6. 8. *See* Cetacea.
Portal vein, how regarded by A. and Galen, iii. 4. 15.
Potentiality, i. 1. 23.
Poulp. *See* Octopoda.
Prepuce, ii. 13. 4.
Problemata, iii. 15. 6.
Proboscis, of insects, iv. 5. 7; of elephant, ii. 16. 3.
Proportions, of body change with age, iv. 10. 10.
Pulse, A.'s explanation of, iii. 6. 7.
Punctum saliens, iii. 4. 2.
Purpura, ii. 17. 15.
Pus, formation of, iii. 6. 7.

Rain, how formed, ii. 7. 13.
Rays, species and habits, iv. 13. 9; teeth, iii. 1. 7; fins and manner of swimming, iv. 13. 7; testes, iv. 13. 34; skin, iv. 13. 33.
Razor-fish, iv. 7. 4.
Refrigeration, the end of respiration, iii. 6. 3; organs of, iii. 6. 3; how effected in insects, ii. 16. 10; produced by fanning motion, iii. 6. 14; due to innate spirit, iii. 6. 2.
Regeneration, of bone and cartilage, ii. 9. 11.
Rennet, iii. 15. 1; of hare, iii. 15. 2.
Reptiles, characters and divisions, iv. 11. 3; scales, iv. 11. 14; eyelids, iv. 11. 15; nictitating membrane, iv. 11. 17, ii. 13. 2; bladder, iii. 8. 3; lung, iii. 8. 5; tongue, iv. 11. 5 and 10; teeth, iv. 11. 12; cloaca, iv. 13. 36; can live without air for long time, iii. 6. 12.
Residuum, various senses of term, ii. 3. 8; turned to account sometimes, iv. 2. 12, iii. 14. 32, iii. 2. 7 and 8.
Respiration, restricted meaning of term, ii. 16. 8, iv. 13. 22; A.'s theory of, iii. 6. 3; mechanism of, iii. 6. 6.
Retromingent animals, iv. 10. 36.
Rhine, and rhinobatus, iv. 13. 9; its skin, iv. 13. 31.
Rhinoceros, iii. 2. 10.
Ribs, true and false, iv. 10. 23; absence of abdominal, ii. 9. 3.
Right, nobler than left, ii. 2. 6; motion commences from it, iii. 9. 12; hotter than left, iii. 4. 28, ii. 2. 6; nourished by aorta, iii. 4. 28.
Roots, of plants, ii. 3. 10.

Rot, in sheep, iii. 9. 19.
Ruminants, oral cavity, iii. 14. 6; multiple stomach, iv. 1. 6.
Rumination, use of, iii. 14. 15.

Sacrificial victims, source of anatomical knowledge, iv. 2. 9.
Salivary glands, unknown to A., ii. 3. 5.
Sauræ, the instruments so named, iv. 9. 16.
Saw-toothed animals, have no tusks nor horns, iii. 1. 3.
Scales, formation of, iii. 8. 2; of reptiles, iv. 11. 14; of fishes and reptiles, iii. 8. 2.
Scapula, of birds, iv. 12. 9.
Scarus, teeth, iii. 1. 7; said to ruminate, iii. 14. 15.
Sciences, how classified, i. 1. 4; their methods a part of education, i. 1. 1.
Scolopendra, iv. 5. 70.
Scorpion, iv. 6. 12.
Sea-anemone, iv. 5. 61.
Sea-lung, iv. 5. 54.
Seal, a stunted quadruped, ii. 12. 4; why without external ears, ii. 12. 3; gall-bladder, iv. 2. 7; kidneys, liii. 9. 5; tongue, iv. 11. 10; dentition, iv. 13. 44.
Sedum, vitality of, iv. 5. 57.
Selachia, iv. 1. 5; skin, ii. 9. 8; gills, iv. 13, 23 and 24; testes, iv. 13. 34; cloaca, iv. 13. 36.
Semen, nature of, iv. 10. 33; inversely related to fat, ii. 5. 9.
Senses, general and special, iv. 10. 8; media of, ii. 1. 12, ii. 10. 10; each limited to one class of sensibles, ii. 1. 13; each ascribed to a separate element, ii. 1. 12; connection of their external organs with sensorium, ii. 10. 19; their external organs not connected with brain, ii. 10. 9; why their external organs are near brain, ii. 10. 11; soul the passive recipient of sensory motions, i. 1. 16.
Sensorium Commune, heart not brain, ii. 7. 27, ii. 10. 10.
Sepia, description of, iv. 9. 1; retractile tentacles, iv. 9. 11 and 13; how tentacles are used, iv. 9. 14.
Serpents. *See* Ophidia.
Serum, its nature, ii. 4. 11.
Silurus, anal fin, iv. 13. 8.
Simplicity, of structure correlated with simplicity of life, ii. 10. 5.
Sinew, iii. 4. 20.
Skin, parts developed from it, ii. 9. 12; its character determines that of the hair, ii. 13. 7; when hard is unsuitable for certain uses, ii. 12. 2, ii. 13. 5.
Skull, bones, ii. 7. 21; use of sutures, ii. 7. 23, ii. 14. 6; supposed difference of sutures in man and woman, ii. 7. 26; closure of sutures, ii. 7. 22; sutures said to be more numerous in man than in other animals, ii. 7. 25.
Sleep, A.'s account of, ii. 7. 15.
Smell, medium of, ii. 1. 12, ii. 10. 10; how dependent on respiration, ii. 10.

24; central position of organ, ii. 10. 25; how related to taste, iv. 11. 8; this sense less developed in man than other animals, ii. 16. 14; in insects, ii. 16. 10; in cetacea, ii. 16. 9; in fishes, ii. 10. 13.
Smuræna, iv. 13. 11.
Solen, iv. 7. 4.
Solid, definition of, ii. 1. 3.
Soul, its nature and genesis, i. 1. 14; how related to several modes of vital motion, i. 1. 16; how far within the province of natural science, i. 1. 17 and 18; heat only its instrument, i. 1. 13, ii. 7. 7, iv. 10. 11; Plato's account of it, iii. 10. 4.
Spallanzani, as to temperature of fishes, ii. 2. 8.
Species, i. 1. 2.
Speech, foundation of human excellence, ii. 2. 5.
Spinal cord, confounded with marrow, ii. 6. 4.
Spit and candlestick, in one, iv. 6. 15.
Spleen, and liver, iii. 7. 1 and 4; shape in different animals, iii. 12. 6 and 7; its uses, iii. 7. 15; very liable to disease, iii. 4. 38; enlarged in marshy districts, iii. 7. 16; size in different animals, iii. 7. 4 and 14; said by Plato to be bloodless, iii. 7. 12.
Sponges, sensibility of, iv. 5. 53; no intestinal cavity, ii. 3. 9.
Spontaneity, i. 1. 9.
Spouting, of whales, iv. 13. 39.
Spurs, of birds, iii. 1. 6.
Starfish, iv. 5. 53; mischief done by, iv. 5. 63.
Sting-ray, iv. 13. 4.
Stomach, upper and lower, ii. 3. 6, iii. 14. 31; is multiple in ruminants to atone for want of teeth, iii. 14. 4 and 15, iv. 1. 6; types of shape, iii. 14. 25; of birds, iii. 14. 10, 11 and 12; of mullet, iii. 14. 19.
Suet, and lard, ii. 5. 1. *See* Fat.
Sweat, bloody occasionally, iii. 5. 8.
Swimming, resemblance to flight, i. 4. 1.
Symmetry, of organs bilateral, iii. 7. 2; more perfect in organs of animal than of vegetable life, iii. 5. 4.

Tadpole, the only footed animal that has gills, iv. 13. 40; not recognised as larval form, iv. 13. 7; its tail, iv. 13. 8.
Tail, various uses, iv. 10. 43; how used by birds, iv. 12. 24; supposed correlation with other parts, ii. 14. 4 and 5.
Taste, relation to touch, ii. 10. 22; relation to touch and to smell, iv. 11. 8; its organ and medium, ii. 10. 10; acute in man, ii. 16. 14; dull in fishes, iv. 11. 7.
Teeth, inverse relation to horns, iii. 2. 19; resembling horns, iii. 2. 21; of carnivora, iv. 11. 19; of seals, iv. 13. 44; of camel, iii. 14. 3; of reptiles, iv. 11. 12; of fishes, iii. 1. 7 and 9, iv. 13. 30; of sharks, iii. 1. 8; of cephalopods, iv.

5. 4; of crustacea, iv. 5. 5; of snails, iv. 5. 10 and 26; how represented in insects, iv. 5. 7.
Temperature, no measure of, ii. 2. 18; of different animals, ii. 17. 19; maintained by food, iv. 5. 77.
Tendons, iii. 4. 20.
Testacea, characters and subdivisions, iv. 5. 25; tongue, iv. 5. 6; teeth, iv. 5. 26; proboscis, iv. 5. 27; crop, iv. 5. 28; operculum, iv. 5. 31; liver and stomach, iv. 5. 29; heart, iv. 5. 67; ovary, iv. 5. 44 and 47; without generative secretions, iv. 5. 68.
Testes, A.'s notion of, iv. 13. 34; of ophidia, iv. 13. 35.
Tethya. *See* Ascidia.
Teuthi, iv. 9. 1.
Theoretical, and other sciences, i. 1. 4.
Tickling, iii. 10. 8.
Tissues, relation to organs, ii. 1. 5. 7, 8 and 9, ii. 2. 3; attempt of Theophrastus to resolve them into simpler elements, ii. 1. 5.
Toes, number of in various groups, iv. 10. 21; number supposed to be related to number of mammæ, iv. 10. 26; of pig, iii. 12. 8; of elephant, ii. 16. 6; of birds, iv. 12. 30; of waders, iv. 12. 22 and 31; of grebes, iv. 12. 8; of birds of prey, iv. 12. 17; of scansorial birds, iv. 12. 33.
Tongue, of seal, iv. 11. 10; of parrot, ii. 17. 3; of reptiles, iv. 11. 5; of serpents and lizards, ii. 17. 7, iv. 11. 10; of crocodile, ii. 17. 9 and 10; of cephalopods, iv. 5. 4; of crustacea, iv. 5. 5; of testacea, iv. 5. 6; of insects, iv. 5. 8; of echini, iv. 5. 37.
Torpedo, iv. 13. 3.
Tortoise, habits, iii. 8. 4; lung, iii. 8. 5; bladder, iii. 8. 3, iii. 9. 3; kidneys, iii. 9. 1.
Touch, whether one sense or many, ii. 1. 13; why the primary sense, ii. 8. 1; flesh its medium, ii. 8. 2, ii. 10. 10; its close relation to taste, ii. 10. 22, iv. 11. 8; acute in man, ii. 16. 14.
Trachea, position of orifice, iii. 3. 5; use of length, iii. 3. 8; relation to heart, iii. 3. 9; of birds, iii. 6. 1.
Trans-olent, and trans-sonant, ii. 1. 12.
Treatises, on Health and Disease, ii. 2. 10, ii. 7. 14; on Natural History, ii. 1. 1; on Nutrition, ii. 3. 16; on Motion of Animals, iv. 13. 13; were illustrated, iv. 5. 34, iv. 9. 5.
Trygon, iv. 13. 4.
Turbinata. *See* Gasteropoda and Testacea.
Tusks, not present in horned animals, iii. 1. 3; weapons of defence or offence, iii. 1. 1; of elephants, iii. 2. 19; of Babirussa pig, iii. 1. 1, iii. 2. 21.
Type, laws of, iv. 13. 15.

Umbilical, vesicle, iv. 12. 15; cord, ii. 3. 10.

Unicorn, iii. 2. 10. and 12.
Upper, why superior to lower, ii. 2. 6.
Ureters, iii. 9. 8.
Urine, where formed, iii. 7. 8, iii. 9. 1; contains earthy matter, iv. 1. 4.

Vapor-bath, of ancients, ii. 4. 7.
Vasa deferentia, thought to be seat of seminal secretion, iv. 13. 34.
Vegetative repetition, a sign of inferiority, iv. 5. 72.
Veins. *See* Arteries.
Vertebrata, number of limbs, iv. 12. 11, iv. 13, 15; how spinal column came to be segmented, i. 1. 7.
Viscera, what meant, iii. 4. 1; relation to vessels, iii. 4. 10, iii. 8. 2, iii. 13. 1; use of, iii. 7. 8 and 10; of new-born animals, iii. 4. 4.
Vision, medium of, ii. 10. 10. *See* Eyes.
Vital, principle, i. 1. 14; motions, i. 1. 16; heat distinct from common heat, ii. 6. 7, ii. 16. 11.

Viviparous, and sanguineous animals, *see* Mammalia; and ovo-viviparous, iv. 1. 5, iv. 11. 24.
Vivisection, of chamæleon, ii. 7. 4 and 5, ii. 10. 9; of tortoise, ii. 7. 12.

Water-animals, temperature of, ii. 2. 8.
Weapons, offensive and defensive, iii. 1. 1; larger in males than in females, iii. 1. 4 and 6; no animal as a rule has more than one, iii. 2. 9; of fishes, iii. 1. 10.
Wet, definition of, ii. 1. 3.
Whales, iv. 13. 38. *See* Cetacea.
Wing, and feather, iv. 6. 6; of insects, i. 3. 1; of bat, iv. 13. 45.
Woodpecker, beak, iii. 1. 14; toes, iv. 12. 33.
Worms, iv. 6. 1, iv. 5. 70.
Wryneck, iv. 12. 33.

Xenophon, simile borrowed from, ii. 15. 1.

Zoophytes, characters of, iv. 5. 53.

HERTFORD: PRINTED BY STEPHEN AUSTIN & SONS.

www.ingramcontent.com/pod-product-compliance
Lightning Source LLC
Chambersburg PA
CBHW030748250426
43672CB00028B/1361